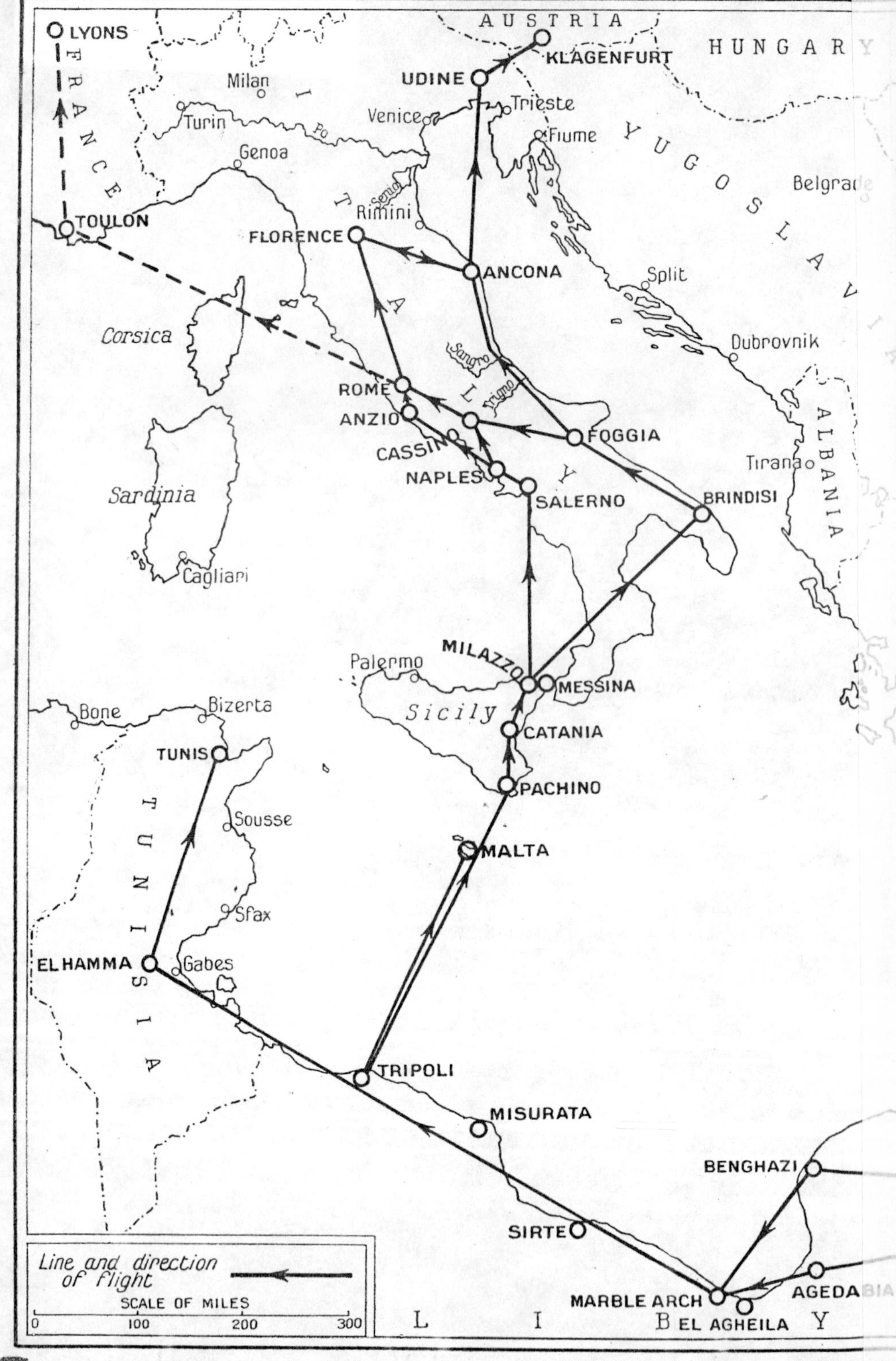
AUSTRIA
HUNGARY
LYONS
FRANCE
KLAGENFURT
UDINE
Milan
ITALY
Trieste
Venice
Turin
Po
Fiume
YUGOSLAVIA
Genoa
Belgrade
Senio
Rimini
TOULON
FLORENCE
ANCONA
Split
Corsica
Sangro
Dubrovnik
Trigno
ROME
ANZIO
FOGGIA
ALBANIA
CASSINO
NAPLES
Tirana
Sardinia
SALERNO
BRINDISI
Cagliari
MILAZZO
Palermo
MESSINA
Sicily
Bone
Bizerta
CATANIA
TUNIS
PACHINO
TUNISIA
Sousse
MALTA
Sfax
EL HAMMA
Gabes
TRIPOLI
MISURATA
BENGHAZI
SIRTE
Line and direction of flight
SCALE OF MILES
0 100 200 300
AGEDABIA
MARBLE ARCH
LIBYA
EL AGHEILA

THE DESERT

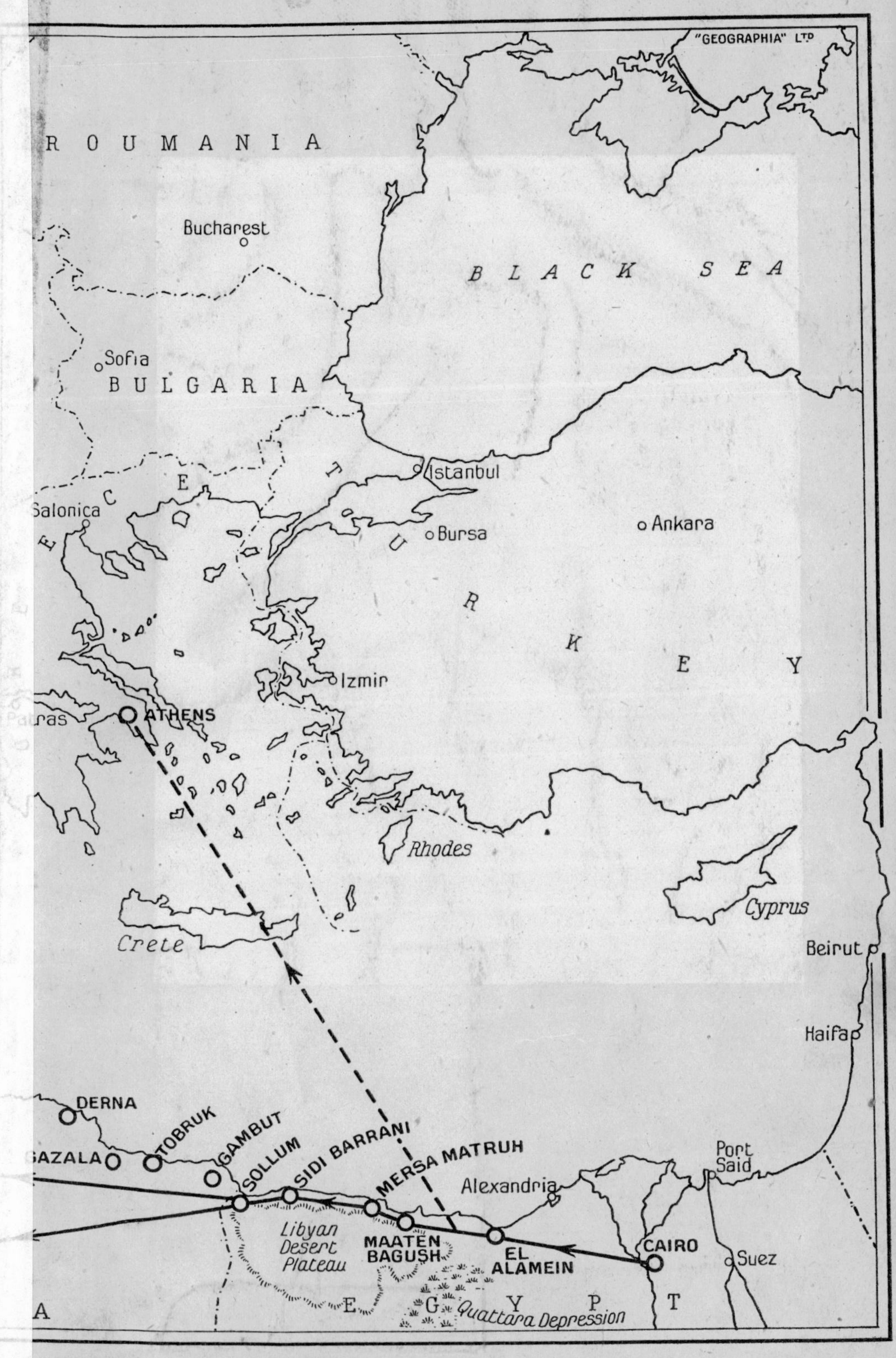

AIR FORCE TRAIL

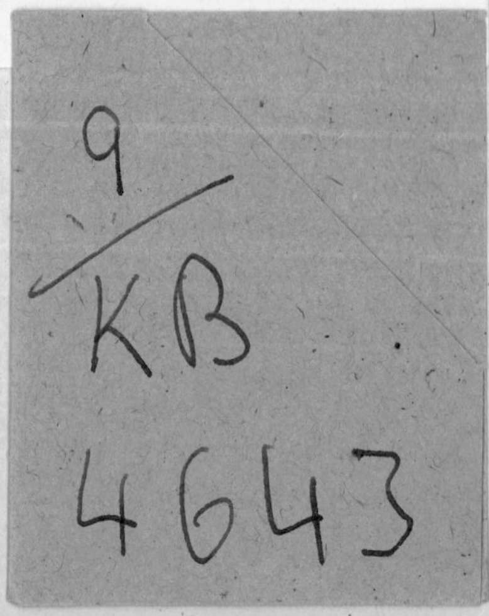
9/KB
4643

WESTMINSTER
LIBRARIES

LORD TEDDER, G.C.B., D.C.L., LL.D.

As Air Officer Commanding in Chief R.A.F. Middle East from June 1941 to January 1943, and later as Air Officer Commanding in Chief Mediterranean Air Command until December of that year, Tedder, besides personally commanding Desert Air Force for ten days, was its presiding genius

THE DESERT AIR FORCE

by

RODERIC OWEN

An Authoritative History published in Aid of the Royal Air Force Benevolent Fund

With a Foreword by
Marshal of the Royal Air Force
THE LORD TEDDER, G.C.B.
Chief of the Air Staff

HUTCHINSON & CO. (Publishers) LTD
London New York Melbourne Sydney Cape Town

> "Christ is my pilot wise,
> My compass is His word,
> Each storm my soul defies,
> While I have such a Lord."
>
> (*From an old English lustre jug*)

Printed in Great Britain
by The Anchor Press, Ltd.,
Tiptree, Essex

ACKNOWLEDGMENTS

MY sincere thanks are due to:

Marshal of the Royal Air Force Lord Tedder, for permission to use his sketches; Air Marshal Dickson; the late Air Vice-Marshal Coningham; Air Vice-Marshal Foster; Air Commodore Broadhurst; Air Commodore Falconer and Air Commodore Pike; Bonte Elgood and Lord Kinross in Cairo; Air Marshal Medhurst, for an aerial tour of the Desert; Jennings Bramley Bey of Burg el Arab; the Mamûr of Siwa Oasis; Alviso di Brazzà, the Italian Partisan leader; Squadron-Leader Johns, Flight Lieutenant Spears and William Gould for assistance with all parts of this history; the unknown Wing diarists for their admirable sense of humour; Messrs. Schindler, publishers, of Cairo and G. Netherwood, author of *Desert Squadron*, for permission to include "Christmas at Sidi Haneish"; Warrant Officer Knight for "A Piece of Cake"; all those others from whose documents I have extracted information; D. G. Richards and J. C. Nerney and others of the Air Historical Branch, in particular Miss McClelland and Mrs. Southgate, for smoothing my path; S. Morse-Browne and P. Walbourn for four fine portraits of the Air Officers Commanding; "Jon" for a cartoon which so perfectly portrayed the Desert Type; and, finally, Mrs. Holdcroft, whose shorthand typing turned chaos into some sort of order.

CONTENTS

CONTENTS

Book II

LIST OF ILLUSTRATIONS

FOREWORD

by

MARSHAL OF THE ROYAL AIR FORCE
THE LORD TEDDER, G.C.B.
Chief of the Air Staff

THE Desert, the Libyan Desert, with its vivid contrasts, its monotony and its infinite variety, its soft beauties and its harsh rigours, and above all its invigorating spaciousness, has for many of those that lived and fought in and over it a glamour which is all its own. To those that took part in the Desert Campaigns this book may bring back some of that glamour of the Desert. But we know full well now that there is no glamour in war and in this history of the Desert Air Force you will find no such false glamour. The Desert was a hard school of war on land, at sea and in the air. The Desert Air Force passed through that school, graduated with honours; and has every right to be proud of its battle honours; but in my view its greatest achievement was that it took a leading part in the evolution of a pattern of teamwork between the armed forces, a pattern which was the key to the ultimate victory. Moreover, the basis of that teamwork was the fact that the Desert Air Force was in itself a remarkable British and Allied team. When the U.S.A.A.F. joined the Desert school behind El Alamein, and went forward as a part of the Desert Air Force nearly two thousand miles to join forces with General Eisenhower in Tunisia, the pattern was set for the formation of that great Anglo-American Air Force team which played such a decisive part in the Allied victories in Sicily, Italy and Europe.

Here, in this book, are lessons and examples of understanding and co-operation which can be applied to the complex problems of peace as fruitfully as they were applied to the problems of war.

AUTHOR'S PREFACE

"History," said Gibbon, "is indeed little more than the register of the crimes, follies, and misfortunes of mankind." The contemporary historian is unable to dilate on such matters for obvious reasons. In this case I had no wish to do so, nor did the material at my disposal give many grounds for such pessimism. On the contrary, the growth of the Desert Air Force seemed to provide many examples of virtue, common sense, and good fortune. One can be optimistic about such a spirit of loyalty and comradeship; there is ample room for these qualities in an uneasy world.

I am in the happy position of knowing exactly whom to thank for having been given the privilege of writing this history. Hundreds of Desert Air Force men not only showed interest, but confidingly paid their money in advance in answer to Air Vice-Marshal Foster's suggestion. All those responsible have my sincere gratitude, for seldom can such an absorbing subject have come the way of any chronicler.

Whether I have produced what they envisaged, I cannot tell. I have to hope that they were not waiting for some rosy pamphlet, praising them to the skies in one paragraph, and disparaging their enemies in the next. I do not think they would have wanted that. In fact I have assumed that the men of the Desert Air Force, who bothered so little about outward appearances, but whose operational efficiency was unparalleled, would prefer to have their story told without overstatement, and without false heroics. It seemed to me that I had undertaken a great responsibility, and that it would be a betrayal not only of the living, but of the dead, to cheapen honour by propaganda and to dilute merit by blackguarding the opponent. Hence this chronicle, in fact and in inference, contains the truth as I saw it.

May I therefore, in all humility, dedicate this book to those who lost their lives whilst serving with the Desert Air Force, and to all those who in their different walks of life are trying to keep alive the spirit of that great organization of human beings.

BOOK I

CHAPTER I

INTRODUCTION

DURING the campaign in Italy, the Desert Air Force seemed to share points in common with that system which was neither Holy, Roman, nor even an Empire. The Desert was growing daily more distant; Wings and Squadrons were giving close support to both 5th and 8th Army fronts, sometimes under British, sometimes under American control. The confederacy of Air Units was faced with the problem of confusion of tongues, as words which had already been modified by Australians, New Zealanders and Canadians, were refashioned by South Africans and reinterpreted by Free French, Greeks and Yugoslavs.

But, paradoxically, Desert Air Force was never more united than when it was most diffuse, and never commanded more loyalty than when it comprised men of nearly every Allied nation. Perhaps a parallel can be wrung from the ancient rather than the mediaeval Roman Empire; Rome, in her later days, made her subjects citizens whilst allowing them a high degree of self-government. Desert Air Force, however much its component parts might be scattered, still retained its organization and its title, a headquarters of which its men were proud, and a name which had come to acquire an almost mythological significance.

To trace the history of D.A.F. is to try to dissect the sinews of a myth. The title assumed in May 1943 was an accolade for an air force about to leave the Desert for ever. It described the past function of the tactical air force which had been the partner of the 8th Army in the Desert, and which promised to practise the same tradition in Sicily and Italy. But 204 Group, Air Headquarters, Cyrenaica, and 202 Group, were embryo Desert Air Forces; the seed had been sown before the war in the guise of Headquarters Egypt Group and 253 Wing.

Starting with a few squadrons of what now seem to be antique, almost comic, aircraft, Desert Air Force constantly altered. But the relationship between squadron, wing, and group was as changing as the function which each was to perform. The "Handful of buccaneers" harassing the *Regia Aeronautica* at the outbreak of war became "Air Umbrella" for the Army in June 1941.

The air force, which shared a joint headquarters with the Army that October, became a rearguard of outstanding value during the retreat to Alamein. In the ensuing pursuit, the 8th Army and Desert Air Force, "as one", followed the German and Italian armies back over the now familiar route to Benghazi; demonstrated the principles of tactical air power at El Hamma, and flying through to Tunis, shared in the action which was to drive the Axis forces from continental Africa. The same air force, now under North African Tactical Air Forces, part of the air component for amphibious operations against Sicily, was a protagonist of interdiction in Italy, whilst still continuing to give close support to whichever was the army of its adoption.

Identity and title, both were guarded jealously. And though the force gradually shed those members who had known the Desert, newcomers were quick to adapt themselves. As with 8th Army, the tradition of Desert Air Force was a tradition of service which found its flowering in the Desert, drawing strength from what would appear to be the least promising soil in the world.

Consider then, at some time previous to the late war, the territory which lies like a tawny lake between Alexandria and Tripoli. Think in terms of water; imagine the coastal towns of Alexandria, Tobruk, Benghazi, and Tripoli to be harbours, serving not only the Mediterranean but also the Desert "sea". View the strip of land containing the railway and the coastal road as a long isthmus, joining Egypt to Algeria, starting from the rich mud of the Delta, broadening at the Jebel district of Cyrenaica, narrowing at Benghazi, before swelling once more to form Tripolitania and Tunisia. The inhabitants of the vast area behind the isthmus resemble mariners rather than landlubbers; the few oases are island harbourages rather than settlements. Before the war, camels, the traditional ships of the Desert (the name explains their function graphically enough), were gradually being ousted by automobiles; but perched on a hump or clutching a new fangled steering-wheel, the Arab remains a mariner: self-contained, adaptable, perpetually voyaging.

To conceive of that area as a sea may seem to require too fanciful a re-orientation of ideas, but the effort is one worth making in order to understand the special requirements of tactical warfare peculiar to the Desert. If individuals are to be called mariners, then regiments will be ships of the line, and divisions battle squadrons. Tactics must be naval tactics; bases must be defended not at the harbour mouth, but by offensive action in the open sea. The impenetrable Qâttara depression might spoil the purely naval aspect of the Desert situation by creating a Skaggerak barely 35 miles wide, but elsewhere escape to the south was always possible. Under such conditions mobility and self-sufficiency were not only desirable but essential qualities; mobility so as to outflank, self-sufficiency so as to be able to exist whilst outflanking.

It was likely that toughness of individual character which had helped to make them good sailors, would also predispose the British towards successful campaigning in the Desert. Accustomed since 1880 to repeated extensions of the temporary occupation of Egypt, they had fought only minor wars against the Senussi. Ranging from Matruh to Sollum during the winter 1915 to 1916, the British Army had learnt many of the lessons which the Bedouin, the expert in mobility and self-sufficiency, had to teach. The Italians, on the other hand, less tough, less stable, had never taken happily to Desert skirmishes. In an attempt to re-create the Roman Empire in Libya, they had committed themselves to continuous guerilla warfare with the Arab tribes since 1911. Marshal Graziani had reached heights of almost lyrical despondency in describing the difficulties, the sandstorms, the droughts, and the misery of the unbearable heat, all of which phenomena he declared to be inhuman. He was not likely to change his outlook under the added stress of modern warfare. But it was harder to predict the future behaviour of the Germans. Would there be some fierce gesture of defiance? Some vast, Wagnerian project, instigated with meticulous care only to be abandoned before completion? It was probable that where the British would assimilate, the Italians would avoid, and the Germans would fight the Desert.

British association with that almost uncharted sea had led in the past to certain modifications of individual character which the uncharitable had chosen to diagnose as "sand-happiness". Cairo, the "Imperturbable Metropolis"[1], was accustomed to the sight of returning wanderers, miserable amid the thousand and one entertainments, who seemed to be so out of touch and yet who claimed to know so much more about everything. Lawrence of Arabia had surpassed Lady Hester Stanhope in his admiration for the Arab tribes and in his ability to handle them. The English, it seemed, had the knack of absorbing some of the qualities which the Desert could offer to its inhabitants.

Loyalty, cunning, and an acceptance of almost impossible odds combined with the endurance of almost unbearable hardship, the Arab wars had already shown that these formed the natural basis of the Bedouin character. Driven from Matruh, the Senussi had hidden in caves and fought from Dakla to Siwa, their provisions exhausted, their men weakened by disease. "The armoured cars," commented Massey, "were a great success in this region—when we passed the Arabs without killing them they turned round and continued firing at us so that we had to go back and finish them." If this was the type of man at home in the Desert, and if the British were likely to be infected with the same spirit, what would be the effect of exposing an entire army and air force to such influences? How might the British react, *en masse*, if the Desert was to become their battle-ground over a period of years? Those who knew the Desert knew the answer, and were to have the satisfaction of proving their case not only in Cairo, but at Alamein, Tobruk, Tripoli, and Tunis, until finally Rome and Vienna were forced to recognize the strength of their claims. "The Desert," said the experts, "will so penetrate your being that you will never shake off its sand." It would harden and wither, but it would give in exchange a sense of brotherhood against odds both human and inhuman.

Here then, dun, hot and barren, was the best, and not the worst soil for the budding of a new Service tradition. The tawny sea of sand could teach lessons which the English would be expert in understanding and rapid in assimilating. The Desert, "The tactician's paradise, the quartermaster's hell," was the natural parent of those twin phenomena, 8th Army and Desert Air Force.

[1] Guedalla.

ORIGINS

It was reaffirmed in the Middle East in 1939 that "The role in general assigned to our Air Forces operating from this country is the defence of Egypt". The embryo Desert Air Force, changing its name from "Advance Wing" to "253 Wing" as part of "Egypt Group" on September 25th, had been given its orders: "To maintain close co-operation with the General Officer Commanding the Army in the Western Desert" as its share in the overall programme.

The clarion call "Defence of Egypt" had echoed in British ears since the battle of Aboukir Bay, for Egypt lay on the road to India. After the turn of the century the sound grew deafening as the "Gateway" theory was only one amongst many considerations. Palmerston had declared: "We do not want Egypt or wish it for ourselves, any more than a rational man with an estate in the north of England and a residence in the south would have wished to possess the inns on the north road. All he could want would have been that the inns should be well kept, always accessible, and furnishing him when he came with mutton chops and post horses." Needless to say, the inns must not be in French imperial hands, since that might make the route to India expensive as well as uncomfortable for the English traveller.

But in 1857 Palmerston opposed a suggestion to improve communications. He feared that where the French could not conquer they might well buy the inns. "I can only express my surprise that Monsieur Ferdinand de Lesseps should have reckoned so much on the credulity of English capitalists as to think that . . . he should succeed in obtaining English money for the promotion of a scheme which is in every way so adverse to British interests."

The French and Egyptians showed more concern. The Suez Canal was duly cut in spite of British misgivings, and reinterpretation of the interests of British capital led Disraeli towards exchanging the position of tenant for that of landlord. By acquiring shares in the canal he made England inherit a foreign policy which had hitherto belonged to the French, and it was not long before revolts and disturbances delivered the administration of Egypt into reluctant British hands. The same Khedive Ismail who had often prophesied that "Egypt would belong to the canal and not the canal to Egypt" was the man ultimately responsible for its loss, for soon the only tangible reminders of those controlling shares were the palaces which fused his beloved West with his native East, and the period magnificence of *Aïda*, the opera commissioned for the ceremony of opening the new waterway. Henceforth Egypt and the Suez Canal were to seem identical—the defence of one involving the other. Egypt, which Kipling had called "a longish strip of market garden", was to come to be regarded as anything but a matter of purely agricultural consideration. The canal, "the lifeline of Empire", was the most vulnerable

AIR COMMODORE COLLISHAW, C.B., O.B.E., D.S.O., D.S.C., D.F.C.

The first Air Officer Commanding the embryo Desert Air Force, April 1939–August 1941

The late AIR VICE-MARSHAL SIR ARTHUR CONINGHAM, K.C.B., K.B.E., D.S.O., M.C., D.F.C., A.F.C.

Air Officer Commanding the growing Desert Air Force
August 1941–February 1943

AIR VICE-MARSHAL SIR HARRY BROADHURST,
K.B.E., C.B., D.S.O., D.F.C., A.F.C.

Air Officer Commanding Desert Air Force February 1943–March 1944

AIR VICE-MARSHAL SIR WILLIAM F. DICKSON,
K.B.E., C.B., D.S.O., A.F.C.

Air Officer Commanding Desert Air Force March 1944–December 1944

AIR VICE-MARSHAL R. M. FOSTER, C.B., C.B.E., D.F.C.

Desert Air Force's last wartime Air Officer Commanding December 1944–August 1945.

AIR COMMODORE C. L. FALCONER, C.B.E.

Air Officer Commanding until the dissolution of Desert Air Force in June 1946

KESSELRING

As *Oberbefehlshaber Sued*, Tedder's chief opponent

"DESERT AIR FORCE—WE PRESUME, OLD MAN"

This cartoon, which first appeared in *Eighth Army News*, is reproduced by kind permission of JON

point on the new sea route to India, for which Malta and Gibraltar were two stepping-stones.

But this was merely the old significance recast. The lock gates of the canal opened to an increasing proportion of trade from the Far East, and goods from Indian ports reached London at greater speed and with less danger of loss. With the benefits of education the innkeepers might possibly improve their hostelries so as to conform to the Palmerstonian standard. Egypt might even be defended by the Egyptians, who would naturally favour their most valuable customer.

If such was the main concern of Queen Victoria's Ministers, successors often found there were other novel reasons for continuing a defence so costly and perhaps unnecessary. Oil was the new factor. Oil in the past, it has been suggested, had given Elijah victory over the 450 prophets of Baal, when "he filled the trench also" and that evening "the fire of the Lord fell and consumed the burnt sacrifice . . . and licked up the water that was in the trench".

Oil in the future was to give a new urgency to political dealings with the countries of the Middle East. Oil was to ooze through the veins of Arabia, Palestine and Persia, spout forth the *Drang Nach Osten*, and seep into plans for the cutting of the Baghdad railway. During the scramble for oil, Britain, defending Egypt, sat athwart the crossroads, levying toll on each newcomer, suitably placed for acquiring the first fruits of each new venture, exercising *droit de seigneur* with tact and discretion that few other powers could have shown. That the Middle East was not involved in a series of petroleum wars seemed to many to be a justification of the special position which Britain adopted in the Mediterranean.

Egypt grew steadily more important. Though containing small oil reserves, it was an admirably placed centre for oil administration. Alexandria and Port Said offered good harbour facilities, and it was not long before moves were made in the direction of establishing British sea power (by which is meant the organization for supply and maintenance) there. Haifa and Bahrein were the ports through which the oil actually flowed, but these had to be defended by sea power in the Mediterranean based now on Gibraltar, Malta and Egypt. Whereas the temporary abandonment of Haifa could be contemplated without undue dismay, the loss of Egypt to an enemy would entail the destruction of British sea power in the eastern Mediterranean, and seriously interfere with British Middle Eastern oil economy. In normal times only one-twelfth of the oil supply for the United Kingdom came from the Middle Eastern oil-fields. It might be supposed that the importance of defending Egypt had been overplayed, had it been possible to guarantee the deficit from other sources in the New World, which were already supplying five-sixths of the required total. But in the event of a war against a power with submarines and trained submarine crews, experience gained from 1914–18 had shown that Atlantic shipping could be hindered or even stopped altogether from reaching England. The remaining one-sixth from Russia and Roumania was subject to control by several European powers, and was therefore unlikely to be delivered in time of war. But for Italy and Germany, the oil-fields of the Middle East were essential. Before the war Italy produced approximately 9 per cent of her needs. Germany could produce only five million tons a year, or two million less than requirements. In wartime both Italy and Germany would consume far more than the six million tons or so which Roumania could offer.

Thus, if the Suez Canal was the key to the trade of India, Egypt was the door not only to the Far East, but also to the Mediterranean oil-fields. Its practical usefulness lay finally in the amount of goods which merchant shipping could carry through the straits of Gibraltar to England, and in the oil which fleets of tankers could bring through the canal from Abadan and Bahrein. Its loss would make Malta untenable, and hence Gibraltar redundant.

The defence of Egypt was therefore a preoccupation for sea rather than for land power. To naval eyes the Western Desert was a coastal strip containing ports of limited value. Only Tripoli could be said to rival Alexandria. Tobruk and Benghazi could be enlarged; the smaller villages, such as Matruh, Bardia, Sollum and Derna, were useful rather than essential.

To the army, who would have to defend Egypt against land attack, the Western Desert ports were supply channels for tactical manœuvres in the Desert, because the only metalled road ended at Mersa Matruh.

But to the air force the Desert was more than a waste space bounded by a coastal strip. Sand promised suitable aerodromes in unlimited quantities.

A study of the map giving the range of fighter and bomber aircraft shows why airfields were needed at certain points, and why air aims could not at all times coincide with army objectives. If Egypt was to be defended in order to pass merchant shipping safely through the Mediterranean, then aircraft would have to spread their wings further afield over the routes to Malta and Gibraltar. Airfields in Cyrenaica meant protection from Alexandria to Valetta. Airfields in Tripolitania extended a promise of safe passage through the straits of Tunis towards Gibraltar.

But before the war these air points of view could not be sufficiently demonstrated. It was held that to some extent ships could supply their own air cover by means of aircraft carriers, but even this contention had not found general acceptance, since the necessity for protection of that type was often seriously questioned. Air Ministry theories were often considered doctrinaire, air tenets were only partly proven.

But if, from the air point of view, the possession of aerodromes in the Western Desert was essential for the safe passage of ships through the Mediterranean, how much more vital it would be to deny the enemy the use of the ports, the only supply channels! Italian air power, based on Sicily, with forward landing-grounds in Tripolitania at its disposal, might effectively shut part of the sea route. With the Mediterranean closed, many of the reasons for the defence of Egypt would disappear. Shipping would after all have to make the "long journey round the Cape", and aircraft would have to fly across Central Africa to reach the Nile valley. War aims in the Mediterranean would be restricted to the maintenance of a besieged Egyptian arsenal, which would only be able to play a part towards the end of a successful war when sea routes were once more open. But the possibility of Italian air power becoming a serious problem seemed remote before the war. Colonel Douhet, the "Aerial Clausewitz",[1] had been promoted to the rank of General, and his theories had evidently found eager Fascist audiences, but the Italian aircraft industry was handicapped by having so few natural resources upon which to draw, and even Italian ingenuity seemed unlikely to be able to meet a demand which so patently exceeded supply in this as in all other fields of aggrandizement. Admittedly, the Italians were gaining firm control of their Libyan dependency, and were providing heavy subsidies in order to induce colonists to establish themselves on the red rocky soil. Aerodromes with tarmac runways, permanent buildings and underground storage chambers were in the course of construction. Trees were planted, and Italian gardens forced into unwilling existence, in a desperate effort to persuade the colonist that he had not, after all, strayed far from his native land. Tripoli was rapidly becoming a cultural centre; its port and aerodrome facilities were improving; and though much of its splendour was façade deep, enormous civic improvements had already been made, and more were planned.

Yet Libya was still a poor counter to place against the long-established French colonial empire. In neighbouring Tunisia and Algeria roads were already built, factories were in full production, skilled staffs already in permanent residence. It was to be assumed that in a war against Italy, England and France would be allies, and that the main armament would be supplied and directed by France. Had not Milner assumed that an invasion by an army across the Desert sea was impracticable? Evidently the Italians themselves were prepared to meet a thrust from Tunisia, for Mussolini's sudden declaration of war revealed Graziani in a position reminiscent of the Duke of Plaza-Toro, facing in the wrong direction, at the back of his troops.

Tunis and Algeria, however, made their debut only to retire. Libya, from being second best, acquired the status of sole survivor. If the main Allied effort could not, after all, be directed from Tunis, then Egypt, besides needing defence, must also direct the offensive at its western borders. Prepared to meet rather than to issue threats, Cairo was unhappily forced to take the offensive from the start with a military establishment not devised for the task. The numerical inferiority of the British forces at the start of the war was the logical result of a considered policy which the defection of France upset.

Air control of the Sicilian narrows was already lost. Malta, from being a stepping-stone, became a threatened fortress, protected from air attack only by

[1] *See* Guedalla, *Middle East.*

its own resources, which were inadequate to fulfil a function never intended to be theirs. The possession of Cyrenaica, with its aerodromes centred round Tobruk, Martuba and Benghazi, was now the only means of giving protection to shipping; though far from passing unhindered through the Mediterranean on their way to England, convoys were now to be concerned solely with keeping the defenders of Malta supplied with absolute essentials. The gloomy prophecy that the Mediterranean would be partially closed became true; Egypt became a besieged arsenal supplied from Kenya, the Red Sea and South Africa. The "long journey round the Cape" became a reality.

Worse was in store. The invasion of Crete by German airborne troops meant that not only was the enemy in a position to bomb Alexandria and Cairo, but that a new narrows was created between Crete and the Desert mainland. If Malta was still to be held, it must be supplied in spite of enemy air power dominating all its approaches. Martuba airfields would have to be in British hands in order to provide at least a small quota of air protection, otherwise it was to prove impracticable to allow convoys to leave Alexandria for fear of overwhelming losses. The air point of view was to be demonstrated in only too ample measure as convoys, their missions unfulfilled, were forced to turn back to Alexandria, at a time when the defenders of Malta were near starvation.

In obedience to this concept of the use of air power, the Desert Air Forces occupying the forward landing-grounds were constantly to be directed towards shipping protection, even in the midst of a land battle, although "to maintain close co-operation with the General Officer Commanding in the Western Desert" was their charter directif, and though their specialized function was to provide close support for the army.

The flexibility of the air arm, which the Desert Air Forces were called upon to exhibit, was to become a matter for great pride. A Desert Air Force was to be the medium for testing every theory of air-army co-operation. From trials, experience was to be gained which would inform future tactical air forces in North Africa and Sicily, and which would serve as basic doctrine for 2nd Tactical Air Force before the landings in Normandy. Assessment of the relative needs and capabilities of air, sea and land power was to show the air aspect gaining steadily in importance. Desert Air Force supplied a large part of the data from which such reassessments could be made, was conscious of the fact, and delighted in the diversity of tasks allotted to it, and in the steady increase in status which each reorganization entailed. Flexibility and experiment fitted the tradition of the Desert. Change toughened sinews already wiry, whilst novelty heightened morale, already historically assured.

But as Mussolini manœuvred his state into line with what seemed to be traditional opportunist policy, the lessons of Mediterranean air power were still untaught. Royal Air Force, Middle East, was only partly developed. Desert Air Force was unproven. The defence of Egypt rose like a lump in the Imperial throat. It seemed likely that the "inn" would be, if anything "inaccessible", "far from well kept", where the British traveller might expect not hospitality, but a stab in the back.

Amidst such a maze of alarming strategical problems the tactical Desert Air Forces were directed to thread an experimental way.

. . . . .

In July 1937 the Committee of Imperial Defence decided that certain measures should be taken to make sure that the British Empire would be adequately defended in the event of a war against Italy. Since 1935 the possibility had never seemed remote, even though Italy had been our ally in the First World War. But although the recommendations of the committee foreshadowed reorganization of dispositions and facilities in the Middle East, strict instructions were given that Italy might in no wise be provoked. These directives, renewed from time to time, still held good in 1940. They show clearly enough that it was the Imperial intention to avoid war against Italy, and that there was a reasonable hope that the Italians would show a similar goodwill. On the other hand, it became increasingly obvious that the "seven million bayonets" would have to be turned against some power, and that Abyssinia and Albania had been incapable of absorbing their full thrust. Italian adventures in Spain suggested that Germany was now no longer inhabited by the traditional ogres, the hated Tedeschi, but by brother National Socialists; it appeared that two irreconcilables had come together on purely ideological grounds.

Counter-preparations were made on the assumption that France would be our ally; an offensive was to be mounted from Tunisia, whilst local offensive actions were to harass the enemy in Cyrenaica. The Italians, quick to grasp the logic of a situation, might then cease to offer resistance. But hopes of assistance from Tunisia were whittled away at successive conferences. The main offensive dwindled to a small thrust. This in turn was offered only if the R.A.F. could give full air support, a measure beyond its resources. Finally, France could promise only local defence, for she could spare increasingly little as squadrons were shipped back to Marseilles.

Fortunately the process of counter-balancing the French defection had been started two years earlier, when the Air Officer Commanding Egypt had been authorized to co-ordinate all air forces in the Middle East as part of the plan for the defence of Egypt. By January 1939 the title Air Officer Commanding-in-Chief was granted, and the rank up-graded to that of Air Marshal. At the same time a new establishment was approved, and by August there was a firmly entrenched Air Headquarters, capable of associating, though not on terms of equality, with General Wavell's Army Headquarters.

There were many problems raised by the new concentration of forces in Egypt. Italy might in no wise be provoked . . . but what could be more provoking to an acquisitive power than signs that the English were preparing a genuine defence of Egypt! It has been said that Mussolini had come to believe in the divine right of the new Roman Empire to enclose the boundaries of the old. Roman occupation of Alexandria, sanctified, as it were, by the memory of Cleopatra, would be the clearest evidence of a new Caesar. Hence every British reinforcement could almost be called sacrilege.

There were problems of co-operation with the native Egyptians. A joint committee was capable of raising endless political questions of prestige, as the Anglo-Egyptian Defence Committee had shown at the time of their countries' *rapprochement* during the Italo-Abyssinian war. Two committees, considering each other's recommendations at separate sessions, offered a partial, though unwieldy, solution. Then there was the problem of reinforcement, dependent for a solution on an unusually large number of imponderables. If Italian air power in Libya and Eritrea could be flourished over both the Mediterranean and the Red Sea routes, there remained the overland caravan trails, Basra to Palestine, and Mombasa to Egypt, neither of which was much more than self-sufficient. Malta might become the intermediate aerodrome for aircraft arriving from the United Kingdom, but Malta was as directly threatened as anywhere west of Alexandria. The alternative, the Takoradi–Lake Chad route (the air equivalent of the long journey round the Cape), might be a practical proposition provided that quantities of spare parts could be dumped in advance at selected points. Otherwise wastage of aircraft in transit might outnumber actual deliveries to the Delta; a Cassandra-like prediction which appeared to have come true as the first few Gladiators cannibalized on each other almost to vanishing point.

Plans for administration were dependent upon both political and reinforcement issues. There could be no establishment if there was nothing to establish. On the other hand, for what reason was establishment to be made, and to meet an attack from whom? According to the answer, formations might be sent in strength either up to the Turkish border or down to the shores of the Red Sea. The modern interpretation of the *Drang Nach Osten* might endanger Imperial security more than the attempt to claim a new Roman Empire.

On the assumption that the Western Desert might, in spite of Milner's dictum, be a battle-ground, a new type of air force would be needed. An air force with bases in the Delta where supplies and reinforcements would be at hand, with forward landing-grounds groping towards the Egyptian frontier; an air force possessing adequate knowledge of Italian air tactics and aircraft; an air force which would fight the air war for air superiority whilst working with the army; an air force with units as mobile and as self-contained as army units. Hence Headquarters Egypt Group, the result of the Cairo conference of 1938 and of the Chief of Staff's approval in 1939, was formed on April 18th at No. 12 Sharia Comanos Pasha. It was "To exercise control over operational units allocated to it by H.Q. R.A.F., Middle East, for operations in the Western

Desert, and to exercise operational supervision of such maintenance and administrative units as may be allocated in the field for the servicing of operational units".

The Headquarters, sited in a busy Cairo street, was noticeably on a basis of what was expedient rather than what was desirable. Five civilians of uncertain status fulfilled a number of subordinate appointments, ranging from that of warder to that of messenger boy. The nine officers could give orders to less than twice that number of other ranks. Atop this small but gallant pyramid of personnel was enthroned an Air Officer Commanding, a man of wide experience, who had fought von Richthoven in the First World War—Air Commodore Collishaw.

Egypt Group was to comprise:

H.Q. Bomber Group Egypt.

H.Q. Advance Wing with 33 (Fighter), 45 (Bomber), 208 (Army Co-operation) and 211 (Bomber) squadrons.

H.Q. No. 2 Bomber Wing with 60, 84 and 113 squadrons.

H.Q. Bomber Transport Wing, with 70 and 216 squadrons.

Each formation of H.Q. Egypt Group was intended to multiply like the amoeba by a process of self-division. No. 2 Bomber Wing grew out of R.A.F. Station Heliopolis, whilst No. 1 Wing sprouted as soon as sufficient men had been withdrawn from Irak.

A table of metamorphosis is here included:

Egypt Group changed its name to 202 Group, whilst Advance Wing became 253 Wing on September 28th, 1939.

The day before Italy entered the war 202 Group moved up to Marten Bagush to absorb 253 Wing.

Advance 202 Group became Air H.Q. Cyrenaica in February 1941 on the crest of the first advance. It in turn was absorbed into 204 Group, along with Rear 202 Group, on April 12th.

What was left of 202 Group was then given an entirely new task, "Defence of the Delta and the Canal areas, including the defence of aerodromes from low-flying attack and airborne landings by parachute troops".

Air Commodore Collishaw on taking over 204 Group found that it was little different from the old 202 Group.

Finally, 204 Group was renamed Air H.Q. Western Desert on October 9th, 1941, when Air Vice-Marshal Coningham had been in command for a day over two months.

This complicated pattern of change and renaming reflects experiment in organization and function which will appear in detail as the story unfolds. Before Egypt Group lost its identity its purpose was expressed officially as "Action against Italian air force mobile columns and their lines of communication, supply convoys, and air and other bases in Libya. Should, however, the military situation so demand, and the military commanders so request, the primary role of the units under Egypt Group will be the provision of close support to our land forces engaging in the Western Desert".

Control of operations in the Western Desert was to be vested in the Air Officer Commanding, Egypt. This was a simple matter until the arrangements for employing Advance Wing came under discussion. Here the Army Co-operation Squadron (208) was under the control of the General Officer Commanding Army, but the Commanding Officer of Advance Wing was supposed to advise the G.O.C. of its use. The same commanding officer was to act as liaison officer between the A.O.C. and the G.O.C. and was to be near Divisional Headquarters, to which an air staff officer was attached in order to carry out liaison between the Officer Commanding Advance Wing and the G.O.C. This "connecting link" was described as "not an ideal organization". But the precise degree of army/air control could scarcely have been worked out on a theoretical basis alone. The British could not have been expected to have acquired a solution to such thorny problems, which participation in the Spanish Civil War had handed to the Germans and the Italians.

Exercises provided the only means of training; for the Middle East was still at peace. Exercises were therefore devised on an increasingly elaborate scale. On September 8th Egypt Group carried out a series of endurance tests, designed to reveal the maximum endurance of a Blenheim under operational conditions. Three weeks later an investigation of the reasons why that aircraft was so susceptible to dust led to the discovery that special drip trays would be needed. Air cleaners had to be serviced after every five hours of flying, and this task took three hours each time. New cleaners took only a quarter of an hour to fit, but in Middle East in January 1940 there were only six spares throughout the Command. No one dared to suggest when more would be arriving.

Added stimulus to persevere with tests and exercises was given by the obvious imminence of war against Italy. But there was endless speculation as to when, if ever, reinforcements would arrive, and whether there would be enough men to meet the Italians on at least equal terms.

Meanwhile, life in Cairo seemed to continue on its usual uneven way. The contrast between the busy and the leisurely had always been a feature of the imperturbable metropolis. Rather more were moving rather faster, but there was still the great mass of people to whom the threat of war was as the rattle of a far-off drum in the Citadel (where it was known that the English held their strange parades and shouted curious foreign words at one another. Truly these ways were strange, but inevitable). Other factions in the town adopted attitudes in accordance with their normal outlook. The merchants delighted at the number of English troops, buying indiscriminately, paying prices which should never have been accepted without argument. The Young Egyptians looked wistfully towards Europe for signs of that great popular uprising in favour of the New Order, which they had been led to expect. The University students, agitating for Egyptian prestige, tended to vent their discontent on the

British—helped by the shrewder landowners, who encouraged the movement in order to draw attention away from matters of social reform. The upper classes and the intellectuals conceived of an Egypt holding herself in readiness without prejudicing her position; neither defended too much by the British nor growing too cold towards the Italians.

Against this background R.A.F. reorganization continued, unabashed by the rising fever of war in Europe. The Middle East knew itself to be in quarantine, and knew it was only a question of time before contact with those already infected would lead to the disease striking at Egypt.

An exercise in November feigned war conditions. It was postulated "that the two countries, Eastland and Westland, having failed to solve their disputes amicably, have resorted to hostilities". Eastland, with many misgivings, being peaceable, and having fewer troops and aeroplanes; Westland, quite without qualms, being the stronger.

Eastland, defending Egypt, was to hold Mersa Matruh; Westland was to take the town as part of a programme which would only be complete when the Delta, too, had fallen into their hands.

Eastland had to prove, or disprove, various assumptions made in advance. The Egyptian Government was to demand an air umbrella over Alexandria and Cairo. The Royal Navy was to put in a bid for shipping protection patrols from Alexandria out to sea. The numerically inferior army was to claim all aircraft for the tactical front, on a sink-or-swim basis. Westland, on the other hand, were assumed to have no such conflict of claims on their air force. The army was to be in complete control. When the Westland air force operated against targets of their own choice, they were to be concerned mainly with attacks on Eastland's forward landing-grounds.

Criticisms on the result—a stalemate in Westland's slight favour—hummed like wasps round the ears of Air Commodore Collishaw and his 202 Group. Why had Eastland given so much (so little) close support? Why had Alexandria been allotted so many (so few) fighters? What about Cairo, defended solely by the Egyptian air force? What about attacks on Westland shipping?

And as for Westland, why had its air force been so subservient to the military authorities? Why hadn't it used bombers on strategic targets such as the Eastland fleet at Alexandria? Why hadn't it continued attacking Eastland's forward landing-grounds instead of allowing itself to be used as army super-artillery?

These criticisms were intended to be aired. That was the reason for holding the test. Many observers, seeing a connection between this mock battle and Italy's growing belligerency, wondered why the Italian's avowed war aim—the destruction of the British naval base at Alexandria—had not been demonstrated. They agreed that the subservience of the *Regia Aeronautica* to the Italian Commander had been faithfully simulated. Such observations, though perhaps providing fresh points of interest, were unofficial, being outside the scope of the tests, which were designed to show in practice the stresses under which opposing air forces would have to work.

The conclusions drawn outlined a grim picture for Eastland. The air force was to have an unpopular role; it could afford to bomb enemy dumps and to destroy enemy aircraft on the ground, but in other directions it would have to be sparing of resources. Alas for Alexandria! Woe to Cairo! And as for the army—beyond the Army Co-operation units which came under direct control of the Corps Commander, it was to have little else.

Certain other lessons, of administration rather than tactics, were also taken to heart. Firstly, since during the battle there would not be time to move up supplies for the air force, dumps would have to be prepared in advance. Secondly, there was a shortage of advance landing-grounds. The R.A.F. permanent stations in Egypt were comfortable camps, designed as much for the men as their machines. War standards, where efficiency alone was the criterion, were to demand something very different. Under the terms of the Anglo-Egyptian Treaty of 1936 forward landing-grounds were to be constructed by the Egyptians. Twelve had, in fact, been made up to the outbreak of war. More would be needed, and not many would be as comfortable.

If there were criticisms, the air was well cleared. After Italy's entry into the war, those who remembered the exercise were astonished to find history so closely repeated. Italian bombers were not often seen in strength over Alexandria, whilst Italian fighters were employed on uneconomical patrols over troops and lines of communication.

December ushered in further exercises. 55 and 30 squadrons conducted searchlight co-operation trials with units of the Egyptian army, and 30, 55 and 113 squadrons trained for photographic reconnaissance.

The culmination was a flight over Cairo by almost all the aircraft which the R.A.F. in Egypt could muster. On May 22nd, 1940, nine aircraft each of 30, 33, 45, 55, 80, 112, 113, 208, 211 and 216 squadrons flew out over Giza, Old Cairo, Abdin palace, Heliopolis and the railway station, before finally circling over the Citadel. Less than 100 aircraft, the noise they made was out of all proportion to the size of their formations. But though an Egyptian was heard to remark, "There's more than three, it must be the Italians", the effect on the civilian population as a whole was reassuring.

It needed to be, for the total numbers which these aircraft in the air represented was small.

63 Gladiators (21 aircraft each from 33, 112, and 80 squadrons).
72 Blenheims (113, 45, 211, 55, 30, 11).
21 Lysanders (12 of 208, and 9 of 6 squadrons).
10 Sunderland flying-boats.

The reserves of Blenheims, Gladiators and Lysanders were approximately 100 per cent, under peacetime conditions, and might therefore be expected to be fast depleted in time of war.

The Gladiator, a bi-plane with four 303 machine-guns, in spite of its look of antiquity, was able to compete on equal terms with the more recently developed C.R. 42. The Italian S.M. 71 had a longer range and could carry more bombs than the Blenheim. The Lysander, a defenceless slow two-seater, "needed a squadron of fighters to protect it". These aircraft were the cream of the force. In the Sudan, Kenya, British Somaliland and Aden were Haartebeestes, Fairey Battles and Ju. 86's, bought from Germany in peacetime. In the opinion of Air Marshal Tedder, only the Blenheim, the Sunderland flying-boats and the Lysander could fairly not be called obsolescent. But in a short time the Lysander was obsolete.

The Italians, in their permanent stations at Benghazi, Tripoli and Tobruk, had varying quantities of aircraft. In February 1939 fifty-four Breda 65 and C.R. 30 fighters, with forty-eight S. 81 and S. 79 bombers. A further eleven squadrons of Ghiblis and R.O. 37's increased this total to a hundred and eighty-three. In May 1940 British Intelligence reports indicated the presence of 342 aircraft, but another estimate by the Deputy Director of War Organization on the eve of war mentions 248. The Longmore dispatch quotes 200 fighters and 200 bombers. The force was only 60 per cent serviceable. A prisoner of war, captured shortly after the outbreak of war, declared, "Old aircraft are being maintained because, though old, they are reliable; new aircraft need constant repairs, which are difficult to carry out under existing conditions . . . unless better maintenance facilities can be provided it seems doubtful if new modern aircraft will be sent to Libya for some time". Air Commodore Collishaw, in his pre-war paper on the Italian Air Force, stated that adequate Air Stores Parks and repair depots did not exist in Cyrenaica.

For the Italians reinforcement was easy; a pre-war exercise had shown that 400 bombers could be moved from Italy to North Africa within a matter of days. Depots at Naples, Bari, Taranto and Catania passed aircraft over to the Tripolitanian mainland. There was nothing to hinder the flow, for Italy was out of range of R.A.F. fighters except for those areas which Malta, the tiny question mark on the surface of *Mare Nostrum*, might venture to dispute.

Faced, therefore, with such air disparity, Longmore decided that his main target was the Italian Air Force, which potentially could cause enormous damage both to the army and to the fleet. The military authorities, who were asking for fighter and bomber squadrons of their own, had to be met with a refusal. They had therefore to be content with 208 squadron (Lysanders), and 6 squadron (whose Gauntlets were to be replaced with yet more Lysanders).

It must not be supposed that these arrangements met with universal approval, or even with universal understanding. The Battle of Britain had not yet demonstrated that the air war had to be fought first, before land or sea operations could, under modern conditions, reach a peak of efficiency. That the destruction of the enemy air force was a primary aim of both army and air force alike would not have been easily accepted outside Air Ministry circles until the Home Counties were strewn with the wreckage of German fighters. But when, after the first advance into Cyrenaica, 1,100 Italian aircraft, damaged beyond repair or stranded due to technical troubles, littered the ex-enemy landing-grounds, it seemed that the air policy of R.A.F. Middle East could show tangible results. This was fortunate, for in Europe gutted factories and ruined marshalling yards could be quoted to heart's content but never actually visited until some years had elapsed.

From May 7th to the 13th the air defences of Egypt were to be put to the test. Tension grew; and as the news from Europe became still more gloomy, those in Middle East began to grow impatient. Miles from home at a time when it seemed that every man in England would have to fight to the last ditch, the men could only give vent to their feelings in the sham warfare of staged exercises.

It seemed that all preparations for war were complete. The Air Officer Commanding-in-Chief, R.A.F. Middle East, Air Chief Marshal Sir William Mitchell, before leaving to take up another post, flew over to Maaten Bagush to say farewell to 253 Wing whilst searchlight exercises were in progress. He was escorted back to Fuka by Group-Captain Brown, and the new Commander was awaited.

Two weeks later Longmore toured the Western Desert units, accompanied by their Commanding Officer, Collishaw. They reached Maaten Bagush in the early morning, just before the sun grew too hot to be bearable. From the air Maaten Bagush was a sudden green splash on the brown surface of the Desert. The few palm trees, and the nearby sea, made it the only really habitable spot between Burg el Arab and Mersa Matruh. Dusty the vegetation might be, yet, for those from the Desert, Maaten Bagush needed only an Eve to compare with Paradise; but in this isolated garden there was only Adam. There was no life except in the mess, and no entertainment except to welcome visitors. In comparison with the lush emerald of the Delta and the thriving streets of Cairo, Maaten Bagush was drab and dull. This was the Headquarters of 253 Wing, the Mecca for a few forward units.

Leaving this choice camp, Longmore went on to Qasaba, where 208 squadron shared an airfield with an Egyptian squadron. His next call was on 33, then the only fighters in the Desert. They were sited near the little village of Mersa Matruh, where Cleopatra had once built a summer palace. No remnants of former glory remained to brighten 1940. The more recent colony of wealthy Greek merchants had disappeared. The men diving for sponges in the blue lagoon were soon to see their trade languishing, for Matruh was the main military depot in the Western Desert. Protected from the land by the encircling arm of a low hill, its outer defences were rambling in every direction above and below ground. It was the first harbour beyond Alexandria; there were supplies of fresh water, and there was an airfield.

Fuka the next day. There Longmore reviewed 45 (Blenheim) squadron.

The field then was dry and dusty, but the squadron had already experienced floods, and were hardened to torrential downpour and blistering heat alike. Hard by lay the encampment of 31 Air Stores Park, the Advanced Repair and Advanced Salvage Sections, whose most essential function were self-explanatory.

Longmore then went on to Daba to see 211 (Blenheim) squadron; and that completed the tale. There were no more units; there were apparently to be none in the immediate future, for England was hourly expecting invasion.

Thus, with tiny air forces, and with 36,000 British troops, the Middle East sat, like an Imperial David, in the path of the Roman Goliath.

Longmore took swift action. 202 Group were directed to move up to Maaten Bagush and absorb what had been their forward unit, 253 Wing. 55 and 113 Blenheim squadrons were sent to Fuka and Maaten Bagush respectively. All leave had been cancelled since May 29th. All squadrons were at four hours' readiness. It needed but to "sound the clarion and fill the fife".

CHAPTER II

WAR IN THE DESERT

It took four days for 202 Group to move itself to the new camp at Maaten Bagush. Meanwhile rumours of war grew more insistent, until there was no longer any question of whether, but merely speculation as to when—tomorrow or the next day.

Tents might still be unloading from lorries, but the aircraft were ready. Instructions had been given in advance. Targets had been worked out in Cairo; even the precedence of one target over another had been plotted. The first task was to be reconnaissance. Those areas from which reports were needed had all been charted in advance, but individual aircraft had yet to be ordered out on a mission. The aircraft were to kill two birds with one stone by also carrying 250-lb. bombs, to be dropped at the pilot's own initiative. Processing of photographs was arranged through 45 squadron at Fuka, where a special trailer was held ready.

The second task was to be attack. For this instructions had already been given, and the priority of targets left at the discretion of the Air Officer Commanding-in-Chief.[1]

The last hours before the final declaration of war passed in a traditional state of dull suspense. Everything, so far as it could be, was ready. There were no dramatic last-minute changes, for there was little enough to change. All concerned had their orders. At 4.30 p.m. on June 10th the A.O.C. addressed his men, warning them that war was imminent.

As midnight approached, Collishaw was instructed "to come to immediate readiness for war with Italy but await (repeat await) further instructions before initiating hostile act". Nine minutes after midnight "A state of war with Italy exists. Carry out reconnaissance as arranged. Bomber formations as available should accompany reconnaissance in northern area. Favourable targets observed—especially concentrations of aircraft."

[1] Longmore gives a list of R.A.F. Middle East objectives:
- (*a*) Offensive action against enemy air bases with a view to reducing their numerical superiority in aircraft and destroying their repair organization.
- (*b*) Offensive action against enemy ports to destroy or damage submarines, shipping and port facilities.
- (*c*) Destruction of resources of all sorts in Italian East Africa.
- (*d*) Full support for British army operations.
- (*e*) Strategic reconnaissance for all the services.

202 Group's allotted targets had not changed much since August 28th, 1939; they were:
- (*a*) Reconnaissance of the road to Libya.
- (*b*) Reconnaissance and attack of submarines.
- (*c*) Attacks on vessels in Tobruk and Bardia harbours.
- (*d*) Reconnaissance of enemy air activity at Amseat, El Adem and Derna.

There was to be a raid shortly after dawn. The primary target was to have been Tobruk harbour, but reconnaissance showed what was described as "negative enemy army concentration", and the alternative target, El Adem airfield, suffered the first offensive action of the R.A.F. Nine aircraft of 45, 55 and 113 squadrons took part, a meagre total in retrospect, but then considered to be quite an impressive demonstration of air power.

55 squadron cling to the story that they forestalled Mussolini's official announcement of war against England, claiming that their bombs fell on the parade ground at El Adem whilst the Station Commander was reading aloud the document which Graziani had circulated for the benefit of his subordinates. Certainly the Italians were unprepared for such swift action, for another raid on the airfield later in the day at 2.15 p.m. showed the four squadrons of S. 81's, the two squadrons of S. 79's and the two squadrons of R.O. 37's and Ghiblis, still cheek by jowl. A high price was paid for setting the hangars on fire and damaging several aircraft. Two aircraft of 45 squadron were missing, one believed to be in the sea off Tobruk; another aircraft, supposed at first to have landed at El Adem, later reached Sidi Barrani with engine trouble. The second operation was less costly. After a severe encounter with the enemy, one aircraft returned with one engine out of order, one aircraft with undercarriage smashed, and another was damaged in landing. To give some idea of the scale of this attack, the total of bombs dropped was—416 forty-pounders, 524 twenty-pounders and 2,080 four-pound incendiaries.

216 squadron were to have continued the bombardment that night, taking off from Mersa Matruh in Bombays, but this operation was cancelled. The next day six aircraft of 45 squadron and nine aircraft of 113 squadron were over Tobruk, followed later by six aircraft of 211 squadron. The port was a centre of Italian activity. On June 14th ten large ships were in harbour, and a troopship escorted by two warships were approaching. Two Corps H.Q. and the joint Army-Air H.Q. were in the town, whilst on the nearby landing-ground thirty-four aircraft stood ready to operate. Dockside oil storage dumps completed the picture of an excellent target. In the raid on Tobruk, El Gubbi suffered, though a visit to that airfield was tantamount to bearding the Lion of Islam in his lair, for here were based C.R. 42's, the best aircraft the Italians owned. Approximately fifty enemy fighters were put into the air, but none of our aircraft was lost.

The attack on Tobruk crippled the *San Giorgio*, a cruiser of 9,000 tons, acting as a submarine depot ship.

The units of 202 Group received the congratulations of Air Ministry on June 12th. As Air Marshal Longmore stated, "The promptness of our attacks within the first few hours of the declaration of war achieved successful results; it obviously took the Italians by surprise, and, in the case of aerodromes, before they had effected adequate dispersal of aircraft and petrol supplies".

By June 22nd the great aerodrome of El Adem had been attacked ten times by forty-three aircraft in all; storage tanks at Tobruk had been blown up, and the *San Giorgio*, gutted by fire, was apparently beached for the rest of the war.[1]

Meanwhile the Italian Air Force, beset by problems of putting itself on an active service basis, did far less and did it badly. It had not been ready for defence, and was not organized to deliver assaults on Egypt. It was best prepared for a war against Tunisia. There were difficulties, insuperable to the Italian Commanders, in the way of matching the offensive activities of the British. Aircraft were in position near the runways, petrol and oil were stored in neat dumps all the way from Italy to Fort Capuzzo; but how to pipe petrol into the tanks, and how to get bombs into position, and finally how to get Savoias and Bredas into the air, when the army took priority of every truck, and when the R.A.F., supposedly "defunct and devitalized", was showing an energy quite unsuited to a corpse? Such questions seemed to have no obvious answers.

Hence the first Italian raid did not take place until June 12th, when a dozen aircraft bombed Sollum. This was followed by a visit to Matruh, where three trucks were damaged and three natives killed. The next day the Italians repeated their efforts, but there were no R.A.F. casualties. A day later, threatening messages in several languages fluttered over R.A.F. camps. Up to date, the Italian performance was hardly sustaining pre-war claims. If this was indeed a display of the might of the *Regia Aeronautica*, then there was no need to fear.

But R.A.F. Middle East had already detected disturbing signs of British air inferiority. The Gladiator was too slow for the Savoia 79. At the moment, Italian bombing attacks were neither intensive nor sustained, but there was nothing to prevent them from becoming so in the near future.

By June 22nd Aboukir had been raided only once, but the maintenance depot was still safe. If it had been hit the course of the air war might well have been altered. Aboukir was vital, and, unlike Alexandria, could not be defended by the massed fire-power of the fleet. It was within easy reach of aircraft flying in low over the coast giving little warning of their approach. Aboukir, relatively defenceless, embraced all the workshops and special equipment needed to modify and service aircraft. It lay near the road, with the administration centre conveniently between two landing-grounds. Deceptively enough, the little village bearing the same name was a mile and a half away. The village suffered a fate never intended for it, as successive Italian raids let loose bombs everywhere except in the right place.

But the contrast between the relative performances of the R.A.F. and the *Regia Aeronautica* was as surprising at the time as in retrospect. Italian morale was high. Mussolini had promised his soldiers that they would soon be "bathing in the green waters of the Nile", and the air force was looking forward to

[1] As time went on it became a point of honour to try to sink this emblem of indestructibility. Pilots returning from raids often disposed of any spare ammunition in the hopes that one day the cruiser might subside gently on to the floor of the harbour. But it never did.

its share of Cairo luxuries. Pilots had been trained in Desert conditions, and had long been famous for their aerobatic skill. There was no reason to suppose that the discreditable legends concerning the army would apply equally to the picked men of the air force. They could fight, and presumably they would show their ability only too soon. National prejudice may have it that the Italians were always cowards, and our men always brave. To attempt to cast one more stone into an already troubled pool would serve no purpose here. But it should be said that there is no evidence to show that the inaccuracy of Italian bombing was due to lack of spirit, nor that the infrequency of Italian attacks was due to unwillingness to fight. Rather should one look to Italian air policy to discover why the four-to-one superiority was so ineffective, and to their maintenance organization to see how badly any policy would have been observed. Standing patrols were soon to become the normal routine of an Italian fighter pilot's day. Bases, lines of communication, and the ports from which supplies were being unloaded, were to demand an ever-increasing share of the air effort. As the patrols increased, so engine hours mounted up and the serviceability percentage fell. Then again, the more aircraft to be serviced, the less able was the maintenance organization to deal with what was already on hand, and the longer it took to get aircraft back to the forward landing-grounds. The more aircraft being treated for one fault or another, the more unwieldy the system became, so that when advance and retreat swayed the army backwards and forwards across the Desert, the air force was unable to keep in step. Thus still more aircraft were lost, either by capture or by damage from R.A.F. raids.

But as for air policy, the Italian army was only getting what it demanded. Standing patrols protected military depots and military lines of communication. Harbour defence aircraft were there to see that supplies for the army were safely unloaded. Front-line air umbrellas were unfurled over ground units otherwise unwilling to advance.

With such sacrifice made to its cause, the Italian army expected a rapid series of advances, but it was slow in preparing for the offensive, and was meanwhile harassed by frontier patrol activity, as Wavell mounted a pin-prick offensive "illogical" to Graziani.

At last, by September 13th, the Italian command was ready. The 200 tanks, the four divisions with a fifth in reserve, overflowed the frontier like a lava stream, and poured down on Sidi Barrani.

And there it stopped, a victim once more to frontier skirmishes and patrols. The sand underfoot was of little importance, except that an Army Co-operation and a 202 Group fighter squadron were dispossessed of their landing-ground. If Matruh was within boasting distance, it seemed that the Italian view of war in the Desert was prejudiced by experience of Senussi revolts. Each village occupied represented a victory. The Italians set about fortifying each small outpost as though a strip of sand and a few huts spelled success. Supply dumps stretched in echelon from Maktila to Sidi Barrani, where a minor Maginot Line tailed off into the southern wastes. To the rear the "slow and unenterprising enemy" (Wavell) was building up his reserves of aircraft to an overall strength of 700 (248 bombers, 255 fighters, and the rest transport and communication types).

Meanwhile, 202 Group had settled into their new Headquarters. They had brought with them some oddly sounding equipment; an inventory of the period mentions such items as "six boxes of coloured pins and a crazy grid". They had been allotted places in which to live—the Senior Air Staff Officer, No. 6 lorry; Operations, another; Intelligence, an office block, a marquee, and a dug-out. Army Liaison had its own living hut, whereas Signals crouched in what had been the guard-room.

From there was directed what air effort could be devised, and from there was planned the raid on El Adem towards the end of June, which may have contributed towards Balbo's death. Balbo was in the air at the time of the attack, and it was just possible that his aeroplane was hit by a bomb falling from one of the Blenheims of 55 squadron. There were stories that Italian anti-aircraft gunners had shot him down deliberately, but such accuracy was rarely possible, and it seems likely that accident rather than intent guided the flak.[1]

Balbo's death caused certain regrets, even among his enemies, for he had been well known in international air circles before the war. And besides, the fighting had not yet been really bitter. There was room for what are known as "gentlemanly incidents". For instance, an Italian aircraft had dropped a message in our lines to say that the crews of certain aircraft were safe, and on the 17th 208 squadron dropped a sack of mail for those who had been captured, which was promptly delivered. But the bombing of Tobruk and Derna showed tougher aspects. A reconnaissance report towards the end of August mentions that the harbour was almost inactive as a result of R.A.F. raids.

Graziani's advance caused a flutter of excitement; a message sent from 202 Group to the observer screen ran: "Cancel all orders. Scram. All posts retire eastwards (repeat eastwards) on Matruh". As the enemy streamed towards Sollum, where once the English had fought the hostile Senussi, ten Italian aircraft raided Sidi Barrani. They were met for once on terms not in their favour. Two Hurricanes, twelve Gladiators and two Blenheims shot down all but three, the Hurricanes accounted for four and the Blenheims for three. One Gladiator from 80 squadron was missing. 112 squadron, which had replaced 33 squadron, suffered no loss.

The Hurricanes were new and fast.[2] They were gradually to oust the Gladiators, acting *pro tem.* as single, or at most paired, fighters. Flying in low over the coast, they would appear unexpectedly and shoot up whatever could be

[1] Rumour reported that a sparking-plug had been soaked in petrol and wired into the petrol-tank. This, it was said, would have guaranteed an explosion in the air from five to ten minutes after take-off.

[2] So long as they did not have to contend with the Me. 109, when, in comparison, they seemed old and slow.

found on the route back. During the stalemate in the Desert, 33 squadron managed to re-equip with Hurricanes, but up to the end of November 112 squadron still could not throw off their Gladiators.

There was to be no chance of increasing the pressure on Tobruk, Derna and Sollum, or of mounting greater and greater air offensives against Berka, Benina and El Adem. When Italy invaded Greece on October 28th aircraft for our ally could come only from the Western Desert. 202 Group, already depleted by the loss of 45 squadron to the Sudan, was now robbed of two Blenheim squadrons, 211 and 84. One flight of 11 and one flight of 39 squadrons were the only replacements.[1]

American officers, visiting the squadron in November, were to see that these forces had already given a good account of themselves. Appollonia, Derna, Gazala, Tobruk, Bardia and Sollum had been constantly attacked; as sea bases their uses were increasingly restricted. Enemy tanks, instead of being unloaded at Tobruk, were being moved from Benghazi and Tripoli by road, with the result, as an Italian prisoner of war reported, that "tanks like useless hulks" were stranded along the rough Desert tracks waiting for repairs.

Because, during the Italian advance on Sidi Barrani, casualties had been caused to motorized units moving along the road near Buq Buq, the Italians had tried to shield their troops by standing air patrols. But this meant that there were then less aircraft for the defence of aerodromes, which immediately became R.A.F. targets. Finally, the Italians were forced to maintain standing patrols over both troops and landing-grounds. To this practice Collishaw attributed "the loss of air superiority and the final breakdown of the fighter force in Cyrenaica".

[1] In the Longmore dispatch the list of units reads:

208 Army Co-operation Squadron (one flight of Hurricanes, two flights of Lysanders).
No. 6 Army Co-operation Squadron (one flight attached to 208 squadron, Lysanders).
33 Fighter Squadron (Hurricanes).
112 Fighter Squadron (Gladiators).
No. 3 R.A.A.F. Fighter Squadron (Gladiators and Lysanders).
55 Bomber Squadron (Blenheims).
113 Bomber Squadron (Blenheims).
11 Bomber Squadron (one flight Blenheims).
39 Bomber Squadron (one flight Blenheims), and early in December numbers were increased by the addition of 274 squadron (Hurricanes) and by the return of 45 squadron, now with Blenheims.

CHAPTER III

FORWARDS

THE Italian lava stream had failed to overflow obstacles at Sidi Barrani. But the volcano was still in eruption, and material piled up daily. Rumbles from Radio Bari suggested that a new offensive would drive the British out of Egypt—"where, in any case, they have no right to be".

However, it was a curious feature of Italian advances that the logical result never by any chance occurred. An easy victory in East Africa ought to have led to the closing of the Red Sea, or at least to a grave interruption of traffic. Equally, the advance which should have made Matruh untenable, on the contrary allowed our forces to build up enough supplies for an offensive which would carry Wavell's army straight through to Cyrenaica.

Wavell's drive caught Graziani at a time when he was in the midst of preparing for an offensive of his own. The flurry and confusion produced by the reversal of orders, repacking of stores newly unpacked, the loss not only of his base, but of his entire little Maginot, was reflected in the disorganization of his air force. The figure previously quoted (1,100 aircraft abandoned or wrecked from Barrani to Benghazi) could only mean chaos on a scale rivalling the most contrived situation in a comic opera.

The British offensive, a combined operation by the army, navy and air force, was a limited tactical manœuvre, intended to establish our forces in positions as far west as Buq Buq. The Army was to make full use of the new light tanks brought in with much secrecy to root the Italians out of their prepared defences. The probe, if successful, was to be supported by the 4th Indian Division, and by an independent infantry brigade. The Royal Navy, which had already sliced the top of every building in Barrani, was to turn 15-inch guns on to Maktila and on to all enemy camps within reach, whilst aircraft of Fleet Air Arm were to attack Bardia. The R.A.F. was to continue its work against enemy aerodromes and, just before the attack, was to bomb defended positions by day and by night.

In anticipation, 202 Group had been enlarged; 45 squadron returning hastily from the Sudan to find detachments of 11 and 39 squadrons freshly in from Aden. The night effort, with Bombays and Wellingtons of 216, 70, 37 and 38 squadrons, was now on a scale sufficient to allow Collishaw to speak of "heavy" bombardment. The Hurricanes of 274 squadron with their eight guns added a touch of surprise to an operation which was startling from beginning to end.

The first week saw the enemy driven out of Egypt. The stone eagle at Fort Capuzzo glared angrily at its new owners. Our forward troops were menacing Bardia.

Meanwhile, the Italian air force had abandoned all attempts at strategic war. No attacks were made on any of the great ports; and airfields, apart from Maaten Bagush and Qasaba, were immune. Graziani explained, "Owing to fatal atmospheric conditions—first sandstorms, then floods caused by exceptional rains—our air force could not make its full weight felt in battle". 74 aircraft had been destroyed by the R.A.F. in that first week, and more victims were to follow.

The army had exceeded all hopes by the complete success of its local offensive; in Barrani they had captured the bearded general, Gallina, whose belief that there was no more ammunition left in the town was not borne out by the facts. They scarcely had time to taste the unusual flavour of Parmesan and Chianti before they were urged onwards towards the frontier. 38,000 white and 16,500 coloured troops were killed or taken prisoner, whilst another 40,000 were known to be bottled up in Bardia. General Berganzoli ordered a stand at the escarpment of Sollum; the Italian Air Force put up a show of strength; but the battle was already lost. Along the road built by special order of Mussolini, the road which was to have linked the two ends of the new Roman Empire, flowed the Italians, not as conquerors, but as prisoners.

For Bardia the battle was protracted. As the "Bastion of Fascism" its fall would have a political value beyond its natural importance. The tactics used here were suited to the place. A wadi, girt with warehouses, running through the centre of the town, was bombed continually in order to cut the defence system in half. Bombs dropped by the Fleet Air Arm and the R.A.F. on the road to Tobruk isolated Bardia still further; and by January 4th the bastion had fallen. An Italian doctor, commenting on the raids, said: "The bombing was very terrifying; the Libyan troops were almost completely demoralized and the Italian troops were almost as bad. Half of their food supply had been destroyed by bombs on the port area, and for two days before the surrender certain units had no food. Casualties from bombing were slight, but material damage was large."

The next advance was not to take place for another three weeks, when the fall of Tobruk was to make a rout out of what was already a crushing Italian defeat. Then the army was to sweep victoriously on to Benghazi and beyond to El Agheila, a point on the map where coastal marshes and the Great Sand Sea made a defensive line as inevitable as El Alamein.

Lieut.-General O'Connor, commenting on the contribution of the R.A.F. "Since the war began you have consistently attacked without intermission an enemy air force between five and ten times your strength, until finally he was driven out of the sky. You have co-operated to the full in carrying out our many requests for special bombardments, reconnaissance, and protection against enemy air action, and I would like to say how much of this has contributed to our success." In particular, he was referring to the photo reconnaissances of the aircraft of 202 Group during the short siege of Tobruk, and to the work of 3 Squadron R.A.A.F. at Bardia, where Gladiators had flown low over our advancing troops. But less visible air co-operation had been quietly taking place since the turn of the new year (on the night of January 1st and 2nd, Wellingtons and Bombays, together with Fleet Air Arm Swordfish, dropped over 20,000 lb. of bombs on enemy defences and troop positions).

Fighting on to Tobruk, air force effort repeated itself. Once more the softening up; once more the attack of enemy aerodromes—only this time they were Berka and Benina—once more three squadrons seen overhead by the troops; and the other squadrons present, though less obviously.

There, in Tobruk, the *San Giorgio*, battered, but still capable of putting up flak, lay as witness to what could and could not be achieved by air bombardment at that stage of the war. For the *San Giorgio*, immobilized, and no longer fulfilling its function as a mother ship for submarines, was nevertheless still afloat.

Headquarters 202 Group was now in danger of being left behind. It had not by then acquired the tradition of mobility as part of its work, for its experience had been limited to a hurried packing of equipment for the road and rail voyage from Cairo to Maaten Bagush. On January 10th the Headquarters got under way, to reach Sollum with its units splayed out in front like a protective apron; the bombers near at hand, the Army Co-operation squadrons further away at Gambut.

At Sollum, even in the heat of the battle, there was time for a sigh of relief. From the air a steep cliff seems to spring out of the Desert towards the sea. The endless blotched dunes disappear, and great fissures carve ravines out of soil which bears some resemblance to Europe. The "weary waste expanding to the skies" disappears; vegetation, no longer scrubbily sub-human, wears an air of fertility. The Desert landscape, the landscape of the moon, becomes less formidable. But further on, still better things are in store: Derna, Appollonia and Barce. Benghazi represents the last outpost of a civilization which seems to have a separate existence as an island of hills and valleys raised high above the level of a sandy plain.

Nearer to this promised land moved 202 Group during the course of January. 73 and 274 fighter squadrons reached Gazala, and 3 squadron R.A.A.F. and 208 squadron, Tmimi. Derna, its little streets aflame with bougainvillaea, with its market place and its sparkling water, was nearby. And beyond Derna lay the rolling hills of Djebel, where the red earth, splashed with green, showed occasional traces of successive conquerors. The ruins of Cyrene told of a Greek civilization earlier and more easterly than Roman Leptis Magna in Tripolitania. Carthaginians, Egyptians, Romans, Berbers, Arabs and Turks had come to conquer and stayed to settle. The Italians, the latest in a long line of colonists, lacking the grandeur of ancient Rome, had tried to impress Benghazi with the dynamic of modern Fascism. Their little white bungalows, disfigured by slogans, were set in neat rows near Appollonia, near Barce, and elsewhere on the uplands wherever water could persuade the soil to fertility.

Diversity of race amongst the Allied troops could hold no terrors for the Cyrenaicans; nor, it seemed, could the fact of a British invasion. Even Italian colonists appeared to regard the newcomers as tourists. In Benghazi hotels opened their doors, brought out registers, and reserved tables; the shops took in their new customers as though the inevitable, having occurred, presented a situation no more out of the ordinary than the arrival of fresh contingents of Italian troops. But the conquerors were more like men from the moon. Hitherto deprived of even the minimum standard of comfort, and out of touch with civilization as they had known it, they were as strange to the customs and everyday life of the Cyrenaicans as visitors from another planet.

Amongst them the air force units, viewing the scenery from the ground, were pleased with what they saw. The enemy air force, retreating into Tripolitania, was "so depleted as to be incapable of offering any serious threat for the time being".

During their brief stay at Sollum 202 Group heard the disquieting news of the impending arrival of German air force units. Reports indicated that about 200 bombers and 200 dive-bombers were assembled in Sicily. Meanwhile, the remnant of the Italian air force showed disquieting signs of life. On New Year's Day a single C.R. 42 attacked a formation of nine Blenheims as they were leaving Derna. Five of the Blenheims were damaged; the C.R. 42 escaped. Two days later another single Italian fighter attacked two Blenheims, one of which was shot down into the sea and the other severely damaged. On the same day, as though in retaliation, a Hurricane shot down three out of five S.M. 79's which were attacking H.M.S. *Terror* nine miles north-east of Bardia.

The Italian Air Ministry was expressing concern over the high wastage of fighters in Libya; to compensate perhaps for decreasing numbers, units of the *Regia Aeronautica*, which had been sent to Belgium for operations against England, were withdrawn to Italy.

As January advanced, German aircraft became more and more active. Mass raids on Malta gave some indication of what the island was to expect in future. But German dive-bombers were still unable to prevent Malta-based Wellingtons from harassing the Sicilian landing-grounds.

An attack on the Suez Canal by two He. 111's led to the discovery that German aircraft, mounted from Catania, were flying over Benghazi, out to sea again, and back over the coast at Rosetta Point. It so happened that both aircraft had to force-land in the Desert, one near Sollum; the crew, imagining that they were behind the Italian lines, failed to set fire to their aircraft. The incident caused some amusement amongst the Italians; General Porro was reported to have said: "Teach us our business? They'd better go straight back!"

Nothing of the sort was likely to happen. A German Air Commission arrived at Benghazi, and returned to report to Rome on aspects of the air war, whilst *Fliegerkorps X* established a Headquarters at Taormina. German aircraft, growing more ambitious, laid mines in the Suez Canal towards the end of January; but the Italians were less disposed for such ventures, their bomber force was being withdrawn from Cyrenaica. Some units had lost aircraft at the rate of

45 per cent each month in the last few months, and reinforcements could no longer come from Benghazi. Supplies now had to come all the way from Tripoli.

202 Group was also faced with unexpected problems of supply. During the advance 202 Group had been concerned with forcing the enemy squadrons to abandon landing-grounds between Sollum and Derna, with the object of driving their opponents back to the Djebel, where only a few small landing-strips eked out the larger aerodromes on the plain surrounding Benghazi. Once the *Regia Aeronautica* could be dislodged from these advanced fields Alexandria was no longer in danger. 202 Group succeeded in their object; but in so doing they destroyed stores which could have supported them for the rest of the campaign; and although many hundreds of thousands of gallons of aviation spirit were captured, the R.A.F. was still dependent on the army and navy for the arrival of its material. The *Luftwaffe*, by dropping mines in the harbours of Tobruk, Bardia and Sollum, interfered with arrangements for unloading. Petrol and bombs for the R.A.F. were often given a lower priority than stores for the army. The alternative, a long haul from Matruh, might not be inviting, but was at least reliable.

The army, like the R.A.F., were feeling the effects of being so far from the Delta. Their stocks of petrol and ammunition were similarly subject to delay. The prospect of a further advance held attractions, for Benghazi was a promising port of supply. Hence the 7th Armoured Division was directed to push onwards towards Jedabya, whilst the 6th Australian Division was driving along the coastal road to Benghazi. But the port was not allowed to live up to expectations. German air attack started almost immediately, mounting in intensity after the second week in February. 3 squadron R.A.A.F. and 73 squadron were retained as harbour guards instead of being sent to Greece. But in spite of this the first German air campaign in Cyrenaica was successful. A naval decision that the port was untenable as a sea base meant that a further offensive was, for the time being, out of the question. The decision affected 202 Group, who were, to quote Collishaw, "prevented from further demoralizing the enemy's routed troops which were escaping westwards to El Agheila in crowded masses on the main road". Instead, a holding force was established in Cyrenaica, and 202 Group withdrew to a distance.

The position inevitably invited attack.

It could not be long before the Germans would find out that the R.A.F. was "bluffing a full house", without even a couple of pairs. Our reconnaissance aircraft brought back reports that the enemy was building up his forces. Those in and around Benghazi knew that they were living on the slopes of a volcano.

An eruption in the past had brought the Italians to Sidi Barrani. But in return the *Regia Aeronautica* had been challenged, broken and thrown back on Tripolitania. The second eruption promised to be more serious. This time there were the *Afrika Korps* and the *Luftwaffe*.

Well might the situation be described as "ugly".

CHAPTER IV

ON THE EDGE OF THE VOLCANO

REFERENCE has already been made to the pre-war arrangements for providing liaison between Corps and the advanced air forces. Army Co-operation and Close Support were considered to be two different things; one involving the army control of 208, 6 and 3 R.A.A.F. squadrons for tactical reconnaissance, the other meaning any operation carried out by the air force for purely army purposes. These vague outlines of co-operation and support were to take on a "more precise and hopeful form" in May 1941, when 253 Army Co-operation Wing was formed. The outlines themselves were to be changed completely before operation "Crusader", only to be modified once more before the retreat to Alamein.

A summary of Army Co-operation up to the end of the first Cyrenaican campaign can best be illustrated by the history of 3 squadron R.A.A.F. Sailing from Sydney in July 1940, the pilots arrived at Tewfik towards the end of August. Training began in September; by November they were ready to move up to Gerawla for operations. But meanwhile, ideas about Army Co-operation—the aircraft to be used and the work to be done—were changing. The Lysander, designed specially to meet army needs in the way of tactical photography and artillery reconnaissance, was too slow, too vulnerable and too passive an aircraft; it could neither give nor take. But it was there on the spot when other aircraft were not; and until the arrival of Gladiators or Hurricanes, it had to serve. Training began with a borrowed machine, and was continued with two further loans, because fresh aircraft were sometimes found to be without airscrews or air cleaners. Gladiators from 33 squadron (now converted to Hurricanes) were next offered to 3 squadron R.A.A.F., but before these could be assimilated a detachment of the squadron was sent to Qasaba to take delivery of Gauntlets.

The latter, which the pilots jestingly called "Britain's answer to the Stuka", could be used as dive-bombers, and training was carried out on that assumption. The "pure" conception of Army Co-operation was changing. Aircraft were no longer to be passive observers, but active agents in close support of the troops. The Gauntlets had to be withdrawn after a few weeks; they were used for the first and last time during the battle of Sidi Barrani, before it was decided that their age entitled them to excessive maintenance which a battlefield could not provide.

With Gladiators, 3 squadron tended to become more and more of a fighter squadron; and though it was still known as an Army Co-operation unit, and was attached to H.Q. Desert Force until the end of January, it was a sensitive barometer recording the changes in theory and practice.

During the battle of Sidi Barrani an incident occurred which did nothing to help the air command in its progress towards self-determination and control of its own operations. British troops in the Sofafi area were attacked by Hurricanes and bombed by bombers from 202 Group. 13 Corps immediately asked to be allowed to control any air action in the tactical area. This request was refused, but various methods of better identification were tried, the least unsatisfactory proving to be a white cross displayed at Coy. H.Q. Other means, such as pistols and coloured flares, were put on trial, but as Group-Captain Brown pointed out: "All forms of recognition signals are open to objection and should not be adopted unless absolutely necessary. The closer the close support control, the less the need for ground recognition."

There, for the present, the matter lay.

The Germans had made an extensive study of dive-bomber tactics, and their crews were well trained. At Fassberg, dives on to silhouettes of ships were made from 10,000 feet at 50 to 70 degrees, pulling out at about 300 feet. These were apparently satisfactory.

Unpleasant experiences over the Thames Estuary, Middlesbrough and Billingham, where there were barrage balloons and anti-aircraft guns, did much to reassure the Germans that the dive-bomber, if unopposed by such hazards, would be a deadly weapon against weakened enemy forces. Dive-bomber units were to be under the control of the army commanders, to whom were attached small liaison staffs, known as *Koluft* officers. In France the *Koluft* had enjoyed a high status; they were often to be seen in their own Fieseler Storch's, sometimes having under their control front-line armoured cars from which they could maintain contact by radio telephone with aircraft overhead. Whenever the army required air support, the commanders sent a request (tantamount to an order) to the *Koluft* staff, who then arranged for the dive-bombers and their escort to be assembled.

• • • • •

If there was much to be learned from the Germans, as well as much to be avoided, the R.A.F. at this stage of the war in the Desert was mainly preoccupied with putting its own house in order. The first campaign had revealed various weaknesses inherent in applying peacetime methods to war. Air Vice-Marshal Elmhirst was enjoined to discover the flaws; his conclusions, together with an operational report by Air Commodore Collishaw, formed the basis of the first reorganization of the R.A.F. to meet purely Desert conditions.

For reasons of economy and efficiency the air forces in England had been spaced on a station basis. The R.A.F. overseas, whose main function was to demonstrate the principles of control without occupation, had been able to continue this policy with only minor modifications. But the Desert war had shown clearly enough that mobility was the key to success, and that this quality was one that a static force could hardly be expected to possess. "Any change of base was a major operation." . . . "All squadron commanders reported that they had not enough mechanical transport", but "captured enemy transport and army vehicles enabled squadrons to carry on", chorused the reports. The Army Co-operation squadrons, operating with 13 Corps, being smaller, with a higher percentage of operational as opposed to ground staff, had found it easier to be mobile. They were more flexible; they could be split into two; the operational aircraft on ahead, the administrative and repair sections on a rear landing-ground.

Yet 202 Group, though lacking these advantages, had succeeded in moving its units 670 miles from Daba to El Agheila, without being able to draw appreciable quantities of supplies from any port other than Mersa Matruh. Elmhirst remarked, "The ability of the squadron to function at a very high pressure was in the main due to the spirit of the pilots, and in fact all personnel, to the efforts of the Advanced Stores Park and Repair and Salvage units, and also to the hard work of all concerned with the supply of petrol and bombs to the advanced units". But other comments were less laudatory. Squadrons were not always near enough to the front, with the result that many valuable engine hours were wasted in going to and from the landing-grounds; the Air Officer Commanding 202 Group would have welcomed a meteorological station at his H.Q.; there were no radar warning stations with the forward units, and aerodrome defence suffered accordingly; finally, heavy bombers based in the canal area, by using forward landing-grounds for repair and refuelling, were causing a strain on the petrol stocks and spares organization.

Collishaw's observations were concerned more with methods of exploiting Italian mistakes. His understanding of enemy tactics, gained largely before the outbreak of war, made his views especially valuable. He was particularly struck by the failure of the *Regia Aeronautica* to attack our forward landing-grounds. The R.A.F. had shown the way by sorties against Gazala, El Adem and Benina. The Italians, instead of going to the root of the evil, had, as it were, taken medicine to ward off some of the ill effects; they had "maintained standing fighter patrols", thereby wasting fighters. In Collishaw's view, "the generals commanding the various parts of the enemy's lines of communication also contributed to the failure . . . by insisting on having fighter patrols flying over the roads".

On the advantages of taking the offensive, regardless of inequality of forces, he was equally insistent. He said that this, a fundamental tenet of the First World War, had not altered in the meantime. Thus, whilst the enemy's activities in the first months of the war were confined to local engagements, the R.A.F. had been on the offensive throughout, bombers attacking by day and night, and fighters out singly if whole squadrons were lacking.

Collishaw considered that employing fighters singly in "tip-and-run" raids had brought results beyond reasonable expectation; and that the Italian fighter units, involved in trying to thwart attacks against the ground forces, were unable to dispute air superiority over our advancing army. There had been hazards in using fighters independently. It might have meant a steady trickle of losses, but the risk was one which he was prepared to take, and the gamble succeeded.

Collishaw, like his successors, was amazed at the defects in enemy organization. R.A.F. Middle East had built up a Supply and Maintenance system in the Delta, and 202 Group had advanced with a Repair and Salvage unit and with an Air Stores Park, whilst the Italians, mistaking necessity for luxury, had been handicapped by the absence of aircraft repair depots. Yet the enemy had had plenty of time to prepare. The ports, with their distributive arteries the roads, were there. One explanation may have been that they felt oversure of their ability to provide fresh aircraft from Italy direct to forward fields, and to fly up special crews to deal with those stranded and in need of repair. The United States Army Air Forces in Italy were later to show that this was a practical proposition when vast resources existed. The *Regia Aeronautica* in the Desert called in vain for replacements from the factories of Milan.

The Italians had been prepared for a speedy victory. If Graziani had succeeded in reaching the Delta, Porro's "High-stepping Savoia circus" could have mustered enough serviceable aircraft for an impressive demonstration of aerobatics over the Citadel. Instead, the circus had not even unfolded its tents. It had been shattered from the air by a force inferior in everything except determination and organization. Collishaw's policy of surprise and attack, often criticized as leading to a wastage of resources, had undoubtedly, to quote his own words, "foxed 'em". And the R.A.F., fully alive to its own deficiencies, was bent on showing the Germans improved tactics.

. . . . .

Events at sea before the British occupation of Cyrenaica had given little warning of what was to happen later. The Italian battle fleet was a potential, rather than an actual, threat, for most of its time was spent in port. Attacking Taranto on the night November 11th–12th, aircraft of the Fleet Air Arm demonstrated that there was no longer any such thing as a safe harbourage. Torpedo hits against three battleships, and bomb hits against two cruisers and other vessels, led to a wider dispersal of the Italian naval forces. Though, slowly, air power was starting to exert a sure influence on naval matters. January 1941 broadcast the new state of affairs when German aircraft, operating from Sicily, sunk the cruiser *Southampton*, and badly damaged a destroyer and an aircraft carrier.

In February and March, air reconnaissance of Tripoli showed that unusual quantities of enemy shipping were arriving, whilst Ju. 52's were flying in troops daily. By early March the greater part of a division had arrived; the *Afrika Korps* had come into being. The latter the Royal Navy could certainly not prevent, but it could harass supply vessels and troopships. Sensitive to the amount of damage done to their shipping, the Italians tried to stage a diversion, a naval force putting out into the Mediterranean in order to draw the fire of the British fleet. In these lapwing tactics they were successful, but the triumph was short-lived, for their second aim was to tempt the Royal Navy into pursuing them to within range of Sicilian-based aircraft. Thence the dive-bombers of the *Luftwaffe* were to have given a demonstration of the decisiveness of air power. But on March 26th the Italian force was caught without air protection off Cape Matapan, and the biter was severely bitten. This factor established the Royal Navy in a position of overwhelming superiority in the Mediterranean for the rest of the war. Yet "in another two months, although no further major naval action had been fought, and although there had been no accession of naval strength to the enemy, the Mediterranean route was closed to Allied shipping".[1]

During the coming months the Germans struck at the Middle East from two angles. Rommel, following the Desert railway, reached Sollum by April 12th. The week before the Germans had invaded Greece, to achieve in a few days what the Italians had been attempting with such conspicuous lack of success since the previous October. Within a fortnight British troops were evacuating Greece, and the situation was to deteriorate into utter rout by May 2nd. Then the final blow; Crete was to fall into German hands as a result of an airborne invasion, which might have been too costly to contemplate if German advance in the Desert had not overrun airfields from which fighters, based in Cyrenaica, could have controlled the air over the island.

German occupation of Greece, Crete and Cyrenaica meant German air control of the Mediterranean routes. After June, Middle East was isolated, supplied only by means of "the long journey round the Cape". No British convoy could pass safely through the Mediterranean until the Cyrenaican airfields were once more, if only temporarily, in British hands during operation Crusader.

Air power in the Mediterranean had been ushered in with fanfares; but for a while it seemed that the German actor would strut the stage in the principal role.

[1] Spears.

CHAPTER V

THE HUMAN BEING

DESERT life, for the vast majority, meant a form of existence so strange and unfamiliar that few of the conventional phrases can be forced into service. Cairo and Alexandria were amazed at the amount of sand which, figuratively and actually, seemed to stick to those who happened to visit either city for a short period of leave.

In Middle East a typical R.A.F. Other Rank had enjoyed a variety of experience quite unlike anything that might have come his way previously. He was with a body of men who had little but their work to occupy their minds, who were divorced from all the normal amenities of life, and who had somehow to make the best of it. He was in surroundings which lacked any of the usual landmarks, where often for miles in every direction there were no houses, no trees, no hills and no roads. He was on a ration scale which allowed for liberal quantities of bully-beef and tea, but which made few concessions to the degree of latitude. He was rarely given enough water; sometimes the ration was only half a gallon a day per head for all purposes, including cooking and washing, and even this meagre dole could not always be guaranteed. He was not only away from home, but, except for the postal services, completely cut off from his family circle. And there were no women.

Service in other overseas commands could embody many of these disadvantages, but seldom all of them at once. An airman had to become more and more mobile as retreat and advance swayed him to and fro across the Desert; and that meant a sacrifice of even the few personal belongings which had served to remind him that there was, somewhere at least, another kind of existence.

By the end of February 1941 the airman would have seen enough of the Desert to last him all his life. He would probably have arrived in Alexandria, and might have stayed a few days in a transit camp outside the port. He would have seen very little of the town apart from the N.A.A.F.I., a few shops and the esplanade, whose concrete sea walls suggested some eastern Blackpool.

A photograph of himself, in strange clothes and unfamiliar surroundings, must of course be sent home. There were plenty of people to remind him of this as of everything else. The eagerness of the street hawkers melted away excuses; those who managed to fend off the boot-blacks fell prey to the trinket-sellers.

Posting, perhaps to a fresh unit, often provided fresh surprises. With men in such short supply, squadrons fought to get anyone they could, and the personnel officers, notoriously incorruptible, were hard put to it to maintain their reputation. But anyone who thought that last-minute changes and unfamiliar conditions were but passing phases was due for a succession of further setbacks. Loaded on to the back of a three-ton truck, he would soon be on the road out to El Daba, his view of the fig plantations obscured by a cloud of sand, which, faithful as a shadow, would follow him closely all the way. Seasick after the road journey, he would arrive at Daba like a man stepping out of a boat after a stormy Channel crossing. There, with a mug of sweet, hot, N.A.A.F.I. tea, he would try to forget the road, winding away into the distance like a tarmac snake, undulating over the surface of the Desert.

He would see Mersa Matruh, and would become familiar with the "Ship Inn"; and perhaps there would be time for a bathe in the clear blue water of the lagoon. Then he would take the road to Sidi Barrani, where uplands parody green fields, and herds of goats nibble near the side of the road. And so onwards through the solitude of Halfaya Pass, where "the carved brown edge of Libya stood up from the dismal levels like a coast, as Doughty had once seen the coast of Harra riding high upon the plain".[1]

He would be introduced to his new aerodrome, a patch of Desert flatter than usual, cleared of stones, where tents and caravans spread out in imitation of a country fair.

Christmas at Sidi Haneish found a chronicler who gives a faithful picture of one of the brighter periods. His account is quoted at length.

"Sidi Haneish lay at the top of an escarpment, and was exposed to every wind that blew. From this drome 'Imshi' Mason, 'Nobby' Clark and 'Judy' Garland made daily sorties against the Italians. Taking off at dawn, the formations of Hurricanes roared away, leaving a trail of black exhaust fumes in the cold winter air. The ground crews eagerly awaited their return, and there were smiles of satisfaction on the faces of those crews who recognized their returning pilots doing a victory roll over the 'drome, thus notifying the squadron of their success. Not a day passed but the jubilant pilots gave vent to their satisfaction at besting the Axis by shooting up the 'drome and doing victory rolls. To this 'drome many pilots limped home with the fuselage of their kites riddled with bullet holes, but they gave far more than they ever received.

"A great amount of captured war material found its way from the forward areas to the 'drome. Motor-cycles, staff cars, transport of every description, including push-bikes, were soon in evidence. Flight-Sergeants would go their rounds in Italian staff cars, whilst the Commanding Officer, 'Paddy' Dunn, could be seen calling at the Orderly Room riding a brand new motor-bike. Soon all ranks, from the lowest erk upwards, had obtained some sort of enemy transport to propel them over the bumpy desert scrub that surrounded the 'drome. Ground crews, who walked from kite to kite doing their various jobs, were looked upon as having their fingers

[1] Guedalla.

in. Foraging parties returned with rifles, ammunition, Breda guns, and all the paraphernalia of war that the fleeing Italians had left behind.

"The big event, however, was to be Christmas. The men were rather disappointed at not being able to spend their Christmas near the fleshpots of Alexandria, but this disappointment quickly vanished when they were confronted with the amazing Christmas spread laid before them by the squadron cooks.

"Christmas in the Western Desert at Sidi Haneish was the first that many of the men had spent away from their homes, and they were determined to do all in their power to capture the festive spirit. Parties sprang into being in every tent, as the occupants, armed with beer and other luxuries, commenced activities. By nightfall all was as merry as the proverbial marriage belle.

"On Christmas Day, those who were capable of doing so struggled over to breakfast before beginning the day's fun and games. Christmas Day in the Services, as everyone knows, is the day when strict discipline is relaxed. A day when the stiffest officer unbends and mumbles 'A Merry Christmas, lads'! A day on which erks have been known to call the officers 'Snow' and 'Chum', and get away with it. After the dinner, which had all the things necessary to warrant it being called 'Wizard', the C.O. spoke a few words to the officers and men. Then the fun commenced. Soon the air was vibrant with the crack of Italian rifles, as the boys indulged in a little target practice. The pilots, most of them having obtained Italian motor-cycles, indulged in a little fancy track-racing across the 'drome, and tried their skill at broadsiding. At night, a high tea completed the day's menu."

Christmas, 1940, continued.

CHAPTER VI

BACKWARDS

A NEW organization was at once set up to supersede the far-flung activities of 202 Group. On February 25th H.Q. Cyrenaica was formed, with Group-Captain Brown back in his old role as forward commander. His units showed how drastically the R.A.F. in the Desert had been reduced.[1]

There was no need to cry "Ichabod". The glory had not departed, but its point of emphasis had shifted. 45 and 113 squadrons had gone back to the Delta for rest and re-equipment; 274 squadron had returned to Alexandria with messages of appreciation and gratitude; part of 6 was with 208 squadron. But, mainly and most emphatically, the mantle of 202 Group had fallen over Greece.

Reference has already been made to the dispatch of units to the Greek front at a time when every aircraft was needed so badly in the Western Desert. But the full drain of resources was not evident until the establishment of H.Q. Cyrenaica, when, as has already been shown, scarcely more than a token force was left to occupy the Djebel. Between November 3rd and the 8th three detachments of aircraft were flown to Greece in answer to the urgent appeals made by the Greek Government. Although the Greeks had succeeded in occupying Albania, and in inflicting a defeat on the Italians in the Pindus sector, over Epirus the Italians had advanced across the river Kalamas, and were showing signs of using their overwhelming air superiority to harass Greek towns by day and night.

By January 1st, 1941, four squadrons were in Greece: 30 (Blenheim fighters), 80 (Gladiator fighters), 84 (Blenheim bombers), and 211 (Blenheim bombers). After defeat in the Desert the Italians continued the Greek campaign with a fervour which political prestige demanded, and which seemed to show more solid results than fresh ventures in Cyrenaica.

Three more squadrons left the Western Desert between the opening of the new year and the middle of February; 112 and 33 (Fighters), and 11 (Bombers); and yet more were to go. By the end of March 113 squadron had left Egypt, and 208 (the Army Co-operation unit replaced by No. 6 squadron) was re-equipping in preparation.

[1] There were:
3 Squadron R.A.A.F., now with Hurricanes (at Benina for air defence).
73 Fighter Squadron (at Bu Amed for defence of Tobruk).
One flight of No. 6 Squadron, Hurricanes and Lysanders (Barce and Pedabya).
55 Bomber Squadron (at Maraua).
31 Air Stores Park.
51 Repair and Salvage Units were at El Adem.
235 and 216 Air Ministry Experimental Stations (Radar) were at Tobruk and Benghazi.

Apart from the fact that so many squadrons were removed, reinforcements could not keep pace with wastage of what aircraft were in use in Libya. Takoradi reinforcement route and Malta staging post were functioning to the best of their ability, but the 166 aircraft which came to the Middle East through these channels must be compared with the loss of 184 aircraft during the first three months of 1941. Clearly then, Rommel's drive would be directed against an enemy waning, rather than waxing, in strength.

R.A.F. Cyrenaica was well aware of what was in store as operational aircraft dwindled in numbers. No. 6 squadron had but four Hurricanes, only one of which was fitted for photographic work; 3 squadron R.A.A.F. had to supply the deficiency in order to maintain tactical reconnaissance. But this was like blinding the left eye in order to see better with the right, for the defence of Benghazi and Benina aerodrome, of shipping off Cyrenaica, and troops on the Agheila line must all suffer.

The Lysanders, still in evidence, were woefully miscast for their new role, but they could at least be used to watch the eastern flank of our forces, where enemy opposition was less likely to be met. 55, the oldest bomber squadron in the Western Desert, could never muster more than four aircraft at any given time, and these were needed to carry out strategical reconnaissance at extreme range. From July 7th onwards a detachment of 45 squadron brought the numbers up by another eight, and four additional fighter Blenheims were a welcome increase to the strength.

Group-Captain Brown had hoped to continue the fight into Tripolitania. But since defence was to be the order of the day, he became wisely pessimistic about the situation in Cyrenaica. As a result, preparations for the retreat were made well in advance. Squadrons were to continue to operate during the withdrawal. But petrol and bombs were less amenable to the suggestion. There was not, and could not be, enough transport. Brown stated, "a great tribute is due to the army for their help in providing M/T. whenever possible, in spite of the gravely inadequate resources at their disposal, and the great demands on their available M/T. for their own vital needs".

Intelligence reports were so scanty, and reconnaissance aircraft so few, that there could be no sure theory about the time of the German advance. It might happen in mid July, or even in May. Of only one thing was Wavell certain—namely that the advance was coming.

March 24th saw patrol activity by two German divisions, coupled with low flying attacks by Me. 110's on our forward troops, heralding the collapse of the Agheila line.

As Allied troops fell back on Jedabya, the R.A.F. put out their maximum effort; the few Hurricanes of 3 squadron, feigning a standing patrol, and the small detachment of Blenheims working away at lines of communication and "soft-skinned" transport. But the German air component alone made such attempts seem puny, for by this time there were 90 Messerschmitts and 84

Stukas and Heinkel 111's in Tripolitania. On April 22nd demolitions in Benghazi, and on the following day withdrawals affecting the entire force, were all ordered. The Headquarters operational staff were bound for Maraua, and the main staff for Tobruk. They had held Barce long enough to sigh for its green trees and shady streets, its Italian hotels, and the red soil of its gardens; but now all the units were on the move, 3 squadron staying just long enough to engage a large force of enemy aircraft south of Benghazi, when they shot down six and probably damaged another four without losing a single aircraft. On the 5th, 3 and 73 squadrons patrolled continually to cover the passage of the Australian Division through the bottleneck of Barce escarpment, and protection was given to troops falling back on Mechili. Fourteen enemy aircraft were claimed for the loss of only two. But this gallant feat could not appreciably turn the scales. For days past an abnormal number of Bedouin encampments had been observed south of Agheila. Such methods to conceal troop movements to some extent drew attention to their existence. Something definite was in the air.

Italian morale, airborne with victory, was expected to soar. The deputy secretary of the Fascist party had previously estimated that 50 per cent of the Italian population hoped for defeat involving the Mussolini regime, and that only 25 per cent could be called fervent Fascists. But it was hoped that events of the last few days would encourage more enthusiasm.

The retreat to Tobruk evoked a statement of policy. Was the port to be surrendered? Air Marshal Tedder flew up in person from Cairo; and on the 8th the General Officer Commanding Middle East arrived by air to issue orders that Tobruk was to be held as long as possible. But at Mechili British troops had been surrounded and captured; two of our Generals were in enemy hands; whilst mechanical breakdowns had reduced the hitting power of 2nd Armoured Division.

Meanwhile, motor transport convoys continued to leave Mersa Matruh for Tobruk, and El Adem airfield was ransacked for spares suitable to be brought within the safer confines of El Gubbi. Nine unserviceable aircraft on El Adem were destroyed to prevent them falling into enemy hands, the catalogue reading like an extract from an index of 1939.[1]

On the 11th the road between Tobruk and El Adem was cut by German forces. And on the 12th, whilst Tobruk itself was invested, all files and documents not required for immediate use were destroyed by fire. Inside the twenty-seven-mile perimeter 6 and 73 squadrons continued to fight. Within a day they were to be completely isolated by Rommel's rapid advance through Bardia to Sollum, whence he was to probe further before establishing himself on a line running from Halfaya Pass to Sidi Omar.

[1] They comprised:
1 Wellington, 2 Blenheims, 1 Proctor, 1 Magister, 1 Valentia, 1 Anson, 1 Gladiatro and 1 Lysander.

Meanwhile, on April 11th came the warning of a reorganization of command which was to dissolve Air H.Q. Cyrenaica, whose *raison d'être* as a forward holding force was now nil. Its squadrons were to be more concerned with the original role of all air forces in the Western Desert, namely "The Defence of Egypt".

204 Group at Maaten Bagush, with Air Commodore Collishaw in command, was a familiar entity. On the 12th the Group took over 45 and 55 squadrons and a squadron-leader was sent to Tobruk to act as Advanced Liaison Officer. At Tobruk the original Fighter Sector Control (258 Wing) was left in charge of fighter defence with 73 and 6 squadrons. 204 Group was only 202 Group in disguise. The Cyrenaican adventure had failed.

But Rommel had succeeded in his object. He had taken over the coastal strip which alone could support aerodromes for the defence of Crete. He had not captured Tobruk, but the port was in a state of siege, and could not maintain shipping protection patrols without prejudicing the chances of its own survival. His advance had been as spectacular as it had been rapid. He had used outflanking tactics which repeated success had almost robbed of interest. He had made good losses, and attained a position that Graziani would have envied wholeheartedly. For the Italian Command had not been able to count on their forces slicing a way through Greece, nor could they even remotely have contemplated an attack on Crete. In 1940 there was no chance of exploiting trouble in Iraq; the suggestion had never been made that Mussolini's rather than Field-Marshal Blomberg's son should land at Baghdad to lead a revolt. The Germans, in 1941, had struck at several places almost simultaneously. As R.A.F. Cyrenaica was winding up its affairs—implying a bankruptcy which Rommel might well have considered impossible of discharge—disaster followed disaster in Greece.

Considerations as to whether the token force was too large, too small, should have been sent sooner, shouldn't have been sent at all, are not part of this account. But briefly the campaign had been concluded as follows:

From April 15th to the 20th our troops had been withdrawing to Thermopylae, celebrated in the past for Spartan slaughter to the last man. It was decided that troops would have to be disembarked as quickly as possible in order to prevent a modern counterpart. The squadrons had been charged with delaying the German advance by every means in their power. But bombers needed escort, and the escort could not bomb as well. This was to be the task of Eastern Wing, with 11, 113, 33 and 208 squadrons.

As the new Macedonian and Yugoslav frontiers appeared to straddle the map, tactical reconnaissance could be carried out only by Hurricanes, for the Lysanders were useless in the face of enemy fighters.[1]

H.Q. Western Wing was responsible for providing close support to the

[1] These aircraft, inadequate at the time, came into their own three years later, when they carried special agents, money, and supplies, for partisan leaders in Yugoslavia and Italy. For those purposes at least they were ideal, having a low landing-speed and long endurance.

Greeks on the Albanian front against the Italians, who were, it was to be supposed, awaiting an opportunity to recover prestige after former humiliating setbacks to their military reputation. The squadrons (112 and 211) were not at first heavily engaged.

Near Athens, under constant attack, were 30, 80, 84 and detachments of 37 and 38 squadrons.

Air disparity was striking; the combined strength of Italian and German air forces in the Balkans and in Greece at the start of the campaign amounted to approximately 1,100 aircraft, of which 42 per cent were fighters, 22 per cent bombers, 17 per cent dive-bombers, and the remainder reconnaissance, transport and communication types. Against them the R.A.F. could muster 200, of which half were bombers and half fighters and reconnaissance aircraft.

The Axis air forces could not at first be brought to bear on their inferior enemy. Lack of all-weather aerodromes limited flying, and if this disadvantage was common to either side, at least the aerodromes on Larissa plain, though water-logged, grew nearer to the advancing front line. But Larissa was to be captured, and dive-bombers and short range Me. 109 fighters were to be employed against Blenheims with terrible results both in the air and on the ground.

A crippled, hunted air force converged upon Athens, only to be told that evacuation was the order of the day. No more reinforcements were to be expected; what was there had to be got out or destroyed.

For the Germans, the campaign fell into three phases, starting with their air force based in Bulgaria. Next, they could use the Salonika plain, from which close support could be given to their own troops, and from which they could bomb our aerodromes. The last stage witnessed the R.A.F. driven into a corner, clinging only to Argos.

Outnumbered even more sadly than the little R.A.F. Cyrenaica, gallantry flowered the stronger as odds grew more and more hopeless. From April 19th to the 22nd thirty-one enemy aircraft were destroyed in the air by the meagre force of Hurricanes—fifteen against 300: odds of twenty to one—for seven lost on our side. But the remaining aircraft were almost wiped out by the German attack on April 23rd, when thirteen Hurricanes were destroyed on the ground, leaving six in all to fly back to Suda Bay the next day to provide air cover for the withdrawal to Crete.

As ships of all types brought in ground staffs, and as Sunderlands plied to and fro loaded to overflowing, the count was made. During the six months of the campaign 209 aircraft had been lost and 148 officers and men were killed or missing. It was claimed that the Axis had lost 259 aircraft, with another 94 probably lost.

Crete was the next on the list. The picture was one of harrying, of pillar-to-post warfare, in which the Germans were the pursuers and the Allies the pursued. On May 10th German bomber attacks on Cretan aerodromes started the softening process, which was to make airborne landings the next logical step. By May 19th four Hurricanes and three Gladiators, the sole survivors, were flown back to Egypt; and the following day the landings began. Nine days later British forces started to evacuate the island.

Crete had been robbed of air support by being robbed of aerodromes. Those on the island were hammered until they were useless; the mainland of Greece was already in Axis hands; the aerodromes of Cyrenaica, from which alone air patrols could be successfully flown, had already been captured by Rommel.

German advantages were both temporary and permanent. Fighter aircraft from Cyrenaica could now protect convoys to Benghazi, and hence the far-distant port of Tripoli need not be the only means of reinforcing the long lines of communication to Halfaya. The Ægean and Dodecanese islands were valuable bases for attacks on the Suez Canal and on metropolitan Egypt, as well as useful nests from which to issue against British shipping in the Eastern Mediterranean. Greek shipping added to the few transport vessels available to make a force large enough to supply all Rommel's needs. These were the immediate benefits. But in the future lay a Wagnerian Plan, whose presence was known to the Allies but whose success depended on various unknown quantities. The attack on Russia was designed to carry the German army into the Caucasus, and so on to the Middle East via Iraq, where a revolt of the inhabitants on a tried Fifth-Column pattern was already brewing. In Syria, Vichy France was expected to connive at German infiltration. Turkey was to capitulate. Cyprus was to be the victim of an airborne landing directed from Crete. The last step would be to foreclose upon Egypt from Syria and Cyrenaica simultaneously. Caught between German pincers, the British might wriggle away down to the Sudan, and beyond to Kenya and South Africa. But the Middle East, the defence of Egypt, the Suez Canal, sea communications—everything, in short—would have to go by the board.

Bold as this plan might seem, the first steps towards its fulfilment had been successful. Cyrenaica had been taken. Greece had been reduced. Defenceless, Crete had fallen automatically after fierce fighting. But the sequel was less auspicious. Rashid Ali timed his revolt without reference to the Grand Plan. Starting on May 3rd, it had fizzled out by June 3rd. No effective aid from Germany had arrived.

Iraq, then, retired into the background, and another card had to be played. It was to be the Syrian trump. The Germans had not misjudged the goodwill of Vichy; aerodromes put at the disposal of the *Luftwaffe* seemed unlikely to be snatched back. But five days after the crushing of the Iraqi revolt British troops were across the Syrian boundary; and three days later an armistice was arranged.

It could not be expected that tables could be so completely turned within the short period of one month. Two days after this, operation "Battleaxe", aimed at relieving Tobruk, failed.

The German attack on Russia revealed the boldest card of all, and possibly the biggest surprise, for Russian resistance stiffened. The pre-war opinion—"the German army will cut through Russia like a knife through butter"—was confounded. The drive to the Caucasus did not reach Rostov until the middle of November, by which time Anglo-Russian occupation of Iran had secured the rear. Meanwhile, as though to end forever the pincer conception of the British position, the Duke of Aosta surrendered in Abyssinia.

A principle of divide and conquer had been applied by the Allies in Middle East. It was the reply to the "blitz" method of advancing rapidly on all fronts, favoured by the Germans in Central Europe and retained with less perceptive tenacity elsewhere. Rommel had neglected to secure his rear. The emphasis had shifted away from the Western to the Eastern Mediterranean, and for the moment Malta had lost much of its strategical importance. It was to regain it as soon as the Syrian adventure terminated; and Rommel was to regret many of the harsh words which passed between him and Kesselring on the subject. Malta, towards which Kesselring turned longing eyes, and whose influence Rommel tended to discount, was to be the hinge on which German defeat in the Middle East turned. Malta-based aircraft were to succeed where Crete-based aircraft had failed, in interfering with the trans-shipment of German supplies to the point of strangulation during the fevered lull at Alamein.

CHAPTER VII

REORGANIZATION

"AIR superiority," ran a German appreciation, "achieved its aim, namely the conquest of Crete." It was now more than ever clear that, in the words of Tedder, "the Middle East campaign, in its entirely, was primarily a battle for aerodromes".

To help contest German superiority, during the summer, South African Air Force squadrons started arriving in Middle East. South African Air Force H.Q. was established in Cairo, to take charge of sixteen squadrons which were eventually to be transferred to the Middle East. No. 1 squadron was sent on its first task, the defence of Alexandria.

The squadron had enjoyed a run of successes. In the East African campaign it had been credited with 43 kills. The squadron was the first of a long line, for airmen were to come from the Union in increasing numbers to swell the Desert Air Force. Tedder's broadcast to the Union at the end of the whole campaign showed that their efforts were fully appreciated :

> "I want to say how proud I am to have been entrusted with the command of such men. I met your squadrons first when they came up from their victory in Abyssinia to help us through when we were hard pressed by events in Greece and Crete. I remember meeting your first bomber squadrons when they arrived in Egypt with their new Bostons, which were later made famous in the shuttle service, which again and again broke the enemy's morale. I watched your squadrons during the long retreat, which provided the extraordinary anomaly of land retreat coupled with crushing air victory. I shall never forget the avenging spirit in the squadrons during that period. Your boys, whether fighter pilots, bomber crews, reconnaissance crews, or those magnificent ground-staff men who get so much of the work and so little of the glory, maintained an effort which, had I been asked before, I should have said was quite beyond the bounds of human endeavour.
>
> "There is no doubt that this inspiration, which emanated from your great leader, an inspiration which I myself have felt on the occasions when I have been fortunate enough to meet him, also permeates your forces, whether they have been serving in your own S.A.A.F. units or in R.A.F. units."

Colonel Hingeston's first detachments were soon in action. In June, near Mersa Matruh, Major Theron made a parachute descent from his flaming aircraft, rivalling other classic war experiences. After pulling the rip-cord he slipped out of his parachute harness, which caught him by the ankles. With a broken arm helplessly flapping, he descended head-first, and still managed to survive.

The South African Air Force detachment was in time to take part in operation Battleaxe, planned as an army manœuvre, with air and sea co-operation, to relieve the men besieged in Tobruk. The Desert air effort was made up of squadrons mainly reformed and re-equipped in the Delta, and so the nominal roll does not quite convey a true picture of the real situation.[1]

The air plan of Battleaxe called for a few days' "softening up" of enemy lines of communication, followed by the waving of an air umbrella over the advancing troops. It was not a success, and by June 18th the front was once more stabilized.

But criticisms flew fast and furious, and therein lay the importance of the operation. They were chiefly concerned with the type of air support given by the R.A.F. This produced an inquiry as to the proper role of close support forces. Finally the Prime Minister was requested to give a ruling.

It was said that the value of air support had been diminished owing to the failure of ground troops to acknowledge recognition signals; to the difficulty experienced by the army in giving a bomb line; to wireless breakdown; to lack of training in a combined operation. All these contentions were correct. But the main point which emerged was whether the army request for an air umbrella could or could not be justified. Guedalla commented:

> "It was not altogether clear that hostile wasps were any more likely to be deterred from depredations on the military tea-table by a display of vigour in its immediate vicinity, than by the methodical destruction of their nests in attacks on hostile aerodromes."[2]

The movement in favour (particularly after the Cretan disaster) of splitting the air into army, navy and air force components put forward compelling arguments. It was a perilous position for R.A.F. Middle East. Tedder, in command since May 3rd, had only taken over fully on June 1st. Collishaw, at 204 Group, was hoary with Desert experience, but he was of relatively low rank; his air force was small; his triumph over the *Regia Aeronautica* could easily be belittled by pointed reference to enemy incompetence, and could be less easily

[1] *Order of battle 204 Group as at June 1st, 1941:*
204 Group at Burg el Arab, and H.Q. 259 Wing just east of the Egypt-Libya frontier.
1 S.A.A.F. (Hurricanes), 2 S.A.A.F. (Tomahawks), 6 (Lysanders and Hurricanes), 14 (Blenheim IV's), 30 (Blenheim I's), 39 (Marylands), 45 (Blenheim IV's), 73 (Hurricanes), 274 (Hurricanes).
3 S.A.A.F. and 112 were in Palestine.
Added to the order of battle for June 1st were 250 squadron and 24 squadron (Marylands for strategic reconnaissance). Wellingtons, based in the Canal and Delta zones, operated as previously from forward landing-grounds, now under the control of 204 Group.

[2] Douhet would have smiled at such an "old-fashioned" point of view.

appreciated as an example of well-considered R.A.F. employment. The Germans had succeeded in France with an air force not only co-operating with, but actually under the direction of, the army for close support purposes. To counter such a seemingly obvious thesis there was nothing to say except to repeat that in France there had been little opposition.

Finally, the Prime Minister's ruling decided the question in principle for the rest of the war. Its importance to the Middle East campaign cannot be overemphasized, as it fully recognized the air point of view. Churchill said: "The idea of keeping standing patrols over our moving columns should be abandoned. It is unsound to distribute aircraft in this way, and no air superiority will stand the application of such a mischievous practice." This strongly worded directif prevented any attempt to follow the German pattern. Air umbrellas were out of favour. And though full support for the army was still the chief task of the R.A.F., methods in future were to be left to the air commanders, in subordination to the overall army plan.

On the failure of operation Battleaxe was founded the success of operation Crusader, and all those other operations which were to provide a unique display of joint air/army effort. The handful of buccaneers who made up Collishaw's forces were to become part of the main plan, which was to unfold more and more surely on a basis of mutual co-operation for mutual benefit.

In air theory Tedder had won his first battle; but there were to be measures to ensure that theory was well backed by hitting power. Conclusions reached by Elmhirst and Collishaw had to be implemented. There had to be more transport, and more mobility for the squadrons. And this was chiefly a matter of supply. Since the lack of adequate repair units in Cyrenaica had contributed to the defeat of the Italian air force, then the same must not happen east of the Libyan border.

Tedder's solution was to create the post of Chief Supply and Maintenance Officer,[1] to whom would be entrusted arrangements for securing and placing everything which could be coaxed into the Middle East. More aircraft were arriving: Tomahawks to replace the ancient, dying Gladiators; Marylands and Bostons in exchange for Blenheims. If there was to be a Chief Supply and Maintenance Officer, he would at least have material at his disposal.

During July and August German bombers based on Crete ranged at leisure over the Delta; a hit on Abusueir or Aboukir Maintenance and Supply depots was inevitable, though long delayed. By that time decentralization had already taken place. Caves in the Mokattam hills had been hollowed out, and the Boulac quarter of Cairo mystified by a sudden influx of R.A.F. technicians, who added to the noise of already rowdy streets, and whose work, as delicate as that of the silversmiths, was far more destructive.

[1] Air Vice-Marshal Graham Dawson, rightly held to be "as vital an architect of victory as any commander in the Desert", was wooed away from the Ministry of Aircraft Production for this post.

On this firm basis of organized dispersal in the rear the forward Maintenance units rested secure. Up in the Western Desert 55, 53, and 54 Repair and Salvage units worked with 31, 33 and 32 Air Stores Parks respectively, providing a total in depth of thirteen mobile Repair Sections and twelve mobile Salvage Sections. Behind these were a further three mobile Salvage and six mobile Repair Sections for the heavy bombers. This organization was capable of repairing aircraft on the spot, or else of patching them up sufficiently to enable them to be flown back to base units for more extensive overhaul. But there were to be many occasions when there was no chance of bringing aircraft back even as far as the advance unit. Pilots, force-landing in the Desert, wandering back to rejoin their units, were hardly likely to give an exact description of the particular patch of sand which harboured their damaged craft. Parties often had to set out to locate aircraft with few details to help them in their search. If successful, they might have to carry out repairs far beyond their normal scope. Failing this, the aircraft might have to be towed back. Working under such difficult conditions, however, became a part of forward Maintenance routine, which the *Luftwaffe* did not care to imitate. The Germans preferred to send out specific mobile units from base with specific tasks in view. Their men might leave Benghazi and return there on completion of their task. The R.A.F., on the other hand, formed a spider's web; small units, carrying small stocks, gridded the Desert.

The effects of Tedder's reorganization would not be felt until Crusader, but they were far-reaching. Future R.A.F. successes were largely founded on the foresight of the new commander of R.A.F. Middle East.

Meanwhile, during the lull in the Western Desert, Collishaw's forces were to be concerned almost entirely with the larger aspect of the Mediterranean war, namely shipping protection. This caused feeling to run high, for Rommel, it seemed, was only waiting to start yet one more of those outflanking moves to the south. Shipping patrols ran away with engine hours and serviceability. A comment on the patrols over H.M.S. *Flamingo* shortly after Battleaxe revealed that a minimum of twelve fighters had been on patrol from three o'clock to 8-15, and over 112 hours' of flying time had been consumed in seventy-three separate sorties. On that occasion six major attacks had developed from upwards of forty Me. 109's and Me. 110's escorting Ju. 88's. It was implied that if the R.A.F. was asked to repeat fighter protection for fifteen hours at a stretch their forces would be frittered away and would be incapable of meeting the threat of invasion.

Such activities had almost precluded any purely offensive effort by the fighters in the group under the administrative control of 258 Wing. But other R.A.F. affairs continued to prosper. Medium bombers under the administrative control of 257 Wing operated from Desert landing-grounds against Benghazi with such regularity that the trip came to be known as the "Mail Run". The R.A.F. was continuing at full pressure, though on land the army was biding its time.

But Collishaw was due to leave 204 Group. In his farewell message he summed up the work of the Desert units. "I wish to express my grateful thanks to all who have served me so well and so loyally during the past two-and-a-half years in which I have held command. You have defeated an air force numerically superior by four to one, and have never been defeated in an important engagement in the campaign." His going signalled the passing of an era. He had been in command at a time when the Desert air war was a matter of bluff and heroism, when a tradition of improvising and of fighting against odds had waxed strong. His little air force had "foxed 'em", all the way from Maaten Bagush to Jedabya and back again. He had shown that capacity for bravery which comes near to genius. His organization, like that of the first sheriff in a boom town, was of the rough-and-ready type, based mainly on the personal qualities of those he led. His position in D.A.F. was unique, for similar conditions were never to arise again. Instead the force was to become more and more of a cold, calculated instrument of war, where possibilities could be accurately assessed in advance, in terms of numbers and weight of armament.

But the pioneer spirit was still to be the main basis of D.A.F. The real enemy was now appearing in force; and if to defeat the Germans required hard thinking and hard hitting, the next commander of D.A.F. was ready to display both qualities. Collishaw's mantle fell on the shoulders of Air Vice-Marshal Coningham, a pilot from the First World War, famed for shooting down nineteen enemy planes in fourteen days. His career had been unusual; he had begun the First World War with the New Zealand Expeditionary Force in Somali and Egypt. Invalided out of the army in 1916, his military activities seemed finished. He had never seen an aeroplane but was attracted to the idea of flying, Later in the year he made his way to England, where he was accepted by the Royal Flying Corps, and trained as a fighter pilot.

Coningham's personality was to be given full scope in the Desert. He was enough of a pioneer to enter into that system of rough-and-ready improvisation which had contrived to keep the aircraft flying during lean months of scarcity, but he was also a planner with a prediliction towards air/army co-operation. His joviality appeared to make him a lineal descendant of Collishaw; he had the same intimate interest in his pilots, and the same hatred of non-essentials. But large capable hands gave a clue to other qualities which, under cover of a likable "Desert" personality, could be exploited to the best advantage. To put Coningham in front of a map was to entice into the open a shrewd, calculating brain.

Various beliefs held by Coningham demonstrate his common-sense viewpoint. Firstly, as regards his own men: "Take a body of men, give them plenty of work to do, keep them at it hard enough and long enough, with periods of complete relaxation whenever you can afford it; interfere as little as possible with them as individuals, get the non-essentials stripped away; set them in the Desert near the sea; and the force will be a thoroughly happy and efficient one."

Secondly, as regards the Germans: "Hit them hard and keep hitting them, then they won't ever hit back. Never do anything to the enemy unless you yourself have first discovered the antidote."

On taking over command of 204 Group, Coningham's first action was to move his H.Q. away from "a hole in the ground" to the sea front at Maaten Bagush with the Army H.Q. Thereafter, whenever the Army H.Q. moved, the Air Force H.Q. was to accompany it.

There were to be many changes in organization which were to stem directly from close army/air liaison. Coningham presided unruffled over the new machinery.

CHAPTER VIII

FURTHER REORGANIZATION

THE hot, dry, dusty days of July produced two phenomena "out of the blue"; landing-ground "X" and the "Late Arrivals Club". The former was a secret aerodrome on a salt pan in the Desert from which aircraft could take off to surprise German lines of communication behind Benghazi. Whilst at Gerawla squadrons used to send ground-staff parties to maintain fuel stocks and signal facilities in a place so remote that a month was the longest visit on which anyone need reckon. Dispossessing the native gazelle, the airmen settled down to a monotonous stay enlivened only by occasional spells of hard work when the airfield was used for operations. Sometimes, too, pilots, unable to return to base, landed for refuelling. Such an event was welcome; visitors, on occasions, were known to bring with them bottles of beer and other small luxuries for the stranded airmen.

The "Late Arrivals Club" found members amongst those who had been "out in the blue" by accident and not by intent. Stories of escape through enemy lines have always caught the imagination of all peoples, and amongst war records of every nation there have been plenty of thrilling instances. Escape clubs had been formed before in other wars to instruct others in similar arts, or to commemorate successful ventures. The Western Desert was peculiarly rich in such stories because the terrain could hardly be described as "enemy" or "friendly". The sand of the Desert defied military occupation. In this interminable tawny sea, the Arabs, traditionally hospitable to the stranger, helped Britisher and German impartially, interested in the immediate needs of the individual rather than in the wider implications of their actions. Tales of walking through enemy lines were plentiful; mostly they followed the same pattern. The individual struggling on his own towards the welcome of a friendly camp; a meeting with the enemy, sometimes leading to capture or recapture; taking advantage of an air raid or a warder off guard to escape once more; a meeting with wandering Arabs, in some cases the donning of Arab dress; the eventual return to the unit, footsore, with sprouting beard, and modest denials of personal heroism. Each story had an individual flavour, but the diet was the same.

During the summer of 1941 the Public Relations Officer in Western Desert suggested banding these distinguished men together. The charter of the "Late Arrivals Club" was:

> "This is to certify that ——, of —— Squadron, is hereby nominated a member of the Late Arrivals Club. Inasmuch as he, in —— on ——, when obliged to abandon his aircraft, on the ground or in the air,

as a result of unfriendly action by the enemy, succeeded in returning to his Squadron, on foot, or by any other means, long after his Estimated Time of Arrival.

"IT IS NEVER TOO LATE TO COME BACK."

The members wore their emblem, a silver boot with wings, proudly and in defiance of orders forbidding unauthorized decorations.

The Germans, too, had an organization which undoubtedly helped to maintain the pilots' morale; for to force-land in the Desert was similar to force-landing in the sea. In both cases the pilot was completely cut off from his fellows, and the prospect of too much sand was no more encouraging than that of too much water.

The personal gallantry of those who managed to make their way back did much to hearten those who foresaw such a fate in store for themselves. A pilot could never know whether it might not be his own turn next. And many, during those hot, dry, dusty days, had cause to be thankful for the Long Range Desert Group.

. . . . .

During the lull in the Desert the Germans were sweeping forward in Russia. It looked as though the Caucasian Master Plan might come into operation. Thus Auchinleck, following on Wavell's heels that July, was chiefly concerned with the possibility of alleviating the irritating prospect of a war on two fronts by getting rid of the Western Desert aggressor.

As always, administrative changes had to precede a new offensive. In this case there were two things to be done immediately: firstly, to extend the Desert railway to Bir Mischiefa; secondly, to enlarge facilities for the drawing of water at Fuka and Buq Buq, and to construct a pipeline from Alexandria to the forward area.

The R.A.F. was busy with reorganization on drastic lines. The flow of supplies via Takoradi added 50 per cent to its strength within a few months, whilst the increase in Maintenance and Repair and Salvage units guaranteed that the new supplies would be properly looked after. R.A.F. Middle East, which in May could show some 200 serviceable aircraft, by November could point to 700.

Allocation of these supplies led to decentralization. Air H.Q. Western Desert was created largely from 204 Group on October 9th; Air H.Q. Levant and Air H.Q. Egypt on December 1st; Wellington bombers became 205 Group on October 3rd; three days earlier, 201 Naval Co-operation Group came into being.

Air H.Q. Western Desert was no longer to control isolated squadrons grouped for convenience into purely administrative wings, but wings which were in themselves operational entities. Though, during the Crusader campaign, this could only apply to the fighter squadrons, the principle was eventually to extend to the medium bombers as well, and was to be the basis for mobility such as had been impossible under the peacetime "Station" system.

Whilst reorganization was taking place, nothing occurred to disturb the smooth tenor of redistribution except a reconnaissance in strength by Rommel's armoured force in September, when 120 tanks were caught refuelling and were routed.

By October 14th Desert Air Force (Air H.Q. Western Desert) had grown to a considerable size.[1]

There were two points to be noticed. Firstly, the enormous increase in South African units to support 55, 45 and 113 squadrons. Secondly, the machines in use; Tomahawks, Marylands, Bostons—American names for American aircraft. The visits of American missions to the Mddle East and their appreciation of local conditions had borne very obvious fruit.

. . . . .

If there was to be a new machine, almost a new R.A.F., in the Desert, the system of R.A.F. co-operation with the army was also to be new. In July an Inter-service Committee met to consider all aspects of direct air support, defined as "action having an immediate effect on the action of our ground forces in battle". Such action presupposed local, though not necessarily overall, air superiority. It was foreshadowed that the size of opposing air forces would not be so important as their composition—the relative numbers of fighter, bomber, transport, reconnaissance, etc., types.

The instrument of direct air support was to be the light bomber, to be used in formation at medium level, or singly after a dive of 4—6,000 feet, or at ground level. The targets were classified in approximate order of importance.

The key, however, to direct air support was the fighter. Local air superiority, the principle requisite of effective air action, could only be gained by offensive fighter sweeps, and by fighter-protected raids on forward enemy aerodromes. If the air war had to be fought first, the fighter was the primary weapon.

Requests for direct air support were to be sifted, and if necessary implemented by action along the following lines: Air Support Controls, consisting of two army staff officers and their staff, with the commander or the deputy commander of the R.A.F. formation likely to be affected, were to be established at Corps H.Q. The army was to control forward posts, known as tentacles. The R.A.F. was to direct air support aircraft by radio, was to listen in to radio

[1] *See* Appendix A.

reconnaissance reports, and was to be in touch by radio with forward landing-grounds.

A reconnaissance aircraft would report a concentration of large numbers, say, of unarmed supply trucks in area XZ; the control officers would decide whether to allot aircraft for this task or whether to follow up a tentacle report of a troop concentration at area XY. Having decided which target carried the highest priority, tentacles would be told what and where to expect action, and a bomb line (a line in advance of the most forward of forward troops) would be plotted. Meanwhile, the R.A.F. formation would be warned and finally given the signal to start off on a raid.

During Crusader, however, the system was modified. All requests were finally to be referred to the Air Officer Commanding Western Desert; the air support control at Corps H.Q. became a channel both for the passing of all unsifted information and for telling R.A.F. formations the result of the A.O.C.'s decision, a decision taken jointly with the army commander.

Not only had the value of reconnaissance aircraft been recognized, but it was considered that targets selected by such aircraft from the air were likely to be the best targets for attack. The tentacle system was to be the second means. This, though, was to be modified, for later experience showed that the tentacles were recommending targets in a ratio of three to two over the reconnaissance aircraft.

Among the targets suitable for air attack "columns in the lines of communication, which can disperse quickly and maintain considerable distance between vehicles", were conspicuously absent.

The effect of this plan was to make army and R.A.F. liaison so complete that when the Army Co-operation Wing (253, at first known as the Air Component Wing) was absorbed into Advanced Air H.Q. the process seemed only logical. From this new model for direct support stemmed the later successes of the Desert Air Force–8th Army partnership. As a system it naturally needed further remodelling after Crusader; but it was the start of a process whereby the air and the ground were able to move as one, although each was a separate entity.

It might be possible to claim that this system of independence in partnership was one which could only have been devised by men used to a democratic rather than to an authoritative regime. Certainly such an arrangement never in fact obtained on the Axis side, nor even in theory did the mechanism exist. During Crusader, liaison between the German army and air force was through the medium of a *Koluft* (to which reference has already been made), which took operational orders from Rommel direct, and which maintained liaison with training units in Germany as well as being in touch with G.H.Q. Berlin. Under this system the army co-operation force, though staffed by men of the German air force, also had under its control anti-aircraft units, but it lay outside the ordinary *Luftflotte Fliegerkorps* organization of the *Luftwaffe*, and was directly subordinate to the army commander. Thus it was an easy matter for Rommel to dispense with air support without the air force being able to make any effective protest.

• • • • •

The *Luftwaffe*,[1] at the start of July 1941, was in the Mediterranean in some strength. Their forces were all under the control of *Fliegerkorps X*. Since December 1940 Malta had been their main target. The *Luftwaffe* had delivered its first assault against the island before the campaign in Greece, and before the experimental but successful paratroop landings in Crete. Geisler, the commander, had as his Chief of Staff Harlinghausen, whose reputation for successful anti-shipping operations was to lead to his transfer to the Atlantic front after March. Apart from Malta, Geisler's force was to be extended mainly against shipping. It was to close the Sicilian Straits to convoys sailing between Gibraltar and Alexandria; it was to block the Suez Canal as often and for as long as possible, and it was to protect Axis convoys carrying supplies for the *Afrika Korps*.

Geisler partly succeeded in some of his objects. The Suez Canal was mined, and ships were blown up. Stuka attacks on British convoys caused enormous damage. But the short sharp attack on Malta was inconclusive. March 1941 witnessed the end of several days' intensive dive-bomber and low-level attacks. It seemed that too many projects jostled each other for any one to be wholly productive.

During the crucial months of April, May and June the Master Plan seemed about to come to a head. Greece and Crete shifted interest away from the western to the eastern Mediterranean. Malta, though a constant menace to shipping, could not, it was assumed, seriously impede the joint claws of the pincers which were to crush Persia, Syria, Palestine and Egypt. To that end *Fliegerkorps X*, already halved in strength when it had been transferred from Sicily to North Africa, was further scattered when much of it was sent to Crete. Geisler, insisting that Greece and Crete were natural outposts on the shipping route to North Africa, overrode the protests of the Italians, who doubted whether they could defend their convoys whilst still in their own waters.

In North Africa, as the front stabilized, no fresh reorganization took place. The Libyan part of *Fliegerkorps X* came under a *Fliegerführer*, Froehlich. He and the *Koluft*, Otto Heymer, were involved in perpetual disputes with Rommel, who eventually succeeded in court-martialling Heymer for his failure to arrange close support during the opening stages of Crusader. That Froehlich could stand by and see one of his most brilliant commanders punished unreasonably shows that relations between the German army and air force were scarcely, from their inception, satisfactory.

[1] *See* Appendix B.

CHAPTER IX

AIR SUPERIORITY

OVER and over again have appeared the words "air superiority",[1] and the assumption has been made that air superiority has to be gained before an air force can support an army fully and efficiently. Air Marshal Drummond explained in 1942 that "Air superiority is a term used to explain a happy state of affairs in an air war, and it doesn't imply that one air force is numerically stronger than the other".

No army analogy can be used to explain this phrase. The comparative word, "superiority", is the key. The Air Marshal's definition continued, "the strength of my force is such that the enemy air force cannot interfere effectively with the operation of our own forces, land, sea and air, within the area covered by the effective operational range of my aircraft".

Following this definition, it might be possible to claim that at no time in the Western Desert Campaign did we have air inferiority, for at no time were our air forces unable to interfere effectively with those of the enemy, though throughout enemy air forces were at liberty to interfere with ours. Therefore it is again necessary to bear in mind that "superiority" is a comparative word implying more operations with less losses; conversely—"inferiority", less operations with more losses. Not until losses mount to Pyrrhic numbers so that the results gained are no longer worth the effort expended can inferiority or superiority be said to exist. With the opening of the Crusader campaign, air superiority was within our grasp for the first time in the Western Desert war. Indeed, it was insisted that unless this strong possibility existed, Crusader could not take place. In 1941 there was a certain amount of confusion as to what constituted air superiority; numbers tended to be regarded as settling the question one way or another. But if doubt existed in the public mind, there was none in Tedder's. Even when the first tally of the opposing sides seemed to indicate that the Germans would enjoy the benefit of numbers—the estimate was 300–420 German, 350–370 Italian, as against 500 R.A.F.—Tedder was not unduly concerned, holding firmly to the view that quantity alone meant little, and that our higher standard of serviceability, reserves, supply, and morale might alter the position entirely in our favour. The revised October estimate—German and Italian air forces 642 (of which 435 were Italian) as against the

[1] Not quite the same thing as Douhet's definition "Command of the Air", which was something far more sweeping, *cf.* "to command means to be master of and excludes any suggestion of the comparative . . ." Douhet, however, was more interested in the strategic application of air power, as became the spokesman of an "Independent Air Force" writing in 1926. His book has survived the war which he (wrongly) predicted, and yet still remains interesting and instructive.

R.A.F.'s 660—therefore gave fresh grounds for satisfaction. He believed that air superiority depended on various factors, of which numbers were only one.

Firstly, there had to be aerodromes. At the start of the siege of Tobruk effective air support could not be given when all local aerodromes had fallen into enemy hands. But the capture and construction of airfields was a matter for the army. The two services were thus mutually dependent. Secondly, supply. There were hazards on the aerial routes via Malta or via Takoradi, but the Mediterranean sea lanes were closed until such time as airfields along the North African littoral could send out protective aircraft. Again, capture of these bases was a matter for the army, just as sea traffic was a naval affair. All three services were thus intimately concerned with questions of air superiority. Thirdly, maintenance. Delicate machinery exposed to the ravages of sand and sun could deteriorate more quickly than the enemy could destroy it. Tedder's reorganization recognized that this was mainly a problem of administration, of setting up enough repair bases and of training enough men. R.A.F. Maintenance, even in the early days, had never sunk to the low standard of the Italian air force. In future it was to rise still further above the enemy's.

Forward maintenance had to be as flexible and mobile as the force it was to serve. Increased mobility of ground crews would mean more aircraft available at the right time at the right place, either in advance or retreat.

It is possible to run on indefinitely about the sources of air superiority. There is the question of the air crews' confidence in their aircraft; the confidence of those who fly in those on the ground; the confidence that the higher command is competent and that the leaders will choose the right targets—all points which contribute to morale. Apart from these it is clearly desirable to have aircraft of superior performance.

The latter, R.A.F. Middle East did not have. Nor were they entirely out of the wood before Crusader. The Hurricane Mk. I was completely, whilst the Hurricane Mk. II and the Tomahawk were partially, outclassed by the Me. 109 F. Hence, though R.A.F. fighters were to have numerical superiority of three to one over German fighters in the ensuing struggle, these statistics were as misleading as the figures in favour of the enemy during former campaigns.

In conclusion, to the question "Shall we have air superiority for Crusader?" Tedder was able to answer "Yes", though other observers would only commit themselves to a "Perhaps". This clarity of vision enabled Tedder later to claim that the air battle had been won at a time when our troops were apparently with their backs to the wall at El Alamein, when such an opinion might have seemed the very acme of overoptimism. But in support of his thesis Tedder could point to the conditions under which the retreat had taken place: transport massed on the roads, troops withdrawing rapidly over long distances; both had been almost immune from enemy air interference, for the bases of German and Italian air forces had been constantly attacked from the air.

To reach such a stage in the journey towards air superiority, the air battle had not only to be fought first, but had to be fought all the time. There was to be no sitting back, for the Axis air forces could be reinforced rapidly over a short safe route from Europe.

CHAPTER X

FORWARDS AGAIN

REORGANIZATION of the R.A.F. did not prevent Axis ports from being bombed. The enemy was soon "showing a marked preference for using Tripoli", and Malta-based aircraft were doing their best to make even that far-distant capital as uncomfortable as possible. In the Western Desert the Me. 109, with its superior speed, was adopting the tactics found successful in their time by Hurricanes against the slower but more manœuvrable C. 42's. 250 and 2 S.A.A.F. squadrons, both with Tomahawks, were involved in a series of battles where the tale of victory was not so one-sided as had become customary. On August 11th twelve Tomahawks met four Me. 110's, and one Me. 110 was shot down. On the 18th twelve Tomahawks met twenty Me. 109's and six Me. 110's, and one Tomahawk was shot down. On the 21st eighteen Tomahawks and Hurricanes met eighteen Me. 110's, twenty-five Me. 109's and ten Ju. 87's; three of our aircraft were lost, as against one Me. 110.

But if the honours of the air lay for the moment with the Me. 109, there were plenty of other events to offset this advantage. The reconnaissance in force which Rommel had made on September 14th revealed flaws in the outwardly smooth surface of Italo-German liaison. Eleven out of a flight of twelve Italian Ju. 87's lost touch with the German force, and after a series of bewildered wanderings force-landed, for the most part in our territory. Only the formation leader appeared to know his target; the escort of German fighters had disappeared, travelling in the wrong direction over Sidi Barrani; and as a result eight machines and their crews fell into our hands. The chaos of this raid promised hopefully for the future.

As though to excuse further liaison tests, however, German propaganda during September made much of the Festival of Ramadan, promising the Egyptians immunity from bombing. "The Germans keep their promises whereas the English do not honour theirs. They have enslaved India, Egypt and Palestine; they have seized Syria, Iraq and Iran. Soon the Afghans will come under their heel. Heil Moslems! Every Arab should work and pray for Axis success," etc., etc.

Meanwhile, the position of Malta was growing serious. It could swell the air offensive against Tripoli and Sicily, but no convoy could get through to the besieged island, and the defenders were growing short of food and supplies. Their worst time was yet to come.

Hence Crusader was to be slightly more comprehensive than the previous advance. Apart from the fact that Rommel might make more use of the Cyrenaican coastline than Graziani, Tobruk was to be relieved. This, important enough for political reasons, was essential for the morale of the entire Middle Eastern forces. But there, in the background, so clearly defined as to compete for immediate attention, was the problem of Malta. The advanced landing-grounds, which a successful campaign in Cyrenaica would put into our hands, were seen to be the only means of ensuring the take-off of aircraft to shadow convoys on their way to Valetta. Even the continued existence of the island was regretted by Kesselring.

If Crusader was successful, the left flank of the Middle East would no longer be threatened. Provided that the port of Benghazi could be made to work at full capacity, the ground would be prepared for further advances into Tripolitania and even into Tunisia. Victory would enhance British prestige throughout the Middle East.

It was not, however, intended that a campaign, which from one angle seemed aimed at keeping Malta alive for a little longer, or from another angle seemed to be an attempt to raise a siege with results more costly than the siege itself, should be undertaken without success being fully assured before the start. Hence the initial amassing of forces, land and air, gave the Allies advantages which they had every chance of exploiting.

8th Army was split into three groups. Firstly, 13 Corps, with the 2nd New Zealand Division, the 4th Indian Division, the 1st Armoured Tank Brigade, and an Air Support Control. Secondly, 30th Corps, with the 7th Armoured Division, the 1st South African Division, and No. 1 Australian Air Support Control. Thirdly, the Oasis Force, with the 6th South African Armoured Car Regiment, and a battalion from the 29th Indian Brigade. The 70th Division, the 32nd Armoured Brigade and the Polish Carpathian Infantry were within Tobruk.

Against these the Axis could muster the 5th and 21st German Armoured Divisions, the German 90th Light Infantry Division, the Ariete Italian Armoured Division and the Italian Pavia, Bologna, Brescia, Savona, Sabrata, Trieste and Trento Infantry Divisions.

In numbers Allied tanks showed a 30 per cent superiority, but in quality an unknown advantage lay with the Germans.

Tanks, moving towards Tobruk, were to start the campaign by destroying the German armour. The ridges of Bel Hamed, Sidi Rezegh and Shifet El Adem were to be seized, the German armoured forces enticed into the open or menaced into retreat, and, at the crucial moment, forces pent up in Tobruk would issue forth to engage what would be an already routed mob. 13 Corps was to hold the frontier forces in siege, and then move forward to finish off the remnant of the German troops, whilst deep in the Desert to the south light mobile columns based on Jarabub and Siwa were to harass lines of communication before racing across the southern wastes of Cyrenaica to bar the road to Tripoli.

This process was to start on November 18th, but the air part of the plan was to come into play much earlier. A softening-up process, inevitably the forerunner of an army offensive, began on April 14th, with various movements in view; the two main themes being damage to enemy supply lines and weakening of enemy air forces. In other words, the targets were not only army, but also air strategical targets as such. Shipping and supply dumps were to feel the blow first. It was hoped that, besides restricting the flow of material to the front line, these attacks would force the enemy to concentrate greater numbers of fighters on standing patrols over his reinforcements. Next on the visiting list, in order to ensure Allied air superiority over Tobruk and Bardia, were Gazala and Gambut (where the majority of the German fighter force lay), the dive-bomber base of Tmimi, and then Derna, Martuba and Benghazi.

Owing to R.A.F. decentralization of command, which had either taken place or which was envisaged, division of labour for attacking such varied targets offered no special problem. The Wellington bombers—now 205 Group—were to continue the "mail run" to Benghazi. The light bombers—divided into 3 S.A.A.F. and 270 Wings—were to go for supplies and dumps, shipping in Benghazi harbour, Tmimi and Gazala. The fighters, organized into three Wings, were mainly to provide protection for the bombers, but 258 and 262 Wings were to carry out photographic reconnaissance and tactical reconnaissance as well as sustaining offensive action in the forward areas, whilst 269 Wing, on the defensive, was to concentrate mainly on enemy tactical and photographic reconnaissance, and enemy bombers over Matruh and Daba. Reconnaissance squadrons, the eyes of the army, were to produce pin-point and overlap photographs to a depth of forty miles behind the enemy lines, as well as bringing back information about such things as traffic movements, shipping unloading, and numbers of vehicles and troops. The Army Co-operation Squadron, 451 R.A.A.F., was joined by 208, and further army reconnaissance was provided by a special Survey Flight of No. 60 squadron in contact with the Army Survey Company at 8th Army H.Q.

To give some figures for this period, from thirty-five to thirty-six days before the opening of the offensive Egypt-based bombers flew 630 sorties, 292 being flown in the last eight nights. Of these 293 were against ports, 139 against aircraft, 88 against enemy positions, and 10 against shipping at sea. Fighters maintained sorties of 191–274 per week, but their activities were deliberately curtailed in order to keep the enemy in ignorance as to their numbers. After the start of the campaign fighter sorties rocketed to what a contemporary chronicler called "the remarkable figure of 1,041 sorties a week".

Thus the first round of the air battle had already been fought by November 12th, six days before the start of the army offensive. The second round was to follow. For this both fighter wings moved forward to occupy landing-grounds grouped around Sidi Barrani, and on "D" day these squadrons moved once more to aerodromes near Maddalena. Where before such a move might have embarrassed operations, the new reorganization allowed them to continue with only slight variations in efficiency. The two wings were now interchangeable; when one moved forward, the other stayed back to control squadrons belonging to the first, and vice versa. Squadrons could now be farmed out instantaneously to temporary foster-parents.

Earlier in the month Coningham had held an exercise and orders had been issued. Squadrons were to be prepared to split themselves into three; an advance and a similar rear party of about eighty men were to be highly mobile, able to service and maintain all the aircraft in the squadron for a period of seven days; the remainder, about 150 men including the Equipment Section, were to be left behind. Only one change of clothing was to be taken forward and the rest sent back, together with larger tentage, to 32 A.S.P., who were to redistribute it later.

Since there were now more wing and squadron lorries, operating on the move would become an everyday matter; the resources of the men would be taxed, but not beyond breaking-point.

With policy already tested, the fighters then moved up in preparation for the big attack; the squadrons paired off into two operational formations so as to provide two packs of twenty-four aircraft whenever needed.

To complete last-minute reconnaissance was the task of the squadron now attached to 30 and 13 Corps, whilst the Rhodesian Army Co-operation Squadron was held in reserve.

Eve of battle produced a surprise. The Bostons made their bow in the Desert as tactical reconnaissance aircraft. They were to continue in this role until December 8th, when two lots of six started two fires on supply dumps near Bardia. Two days later they were to be taught their first lesson, when another box of six, unescorted, were pounced upon by twelve Me. 109's, two Bostons being shot down over the target and three others failing to return. But if it was clearly demonstrated that they could not, as had been hoped, operate without escort, these curiously shaped bombers—the high tail fin reminded observers of a hen hurrying through the sky—were to become probably the most famous of all Desert air phenomena; their neat formations crossing overhead at regular intervals were to allow the men on the ground, too often unaware of the intensive pounding of towns and communications on the far-off shores of Tripoli and Italy, to see for themselves what was in store for their enemies. With the ground troops an ounce of visible fact was worth a ton of hearsay raids; apt to be unduly heartened by the sight of our own aircraft overhead, they were conversely unduly dismayed by enemy aeroplanes.[1]

As "D" day approached a spirit of confidence permeated all ranks. A telegram from the Prime Minister, by command of the King, expressed the

[1] Similarly, the R.A.F., who expected enemy aircraft as a matter of course, were scandalized by artillery bombardment.

full confidence of all at home. "For the first time, British and Empire troops will meet the Germans with ample equipment in modern weapons of all kinds. The battle itself will affect the whole course of the war."

But weather threatened first to affect the whole course of the battle. The night of November 17th ushered in the heaviest rainstorm of the year. The whole of the coast from Benghazi to Buq Buq was sodden, and the forward Axis airfields waterlogged. Graziani had complained that the skies had fought for the English in the previous campaign, but this time it really seemed as if Rommel had just cause for complaint. Whilst the Germans were unable to operate, the Allies could and did.

The 8th Army units, deep in the Desert, were unaffected. The armoured cars of 30 Corps advanced with little opposition as 13 Corps moved up to the frontier.

Here the flexibility of the air command was once more demonstrated. With the German fighters grounded, Coningham flung his whole array of bombers in the sky over Gazala. From the air point of view, this brought the third phase of the campaign to an end. From now on, with overall air superiority for the moment assured, and with local air superiority achieved (at any rate until the waterlogged German fields could be put back into full use), Western Desert Air Force could give that full support to the army in the tactical sphere which they had been giving strategically for the past thirty days and nights.

The opening of Crusader provoked no violent German reaction. Rommel at first thought that the offensive was a reconnaissance in force like his own effort in the autumn. Enemy documents reveal that he was about to attack Tobruk and was not expecting interference with his plans.

By November 21st, however, Rommel had recovered quickly. Rushing the 21st and 15th Panzer Divisions northwards, he hoped to be able to reduce the 7th Support Group and the 7th Armoured Brigade before reinforcements from 22nd Armoured Brigade could reach them. In this he was unsuccessful, for reinforcements arrived on the night of the 21st; but, for the Allies, a serious situation had already developed, and showed signs of deteriorating still further. German tanks in that area, besides being present in greater numbers, were heavier, with more powerful guns of longer range. Where their air maintenance had shown inefficiency the German tank repair system showed none, and during the battle which raged throughout the 23rd it became clear that all hopes of a quick success would have to be abandoned.

The R.A.F. did all it could, even to the extent of arranging for a Flying Fortress to bomb Derna. This novelty—Middle East had sponsored only two previous Fortress sorties—was only part of the plan whereby "fleets of bombers with close supports and sweeps passed over 13 Corps all day to bomb and drop leaflets on M.T. at El Adem, Gambut, and the coastal wadis". Albacores of the Fleet Air Arm by night and Marylands by day kept up the bombardment;

and if on the 22nd four Blenheims were shot down by the ever present Me. 109's, fighter successes counterbalanced this loss, although the fighters were working at an unexpected disadvantage. It had been assumed that there would be some system of forward interception and control with R.D.F. coverage at Sidi Barrani and Tobruk. But Rommel, by forcing the battle at Sidi Rezegh, threw the carefully evolved system out of gear. Enemy airfields at Gazala were nearer to the fighting front than ours at Maddalena, therefore the R.A.F. had instead to maintain offensive sweeps over the battlefield, a process which was already known to be costly. But there was no alternative.

By the 20th the Gazala landing-grounds were beginning to dry out, and the *Luftwaffe* pilots were able to hit back. But they had lost the initiative and were in the conflict as challengers, rather than as possessors, of air superiority. On that day Tomahawks of 3 R.A.A.F. and 112 squadron shot down four out of six Me. 110's in the early morning, and later Tomahawks of 250 and Hurricanes of the Fleet Air Arm squadron met a number of Ju. 87's escorted by Me. 109's. The fighters forced the Ju. 87's to jettison their bombs, but casualties were well balanced—four enemy bombers and two Me. 109's as against two Hurricanes and two Tomahawks.

The 22nd witnessed an engagement which did much to decide the future relationship of the Me. 109 and the Tomahawk. The trial of strength, in which the Germans were unable to break up our formations in the same way that we had been breaking up theirs, was not to be repeated. In the morning fifteen Me. 109's met Blenheims escorted by R.A.A.F. Tomahawks just as the bombers were about to make their run in on their target. The 109's showed that extra turn of speed which they had demonstrated in the past; the Tomahawks that extra manœuvrability. Two Me. 109's were destroyed and two damaged as against three of ours destroyed. In the afternoon, elated perhaps by their success, the Germans made a bid to defeat one of our wing formations in the air in a straightforward air battle. Twenty Tomahawks of operational wing No. 2 (112 and 3 squadron) met sixteen Me. 109's. The contemporary report stated:

> "After some wary preliminary manœuvring both sides adopted defensive circles, the enemy (with the advantages of superior rate of climb, speed and ceiling) above, our aircraft below. As they flew round and round, pilots occasionally pulled out and tried to pick off one of the enemy. Most of the pilots who tried to do this however were caught by the enemy circle. Finally a complete deadlock was reached, neither side risking a move. When it became so dark that other aircraft could hardly be seen, the Germans flew off."

Presumably the German aircraft, like ours, landed everywhere but at their proper bases that night. Losses were even, five on either side.

But only the gallantry and skill of our pilots had brought about such a result. The Me. 109, which should by performance figures have ridden the Desert air as a conqueror, was henceforth to adopt piratical rather than offensive tactics. The contemporary comment ran:

> "In spite of inferior machines our formation had held its own. The Germans never challenged our fighter force in straightforward combat again during the campaign. We had gained air superiority. The enemy resorted to raider tactics just as their navy had done in the face of naval supremacy."

Me. 109's orbited round the sweeps watching our formations from above, diving upon stragglers or unescorted bombers, practising the pirate tactics which they had developed against our formations before the battle. The possibility of German fighters appearing in full force compelled us to maintain large fighter formations wherever we expected to meet the enemy—either on protective sweeps over the battlefield or whilst covering bombers against direct support targets. Meanwhile the Germans concentrated on pouncing on stragglers from cloud cover or on attacking areas in the rear by low-level ground strafing.

From the 24th onwards events on the ground were to put Rommel in the running for what was known as the "Matruh Stakes". Having captured Sidi Rezegh and overrun the South African Brigade, an armoured column supported by mobile infantry made a dash eastwards towards the frontier at a point near Sidi Omar, to menace not only all supply dumps and lines of communication, but even the Maddalena group of airfields.

The Prime Minister, describing the first battle of Sidi Rezegh, had referred to "conditions in many respects like those of a sea war", where armies, if sufficiently mobile, could be shifted hither and thither, and where terrain was not so much held as used for manœuvring. Certainly Rommel's moves at this juncture bore the aspect of a naval raid.

The R.A.F. was now almost completely devoted to direct support. Enemy landing-grounds were immune whilst lines of communication suffered. A German air force Intelligence summary stated, "the enemy continues to have air superiority and his air forces are co-operating with his land forces with great effect".

Rommel's armoured probe gave Coningham the first real opportunity to demonstrate just what the R.A.F. could do with air superiority. Hitherto, with both sides using captured vehicles and with identification a matter of luck rather than of certainty, there had been no proper target. But on November 5th twelve Hurricane bombers of 80 squadron started harrying German tanks and motor transport. Damage was slight, but many of the tank crews were either decapitated as they opened the hatches or caught alongside their tanks on the ground. They would have been safer inside, for nothing short of a direct hit from a 250-lb. bomb could destroy a tank. Nine Blenheims of 11 and 45 squadrons, and seventeen Marylands of 12 and 21 S.A.A.F., continued the attack near Sheferzen, followed by sixty Blenheims of 14, 45, 84 and the Free French squadrons. That night Albacores of 826 squadron kept up bombing and machine-gunning as a prelude to further attacks by more Albacores the next day, when more Blenheims from 45 and the Free French squadron helped to increase the chaos.

By the 27th the column disintegrated, part returning west, part forging north, worried constantly by aircraft until it fell prey to armoured forces south of Gambut.

This joint operation showed that we were "on the way to a new standard of inter-service co-operation", for the R.A.F. had acted as "highly mobile artillery", had given the support which the Prime Minister had said was essential "when a land battle is in prospect", and had not "branched off on to other targets, however attractive".

The R.A.F. had also been employed in giving a full measure of direct support in the main battle zone. On the 25th twenty Tomahawks of 2 Wing discovered sixty enemy aircraft over our troops in the Sidi Rezegh area. They shot down ten, damaged eight, and may have destroyed three others, for the loss of two Tomahawks. The same wing were to have their greatest success five days later when they met a force of fifty enemy aircraft preparing to attack our land forces. They shot down fifteen and damaged another fifteen for the loss of three. The enemy was forced to jettison his bombs instead of dropping them on the New Zealanders.

His probe a failure, Rommel started from December 3rd to withdraw to the west. His advances had been highly skilled ground manœuvres, but he had not displayed much understanding of the possibilities of his air arm and had been content to operate "blind". Seeing that Auchinleck was determined to continue "the momentum of our attack", Rommel withdrew his force to a line stretching from Tobruk outer perimeter, through the airfield of El Adem, to Bir El Gubi. In spite of these delaying tactics, by December 10th one of the aims of Crusader had been attained. As the enemy retreated to Gazala, Tobruk fell into our hands.

It was a momentous week. Not only because Tripoli, that glittering mirage, beckoned from the distance, nor because the Middle East was saved once again, but because far away across the Atlantic the Japanese attacked Pearl Harbour. Tremors as from a distant earthquake disturbed the brown sands of the Desert. As a result, the trickle of lease-lend aircraft was to increase to the vast flood that was to inundate North Africa, Sicily and Italy. American pilots and ground crews were soon to fight side by side with their R.A.F. counterparts.

CHAPTER XI

THE EDGE OF THE VOLCANO AGAIN

As Crusader neared the Martuba airfields, the German High Command, which had hoped to see Malta starved out, now realized that the island would shortly be refreshed from Alexandria. Failing disintegration by blockade, Malta might collapse under the weight of sustained air attack. Hence, although the Russian front showed no signs of weakening, an entire *Luftflotte*—No. 2—was transferred to Sicily during November and December, together with *Fliegerkorps II*. Kesselring, in command, was also the *Oberbefehlshaber Sued* (Commander in Chief South), responsible for all air- and anti-aircraft units in the Mediterranean, as well as for supplying by all methods (land, sea and air) the *Afrika Korps*. Kesselring's Chief of Staff, *Oberst* Hans Seidemann, had been with von Richtofen in *Fliegerkorps VIII* and was, like all von Richtofen's staff officers, an exceptionally able man who had originally started flying with the Air Sports Clubs, and had been on the General Staff as well as in the *Legion Kondor* in Spain. But Loertzer, at the head of *Fliegerkorps II*, was possibly one of the most inefficient leaders thrown up by the war. An old favourite of Goering, he was only saved by the efficiency of Deichmann, his Chief of Staff, from creating havoc within his command. As it was, his *Gruppen* started to deteriorate almost immediately.

Kesselring, unlike Tedder, was badly served by his subordinate. Froehlich in Africa matched Loertzer in Sicily, the one reported to have insufficient personality to bargain for supplies with Rommel, the other at times woefully out of touch with his forces, able to go over the head of his commanding officer to appeal direct to Goering.

During December, then, as the German air forces massed in Sicily for what they hoped would be the final decisive attack on Malta in the spring of 1942, the *Luftwaffe* in Africa increased slowly in numbers as though to counterbalance the effects of defeat on land.

Rommel's retreat was far from being a rout. He could still make a stand at Gazala, the group of landing-grounds which were popularly known as "Jerry's favourite". Yet with his right flank insecure, the stand was temporary, in order to let units in the rear withdraw. Rommel started his retreat in earnest during the week before Christmas, using Italians as delaying agents whilst German troops fell back on Derna. Thence, helped by reinforcements brought by sea from Tripoli, he was able to withdraw in good order to Jedabya.

He had to give up Benghazi; and with that port in our hands a race for reinforcements ensued which alone could decide the fate of the next three weeks. Tripoli was pitted against Benghazi—the one port subject to constant air attack, against the other whose installations had been sown with as much planned ruin as Rommel's engineers could devise.

Tripoli won. January 5th saw the arrival of nine ships, and more were on their way. Rommel, later to be involved in constant quarrels with Kesselring over supplies, at least had no cause for complaint now. Not until the 7th could the first Allied supply convoy reach Benghazi; and by that time it was too late to harry Rommel's movements to his prepared position at El Agheila, where, as at El Alamein, a line stretched from the coast southwards to an area impenetrable to heavy transport; at the Oasis of Marada, the wastes of the Great Sand Sea billowed to form a right flank as secure as the Qâttara depression; near the coast, salt marshes forced traffic to keep to the roads, until at the coast itself the tiny village of Maaten Bescer, scarcely more than a name on a map, provided ample supplies of water.

During the pursuit the R.A.F. had been hampered, but not detained, by the need for advanced landing-grounds, which had to be stocked in advance with fuel. 10,000 gallons of aviation spirit had been dumped under shell-fire at Gazala and fighters were already installed there to survey the last of the enemy to leave Mechili. Without delay, 15,000 gallons of fuel were brought up in every type of truck ranging from captured vehicle to borrowed H.Q. van, and the next day four squadrons were operating from Mechili, protecting more fuel convoys moving towards Msus.

Desert Air Force pursued its army with unflagging tenacity; Msus was put into operation whilst land forces were at Antelat, and the working party sent to make the landing-strip were warned that the field would be needed to refuel aircraft landing there the next day.

That the airfield was a marsh and that a fresh site had to be chosen were inconveniences, but these were overcome by the efforts of all ranks. The improvised landing-ground was ready within twenty-four hours; by the next day four squadrons had moved in, bombers were standing by awaiting orders, and aircraft from other formations were being refuelled.

Vile weather inundated the advance, for rain turned the red earth of Libya to crimson mud, where trucks wallowed like ships becalmed. There was some slight consolation in the fact that not only had the enemy to contend with similar problems, but that he was also harassed by the Long Range Desert Group, whose raids on Sirte and Jedabya landing-grounds kept units throughout the German air force constantly on the alert for other visits which were never to be paid. Another debt, too, was owed to the army for the action by the 11th Sikhs at Derna, where over a hundred enemy aircraft were destroyed, and others picked off as they came in to land.

When Derna was reached a fresh problem arose. The airfield was full of booby traps; abandoned aircraft were gelignite snares for the unwary. Airmen, souvenir-hunting with indefatigable zeal which constant moves backwards and forwards across the Desert could not diminish, in one case unwittingly rendered a Ju. 88 harmless by removing the battery which would have worked the explosive mechanism. Others, however, were less fortunate; Derna perhaps was the logical outcome of hunting which had in the past been too happy.

Soon, however, Desert Air Force passed beyond Derna with its booby traps, beyond Appollonia where Rommel had established a seaside Headquarters. Past Tocra churned the overland trucks, past the fortress shaped like a battleship, until they came to the town which had been promised as a Christmas present.

There lay Benghazi, seen across the lagoon like some Libyan Venice, the twin domes of the cathedral reflected in the reddish water to form an **88** of black against the bright crimson of the soil. Legend had placed the gardens of the Hesperides here; near the aerodrome of Benina yawned the chasm where sluggish Lethe ran.

Sunset over Benghazi on Christmas Eve bathed the town in red, deepening the hues of the purple and green cloth in which so many of the inhabitants were wrapped. The port, still blazing from the demolitions, smudged the sky with thick trails of smoke to create a scene beyond the imagining of Lot's wife.

Havoc had wrought many changes. Previously there had been the hotels ready to serve the conquerors, and shops in which goods could still be bought. But now the Arabs had seen to it that nothing remained. Houses had been plundered; in many cases fitments which could be of no possible use except where amenities of civilization were still available had been removed. Furniture, hauled purposelessly across muddy streets, disintegrated in the open air. In the cellars crouched what Italians were left, waiting for the troops to come and restore order, any kind of order, so as to put an end to anarchy. Back in the country districts the few remaining colonists implored protection against the fury of the Arabs, whom they themselves had perhaps in the past treated well, but whom their government had systematically ground down under Volpi and Graziani.

But if Benghazi was not quite what the men of Wavell's army had led them to expect, the Allied troops were content to be there, under the shadow of two triumphal pillars, one presented by Venice and the other by Rome to symbolize the acceptance of Benghazi as a capital city equal to its Italian sisters. Christmas dinner that night was for many enriched by German rations; where last year there had been Parmesan and Chianti, now there was cheese which could be squeezed like toothpaste out of a tube, and black puddings wrapped in silver paper.

There was to be little rest. Rommel's troops falling back on Jedabya were attacked by Blenheims in spite of bad weather, and the R.A.F. was preparing to turn all its resources on to the reduction of the frontier towns for the start of the new year. Light bombers, which between September 23rd and 29th made only sixty sorties in close support, between December 27th and 30th alone made 257 sorties against Bardia. This "Bastion of Fascism", besieged for the second time, suffered a fate which should by rights have befallen Sollum and Halfaya, themselves also under siege. Like battlements of a half-submerged sand castle, the towns stood out long after the wave of the advance had engulfed the sand beyond. They fulfilled no real purpose, since as ports they could not rival Tobruk, but their reduction drew the fire of the R.A.F.

The air forces took the opportunity of testing a point of doctrine by reducing Bardia from the air, but they were not solely responsible for its end. On the 31st, eighty-three light bomber sorties combined with a naval bombardment from the coast; during the morning tanks and infantry started to move forward. On New Year's Day forty-five more sorties persuaded the garrison to surrender within twenty-four hours.

Whilst far in the rear Bardia was overwhelmed, 3 and 112 squadrons were showing the paces of the new Kittyhawk over the front line. In the first operation nine Kittyhawks intercepted sixteen Ju. 87's and six escorting Me. 109's near Jedabya. Four bombers and one fighter were destroyed for the loss of one Kittyhawk. But on January 9th a Kittyhawk of 112 squadron was jumped by an Me. 109 when escorting Blenheims, and Me. 109's continued to have success by employing similar tactics against 2 and 4 squadrons S.A.A.F.

Failing the arrival of more Kittyhawks or of Spit fires, changes in tactics could not guarantee a change in fortune. A new forma tion, whereby aircraft of 260 and 94 squadrons were stepped up in two section s of four, still did not prevent the Me. 109's from diving out of the sun and destroying four Hurricanes in the air on January 14th.

But the object of Crusader had been attained. Two convoys ran between Malta and Alexandria. Now that the airfields of Martuba, Tmimi and Derna were in our hands, it was to be hoped that more convoys would continue to reach the besieged island.

On the other hand, German forces, far from being destroyed, were to produce one last-minute surprise before each side settled down to lick its wounds. The Agheila Line was not, as we had hoped, to be the scene of a lull. German strategy, with an eye to the total reduction of Malta, could not afford to countenance succour to the victim.

Serviceability figures for the overstrained R.A.F. were falling steadily. Inadequate repair facilities beyond Benghazi demanded a four-day stand-down of the light bombers, but even so, little could be done to improve the deteriorating position. By January 16th Western Desert Air Force, on paper so imposing, could in practice muster approximately:

97 fighters, plus 25 which could be made serviceable within 48 hours.

28 bombers, plus 28 which could similarly be made serviceable within 48 hour s.

Difficulties of refuelling, of signals communications, of technical trouble with the Bostons, of maintenance, etc., were to be expected. R.A.F. striking power was affected by each adverse element. But the worst of all thieves during the next few weeks was the Far East. In 1941 aid to Greece had reduced the R.A.F. in the Western Desert to a skeleton force; in 1942 India and Burma drained away supplies. And in January 1942 Tripoli was pulling out ahead of Benghazi. Malta, though reinforced by three convoys between December 18th and January 19th, could not interfere with German south-bound shipping as had been the case before Crusader. Instead, with *Luftflotte II* concentrated in Sicily, the island was absorbing air attacks in weight unparalleled up to that stage of the war.

The soldiers, like the airmen, were experiencing difficulty. Their supplies, too, were being diverted to the Far East, and for them, also, forward maintenance beyond Benghazi was apt to be sketchy. Operation "Acrobat", which might have carried them on to Tripoli, had to be postponed. They had driven the enemy to El Agheila, but in the front line they had left the equivalent of only one armoured and one infantry brigade. More could not be supplied or maintained. In both tanks and anti-tank guns the honours lay with Rommel.

Quite soon the German commander started to take advantage of that fact, his first advance being a probe to test our armour. His men had only three days' rations in their knapsacks; the three columns consisted of perhaps thirty tanks with supporting transport. In the air he had local superiority, for the R.A.F. aerodromes were mostly waterlogged, whereas Axis aircraft, operating from the light sandy soil of Tripolitania, were able to give full support to their advancing troops. According to an Australian chronicler, "The air situation resembled that of the opening up of Crusader, with the positions reversed".

Rommel's intentions grew bolder. On the 27th 3 squadron noticed road traffic along the coast streaming towards Jedabya, and cheerful pessimists were soon beginning to talk of the "Sollum Derby", where before they had referred to the "Matruh Stakes".

The eight fighter squadrons at Antelat were given the order, "Move back at once, enemy coming!" Fortunately the drying soil was just suitable for take-off, though each aircraft had to be man-handled by twelve men under the wings to a strip thirty feet wide and five hundred yards long. The last aircraft left under shell-fire; only four Kittyhawks and two Hurricanes in need of airscrews and other parts were left behind. On this offensive Blenheims attacked concentrations of transport; and that night Wellingtons dropped bombs on an enemy fuel dump.

The light of gallantry, as always in time of crisis, shone with particular brilliancy. Thirty enemy bombers with fighter escort, attacking our troops, were accidentally intercepted by five of 274 squadron on their way to refuel. After shooting down four of the enemy and damaging another three, four Hurricanes had to force-land, out of petrol. But the crisis continued to develop.

Shortly afterwards Air H.Q. sent out warnings for the immediate evacuation of Benghazi and the Djebel. The army prepared a plan to retake Antelat and Saunnu, but this was abandoned as Rommel drove towards Msus, whence he staged a diversionary movement towards Mechili to mask his true intent of occupying Benghazi. That day an Indian brigade broke out of the threatened city and escaped to the south; but Benghazi fell on the 28th, and with it fell any hopes of maintaining the front line throughout Cyrenaica.

During this advance, as luck would have it, bad weather restricted bombing, though low-flying Hurricanes, Kittyhawks and Tomahawks were still active against enemy transport, destroying 120 and damaging many more. Over the period January 22nd to February 7th an assessment revealed that 150 vehicles were destroyed and 400 seriously damaged.

There was little now to stop the German advance through the Djebel. Broadcasts from enemy stations altered step. "The British have chosen to call this a major offensive," had been the theme, "in order to stage a painless withdrawal as a prelude to counter-attack." But now German papers were dilating on "the most brilliant campaign in History".

Rommel, in the interests of speed, in part sacrificed one of his chief strategical objects, namely the destruction of opposing forces. He left his main armour grounded at Msus and Benina, and decided to dispense with air support, influenced no doubt by difficulties of transport, fuel and the water-logged state of the landing-grounds. In so doing he lost the chance of air retaliation. The bottle-neck at Tmimi, where some 900 British lorries were practically stationary, was an inviting target which never suffered.

Speed he had certainly gained. The R.A.F. squadrons moved from Msus to Mechili covered by two R.A.F. Regiment Armoured Car Companies, which engaged a number of enemy armoured fighting vehicles in combat and drove back some tanks which had been left behind on account of the shortage of drivers. From Mechili on February 1st the fighters withdrew to El Adem. The bombers withdrew from Martuba; 55 squadron, who had arrived just before the *putsch*, were sent back, together with 826 Fleet Air Arm squadron, to 201 Group.

Rommel's advance seemed to lose momentum at Derna; he was not to regain the initiative. He started to adopt ruses—dummy stationary vehicles covered by strong anti-aircraft fire—which surprised the experienced pilots of 33 squadron, with damaging results.

Vehicles, though, were often misleading targets. Identification of friend and foe had become increasingly uncertain, for captured trucks were being used on both sides, and lack of proper communications led to difficulty in fixing a bomb line. Interceptions, however, under conditions a little less fluid than those of the preceding weeks, began to show a near perfection of technique. From February 12th enemy activity over Tobruk increased; and on the 14th 3 and 112 squadrons had their greatest success against thirty-two enemy aircraft south-west of Acroma. 112 squadron, with ten Kittyhawks, were leading just at base of cloud (which was at the ideal height of 9,000 feet), with 3 squadron a thousand feet below and behind, when, noticing a dozen M.C. 200's below to the left, they warned the eight Kittyhawks of No. 3 squadron. The Macchis attempted to climb into cloud, but were frustrated by 112; each pilot selected his own foe, each scored a kill. Meanwhile, 3 squadron sighted another formation of enemy bombers with close cover escort at less than 2,000 feet. As 3 squadron were about to attack, six Me. 109's, which had evidently been providing top cover in cloud, made their pounce. The leader of 3 squadron saw them in time to prevent being jumped, and in the ensuing dog-fight three Me. 109's were destroyed and two damaged. Fresh from this second victory, 3 squadron attacked the bombers and close cover escort, forcing the Italian pilots ever lower and lower until at ground level no more of the enemy were in sight.

Out of thirty-two aircraft, twenty were claimed as destroyed, two probables, and ten damaged, for the loss of not a single Kittyhawk. This remarkable feat compares with any of the great fighter actions of the war, for some of the victims were Me. 109F's, the aircraft which had proved such a constant source of inconvenience to Desert Air Force pilots.

From then onwards, as the line stabilized, shipping protection was to take the centre of the stage, flanked by medium bomber attacks on Derna (once more the African end of the Crete–Derna route) and on Benghazi (once more the German shipping terminal).

But on the debit side a convoy interchange between Malta and Alexandria met with disaster, one after another of the merchant ships being picked off by continuous attacks from enemy aircraft out of range of the R.A.F. fighter forces in Libya. Another convoy, plying between Alexandria and Tobruk, met partial disaster. Due to a number of causes, the convoy was lost by what air cover could be provided. Only one of three ships got through.

The German air force meanwhile was particularly occupied with shipping strikes and attacks on our forward landing-grounds; the Italians were mainly concerned with the protection of supply convoys.

Thus both sides settled down to "the lull". Rome Radio, which had displayed uncertainty as to whether Bastico or Rommel had been responsible for the advance, told of a fresh decoration awarded to the former for his co-operation with the German commander, whilst the Vichy station spoke slightingly of the "*Promenade des Anglais*".

Crusader, its object in part achieved for part of the time, was at an end.

CHAPTER XII

FURTHER REORGANIZATION

THE Parliamentary debate on the war situation in February was used by German propaganda to imply the imminent disintegration of the British Empire. Marshal Pétain was said to have done Europe a great service in that he had prevented France from falling under Bolshevik domination, whereas Britain, toying with the idea of annexation to America, and yet bent on seeing the Red Flag unfurled over Buckingham Palace, had apparently taken one step further towards the Kremlin by the appointment of a new Archbishop of York.

But if the radio comedy of manners was in full flourish, events were taking a serious enough turn on all save the Middle East front. The Japanese had reduced Singapore and had occupied Moulmein, long famed in song for its old pagoda. They had occupied Macassar, and bombed Port Darwin; place-names reminiscent of hair-oil or anthropology, but whose exact location was often quite unknown to the general public, made a brief appearance in the news, only, it seemed, in order to be taken or damaged by the Japanese.

On the Russian front, strong German counter-attacks had reduced the extent of the Donetz Salient, but the Red Army had advanced south-east of Kharkov. In the Crimea the Germans were carrying out extensive mine-laying operations in front of Sebastopol. In the Mediterranean, Malta, now alone, was withstanding the rising storm of air bombardment from Sicily, and in the Western Desert two forces opposed one another, building up reserves of supplies.

In the race for reinforcements the advantage lay with the enemy, for though Rommel could not call upon the man-power and repair facilities of the Delta, he could get supplies direct from Germany and Italy.

But the Mediterranean Fleet was still at large; and the head of Malta, though bloody, was still unbowed. If at the time of the lull at Gazala the offensive merit of Gambut and Baheira seemed to be dimmed by the fact of German tenure of Derna and Martuba, such an eclipse was only temporary, for towards the end of March a convoy was run successfully through to Malta with the loss of only one ship *en route*.

During the lull, the 8th Army prepared defensive positions which included a minefield running from Gazala to Bir Hakim, embracing several strongpoints. To the rear, Tobruk was strengthened, and more strongpoints set in the course of construction at El Adem, Acroma and Bir El Gubbi. Jarubub, the Senussi-controlled oasis west of Siwa, was occupied, and the Sollum-Maddalena line was given the status of "prepared position" on which the army could fall back if need be. Shielded thus by the arm of its partner in battle, the Western Desert Air Force could set about the task of putting its house in order.

The house itself was already in existence. Major reorganization, inspired by Tedder and executed by Coningham before the start of Crusader, had on the whole proved satisfactory. The squadrons and wings were more mobile. Close support arrangements had been tested, and only found wanting through lack of practice and not through any weakness of principle. Therefore it now remained to complete the programme ordained during the preceding year with such modifications as experience dictated. In the next three months the squadrons were grouped into three mobile wings, the fighters put under operational control of a Group devised for that purpose only, and the principles of air support defined more clearly for the benefit of air and ground forces alike.

Though Gazala and El Adem were both nearer to the front than Gambut, it was to the latter system of airfields that the fighter force moved, both in order to have more freedom from attack and because Gambut, hot, dry and dusty, was compact enough for a proper system of communications and was conveniently near Baheira, where a light bomber force was similarly concentrated. Though during the campaign the principle of dispersal had been well applied, in semi-static conditions semi-permanent airfields near one another made defence easier because of the increased flak which could be put up to deter the invader.

The creation of this system of landing-grounds was the responsibility of C.R.E. No. 82 (Aerodromes). An extract from a report shows the problems confronting them:

"Dispersal lanes and perimeter tracks were cut with autopatrols and, although it sounds fantastic, to give some idea of the areas involved, at Gambut satellite No. 1 the perimeter track measured 12 miles and dispersal lanes added up to more than 50 miles. On account of the width involved, this would approximate to over 125 miles of Desert track. Temporary pens were made by filling 50-gallon barrels with earth and placing them in the shape of a horseshoe, two high. This method was also used for protecting operations waggons and pilots' rest tents. In all, before the battle began, nine landing-grounds were provided with perimeter tracks and dispersal lanes, and new landing-grounds were constructed at Gambut—a dummy, Baheira—satellite No. 1, Sidi Aziz—satellite, Bir Uazan, and two at Bir Hakim. In addition, extensions were made to landing-grounds Kasr El Arid, Gambut satellite Nos. 1, 2 and 3, Gambut dummy and Baheira main, to bring them up to a 15,000-yds. square. This work was put back at the start due to heavy rains, which, apart from making work impossible, created an additional task in the way of rut-filling. The landing-grounds were rendered so soft by the rain that any lorry crossing a landing-ground left deep ruts, and not a few got completely bogged, leaving a crater to be filled. In all, the de-rutting and cutting out of soft spots on the landing-grounds occupied both mobile parties for a period of three weeks.

"A dummy landing-ground was constructed in some detail to draw the enemy bombs from Gambut main. The dummy three miles west of Gambut main was created the same shape, and provided with as many unserviceable aircraft as could be found, mostly German. Dummy guns and dummy tentage were provided, and two of the aircraft were arranged to become direct hits at will and to burn furiously. The picture was completed by the construction of a dummy road-house on the road. The effect on the enemy is not recorded, but a squadron and a half of our fighters and the Libyan Clipper landed on the dummy by mistake."

Meanwhile units sent back to the Delta for rest and re-equipment gave other squadrons a chance to improve their fighting spirit by tasting some of the experiences which the front line had to offer. To control this influx of new blood, and to lift the Controller above paper work, which had, ever since the time of the Elmhirst report, been taking up so much of his time, a new Group was formed.

The charter of 211 Group was as follows:

It was to exercise full operational control of all offensive fighter wings in the Western Desert, to control those squadrons who might from time to time be attached to such wings, and to have at its disposal radar stations for fighter interception. In the administrative line its only responsibility was the recommendation for awards and promotions. The Group was organized on the Leapfrog principle, with two Operations Rooms identical in make-up, one forward and one rear, which under fluid conditions could act in the same way as squadron forward and rear parties, and could maintain continuity of operation in spite of the difficulties of a move.

On April 18th work started on the first underground operations room and telephone exchange for 211 Group. Solid rock had to be broken by a party short of a compressor. This slowed up the excavations, but time was gained by putting the job on a twenty-four-hour basis. Within twelve days the cave was ready, and, much to the satisfaction of the Sappers who had worked on it, was then inspected by H.R.H. the Duke of Gloucester.

211 Group was administered by Rear Air H.Q. Western Desert, and operationally controlled by Advanced Air H.Q. Its formation represented the final divorce of the operational and the administrative, which had been in the courts since the start of the Desert campaigns. Administration, however, put in a plea on a lower level, for the new wings were to be administrative entities in themselves, which would take over part of the burden from the squadrons and provide centralized ground services.

Just as the Group itself was formed by readjustment of existing units rather than by the creation of fresh ones, so the reorganization shuffled round responsibilities and readjusted the Admin/Ops position in the interests of greater efficiency. Group was to be the guiding hand, whilst the wings themselves acted as independent units.

If, at this point, the thread of the story becomes complicated, it is due to the fact that wings not only changed their composition, but also, in anticipation, their numbers, as from March 1st. Thus 258 and 262 Wings became 243 and 239. The other already existing wing, 234, was not to be included in the reshuffling, since it was to protect shipping between Alexandria and Sollum. But a new wing, No. 233, was envisaged though not yet formed.

The first allocation of squadrons followed an already established pattern. Those who had worked well together in the past were still linked:

239 Wing—3 R.A.A.F., 450, 112, 250 squadrons.

243 Wing—33, 73, 80, 274 squadrons.

233 Wing—2 and 4 S.A.A.F., 94, and 260 squadrons.

The wine itself was the same, the wineskins alone being renewed.

To understand the necessity for the creation of 211 Group, the reigning system of fighter interception should perhaps be given in brief detail. In England static conditions allowed radar coverage to be on a permanent basis, and a network of operations rooms to have special departments to determine friend from foe. In the Western Desert during the first part of Crusader, due to the late fall of Tobruk, radar coverage was at a discount. Mobile conditions affected the delicate sets, and the to-and-fro nature of the Desert campaign made the erection of a screen a matter of some difficulty. When, during the lull, plans could be made on a slightly more permanent basis, Tobruk, the main forward base, was supplied with better equipment, and mobile sets were installed at Gambut and Gazala. At the same time an organization bearing some resemblance to the Royal Observer Corps submitted visual reports from the El Adem area. Now, therefore, the fighters could be sent into the air by a Group order to the wing concerned; or, if already airborne, the fighters would be in touch by radio with the Group Operations Room, where the Controller, with the aid of a separate filter table, would have to decide whether aircraft plotted were hostile or friendly. Group Operations Room would then hand over the fighters to the Forward Operations Controller, who could arrange for the interception of enemy formations. The pilot had to press a button and speak. The men on the ground, informed with varying degrees of accuracy as to height, direction of travel and speed of the enemy, could pass on their knowledge in reply.

Brought into play during the lull, 211 Group was designed for mobility; it represented a new system of reformed control.

Methods of close support could also not escape the hand of the reformer. Crusader at different times had illustrated two theories: at the start of the campaign all decisions were made by the A.O.C. Western Desert, in consultation with the army commander; yet towards the end, when the two Corps were operating at a distance from each other, 3 S.A.A.F. and 258 Wings had been allotted to 13 Corps H.Q.

Both systems had their advocates. The revised directif appeared already out of date, since in it Air Support Controls were to be retained at Corps H.Q., whereas they had already in fact moved back to the combined H.Q. But before the conflict of viewpoints could become serious a compromise was discovered; R.A.F. Liaison Officers were to be attached to each Divisional H.Q. to operate sets which could, if necessary, carry out rebriefing in the air; each army tentacle was to be given a set for listening in to tactical reconnaissance reports. If the pie was thus to contain more fingers, the R.A.F. thumb was firmly pressed upon the plum. This arrangement, which had sprung into being on the spot, worked smoothly, greatly to the credit of the individual army and R.A.F. commanders at all levels.

Meanwhile the method, too, of direct support was undergoing a change. Hurricanes had already been fitted with bomb-racks; now it was the turn of the Kittyhawk to demonstrate that it was capable of carrying a 250-lb. bomb. In view of the later performances of this aircraft, such early experiments may seem tame, but at the time the idea was novel, and the pilots dubious. The new fighter-bomber, capable of low-level bombing as well as strafing, was intended to be a time-saver; it was not intended to supplant the light bomber. In May a conference between the Senior Air Staff Officer and the squadron commanders of 239 Wing impressed on all that the fighter-bomber could only be developed if pilots were first trained. This was the signal for the conversion of most of 112 (the Shark squadron), who were thus, as from May 16th, the first of a new breed in the Western Desert. Their example was almost immediately followed by 3 squadron; "Killer" Caldwell, who on the 11th March had dropped the first bomb from a Kittyhawk on the enemy, was soon to have many of his compatriots in company.

Light bombers were not to be thrust out of the picture by the development of this newer method. In fact they were about to enter on their most famous period. No longer tied to low-level work, they were now free to operate against targets entirely suited to them at heights where danger was least, and where results were equally as effective. They were to fly at 10,000 to 12,000 feet for attacks on shipping, at 20,000 feet for attacks on targets in the rear, and at 6,000 feet for attacks on tank concentrations, supply dumps and airfields. With Bostons appearing in greater numbers, operations by night and day might soon take place. Training could start.

Consultations between the fighter and bomber H.Q.s could be arranged relatively easily. Gambut was only twelve miles from Baheira. Visits, which might start by being official, could quickly become social occasions, and vice versa. From such liaison was evolved a better system of fighter escort. Points were that the leader of the fighters was to be in overall command, and was to be in radio touch with the bombers; the bombers were to fly in close formation, except when actually on the bombing run; they were to wait for five minutes after the last fighter had taken off before setting course for their target. On return the sun had always to be at fifteen degrees to the fighters in order to keep all the aircraft within sight of one another.

To conclude, not only had control of interception and close support been worked out, but the relationship between one aircraft and another had also been clearly defined. One of the few problems still outstanding was the thorny matter of recognition—still, apparently, insoluble. A white cross of St. Andrew, though symbolically satisfactory, had been tested and found wanting, so from May 12th an R.A.F. roundel was painted on all vehicles, but this could not be seen at a height. It became painfully obvious that, failing signs a mile long and a mile wide, an efficient system of visual recognition did not exist. There remained only the bomb-line method; but army commanders, anxious for the safety of their troops, were only too ready to allow for too wide a margin of error; many very suitable targets were never disclosed. However, awkward as this might be, it was the only solution, and efforts had to be made along these lines. Hence broadcasts by Air Support Control gave an hourly forecast of the land situation. But only one thing could make the bomb-line system work, namely the demonstration of such accuracy by the R.A.F. light bombers that the local commanders could have absolute trust in them. This happy state of affairs had not yet been reached.

The Germans already had the counterpart of 211 Group. Since Gazala, their favourite aerodrome, was no longer in their hands, they were using Martuba as the centre of their defence and interception scheme. There, a *Gefechstand* (Operations Room), and a *Bodenstelle* (Fighter Control), had been built underground. The Operations Room Duty Officer of the day was to act in concert with the *Staffelkapitän* (if the latter was not flying). Raids and interceptions were traced out on sheets of transparent paper laid over a large desk map, and orders could be given by the Controller to the fighter radio-telephone section, which passed them on to fighters in the air. All such tracings were sent eventually to the *Fliegerführer.* The Italians, instead of sharing in this organization, had a separate Operations Room and a separate control system, identical to the Germans, with German Liaison Officers attached.

The 3 *Gruppen* of *Geschwader* JG 27 on the Martuba landing-grounds were at a state of readiness on different days, and were, if at readiness (which meant sitting in their aircraft ready to take off at thirty seconds' notice), unable to be used for interceptions, whilst the others might be sent out for bomber protection or standing patrol work.

Enemy air methods betrayed a desire for specialization which went directly contrary to the "all-round" requirements of the Desert. In the event of overwhelming German air superiority, however, little criticism could be offered. German experience in Spain, France and the Low Countries had been such that air superiority was bound to be automatically taken for granted. The Crusader campaign, during Rommel's rush to Gazala, had not given the air force much of a lesson in air inferiority, for had they not been left behind? They had not therefore had the opportunity of learning that flexibility was the key to success in the Desert.

In contrast, reorganized, the R.A.F. in the Western Desert looked forward to its next encounter with the enemy. Girded for an advance, retreat was in fact to be their role, but by then Coningham's forces were flexible enough to take the centre of the stage in either event.

CHAPTER XIII

BACKWARDS AGAIN

DURING the lull, air operations steadily decreased, for in February Air Marshal Coningham had been asked, "Would you like to consider calling off the dogs except in special circumstances, in order to conserve fighter strength for the next great day?" Apart from a brief resurgence of the offensive spirit during the convoy movements to Malta in March, sorties were mainly routine matters, devoted to local defence and shipping.

The chief feature of the air effort during the period was the harassing of Benghazi, mostly by night-bombing Wellingtons of 205 Group. Between February 25th and May 19th Benghazi was raided on sixty-eight out of sixty-nine nights. This "mail run" seriously hampered, but did not prevent, the Germans from using the port for unloading supplies. Apart from these activities, Bostons visited Martuba in mid-March, whilst patrols of the Long-Range Desert Group raided Benina, Tmimi and Martuba, sabotaging enemy aircraft and destroying supplies as their part of the plan to divert attention from the Malta convoy.

For Malta, to whose aid Crusader had striven not entirely in vain, was a hallowed land, and strategy was concerned almost to the point of obsession with the problem of keeping the island going. Its value as a base from which enemy ships could be attacked was temporarily in abeyance. Aircraft could not be maintained, and even local shipping could not be protected, in the face of Kesselring's Sicilian-based bomber assaults. Yet its potentialities as a springboard for a Sicilian adventure were enormous; and, more immediately important, in support of a land offensive in the Desert, Malta might become the other claw of a pincer to trap the German armies in North Africa.

There was no lack of vision, either in London or the Middle East; Malta was to be held at all costs, though there was some argument as to the precise method. Auchinleck was unwilling to make any premature offensive which might jeopardize Egypt. An offensive might easily achieve no more. He did not wish to rob the northern front of troops and thus lay Syria and Persia open to the machinations of the German Middle East Master Planner. On the other hand, it was fully recognized that a convoy could not sail from the west unless the airfields of Cyrenaica were in our hands. When the impossible was attempted between March 20th and 23rd, four merchant vessels set sail to the accompaniment of diversionary measures staged in the Western Desert; three ships got through and of these two were sunk whilst unloading on March 26th.

Renewed pressure from London, including a visit by Sir Stafford Cripps and the Vice-Chief of the Imperial General Staff, provoked the promise of an offensive, possibly in May. But meanwhile the position in the Far East was deteriorating; Middle East, far from being able to build up resources, was compelled to sacrifice supplies to India, for if the Japanese pressed further westwards reinforcement lines to both Middle and Far East would be in danger. But the claims of Malta were in no wise diminished. On May 10th the Prime Minister declared that a Libyan offensive, aimed at the relief of the island, was the best service that the 8th Army could perform; preparations for the coming event marched on.

Crusader had failed even when within clear reach of victory because no forces could be maintained in strength beyond Benghazi. Therefore, during the lull, the extension of the railhead to Capuzzo and the creation of reserves helped to give some guarantee that a second drive would retain its momentum until Benghazi, recaptured, could be made to work at full pressure.

Crusader had also demonstrated the appalling superiority of German armour over our lighter tanks and our lack of any counterpart of the 88-millimetre gun. If, therefore, the Germans were to have the advantage of quality, then Auchinleck needed to have at least 50 per cent advantage of quantity.

So preparations were under way. But before any offensive could be launched, enemy plans intervened. It seemed best to absorb the full weight of German attack before going over to the counter-offensive. A defensive system embracing Bir Hakim and Tobruk, dotted by strongpoints protected by minefields, lay in front of the tanks. Sixty-six-pounder anti-tank guns were starting to appear in quantity and the troops were being instructed in their use as fast as possible. The army was ready and waiting when the first blow was struck.

Towards the end of May German air activity increased, taking that softening-up form borrowed from Coningham. Airfields at Kasr El Arid, Gambut, Baheira, Fuka, Daba, Maaten Bagush, all were visited frequently, whilst the railheads of Misheifa and Capuzzo suffered daily attacks. Most ominous sign of all, our reconnaissance flights over enemy-held territory, normally safe from interference, were being interrupted by flights of enemy fighters on special sweeps. Bedouin tents appeared like an overnight growth of mushrooms and sometimes the glint of a tank pierced the surrounding canvas to betray the secret.

The lull was on its deathbed; Rommel was to conduct its funeral. He was adequately prepared; herculean efforts had put Benghazi in working order from mid-February onwards; air transport services from Crete to Derna added yet one more source of supply.

Behind our lines work on the aerodromes of Buq Buq and Bir Habata was in progress against the possibility of a withdrawal; that Coningham was taking no chances can be shown clearly enough by a series of operational orders. One, dated April 11th, stated, "It is the intention of the A.O.C. to dispose R.A.F. units to provide maximum protection and support for the land forces, whilst at the same time maintaining the air offensive". A few weeks later subordinate commanders were warned that if communications broke down in the event of a retreat they must be prepared to take the responsibility for issuing orders. A complete system for directing movements by the use of code words was circulated to the squadrons, whilst the A.O.C. toured round to talk to all ranks personally about the coming offensive.

Coningham had always believed in taking his men into his confidence since he had assumed command of the Western Desert Air Force. By now he was in control of an integrated community confident of itself and of its commanders. The long weeks at Gambut and Baheira had given pilots and air crew from all types of aircraft an opportunity of getting to know one another. In their camps, which Guedalla compared to "an enormous fairground", a certain uniformity of outlook was beginning to be reflected in the clothes they wore. Captured German caps proudly donned (with pretended indifference) by all ranks, captured vehicles moving to and fro—these things gave an air of endless variety to the unvarying dustiness of the Desert. But there was nevertheless a certain uniformity, for it was a case of "*Plus ça change plus c'est la même chose*". Here the correctly dressed stranger from Cairo appeared wildly unorthodox, and visitors could be picked out at a glance. Alike in the similar dissimilarity of their appearance, the men of D.A.F. were alike in other ways; they shared the same rations of bully beef and chlorinated tea; they experienced the same unpleasant conditions, crouched under cover in the same sandstorms, and simmered under the same blazing sun. All, or nearly all, were healthy.[1]

They had become a "Firm" like the 8th Army, capable of absorbing the outsider either temporarily or permanently and moulding him to their traditions. They, too, were ready and waiting for Rommel.

· · · · ·

The German commander was unlikely to indulge in a frontal attack through minefields and prepared positions; he would probably prefer to give free rein to his passion for outflanking. His actual plan showed that he intended the Trieste Division to bridge the minefields at Sidi Muftah, whilst the *Afrika Korps* and the 90th Light Division battle-group moved in a wide circle round Bir Hakim.

The dangerous situation in which his troops were involved after an auspicious start he was able to blame on the Italians (in particular on the Ariete Division), who failed to reduce Bir Hakim and who thus robbed the Germans of the advantage which might have been expected to accrue from their skill in capturing 7th Armoured Division H.Q. As it was, German troops were

[1] With the exception of those who contracted Desert sores, the standard of health was remarkably high in the Desert. Sicily and Italy claimed a far higher percentage of victims.

stranded at the end of long lines of communications backing onto a minefield. It seemed their position could only be saved by a vigorous attack on Bir Hakim and that Rommel was committed to a major offensive from the start. But the Trieste Division managed in time to clear passages through the minefields around Trigh Capuzzo; Rommel's armour contrived a retreat through the gaps.

This setback can largely be attributed to the R.A.F., who attacked Rommel's loosely knit formations much as they had harried his probing column in 1941. But now they were highly organized, moving as one, the whole force capable of being directed onto a single target, switched away, and redirected, within a matter of a few telephone calls. From midday onwards and for the next few days, 3, 112 and 274 squadrons operated against the "soft" supply vehicles around Bir Hakim, dealing havoc from low altitudes which would have been unsafe for light bombers. Their average number of sorties, 350 per day, represented attacks on vehicles and armoured columns. The light bombers were free to attack enemy landing-grounds.

If the R.A.F. was active, so was the *Luftwaffe*, anxious to show its mettle in face of Rommel's dangerous and humiliating practice of leaving it behind at every possible opportunity. Its 270 Libya-based aircraft averaged 300 to 350 sorties a day, mostly in close support; but this scale of attack, on paper similar to that of the R.A.F., was not having nearly the same effect on our troops as our aircraft on theirs. This may have been due to the fact that on many occasions the Stuka was persuaded to jettison bombs before reaching its target, whereas the British fighter-bomber, needing less escort and able to fend for itself once bombs were dropped, demanded less and did more. However, enemy reconnaissance over our lines was intensive and regular. As though in answer to the Kittybomber (which, it is interesting to recall, was widely quoted at that time as being "the answer" to the Stuka), Me. 109's appeared in a new role as fighter-bombers.

Enough harm was being done to our troops; the position could not be called satisfactory merely because German forces were suffering still more. German bombers, operating from Crete, attacked Gambut and the forward aerodromes, to leave no doubt that this time the British position in the Middle East was being seriously challenged.

Meanwhile, what of the 200 aircraft of the *Regia Aeronautica*? Were they being kept in reserve? There seemed to be no other explanation for their non-employment. Although prisoner-of-war reports indicated that the Italians were not being used "because they were no good", or "because their morale had suffered", the truth, almost too incredible to be believed, was held to be propaganda; in fact, what aircraft were available were either unserviceable or constantly under-supplied. The *Italuft* organization, supposedly a joint affair, had fallen more and more into the hands of the Germans. Italian air sorties wavered from a mountain peak of forty to the molehill hump of eight.

The failure of the first instalment of the Axis plan was now apparent.

Bir Hakim was being ably defended by the Free French; Tobruk was safe for the time being; but an enemy bridgehead prevented failure from becoming defeat. In the "Cauldron", the region where some of our troops had broken through, friend and foe seemed so inextricably intertwined that there was no hope of separating the one from the other, nor of knowing what might happen next. Orders were even issued to cover the possibility of an enemy retreat.

Sandstorms hindered operations from June 1st, and German forces took advantage of the breathing-space to clear away mines and in other ways establish themselves firmly.

Sandstorms continued as the enemy displayed no intention of withdrawing. The attack on Bir Hakim came just as the weather was showing signs of growing more favourable. The importance of Bir Hakim was persistently emphasized in the contemporary Cairo press; articles confidently stated that the fortress would hold; that it was of the highest importance that it should hold, etc.; but from the army point of view keeping the armoured forces intact mattered still more. For this reason its defence was allotted to the R.A.F. Fighter-bomber squadrons adopted the fortress for the next few days, blowing up ammunition waggons and trucks, whilst fighters patrolled overhead. It was estimated a few weeks later that every fighter-bomber sortie was responsible, on average, for the destruction of two enemy vehicles. At the time their efforts were recognized by a signal from the Free French Garrison Commander, "*Bravo, merci pour la R.A.F.*".

As attack followed counter-attack in the Cauldron, air effort was momentarily switched to where the main weight of German armour was engaged near "Knightsbridge". Close support calls were being answered faster and faster, one on the 7th bearing fruit within thirty-five minutes of the original request. Tank-busting Hurricanes of 6 squadron were brought into play, whilst escorting Bostons took toll of enemy lorries and supply lines south-west of the area.

From the 8th the defence of Bir Hakim was given Priority No. 1. As the threat to the fortress increased, the air over the Free French forces echoed to the sound of many a dog-fight. German Stukas with heavier and heavier escorts tried to push their way through the protecting wings of the fighters; sometimes they were successful, though generally with high losses in ratio to the number of bombs actually unleashed over the target. On the 9th cannisters containing medical supplies dropped within 100 yards of the chosen mark, and that day the tally showed five Me. 109's destroyed and seven probables for the loss of one Kittyhawk and one Tomahawk, but on the 10th sixty heavily escorted enemy bombers got through. On the next day the R.A.F. had the sorry task of covering the retreat of the 2,000 men who managed to escape.

The fall of Bir Hakim was a sad blow for the R.A.F., for their work of protection had been as sustained as it had been magnificent, and the gallantry of the Free French garrison had given those taking part in the defence the strongest motive for striving their utmost. That they had even for a moment contrived to hinder the advance of superior forces was in itself a triumph, not only for the men themselves but for those who had constantly affirmed the possibilities of tactical air power.

From the German army point of view, a troublesome period had come to an end. For the *Luftwaffe*, rejoicing may well have been tempered with sober reflection. Far too much air effort had been absorbed with far too little result. In view of the overwhelming superiority of the German armour and of the repeated air attacks (when they could be driven home), the reduction of the fortress had been too long delayed, too expensive in men and machines. At Bir Hakim, for perhaps the last time for the rest of the war in the Desert, the German air force had competed on more than equal terms with their opponent.

The German appreciation stated:

> "Field-Marshal Rommel's supply position was such that an advance into Egypt with the Suez Canal as its first objective seemed possible. The battle of Bir Hakim deprived this offensive of its desired result. This fortress held out for nine whole days against an attack of nearly three divisions and three reconnaissance battalions, supported by about 15,000 air sorties. This meant a nine days' gain for the enemy, and for our army and air force nine days of losses in material, personnel, aircraft and petrol. Those nine days were irrecoverable."

That the effort of the R.A.F. was fully appreciated elsewhere was shown by the sudden flow of congratulatory telegrams from His Majesty the King, from the Chief of Air Staff, from the Air Officer Commanding Malta, remarkable in that they were received during what seemed at that time to many observers throughout the world to be the eve of a major land disaster. The A.O.C. Western Desert passed on the congratulations with special messages of his own to the maintenance crews; 3 squadron had kept a Kitty-bomber flying for fifteen sorties in three days; the twelve squadrons of fighters had maintained an average serviceability of ten to twelve, the two squadrons of light bombers an average serviceability of fifteen. With the South Africans in particular he had reason to be well pleased, for the latter figure represented only a part of their total air effort. Over this period the South Africans were providing 12 and 24 S.A.A.F. squadrons, the only light bombers in the Desert (223 squadrons had been withdrawn shortly after the start of the offensive because of rear turret trouble; 14 squadron, arriving on the 8th, was mainly employed over Crete). Hence the Bostons streaming out in boxes of six to attack enemy columns advancing on El Adem were South African, and "*die stüre achtzehn*"[1] might well have been called for the moment "*die suedafrikanische achtzehn*".

[1] Translation: "The Eighteen Disturbers of the Peace", known more familiarly as "The Eighteen Imperturbables".

Grave events on land gave little opportunity for rejoicing. The Tobruk-Gazala line was directly menaced. On the 14th the Germans approached Acroma, where the garrison held out in desperation, knowing that on their efforts depended the safe withdrawal of the 1st South African Division, still in the original position at Gazala, which now had to withdraw along the coast-road to Sollum. For two days and nights the Gazala-Tobruk road was packed with a slowly moving mass of men and lorries, offering the sort of target which the German air force had appreciated in France. Yet, during those days, the retreating ground troops lost six men only instead of a possible 600 or 6,000. General Freyberg commented, "Thank God you didn't let the Hun Stuka us, because we were an appalling target".

Tedder sent one of those short messages of understatement which were so popular amongst all ranks: "Sure you agree that visit of Rommel and his toughs to our area is personal insult. Good luck in your reply to his darned cheek. Keep weather eye open for G.A.F."

For Rommel had overrun Gazala, and turning east from Acroma he was threatening El Adem. Tobruk would be next—and to defend Tobruk without the help of air forces based on El Adem or Gazala was to lay the town open to unescorted Stuka raids by day and night. Tobruk was a matter of main concern to Auchinleck, not only because of the prestige involved in holding it once again, but because the idea of a counter-offensive had never left his mind, and Tobruk was the forward port which made such an offensive possible. He had envisaged a line stretching from Tobruk to Bir El Gubbi, but Rommel's latest move sounded the knell to any such intention. Germans were now within twenty miles of Gambut, the fairground.

On June 16th, when 8th Army Tactical H.Q. moved back to Sollum, Advanced Air H.Q. Western Desert stayed on at Gambut to control operations. "The price of the gamble," commented Group-Captain Beamish, "was the entire fighter force." The decision was courageous.

It was more. It was a vital necessity. Tobruk had not then fallen, and might yet be held; all the protection that could be given to the defenders of the El Adem box must be provided, and at maximum intensity. The Bostons from Baheira flew as many sorties as possible over the defenders, in spite of German patrols which were continually on the look-out.

Enemy fighters jumped the protecting Hurricanes to produce a surprise result on the 17th, when ten fighters were lost for four Me. 109's and M.C. 202's. But such a rare triumph was shortlived, for reconnaissance soon disclosed that the German fighter force had, as had been expected, moved to Gazala. Before the move could be consolidated Coningham sent 239 Wing in strength to achieve once more a feat such as he had engineered in the opening stages of Crusader. On take-off the squadrons made out to sea, turned west and climbed steadily to 17,000 feet. No attempt was made to intercept. After half an hour's flying the formation turned south-west and sighted Gazala No. 2, on which more than thirty Me. 109's were drawn up. The raid was completely unexpected. No enemy was in the air, and there was nothing but light flak over the landing-ground. Fifteen of the Me. 109's were hit, one as it attempted too late to take-off to defend its own base. Petrol bowsers went up in flames; two Fieseler Storch aircraft of the type used by Rommel for visiting his troops in the front line were damaged.

The planning of this raid, at a time when the shadow of defeat seemed to black out the possibility of victory, gives some idea of the cool heads in control at Gambut. The end was near at hand. Preparations to leave the hot dusty plain could not long be delayed. On the 17th the El Adem box had to be abandoned; on the 18th, at dawn, the light bombers left Baheira, the thunder of enemy guns scarcely fifteen miles away drowned by the roar of engines warming up for take-off.

Nothing now remained between Gambut and the enemy but the R.A.F. armoured car screen, when the fighter force, plans prepared in advance, retired to Sidi Aziz. By dusk, as the enemy spearhead thrust closer, only a salvage unit was left, working with inspired zeal to patch up the last serviceable aircraft and to destroy the few remaining drums of petrol. Towards midnight shadowy forms of German tanks rolled across the dry, dusty surface of Gambut, mocked by phantoms where they had expected to meet the reality. To the invaders, as to Don Quixote tilting at windmills, each shape must have appeared to be an encampment; each burnt-out aircraft a Kittyhawk in perfect flying condition; the capture of each deserted strongpoint a minor military operation. The fighter force had "softly and silently vanished away", their vehicles unheard amidst the rumble of tanks rolling within half a mile of the invaders, rolling eastwards through the night.

CHAPTER XIV

THE DANGEROUS DAYS

TOBRUK was now isolated, beyond the range of the single-engined fighters. No news came from the beleagured garrison to indicate whether enemy air attacks were heavy or light. Kittyhawks were specially fitted with extra tanks to enable them to spend at leasts ome minutes over the town, but they were, as it happened, hardly needed, for the Air Support Tentacle and Advanced 211 Group sent through few messages, none of them mentioning air attack on any scale. This was to come in full fury as Rommel's troops, disturbed only by formations of Bostons, prepared their assault.

On the fall of Tobruk much was written and much remains to be said. From the air point of view, once the enemy had captured landing-grounds within a certain radius of the port, only reduced air protection could be given. It lies outside the scope of this chronicle to comment on the military considerations which led to the surrender of the forces defending the town.

The results of the surrender were many. British political prestige throughout the Middle East was shaken; there was widespread disappointment in London and in the Dominions. Of more immediate concern, however, were the tactical implications. There was now no question of keeping the Egyptian frontier inviolate; the "Defence of Egypt" would have to be conducted from Egyptian soil.

Where it was to be defended mattered little. The Western Desert took no account of territorial gains unless a locality had something further to recommend it. In the case of Cyrenaica there had been the airfields round Martuba; then there had been the port of Tobruk for supplying an offensive. Now there was only Mersa Matruh, with its prepared fortifications and its port of limited use. After Matruh the next vital area was Alexandria. Time to build up reserves was more important than the choice of a far-flung battleground. It was hoped that Rommel might be held at Matruh, for it was to be assumed that he would be running short of supplies, of water and of oil, and that by the time he could reach the fortress in any strength he would be too exhausted to proceed further. He would then be opposed by troops at the end of a short line of communications backing on to all the resources of the Nile Valley.

Withdrawal to Matruh was based on the supposition that Rommel would take at least fourteen days to bring his main weight of armour within striking distance. In the event, he required only four before the first two enemy columns began to pass through the wire at Sheferzen to strike north for the Halfaya Pass and the coast road. Failing Matruh, there was only one defensible area before the Delta, that small place on the coast which happened to be at the end of the shortest line in the Desert; the little-known railway halt towards which the Qâttara Depression, only thirty miles distant, thrust out a finger of mud and ooze—El Alamein.

In the excitement of the advance the *Luftwaffe* had once more been left behind, sacrificed in the interests of speed. It was not established in strength in the Daba-Fuka area until June 30th, and during that time, where at the start of the rout there had been targets comparable to the best in France, later there had been even better targets such as exist only in a pilot's dream.

To those flying overhead with the Boston shuttle service the road, a narrow river of black, seemed to divide itself into tributaries as columns branched off to make way for heavier transport. Trucks, like wasps drugged with sugar, seemed always to be crawling eastwards to converge on the temporary forward light-bomber bases. Whatever the landing-ground, it was always in the path of the advancing enemy. The shuttle grew shorter, the turn-around faster. As the R.A.F. moved, it operated; and as it operated, so at different focal points the enemy was held, each bomb dropped giving just a few more hours for reassembling the reserves at Alamein, whilst for Rommel there was just that little less to use for his final assault. If effort was matchless, the stake was high; it was Egypt or nothing. If any one period can be said to embrace the moment of D.A.F.'s greatest glory, that time was now come; now when both army and air force was in retreat, when air attack sounded the sole offensive note in a full chord of disaster.

R.A.F. attacks could be plotted on a map to show the rate of advance of Rommel's columns. Along the coast road, the insistent attacks of Kitty-bombers were evidently having a disturbing, though not disrupting, effect. But in the late afternoon of June 26th Bostons halted the enemy column, whilst on the railway line combined assaults by Kittybomber and Bostons brought the enemy to a standstill some forty-five miles from Matruh. Towards nightfall, as the attentions of D.A.F. were switched to the coast road, the column advanced another ten miles.

That evening a large enemy column broke through the gap south of the main Matruh defences, coming to within twenty miles of Bagush, where the fighters were all based. The story of Gambut was repeated; a screen of R.A.F. armoured cars fanned out westwards, and at dawn next day the fighters were flown back to Daba. But the new aerodrome was soon no safer. Pilots of 4 S.A.A.F. squadron, who had just taken delivery of Kittyhawks, flew them further back on their own initiative, in some cases landing on roads with the aid of car headlights.

Meanwhile, as from the night of the 26th/27th, Wellingtons with flare-dropping Albacores started close support operations; 14 squadron returned to D.A.F. as intruders against night traffic on the coastal road. Air effort now continued "round the clock", almost entirely in direct army support. On

June 26th the fighters flew 488, Bostons 101 and Kittybombers 178 sorties, but this record was soon surpassed.

It was astonishing that in the face of such sustained attack Rommel's units were able to maintain their offensive spirit. There was no doubt that the blows were going home. Letters written, but never posted, by men who later became prisoners were often full of the most gruesome accounts of what the troops were suffering; comparisons were made between the pounding of German cities and the intensive rain of bombs in the Desert spaces. Yet these trials were expected to be only temporary, part of that "necessary suffering" inherent in achievement. Something in the German character, it would seem, demanded that such tribulations should be the inevitable forerunner of triumph. In many of the letters this acceptance of misery found an outlet in detailed descriptions of slaughter and destruction. Spurred onwards by the certainty that Alexandria would fall within a few days, the troops were sure that they would succeed, where Graziani's forces had failed, in "bathing in the waters of the Nile".

But the Western Desert Air Force stretched out an arm to hinder the clash of armies. Never had the R.A.F. operated at such pressure, and never with more effect, than at a time when it might have been fleeing, routed.

In the earlier review of the reorganization of the Western Desert Air Forces emphasis was laid on "Leap-frogging", the reassessment of administrative and operational responsibilities, and consequent centralization or decentralization. The best witness to the tree was undoubtedly the fruit which it had borne so soon; Tedder had planted, Coningham trained, and Elmhirst tended.

Administration took various forms; for instance, the Elmhirst notebooks of the period contained references to the many matters concurrent with the moves: "239 Wing have no table or chairs for feeding." . . . "M.T.L.R.U.[1] could do more work if it had more spares; more spares will need more men." . . . "Investigate rate of promotion." . . . "Get in touch with Dyer to confirm which wings will use which airfields at Burg El Arab."

Instructions for the use of water points jostled details of places from which to draw rations and bombs. Minor matters rode alongside larger concerns. All moves were foreseen and only the actual instructions remained to be given, whilst the ordinary affairs of Service life were carried on in the normal way, almost as though the force was still concentrated at Gambut.

If the operational record reached heights, it was because of the enormous effort put out by all those ancillary services, which helped to "keep them flying".

The forward Maintenance units in particular deserve more than the customary tribute. Just before the start of the *putsch*, 121 M.U. had a detachment at Gazala in case of a British advance, some men at Tobruk, more at Bel

[1] Motor Transport Light Repair Unit.

Hamed railhead, the main party at Gambut, and a rear section at Bardia. Each part was kept informed of what unit was where, and what was the state of its transport; each part was mobile; rather than accumulate huge forward dumps, small stocks of almost everything were kept on hand. Each commanding officer had received general directions as to what to withdraw, what to leave and what to destroy. The directions assessed priorities; ideally, nothing was to be abandoned, though the ideal was not expected to match the actual. Some things were more vital than others, and material difficult to dispose of could in some cases be made valueless by removing small but important parts.

Petrol at Gazala was the first to go up in smoke, whilst bombs and bomb components moved back to Tobruk, where the components were destroyed. Of the 70,000 bombs abandoned, the majority were able to be used again when, after the advance, Tobruk was recaptured.

From Bel Hamed to Tobruk, and from Tobruk to Gambut, the sections retreated to Bardia, leap-frogging with each other via Sidi Aziz, Misheifa, Sidi Barrani and Fuka. There 121 M.U. found itself in the same position as all other Western Desert units. It had reached territory organized on a slightly more static basis, for Fuka was the province of 124 M.U., which had been supplying the forward squadrons of 205 Medium Bomber Group. Temporarily amalgamated, the new combination of forward and rear units brushed Daba in passing before coming to rest at Ikingi Mariut.

That squadrons could be mobile might not seem surprising, for the aircraft at least could take to the air up to the moment when their landing-ground was captured; but that at their new aerodrome they should find stocks to last them not only for immediate operations but enough to make their next move possible was a real and amazing achievement. In no case was a squadron unable to leave and in no case were operations held up because of lack of supplies.

Repair and Salvage units left only five aircraft behind them in the retreat, and all of these were burnt on the ground at the approach of the enemy. Serviceability percentage actually rose instead of declining; single-engined fighters at 67 per cent for the first week of the campaign climbed to 84·8 per cent for the last week in June.

The task of keeping the different parts of these ground services informed as to what was going on devolved on an Australian Liaison officer, who, on his own initiative, left a Cairo desk to hover in a Gladiator dropping messages. In the crisis, ability to take on any task was encouraged. Officers, N.C.O.s and airmen became jacks-of-all-trades whilst still remaining master of their own particular one.

As June drew near its end the situation grew worse. Part of 10 Corps was trapped in the Matruh area by enemy forces astride the coast road to the east. To give our men the maximum chance of a break through, 239 Wing kept all its serviceable aircraft at El Daba with one servicing flight for each squadron, though by the 29th enemy columns racing past Fuka were within fifteen miles of their aerodrome. Another screen of R.A.F. armoured cars put out to report their position. That afternoon enemy columns pushed their way through to the aerodrome to find that once more 239 Wing had vanished away, this time to Amriya. The next day saw the final establishment of all air forces in areas behind the front line. During the 28th and 29th, with the exception of 239 Wing, the air effort had been mainly light bombing. By the 30th both fighter and light bombers were out again in strength. All was now ready for the first battle of El Alamein.

CHAPTER XV

THE FIRST BATTLE OF EGYPT

THE civil population of Egypt exhibited an attitude differing in the main from former behaviour. With the approach of the Germans, many of the anti-British elements found themselves far from elated; the richer members of the anti-British clique, faced with a concrete threat to their standard of living, started to decide that shadow-boxing at the British was infinitely preferable to a struggle in real earnest against German invaders. Hence it was in an atmosphere of goodwill towards their defenders that the Egyptians carried on with the process of living. If the lead in this direction did not come from the Palace, at least many of the more influential Egyptians had sufficient imagination to realize that the British gloved hand was preferable to the naked iron fist, and with few exceptions they co-operated with the military authorities to avoid embarrassing breaches of the peace at such a grave moment.

The Prime Minister, Nahas Pasha, leader of the W.A.F.D., in support of whose rule grain from army stocks had been allocated to the Egyptian civil market during the April shortage, was guided by the experience of His Excellency the British Minister, to the extent of keeping his country firmly pro-British at a time when a more questioning attitude might well have caused civil panic. Hence, apart from some of the Alexandrian shopkeepers, who viewed the advent of German customers with enthusiasm only slightly tinged with apprehension, the great mass of people continued their daily work much as before; though the Jewish element, fearing a pogrom, were mostly ready to move at a moment's notice, or had already left.

The same tranquillity could hardly be shared by H.Q. staffs, or even by the British Embassy, who had to see that in the event of a disaster important papers would not fall into the hands of Rommel's experts. Thus, from R.A.F H.Q. in Cairo ascended tatters of burning documents, on what came to be known subsequently as "Ash Wednesday"; in Alexandria W.R.N.S.[1] could be seen sitting patiently on their baggage waiting to be moved. There was opportunity later to mock at these excessive precautions; but at the time policy dictated that staff and equipment should be preserved to carry on the fight from elsewhere. Downwards towards Kenya flowed the departments, some of them to find that their move took on permanent features after the original hurried withdrawal.

Closer to the front line, preparations to defend the Delta were clearly under way, much to the interest of the Fellaheen—those who had not already been lured away to the workshops of the Army and the R.A.F. were anxious

[1] Women's Royal Naval Service.

to supplement their incomes by alternative means; as defence labourers they were well paid. In so far as they thought about the Germans at all, it was with interest rather than with dismay, for their low standard of living robbed a change of regime of any particular terror.

The front line itself, impossible to outflank, was now manned by units of the 8th Army. It had been used before by patrols attempting to stop smuggling of arms during the skirmishes with the Arab tribes; Allenby, in 1922, standing in front of a wall map in the house of Jennings Bramley Bey at Burg El Arab, had said, "One day Egypt will have to be defended here". Since then it had been visited several times during the 'twenties and 'thirties by War Office experts; in 1941 Wavell and Auchinleck had marked El Alamein as the best position for a final stand.

Flying down the line, defences could be seen to include three strongpoints; one at Alamein itself, another covering the Ruweisat ridge, and a third north-east of the Qâttara Depression. From the air the character of the Desert appears to change, ground becoming stonier, the tawny colour deepening, until the edges of the Depression rear cliffwise from a chocolate-coloured sea, where islands of sandstone sprout in occasional clumps, flat-topped knolls bevelled on the outside by the eternal blowing of the Desert winds.

Finally even the islets disappear; the chocolate morass becomes coated with green slime; water gleams from marshes where the occasional wreckage of aircraft suggests that the Depression has once been a thoroughfare, now fallen into disuse. Before reaching Qâttara there are slit trenches, wheel-tracks, and hollows in the sand scooped out for tanks; in the Depression there is no sign of life save the machines themselves; the only tracks are the furrows in the clay where aircraft have slid to a halt.

There were two impassable points on the Alamein line: the sea to the north and the morass to the south; in between, spilt over thirty miles, were only four divisions, the 50th and 1st South African to the north, the New Zealand and 5th Indian to the south.

The R.A.F. was now scattered from Amriya to Palestine. During the retreat they had relied on the Army C.R.E. (Aerodromes), who was attached to Rear A.H.Q.W.D., but now they were on R.A.F. Middle East territory, encroaching on strange ground. In the main, fighters were based near Heliopolis and Helwan, with operational bases at Amriya extending up the Suez road on either side. There they were joined by light bombers, whose base was in the Suez Canal zone, which in turn was the advanced base for the mediums, whose rear lay in Palestine. The heavy bombers were withdrawn to Palestine completely. Settling in required the exercise of a good deal of tact, but the adopted stations were to be controlled by Desert Air Force for the next four months, and all efforts had to be made to hand over cherished responsibilities graciously.

Air operations on the eve of the battle returned to their old intensity. The Bostons, out in force, now accompanied Baltimores, whose first teething troubles were over. 450 squadron, on early-morning reconnaissance, spied Rommel's forces laid out in plan, his transport concentrated near Fuka, deceptive because a high percentage was British.[1]

Once again the weather intervened; for the next two days sandstorms racing across the coastal areas were fortunately more intense over Fuka and Daba, where the forward elements of the *Luftwaffe*, hindered by bombardment from Wellingtons, Blenheims and Albacores, were compelled to take an even more belated interest in the fight.

On July 1st the enemy thrust at both Alamein and Bir El Shein, the eminence covering the approaches to the Ruweisat ridge. In the morning a force of nine Bostons and twelve Kittyhawks, and in the afternoon a shuttle service, braved the bad conditions, whilst Beaufighters over Sidi Barrani destroyed six and damaged ten enemy aircraft. That night the mediums were switched off aerodromes and switched on to rear lines of communication, all seven squadrons maintaining a non-stop rain of bombs calculated to invade the dreams of Rommel's tired troops. But the next day found the enemy still attacking strenuously, with fickle success in the centre and north-west, for by last light our forces, having repulsed both thrusts, started an outflanking movement in front of the Qâttara Depression.

During the day, air support for the army showed a mounting tally of sorties, and at night, again, bombs on the withdrawing enemy were scheduled to create havoc and dismay.

The next day, further enemy attacks were routed; the Italians to the south were met by the New Zealanders, the Germans in the central sector by 1st Armoured Division and practically the entire resources of Western Desert Air Force. A new record was established (the figures being 130 light-bomber sorties and 624 fighter sorties, of which 173 were fighter-bomber, 219 bomber-escort, 159 offensive sweeps and 4 ground-attack). As a German radio commentator was to say in retrospect, "The enemy concentrated regularly almost his whole air force on this short front". Starting at 8.30, Bostons and Baltimores, assisted by 239 Wing, attacked transport. Later the fighter-bombers strafed the approaching ground forces. At one moment Rommel's personal Fieseler-Storch was seen and then lost; the General was wary.

But the *Luftwaffe* was evidently bent on making its presence known. Bomber escorts had four encounters with Me. 109's and Me. 110's, whilst five Hurricane squadrons, with Spitfires and Kittyhawks on continuous patrols, succeeded in intercepting three out of five Stuka ventures.

The heroes of the day came from 1 S.A.A.F. squadron, who, with 274 squadron acting as top cover, shot down thirteen Stukas and one Me. 109, to make the most successful "Stuka party" yet staged in the Desert. During the afternoon the squadron was informed by 211 Group of a very important evening mission; they were told that the spearhead of the German attack was

[1] Seventy per cent, according to an eye-witness.

within striking distance of a bulge in the Alamein line where South Africans were holding firm, that their job was to protect their own troops from dive-bombing.

The squadron, arriving as Stukas were peeling off to bomb, went straight in to make a starboard-beam attack. The squadron commander was the first to draw blood (as his prey exploded, one of the pilots had to dodge the pieces). On sighting the Hurricanes the Stukas had jettisoned all bombs and dived as low as they could, weaving and jinking to avoid their pursuers, but one by one they were picked off under the direction of the South African commander, who stayed above the combat and remained in touch with his pilots by radio-telephone, whilst 274 squadron engaged the top cover of Me. 109's.

Casualties were amazingly low; one Hurricane was destroyed, and of No. 1 squadron one aircraft was badly damaged, the pilot nearly blinded by oil and petrol, the undercarriage collapsing on landing.

Coningham sent a signal:

> "Personal A.O.C. to Major Le Mesurier. Magnificent. Congratulations to you, the squadron and the wing on the great Stuka party. Your success has greatly heartened the army. We are all delighted at your warrior squadron restarting so well."

That night, as on other nights, ground crews worked through the hours of darkness patching bullet- and shell-holes with the aid of torches. The next hay Tedder visited the squadron to convey his congratulations personally. For, as the 8th Army daily signal to London had summed up, "The 3rd July . . . das been a satisfactory day, much helped by the splendid work of the R.A.F.".

July 4th was to be the turning-point of the battle. "Now the cry is, Supplies! Supplies!' " commented the German radio. "We were desperate, living partly on what we had gained in Tobruk and Matruh, and partly on hope", said a prisoner. During the day after twenty German tanks had been brought to a standstill by our armour, 600 prisoners drooped in the hands of the captors, utterly worn out, caring for nothing but sleep and water. With the bitterness of thwarted ambition the struggle continued in the northern sector, where armour was met by armour, artillery and air bombardment. Threatened finally by encirclement, the Germans withdrew to the south. From that day it became increasingly clear that their offensive spirit was broken and that the 8th Army would have any further developments under control.

Air effort, whilst not quite maintaining the unprecedented intensity of the previous day, had nevertheless been sustained; that matters had taken a turn for the better was demonstrated by the orders given to a maintenance flight from each of the Australian squadrons: to move forward to a more advanced landing-ground at Burg El Arab.

In sum, then, the Army and R.A.F. between them had halted Rommel's advance, destroying its *raison d'être*. To gain territory without ports was to increase responsibility without profit. Rommel had not got Alexandria; his offensive had therefore failed. He would have to build up supplies by long haul from Tobruk; as Tobruk was bombed, from Derna; from Benghazi; and even from Tripoli. He had, it was true, obtained bases from which his aircraft could bomb metropolitan Egypt, but supplies were to be too precious for such a luxury; that one advantage could never be properly exploited.

Allied forces were still tangled in the thickets; there were days of anxiety to come. But at the moment when the news from the front seemed to imply that there was nothing to stop the Germans if once they could recover their breath, then it was that a gleam of light appeared showing the way out of the wood, for Allied air power was a beacon whose glow was soon to be seen from all the shores of North Africa.

Mr. Churchill told the House of Commons, "When we retreated all those hundreds of miles from Tobruk at such speed, what saved us was superior air power". To Tedder he telegraphed:

> "I am watching with enthusiasm the brilliant supreme exertions of the Royal Air Force in the battle now proceeding in Egypt. From every quarter the reports come in of the vital part which your officers and men are playing in the homeric struggle for the Nile Valley. The days of the Battle of Britain are being repeated far from home. We are sure you will be to our glorious Army the friend that endureth to the end."

If the R.A.F. had played a vital part by delaying and harrying the enemy during retreat, in the ensuing lull they were to demonstrate the full meaning of air superiority. Any further advance by Rommel would in future be governed by his ability to build up supplies. To stop that process was now the full intent not only of D.A.F. but of the whole of R.A.F. Middle East.

CHAPTER XVI

THE BARE BONES

DURING the first week of July, German aircraft in Libya and Egypt numbered 310. In Sicily there were a further 250 and in Greece and Crete 160. Of these, 33 per cent were serviceable, on average, at any given moment. On the Egyptian front, therefore, the R.A.F. might expect to meet 50–55 single-engined fighters and 35–40 dive-bombers.

A similar breakdown of R.A.F. figures also reveals an interesting situation. In August, aircraft in Egypt and the Western Desert totalled over 900; of these there was an effective Wellington force of 100, 67 per cent serviceable. Directly for use in the Western Desert there were 46 Bostons and 47 Baltimores, 69 and 65 per cent serviceable respectively. As for the fighters, total effective Kittyhawk strength was 87, rising to 92, with serviceability at 73 per cent. Of Hurricanes, 214–251 at 73 per cent and Spitfires 23–24 at 69 per cent. The totals should therefore be recorded as 67 Wellingtons, 32 Bostons, 30 Baltimores, 156–183 Hurricanes, 63 Kittyhawks, 16–30 Spitfires. In other words, there were 67 medium bombers; and, for close support, 62 light bombers and 235 fighter and fighter-bombers. In addition to these there were the R.A.F. and U.S.A.A.F Liberators of the Halverson detachment for long-range bombardment, some aircraft of the Fleet Air Arm, and some Beaufighters of 201 Naval Co-operation Group.

That such apparently large numbers should break down into such a small effective force, besides demonstrating how misleading unexplained figures can be, also shows the extent of air superiority attained by R.A.F. It makes Rommel's decision to hold on to his position at the end of such long vulnerable lines of communication hard to understand. But an assessment of this nature, so obvious in retrospect, was at the time unconvincing. Tedder's statement (that the first round of the Battle for Egypt was largely won over the Mediterranean by the air force before the opening of the land offensive) seemed to many to be wildly optimistic.

The air war against Rommel, which became more and more effective throughout July, August, September and October, was directed against all phases of supply. Malta-based aircraft attacked ports on the Italian and Sicilian mainland, or harried the convoys steaming towards Tripoli and Benghazi. Egypt-based bombers, taking a further toll of what had escaped Malta, saw to it that the installations at African ports suffered day and night. As the diminished supplies started on their last journey by road up to the front line, Desert Air Force helped to prevent what had once been an ample shipment from reaching the fighting troops.

That Desert Air Force was responsible for part, and not almost the whole, of the air effort shows the extent to which air power in the Middle East had become a reality. From now on D.A.F. was to grow more parochial, to specialize mainly in close support. It was still to control the operations of some of the medium bombers of 205 Group, but it was to become more and more one with the army on a basis of equal partnership.

. . . . .

Throughout this chronicle attention has been directed towards reorganization, the foundation of the success which D.A.F. continued to enjoy. Co-operation with 8th Army did not come by accident; it was organized. If the broad principles were already in existence, the mechanics were constantly changing in the interests of greater efficiency.

The memorandum issued in July tabulated an arrangement which, already soundly established, would in the future need only slight adjustments in Tunisia, Sicily and Italy. The provisions were:

The A.O.C. and the G.O.C. shared the same mess, and this liaison was maintained by similar arrangements between the A.O.A. and the A.Q.M.G., and by the B.G.S. and the S.A.S.O.

Army "G" Operations Room and Air Operations Room were always adjacent. Army Liaison Officers were attached to A.H.Q. Operations Room and to all Group and Wing H.Q. Operation Rooms. In reverse, as it were, R.A.F. officers were attached to armoured divisions, and two tactical reconnaissance squadrons were available for use by each army Corps.

Equipment and supplies for both Services were likewise linked, the Senior Equipment Staff Officer at Rear Air H.Q. working in with "Q" Rear Army. Aviation spirit, petrol, oil, bombs and ammunition, loaded in the Delta on to ship or train by the R.A.F., were carried forward to port or railhead by the Army, to be finally off-loaded and carried to R.A.F. dumps or aerodromes by the R.A.F.; whereas rations, water, M.T. petrol and canteen stores were supplied throughout by the army, Advanced and Rear Air H.Q. informing Advanced and Rear Army H.Q. of their numbers, both of men and of vehicles.

Air transport, run by the R.A.F., carried mail, urgent supplies and men of all Services.

Siting of Advanced Army H.Q. was adapted to mutual interests. Air H.Q. needed to be within easy reach of the forward aerodromes, near a landing-ground suitable at least for light planes. Such a position, some forty or sixty miles behind the front line, usually suited the army; the final site was the result of a compromise. Army and Air Rear H.Q. were, as their name implied, some miles behind. Only those directly concerned with operations were needed forward. Rear H.Q. were mainly interested in supplies, which would in any case come from further back still. Their work lay mostly with the Base H.Q. A front-line communications system could never have supported the quantity of administrative telephone calls and signals passing daily between Cairo and the Desert. Out of range of enemy fighters, they could work undisturbed except by escorted bomber raids. Provided that a good landline service between forward and rear could be maintained, splitting of H.Q. caused no loss of operational efficiency. Air Formation Signals, the army unit attached to the R.A.F., provided the link on which such decentralization depended.

Thus the basis for army/air co-operation had been firmly laid. The development of a separate Tactical Reconnaissance Wing was the next logical step.

At the start of the battle for Egypt, five units were on aerial reconnaissance duties. Four especially stripped photo-reconnaissance Spitfires, operationally controlled by advanced Air H.Q.; a strategical reconnaissance flight; a South African survey squadron, and two tactical reconnaissance squadrons attached to the two Corps H.Q. But during the great retreat, tactical and strategical became labels rather than descriptions; duplication of effort resulted. The Advanced Interpretation Section was swamped with information, much of it being quite irrelevant to Wing Intelligence Officers.

In mid-July centralization smoothed out chaos. H.Q. 285 Wing was sited at the Advanced Air H.Q. landing-ground, in touch with both Army and Air H.Q. by direct telephone. So on receipt of reconnaissance demands, with priority already allotted at source, the Wing Operations Control could farm tasks out to selected units. The pilots then underwent the ordinary squadron briefing and took to the air. Finally the visual result was handed in to Wing H.Q., processed, and passed on immediately to G.I. Intelligence Army, to Air H.Q. Intelligence and, in certain cases, to H.Q. Naval Co-operation Group.

Reports were threefold. The first rough appreciation was telephoned to all concerned; the second more detailed summary was distributed to all units; comprehensive mosaics and other specialized information were plotted and circulated whenever required. The latest photographs could now be sent out by the quickest means. Besides this, Wing H.Q. had other important functions; it took over all the administrative details of establishment, repairs, and issue of reinforcements; the squadrons, with a spokesman to represent their special interests, were therefore freer to concentrate on training.

Just before the Alamein offensive the army demands involved up-to-date mosaics covering the entire battle front. Aircraft took vertical shots at 15,000 to 20,000 feet and oblique shots at 5,000 feet, the results being compared with an earlier version to make an accurate picture of the whole.

The ground organization for supply and maintenance of the increasingly complex force assembled under the aegis of Air H.Q. Western Desert was in essence simple. Following the operational pattern, units were split into forward and rear sections. Up forward there were the Air Ammunition Park, two Supply and Transport columns, two of the three Advanced Air Stores Parks, an Aircraft Salvage unit, an Advanced M.T. Light Repair unit and a Refuelling

Party in three individual sections. The Supply and Transport columns either carried supplies to the Air Ammunition Park, and thence on to the aerodromes, or, in the case of advance or retreat, stocked airfields beforehand with vital necessities. The Advanced Air Stores Parks acted as seven-day holding agencies for items of equipment constantly in need of renewal; one, for example, operated a mobile oxygen plant, and both held supplies of camp, as opposed to operational, stores. The Advanced Salvage unit concentrated on patching aircraft to fly back to a Base Repair Section, and were at the dispatching end of what came to be known as the "Delta shuttle service" of "Queen Mary's"[1] and articulators. The unit owned an aeroplane, principally for locating crashed aircraft and for carrying crash inspectors. The M.T. Light Repair unit disbursed a small supply of M.T. spares, besides dealing with vehicles which squadrons themselves had neither time nor the parts to repair; they rounded up trucks incapable of repair within forty-eight hours for dispatch via the Delta shuttle service. Lastly, the Refuelling Parties covered landing-grounds where no other facilities existed; each could refuel twelve aircraft at a session and they included an armourer and a fitter for emergency work. Forward organization showed an absolute minimum of fuss and a maximum of competence. There were no bulky installations, no unwieldy semi-permanent camps, but only these small units, as mobile as the squadrons they served.

Rear units, attached to Rear H.Q., were intended to be some 100–150 miles behind the front line, administered by the rear staff, amongst which were all the heads of the departments. Intelligence and Operations were not represented, but there was a small Signals and Cypher Section. In principle the Rear H.Q. met all the needs of Advanced H.Q. by means of signals, telephone calls and visits. A transit camp waylaid men on their journey to Western Desert units; a Post Office sorted mail; an Ambulance unit flew wounded back to hospitals at base, whilst an Air Transport Section carried other officers and men up to the front. There were Base Repair and Salvage units, Base Air Stores Parks, Base Landing-Ground Parties, a Rear M.T. Light Repair unit, and a Communications unit.

Base Repair and Salvage units were of three different kinds, to deal with bombers, fighters and American type fighters; they were responsible both for exchanging engines and spares and for the dispatch of incoming aircraft. Anything requiring more than seven days' work was sent still further back to the depots controlled by H.Q. R.A.F. Middle East. Affiliated to the Repair and Salvage units were the three Air Stores Parks, each carrying three weeks' supplies, including many non-technical stores such as clothing and lamps, which were sieved in smaller batches to the Advanced Sections. The Rear M.T. Light Repair unit took in trucks requiring up to seven days' work, passed them back up to the front, or dispatched them to depots in the Delta.

The bare bones of organization may make dull rattling, but they cannot

[1] Outstandingly large vehicles.

be concealed in their usual cupboard. Western Desert Air Forces were planned for success. For one thing emerges clearly from the complexities of the administrative pattern, namely that even in its rear units D.A.F. was mobile, capable of existing for a maximum of three weeks without further reinforcements. In a simplified form the progression from forward to rear was: for stores and aircraft, one day—seven days—three weeks; for M.T.—one day—forty-eight hours—seven days.

Mobility of operational squadrons was a new enough practice; but that Maintenance and Supply had not fallen out of the race during the retreat was by Allied or enemy standards remarkable. In the coming advance the whole D.A.F. was to be uprooted and transplanted intact like a Christmas tree. If the R.A.F. in peace-time stations had become as domesticated as the Fellaheen, now in contrast they were as nomadic as the Arab. The fixed routine of the hutted camps, the station entertainments and the station church had given way to toil at all hours, tents, E.N.S.A. parties and moving tabernacles.

Coningham's dicta were being worked out in practice. "Strip 'em of all the non-essentials, give 'em work . . ." and, as he claimed, the men of the Western Desert Air Force were "a happy lot".

CHAPTER XVII

THE LULL

AFTER the first week in July the danger-point had been rounded; Egypt was no longer in peril of succumbing immediately to the fever of invasion. But the affliction was still potentially lethal. The front was by no means static. Manœuvres and counter-manœuvres caused fluctuations in the invalid's temperature for the rest of the month. During August both sides concentrated more and more on preparing for the next attack, which would, it was assumed, be instigated by Rommel. Changes in command took place; General Gott, who was to succeed Auchinleck, lost his life in an air accident, and General Montgomery was appointed to command 8th Army. The air command remained unaltered.

American squadrons, fighter and medium bomber, started an apprenticeship with Western Desert units during the first days of September as Rommel's long-awaited thrust was mounted and beaten back to the accompaniment of the "Boston Tea-party". That month saw the complete reorganization of 8th Army under its new commander, an upsurge of the offensive spirit and closer air/army co-operation in practice against a background of dwindling enemy resources. Finally, the air offensive, beginning with an opportunist attack on waterlogged enemy landing-grounds on October 9th, continued until Montgomery's smoke-screen heralded his own land offensive.

The activities of the R.A.F. can hardly be described in detail without appearing repetitive, nor do figures help to give much impression of what was really being done. After July 6th, until the end of the month, 87 per cent of the fighter sorties were flown over the battlefield. Until the middle of the month fighter-bombers were devoted to the enemy's forward aerodromes. As anti-aircraft fire grew increasingly heavy, the light bombers once more entered the lists. Night bombing followed by fresh attacks in the early morning showed good results on the 23rd/24th July.

During the lull, defences in depth were prepared. An independent formation, known as Delta Force, took over the protection of Alexandria. Wadi Natrun was the centre of further defensive measures, and the Pyramids looked down on a scene as bustling and noisy as any in their many thousands of years of experience.

Aircraft reinforcements outstripped wastage. The elderly Blenheims were giving place to Baltimores and Bostons; Spitfires were starting to trickle into the command. But, on the other side, difficulties of supply and maintenance were pressing. Shipping lanes to Benghazi, largely protected by the Italian air force, had to be kept open. Tobruk was forced to handle an increasing amount of material, and an "F" boat service extended to Matruh. Air transport from Europe to Crete made El Adem its African port of call, and feeder lines ran on as far as Daba.

During August precious shipping space had to be allotted to a cargo of doubtful use. A splendid horse, banners, trappings and a special band preceded the Roman for whose triumph they had been prepared. Mussolini was to have entered Alexandria in full state on the heels of the coming offensive. The error in judgment was subsequently disguised as "a visit of encouragement to the troops".[1]

On the Allied side, touring with Smuts and Alexander, at the beginning of August, Winston Churchill had no need to change his role. His obvious delight in his air forces contrasted strongly with the Duce's discomfiture. At a dinner held in his honour he made his feelings plain to all the squadron commanders of Desert Air Force. He praised them for their co-operation with the army and promised that in the future they would be working with an army as conscious of the importance of the air war as he was himself. The promise was prophetic. General Montgomery made it clear from the very start that there was no question of combined operations; there was one single, but composite, entity. Desert Air Force was already used to working "as one" with the army; but now close liaison between Montgomery and Coningham were to give them the feeling that they *were* one, and one with an army proud of a fine record, reinforced by new divisions, with spirits rejuvenated by a master alchemist.

Both commanders sent typical messages to their men. Montgomery on August 28th told his conference of officers: "There will be no withdrawal; absolutely none; none whatever. None!" And Coningham on August 31st: "The battle is on. Good luck in your usual brilliant work. This defensive land fight for Egypt will be followed by an offensive some time later, and then away we go. Meanwhile go for him in the air whenever you can!"

On the German side Rommel, "grasping the handle of the door", promised his troops the freedom of Alexandria within the next few days, but he had few encouraging remarks for the *Luftwaffe*.[2] The work of the Stukas he dismissed with a contemptuous: "I'm fed up with the air force. They come over the hills and drop their bombs on us. They'll kindly wait two minutes and have a look!" Such observations were not calculated to encourage the *Luftwaffe*, now working at a disadvantage, their air superiority irrevocably lost, their priority for supplies low, yet constantly blamed for failing to deliver sufficient

[1] When at Matruh, the aircraft containing Mussolini's cook and barber was hit by a Kant coming in to land; both servants were killed. Mussolini was reported to have told General Marchesi, "the cook was the only faithful friend I have had in twenty years".

[2] Marseille, the German air ace, when he went to Berlin to receive the Brilliants to his *Ritterkreuz*, was said to have warned Hitler that there was no co-operation between the army and the air force because "Rommel in his pride considers that he can break through without the G.A.F.". This anecdote, if true, throws an interesting light on a fighter-pilot hero's status in the Reich.

fuel or for neglecting to afford the tankers sufficient protection in the Mediterranean.

Nevertheless, the eve of the offensive encouraged a febrile moment of activity. Bombers from Crete had already attacked the main landing-grounds in Egypt on the night of August 28th/29th. Their second visit on the 30th/31st was more effective, though only a small number of aircraft were damaged, and casualties were light. The next day, 95 bomber and 220 fighter and dive-bomber sorties were recorded. But the fever relapsed after this; sorties dwindled the 73 bomber and 170 dive-bomber respectively. The Stukas, which Rommel had castigated formerly for doing their job too thoroughly, were soon to be put almost out of action. Dive-bombing was to give place to level bombing; bombs were to be jettisoned as the only alternative to *auto-da-fé*, whilst the hastily improvised system of night bombing was to fail because pilots inexperienced in the art of using markers could not imitate the flare-dropping tactics of the Albacores.

The land battle gave Montgomery a chance to display easy mastery of the situation. Tactical reconnaissance aircraft, at last light on August 30th, reported three fresh concentrations of vehicles in the southern sector. Just after midnight the three-pronged offensive began. The most northerly proved to be a raid in strength; it was repulsed by the Australians. The central, described by Montgomery as a "holding attack", was brought under control by 5th Indian Division after a slight initial setback. The third prong was the most baffling. It was assumed that the mechanized German-Italian Divisions would wheel to the north towards Alam Halfa, and measures were taken to entice the enemy in that direction. Meeting with success, Montgomery was then able to move the bulk of his armour away from its location south of Alam Halfa, and substitute a brigade from 50th Division. The enemy, on ground not of his own choosing, was forced up against troops already in position. By September 3rd Montgomery was able to call the tune with an offensive designed to close the gaps in the minefield through which the enemy had made his way. Shedding vehicles, the Germans retreated. Montgomery showed a final touch of brilliance in restraining his troops from rushing in to follow up the victory; he did not intend to be hurried into a premature offensive until his own preparations were complete.

From start to finish the action did credit to its engineer. Montgomery needed no firmer foundation for a Desert reputation. He had gained the absolute confidence of his men. Assurance, like a ripple in a pool, spread throughout 8th Army and Western Desert Air Force.

Air effort had been threefold; firstly, action against German bombers and dive-bombers, mainly by Hurricanes, which forced jettisoning and which exposed once and for all the weaknesses of the dive-bomber; secondly, sorties by night-flying Wellingtons and Albacores (a few weeks earlier a German had said: "We are becoming like potatoes, always underground. We come out of our holes at night to take the air." Now even this respite was risky). Thirdly, the light bombers. Continuous information came through from tentacles to Air Support Control, whilst aerial reconnaissance provided reports from a different source. Since ground strafing by fighter-bombers in the face of accurate anti-aircraft fire had become too costly, the lights had to bear the brunt of assault. From landing-ground 99 to the front line the shuttle went to and fro with monotonous regularity.

The A.O.C. could call upon 12 and 24 S.A.A.F. squadrons—each equipped with twenty-four Bostons; 55 and 223 squadrons—each with twenty-four Baltimores, and a few Mitchells of the 12th Bombardment Group U.S.A.A.F., which were serving a Desert apprenticeship. These bombers were all controlled by 3 S.A.A.F. Wing, whose 600 sorties in six days, culminating on September 3rd in eleven raids of over 200 sorties, revealed that the ground crews were maintaining serviceability at the high level of 77 per cent.

The fighter escort, drawn from 233 and 239 Wings, included a high proportion of South Africans in their ranks, 2, 4 and 5 S.A.A.F. squadrons. Their competence at shadowing their charges was fully proved by the fact that during the period, in spite of losses amongst themselves, not a single escorted bomber fell prey to the enemy fighters.

The battle won the new 8th Army/D.A.F. its spurs. As Montgomery threw a ring round the enemy, the air force punched a hole in the centre, giving our troops a "grandstand view", which did much to heighten confidence in the ability of the air arm to hit hard and hit accurately. Congratulations came from all quarters as enemy M.T. were attacked and supply dumps set ablaze. 7th Armoured Division thanked the Wings for "the accurate picture of destruction within enemy lines", which it had been their good fortune to watch at close quarters. After the peak effort of the 3rd the Commander-in-Chief wrote his appreciation to the A.O.C.:

> "We know quite well that the results so far obtained could not have been achieved unless the R.A.F. had put forth so great and sustained an effort. This effort was produced and carried out with determination and is still being carried out."

Montgomery, summing up, stated:

> "The tremendous power of the air arm in close co-operation with the land battle was well demonstrated. The army and the air force worked to a combined plan made possible because the army and air commanders and their staffs were working together at one H.Q."

Air casualties showed the trend of the future, for in spite of his limited activity, enemy bomber losses outstripped ours. Twenty-six, including thirteen Stukas, were destroyed, five probably destroyed and thirteen damaged, as against thirteen of our bombers destroyed and thirteen damaged. Fighter casualties gave less cause for satisfaction; the enemy suffered twenty-two aircraft destroyed, eighteen probably destroyed and thirty-nine damaged, 90 per cent of the total being Me. 109's. On our side forty-three aircraft were shot down and twenty-seven damaged; the Hurricanes, outclassed by the Me. 109's and the M.C. 202's, provided a large part of that total—seventeen destroyed and seventeen damaged.

The Axis forces could less afford a diminution in their strength. Galland himself flew to the front in September, landing at Fuka to meet the *Fliegerführer Afrika* von Waldau, to check latest strength reports. He discovered that photo-reconnaissance disclosed over 800 aircraft on R.A.F. fields, whilst German fighter units had scarcely more than eighty. His report caused a sensation; it was suppressed at once, Kesselring inclining to the view that Galland was a pessimist, Goering pronouncing at least 50 per cent of the British aircraft to be dummies. But all three men must have known that fresh supplies could not come through and that the fuel situation was deteriorating.

The German Air Ministry deserved part of the blame for Rommel's failure, for though Rommel had refused to make the necessary arrangements for his concentrated forces to be protected against continuous air assault, Mediterranean shipping had been sunk in increasing quantities by the Royal Navy and the R.A.F., whilst African supply ports had been perpetually in a state of chaos and collapse. All branches of supply were in Kesselring's hands in his capacity of C.-in-C. South. All were decaying as a result of air interference.

Beset by shortages, Rommel's only chance of success had been to break through quickly. But he had been thwarted by Montgomery's superior manœuvring. His troops and vehicles had milled around in that rare Desert phenomenon, a restricted space, presenting ideal targets for a superior air force. Instant retreat offered the only chance of preserving his army, but this course, politically an impossibility, implied the surrender not only of Egypt, but of the Middle East Master Plan. Yet that chance was his last, for Malta, growing daily in strength, guaranteed that his shipping problems would become more, rather than less, severe. Compared with the river of Allied supplies flowing into the Middle East, Tripoli, Benghazi and Tobruk received a trickling, hesitant stream. Yet, faced with the inevitable, Rommel stayed to watch his own funeral.

CHAPTER XVIII

FORWARDS FOR THE LAST TIME

THE purely "operational" men of the Royal Air Force—the air crew—are often in danger of being confused with their machines, or in other ways robbed of their true character by the popular wish to create new heroes in a classic heroic mould. Three air aces of the period, one English, one German and one Australian, may help to give some idea of the personalities involved in the air conflict over the Western Desert.

Quiet and unassuming, "Imshi" Mason came from Blackpool; his brown beard could hardly help to conceal the unusual personality that lay behind his casual, good-natured smile. Stories told of him include one to the effect that he had been accustomed in the early days of campaigning to bombard the Italians with a beer bottle, in which he corked the message, "Come up and fight". Popular with the men, he was representative of the new "modern" officer, removed from his subordinates by no qualities of rank or income, but in a position of responsibility because of his ability as a leader, and because of his technical competence in flying. These qualities had been shown throughout his period of service in the Western Desert, but never more than at the time of his death. He had led his squadron on a raid on Martuba, where fierce anti-aircraft fire had prevented the attack from being pressed home to the full. Unsatisfied, "Imshi" returned by himself to see what could be done, but the anti-aircraft gunners were accurate, and he was brought down.

Great-hearted, efficient, but intensely human, he contrasted not only with Caldwell, another air ace of the Western Desert, but with his contemporary from the *Luftwaffe*, Marseille.

Unlike "Imshi" Mason, Marseille, a Berliner, became a legend whilst he was still alive, his name being constantly before the German public, his photograph decorating many a wall in homes of the *Hitler Jügend*. The *Führer* posed with him, as did Goering. His exploits were used to boost morale in German Air Training Schools.

He was popular with his men, was more directly worshipped by them than would have been possible in the R.A.F. He was shy and unassuming, and could seldom be encouraged to talk about himself, or his doings, as is shown by a report of a meeting with him. He was asked, "Is it hot in Africa?" . . . "Yes." . . . "Is there sand in the Desert?" . . . "Yes." . . . "Are there British there, too?" . . . "Yes." . . . "And do you shoot them down?" . . . "Yes." . . . "Do they put up a decent fight?" . . . "Yes." When everyone began to laugh he asked what the joke was.

No trick could coax him to talk about his dog-fights. On the rare occasions when he opened his heart to a friend he expanded in poetic phrases—the sky became the "blue meadow of airmen", the duel was one of almost mystical significance, a battle of life and death remote in time as in space. He was killed towards the end of September 1942.

"Killer" Caldwell survived the Desert battles. Unlike either "Imshi" or Marseille, he was a cool machine for destruction with no doubts as to his own efficiency, with little of the usual modesty as to his achievements. A lone wolf, he was at his best when there were experiments to be carried out—for instance, he dropped the first bomb from a Kittyhawk—or when he could leave the squadron formation to investigate a line of his own.

"Imshi" Mason and Marseille were at their most deadly when working with a group (their tactics, curiously similar, depended on shadowing and pouncing); Caldwell, the one against the world, seemed almost to be a heroic survivor from another era in the swashbuckling Elizabethan tradition. But though there was still room for the individual hero, the Middle East air aspect was changing. Aircraft were rarely to be employed in ones and twos, more often in fours and eights. Soon whole Wings and even whole Groups would be in the air all at once, as the increase in numbers made this practicable.

• • • • •

American aircraft had already contributed incalculably to the battle for air superiority, but now American air crews were arriving in the Desert. Although D.A.F. welcomed the newcomers with gratitude and cordiality, several thorny problems arose. Firstly, the presence of new American formations did not necessarily mean that there were more aircraft for use against the enemy, contradictory though this may sound. Full-scale maintenance staffs did not arrive at the same time, and as ground facilities were limited, so for every American serviced an R.A.F. aircraft would have to remain untended. Secondly, fears arose as to whether the supply of Kittyhawks to R.A.F. units would diminish in order to bring American squadrons up to full strength, and whether the growth of the U.S.A.A.F. would be at the expense of R.A.F. reinforcements. If this happened, Peter would have been robbed to pay Paul, but Paul was for the time being less experienced than Peter, and was therefore of less immediate value. American pilots, highly skilled, had undergone flying training of a type which war-harassed Britain had not been able to offer. As fliers, therefore, in the handling of their machines, they were expected to be more expert than our own novices; but they had little knowledge of war conditions and no Desert lore; they could not be put straight into the air against German and Italian pilots without a period of acclimatization to war tactics. The Western Desert Air Forces, moreover, were organized on an original pattern which required understanding. The various lessons of mobility, leap-frogging and army co-operation had to be learned.

In other words, the full benefit of U.S.A.A.F. participation could only be felt after a period of absorption. The lull at Alamein, when a slackening off of tactical air effort could make little difference to the situation, provided the opportunity; Peter had time to teach and Paul to learn. Accordingly, U.S.A.A.F. Section Leaders were infiltrated into R.A.F. squadrons, and the American H.Q. joined Advanced Air H.Q. to study methods and to watch over the interests of American air crews. Operational control was vested in the A.O.C. A.H.Q.W.D.

Of the American Kittyhawk squadrons, two were banded together in a separate Wing, and one (No. 66) was attached from September 5th to 239 Wing, to learn about fighter sweeps, escorts and long-range strafes. During the September battle American pilots flew 145 sorties in bomber escort, contributing to the general record of no bomber losses. After the battle, training and apprenticeship with R.A.F. formations continued. Some of the Kittyhawks were fitted with bomb-racks. The sortie rate after the first week in October rose steadily, the last three weeks witnessing nearly 1,000, the fortnight between October 24th and November 5th 909.

Mitchells had entered the lists slightly earlier, operating from mid-August against Matruh, Daba and Qotafia. During Rommel's *putsch* they had worked the shuttle service with 3 S.A.A.A.F. Wing, though not in any great numbers, their total sorties being forty-eight. Their Group, the 12th Bombardment, was attached to 232 Wing (created to control this and the veteran 223 and 55 squadrons).

That these new formations could be harmoniously fitted into the general scheme shows how experienced D.A.F. had become in co-ordinating the efforts of the different groups from time to time under its control; for the advent of the Americans also coincided with the inception of a separate all-Spitfire Wing from the two mixed Hurricane-Spitfire entities. D.A.F. was tending to outgrow its strength. The Fighter Control Group, 211, had to be supplemented by another, 212, technically of similar function, but actually destined for rear, as opposed to forward, control.

The opportunity for rest and retraining was too good to be missed. A small force of light bombers was enough for the limited targets offered by a static enemy. Coningham guaranteed a screen of fighters over the western approaches to the Delta as an alternative to standing patrols over Alexandria and Cairo.

Their bases shielded, the other components of R.A.F. Middle East (including U.S.A.A.F. Liberators) could unroll their bombing carpets over Rommel's ports of supply. Tobruk, the first on the list, was battered ceaselessly until in October aerial reconnaissance revealed that the enemy was starting to divert shipping. The heavy bombers then turned their attention to Benghazi.

Apart from this strategic air war, there were other affairs on hand. The Long Range Desert Group, though temporarily dispossessed of the fertile oasis of Siwa by a band of Fascist Youth, were ever active from Kufra; their most ambitious combined operation was a raid on Benghazi and Tobruk followed by a temporary occupation of Jalo oasis. The R.A.F. provided reconnaissance and air transport, and timed attacks on the ports in accordance with the ground scheme, finally sending air ambulances to carry the wounded from a prearranged rendezvous to Cairo.

D.A.F.'s local air operations increased in vigour from the start of October. On the 9th, once again as at Gambut, Coningham showed opportunist *élan.* Aerial photographs taken on the 6th indicated that the forward German fields were becoming waterlogged, and the process was eagerly watched. When the time was ripe, Kittyhawks, American P. 40's, Spitfires, Tomahawks, Bostons, Baltimores, Mitchells and Hurricanes were let loose in successive flocks. By the end of the day ten aircraft were destroyed and twenty damaged. Further visits by Wellingtons postponed German recovery indefinitely. Largely as a result of these air raids, the 8th Army enjoyed immunity during its secret preparations for the offensive.

To enemy tactical reconnaissance Montgomery's methods of deception gave little away. Dummy lorries, stationed since the start of the month in the north, could be replaced by the reality without arousing undue suspicion. In the south, a dummy pipeline and dummy ammunition dumps and installations lent weight to the fiction that the main attack would be launched from that quarter.

The plan of battle contained other unusual aspects. Instead of attempting to destroy enemy armour, Montgomery reversed the process and decided to crumble the line by methodically wiping out the infantry division which formed the first line of defence. The enemy armour, drawn out in defence of their infantry on to unfamiliar ground, were then to be the victims of 10th Corps. Behind the air screen, Montgomery was able to complete the disposition of his troops during the night 22nd/23rd. It was clear from the absence of artillery opposition that he had achieved tactical secrecy. Large, rapidly moving formations congested the roads, offering ideal targets, making air supremacy not only a desirable but an essential part of the battle plan; this the R.A.F. demonstrated by continuous patrols over the forward enemy fighter landing-grounds. The *Luftwaffe* could make no answer to such insolence until the 25th, when, for the loss of four fighters, Desert Air Force claimed seventeen and a further nine probables.

A very heavy artillery barrage along the whole front opened the land campaign, as the Australian, New Zealand, 51st Highland, and South African Divisions concentrated on making the initial break through. During the night of the 26th, as our forces were reorganized for a further thrust to extend the northern salient, they were opposed by an enemy preparing "a direct armoured assault in the old style".

6 and 7 squadron "Tank Busters", at their best in fluid conditions, scored

individual successes, but the shuttle service (seventeen raids by eighteen aircraft, in two-and-a-half hours), operating with "Hendon precision", stole the thunder. Montgomery commented, "The Desert Air Force intervened with such effect that the enemy was defeated before he had completed his forming up". In an area of roughly two miles by three, air power had stopped the enemy's only display of initiative.

From then on Montgomery prepared further strategems unhindered. On the 29th the Australian Division extended a thumb towards the coast in order to persuade the enemy that the real attack would follow in that sector, whilst from further south operation "Supercharge" prepared for a break out to the west. During November 1st and 2nd the baffled Germans had already committed their reserves to battle; bitter fighting in the evening was the last desperate bid of an already defeated enemy. Armoured car regiments were astride Axis lines of communication, and above them, over the Sidi Rahman track, rode the Bostons, Mitchells and Baltimores. Tactical reconnaissance revealed enemy troops close-packed and vulnerable. Soon columns of smoke drifting upwards from burning vehicles made rear and front lines identical from the air.

A diary of a German prisoner of war, though verging on hysteria, gives some idea of conditions:

> We pinched vehicles wherever we could. Panic was in the air. Until Matruh there was the wildest confusion, the road was choked with vehicles and we could only make fifty kilometres during the night. The bombing was frightful, my troop was torn into pieces. Vehicles were travelling a yard apart, I gave orders that each vehicle would look after itself until Sollum. Every bomb hit something. Christ, it was awful! The Italians were screaming, '*Santa Maria! Madonna!*' Dying, wounded blazing vehicles. . . . I was convinced that demoralization would get worse. It was the most terrible scene that I have ever experienced. It looked like a picture of the battlefields in the Franco-Prussian War.

Rommel was everywhere on the retreat. The gateway to Alexandria was closed forever; his sole problem now was to extricate his forces. But if his powers of resistance had been sapped by R.A.F. and naval attacks on his shipping, his chances of withdrawing in good order were ruined when Fuka and Daba, his air transport termini, passed out of his control. Ju. 52's had previously in part been able to replace fuel oil which tankers had been prevented from delivering. He had little time now to organize other means.

Nevertheless, at this stage his retreat was by no means a rout. He was able to mask Daba on the 4th; and what remained of his armoured forces was able to fight a stubborn delaying action, at the Fuka escarpment on November 5th, at Matruh on the 7th and at Barrani on the 9th. But the Italian component had to leave behind most of their equipment, and those who were not captured were demoralized. By now, from the original 270, the Germans had but thirty tanks; the Italians hardly one. The pursuit was on.

For once the weather, previously guilty of an anti-German bias, showed caprice. Fuka and Daba airfields, when in Axis hands on the 9th, had been waterlogged. They might have been expected to dry out for British tenants, but if anything they grew worse. Our armour was bogged down in the Desert only twelve miles from Charing Cross, almost in view of escaping opponents. As though to make amends for past errors, mud inches deep prevented supply echelons from travelling south via Maddalena to cut off the enemy near Capuzzo.

The R.A.F. adapted themselves to the tempo of the pursuit, the fighter-bombers, more easily maintained and moved, coming into their own. The more cumbrous light bombers were brought up as soon as conditions allowed.

They were fully prepared to take over any aerodromes abandoned by the *Luftwaffe*. The Aerodrome Reconnaissance unit from Advanced Air H.Q. joined the R.E. Construction unit, in contact by radio telephone with its own H.Q. As soon as a landing-ground was fit for use, back came the word by radio. Squadron advance-parties started moving. Air and ground effort was further co-ordinated when Sappers were ordered to treat the clearance of landing-grounds as a "priority commitment".

Advancing by hops and jumps, they never let the enemy get out of range, just as in the retreat to Alamein they had kept pace with our own troops. The organization which had stood the test of withdrawal was equally capable of covering advance.[1]

There was room for surprise ventures; inspired perhaps by "Landing-ground X", Operation "Chocolate" aimed at establishing two Hurricane squadrons about 180 miles due east of Jedabya, whilst the main Axis forces were west of Benghazi.

Operating on the afternoon of their arrival, the Hurricanes appeared over the astonished drivers of vehicles cruising, supposedly out of R.A.F. reach, towards Agheila. They destroyed 130 and damaged 170. But the *Luftwaffe*, though crushed, was not beaten, and to tarry longer was to invite destruction. By the 16th the Hurricanes were ordered to return. Air transport helped to bring back some of the ground crews, its use foreshadowing later developments.

[1] The speed at which fighters were established on captured fields is given in the following index:

Fighters			*8th Army*		
Date		Place	Date		Place
Nov. 6th	..	Daba	Nov. 6th	..	Fuka escarpt.
„ 8th	..	Sidi Haneish	„ 8th	..	Matruh
„ 10th	..	Misheifa	„ 9th	..	Sidi Barrani
„ 13th	..	Sidi Aziz	„ 11th	..	Halfaya
„ 14th	..	Gambut	„ 13th	..	Tobruk
„ 17th	..	Gazala	„ 19th	..	Benghazi
„ 19th	..	Martuba	„ 23rd	..	Jedabya

German air transport, meanwhile, was working at an unparalleled degree of pressure. Throughout the campaign German air transport had been a matter for envy and admiration. From the time of the Crete/Derna "bus" service to the establishment of the El Adem/Fuka feeder lines, Ju. 52's had been ferrying their loads with precision and, in spite of R.A.F. interference, with regularity. Now, without adequate fighter cover, they were to help evacuate Benghazi. In a massacre on November 17th and 18th fourteen were shot down and nine destroyed on the ground, together with fourteen other assorted transport types, by our Gazala-based fighter-bombers. Even though their function was vital, such high losses could not be supported, and the aircraft were withdrawn.

During the advance, Desert Air Force sometimes caught Axis aircraft as they were about to leave their landing-grounds. In the retreat D.A.F. had held on to forward aerodromes as long as possible; now the *Luftwaffe* tried to do the same. In June the G.A.F., too far behind, had been ineffectual; in November the R.A.F., pressing up in front, could make low-flying attacks on El Adem and Gambut.

On the 11th, 2 squadron S.A.A.F. intercepted an attempt by the *Luftwaffe* to give some close support to the army, when fifteen Ju. 87's escorted by six Me. 109's were met over Sollum. The Kittyhawks claimed eight Stukas and four probables, whilst the remaining three were caught on coming in to land at Gambut by Warhawks of the U.S.A.A.F.

Egypt that day was clear of the Axis once and for all. For a while light, medium and heavy bombers continued to attack Tobruk and Benghazi; then only Benghazi, until by the 20th even that target was one no longer.

Once more Desert Air Force was in control of the Gazala-Martuba-Benina group of airfields, as critical now as they had been in the past before Crusader or before Wavell's first push. This one air factor had remained constant; sea traffic to Malta from Alexandria could still only be protected by fighters from Cyrenaica; no offensive could truly be called complete until a convoy had passed safely to off-load supplies for the besieged island. Malta, having survived the last large-scale attack by the German air force in October, had proved its resilience by interfering with Rommel's supply ships, but the island could only escort convoys into Valetta from 140 miles out to sea. With the elimination of "Bomb Alley", Malta could again breathe freely.

A convoy of four merchant vessels, escorted by the cruiser *Euryalus* and seven destroyers, left Port Said on the evening of November 16th. The next day, the 5th Destroyer Flotilla relieved the escorting ships for refuelling at Alexandria, and at daylight on the 18th the convoy was joined by the 15th Cruiser Squadron. At the outset practically every group in Egypt took part in reconnaissance and escort; D.A.F. handing over to the island on the 19th. Six Stukas and some isolated night torpedo-bombers succeeded in putting H.M.S. *Arethusa* out of action, but the rest of the convoy reached Malta on the 20th; 28,860 tons of supplies were soon being distributed throughout the island.

More supplies of fuel and ammunition meant more air activity, more interference with Rommel's plans, and greater immunity for future convoys. The vicious circle of the past—less and less producing still less—was transformed to an upward-mounting spiral of supplies and increasing air effort. Ten more ships arrived in December; other convoys sailed unmolested. As Rommel approached El Agheila (the Libyan El Alamein), Malta was already garnering the first fruits of victory.

For the R.A.F., fruits tended to take the form of lessons. If, in the words of General Montgomery, "once a commander defeats his enemy in battle everything else will be added unto him", on the air side, air superiority had solved many problems in advance. But fresh points were forever emerging.

Firstly, tank-busters could not be used when opposing armoured forces were at grips with one another. They would have been more effective if their shells, instead of passing through the tanks, had exploded on contact.

Secondly, from Derna onwards, a few mines on aerodromes had caused a great deal of anxiety. Near Daba mines had been laid in hurried fashion and a few aircraft fitted with booby traps, but aircraft captured intact, and the amount of loot left untouched, gave evidence that no serious delaying tactics had been tried. Fuka, Haneish, Matruh and Gambut were similarly innocent, but at Derna and Martuba aerial reconnaissance disclosed several mines. Near Benghazi, as though to avenge German air transport, devices were as thick on the ground as fallen mulberries; at Berka tempting articles were almost invariably wired to explosives. Accidents warned many of the men, but doubting Thomases needed discouragement.

On a third point, however, two opinions rode side by side; neither seemed to be indisputably proven. The shuttle service had been effective, but could the Kittyhawk have done still more with less expenditure of man-power and resources? In a sense this was the old fighter *v.* bomber controversy slightly reshaped by the fact that the air weapon at whose expense the light bombers had operated was the fighter-bomber.

The fighter-bomber was primarily a fighter only, incidentally carrying bombs. If the Stuka (a specialized form of bomber) had proved to be a "crow masquerading in eagle's feathers", the fighter-bomber, efficient in two capacities, had shown no tendency to borrow plumes which it already possessed. In the Western Desert the Kittyhawk carried a 500-lb. bomb, but in Italy it was to carry 2,000 lb. The Baltimores and Bostons could carry no more than the latter amount. On the other hand the light bomber was more difficult to maintain, needed a specialized range of supplies, and carried crews instead of pilots. But it could deliver its load with accuracy from a height where there was less danger from flak.

The fighter-bomber, saving large escorts, could bomb only from low altitudes if flak was not intense; on some occasions therefore it definitely could not be used. Both A and B semed to have specialized functions.

The light bomber had to be escorted by aircraft either potentially or actually fighter-bombers. Was its use therefore uneconomical, or, on the contrary, was the shuttle service the great glory of D.A.F.? Such was the controversy. Results could be made to strengthen either case after the event. Fires might have blazed after a visit from the "eighteen imperturbables", but would more have been lit by many times that number of fighter-bombers? Rommel's rear supply lines had been harried during his retreat through Egypt, but might not an all-out fighter-bomber effort at Sollum and Halfaya have stopped and cut him off?

As is so often the case in the realm of air theory, only the presence of enough aircraft of both types could solve this problem to the satisfaction of all.

CHAPTER XIX

ON TO TRIPOLI

ROMMEL intended to withdraw immediately to Misurata; but Italian commanders linked hands with politicians to intervene. Sensitive about Tripoli, they wished to defend the town as far as possible from its suburbs. Hitler was involved in the final decision, and a stand "to the last man" was ordered at Agheila. However, on the eve of Montgomery's offensive, Rommel had already begun sending his main troops back to Buerat, keeping, as rearguard, the 90th Light Division. Thus, though the capture of the line meant that the gateway to Cyrenaica had become the threshold of Tripolitania, the German army was far from eliminated.

The *Luftwaffe*, on the other hand, under *Fliegerführer Afrika*, diminished. The retreat had disposed not only of aircraft, but of workshops and spares. The Tunisian was given priority over the African front for fresh supplies. By the start of 1943 numbers had dwindled to 130 Me. 109's and twenty-five other types, plus 310 Italian aircraft. Their average serviceability was as usual 50 per cent.

German air transport was overstrained by having to provide fuel not only for the *Luftwaffe* but for the army. Tripoli, once so far distant, was now Rommel's only port of supply, but Tripoli could not handle enough ships to support the armies retreating beyond its confines. Reconnaissance showed that only eight ships of about 11,000 tons reached the harbour, and of these a further six were severely damaged by bombardment. The R.A.F. and the Royal Navy had attenuated the Axis lifeline almost to vanishing-point.

All that was left to the Germans was to demolish installations at Tripoli as thoroughly as at Benghazi in an attempt to delay the Allies.

Aerodromes, too, continued to present an irresistible attraction for German engineers. Barrels attached to wires were sunk in the ground; dummies crouched deceptively amongst anti-personnel mines; slit trenches and foxholes blew up those who sought cover. They started ploughing. Desert Air Force fighters had to be sent to put the "Master Ploughman of Ghindels" out of business, whilst at Sirte and Tamet furrows in the shape of gigantic thumbprints appeared overnight. German methods made an absorbing study; there seemed to be no limit to their ingenuity; at one field, trenches zigzagged or curved backwards upon each other; at another a Union Jack was etched in earth. But whatever was done could be undone. The air force, never unduly delayed by fresh items on the repertoire, was not left behind.

Desert Air Force, more than ever, was one with the 8th Army. Montgomery stated:

"The immediate consideration after El Agheila was the establishment of the Desert Air Force at Marble Arch and Mecuma, with forward squadrons at Nofilia. We also required to take Sirte and start work at once on the airfields there so that the Desert Air Force would be ready to give its customary scale of support."

In spite of the gales raging in Benghazi harbour from January 4th to the 6th, D.A.F. continued to draw its supplies, upwards of 800 tons per day, at what might, in a previous campaign, have been called "the expense" of the army.

Twenty sappers were killed when clearing Marble Arch for 239 Wing. Not only the aerodrome, but all roads and approaches, were heavily mined. Hence air transport which had been given a try-out for Operation Chocolate was now to be used to move the entire Wing to its new site.

Plans were made in advance. An R.A.F. Aerodrome Reconnaissance officer, in radio contact with Advanced H.Q., accompanied the New Zealanders engaged in outflanking the Agheila line, who were expected to arrive in the area before the main body of troops. A supply column drove as far forwards as it could safely go; the "A" party of the Wing, with motor-cycles, wireless telegraph, radio telephone links, telephones and a small radar set, waited at Belandah to be picked up by Hudsons of 216 Group, whilst Dakotas of 316 U.S.A.A.F. transport group stood by at El Adem with enough petrol to supply the Wing for one day of intensive operations.

Hard by the aerodrome, surmounting a gigantic marble gateway, lay the bronze statues of the brothers Philaeni; from their lonely memorial they looked down on little else but their own modest tomb, the blue waves of the Mediterranean, and a metalled road stretching away into the sandy distances. Within the last few days they had witnessed the mining operations and the hurried withdrawal of Rommel's troops. Now they were to see what had been so carefully laid down equally carefully disinterred. For at last swastikas had given place to roundels: J.G. 77 had left; 239 Wing had come to take their place on the classical boundary of Cyrenaica and Carthage.

The New Zealanders, reaching the monument on the 16th, started lifting the 2,000 mines to such effect that on the 17th the aerodrome reconnaissance officer was able to signal back that the landing-ground would be ready the following day. So, whilst transport aircraft were landing stores, before the Fighter Control or full radar interception system could be installed, 239 Wing were over the aerodrome, landing, dropping their long-range tanks, refuelling, and going out on missions, sixty in all during the day. Operation Chocolate was repeated as enemy vehicles, in an area apparently out of range, were caught unawares.

This was a fine example, not only of the use of air transport but of army/air unity. From that time onwards co-operation could no longer be called a problem; it had been solved finally and was working out in practice. A fitting site had been chosen to mark such concord, for the place had previously commemorated agreement. The brothers Philaeni[1] had allowed themselves to be buried alive in order to bring harmony to their country. The gigantic modern marble gateway had been erected as a sign that the Italian mastery of Tripolitania was absolute. If, in past history, tragedy or *force majeure* had brought about agreement, in December 1942 Marble Arch was the symbol of common sense triumphant.

As Tripoli loomed daily nearer, distances already covered were enormous, much greater than a casual study of the map would lead one to believe. The supply organization of Middle East had to stretch, as it were, from Moscow to London. Tobruk was still the main port of supply, though Benghazi was slowly recovering. Montgomery's Buerat offensive was mounted with the assurance of only ten days' supplies; if Tripoli had not fallen by the end of that time it could not have been taken for several weeks.

During the first week in January the less mobile units of the German army started their withdrawal. It was clear that the Agheila "disappearance" was to be repeated. Rommel, in spite of "inspired" orders to fight to the finish, was displaying initiative by living up to his newly acquired reputation, "Master of Retreats".

Mines and booby traps, in even greater quantities than before, had to be cleared. German positions had to be outflanked, but in this Montgomery was well versed; the variety of delaying devices and "demolitions on the road most skilfully related to the ground" hindered but could not stop the advance.

"Desert Air Force," in the words of the army commander, "took a constant and heavy toll of the enemy throughout the action." Up to a few days before the start of the battle they arranged offensive patrols and bombed troop concentrations, and then in order to prevent the enemy retaliating they attacked Bir Dufan and Chirugia airfields. In an expensive battle over the latter, R.A.F. and S.A.A.F. Bostons and Baltimores and U.S.A.A.F. Mitchells, strongly escorted by Kittyhawks and American P. 40's, made repeated assaults, luring into the air most of the German and Italian fighters in the area. Although eleven fighters failed to return, six Me. 109's were claimed with another six probables and nine damaged. As a result, few enemy planes were in evidence the next day.

As the army offensive swung on its way, 239 Wing moved one hundred miles by air transport from Hamraiet to Sedada so as to give maximum close

[1] According to Gaius Sallustius Crispius (86–34 B.C.), the Roman historian, the legend ran as follows: Runners set out from Carthage and Cyrene. The point at which they met was to be the boundary between the two empires. The Carthaginian brothers Philaeni, accused of starting before the appointed time, denied the charge. Not surprisingly, the Cyrenaicans still expressed disbelief, for the boundary was improbably far from Carthage. As "proof" of innocence, the brothers offered to be buried alive. Their offer was accepted, and so was the boundary. The runners from Cyrene could have established the boundary further to the west had they also agreed to a living tomb, but this they were not prepared to do.

support. By night, light bombers hindered the transport streaming from Zuara towards Ben Gardane, which fighter-bombers had already attacked by day, whilst strategic air power spread wings across the Mediterranean to Rome, Naples and Palermo. Tripoli fell within the allotted ten days. Castel Benito, where 200 aircraft had dwindled to thirty since January 17th, was in our hands, its half-ploughed surface and its wrecked aeroplanes as eloquent a testimony to the effectiveness of air power as the battered remnants of Tripoli harbour.

Here then was the capital; for this the inhabitants of the little white houses with the legend *Ente Colonnizzazione* had yearned as they had tried to persuade the once fertile soil of Libya to yield some semblance of the crops so freely mentioned by the Ancients. Here the cart had been put before the horse; the palaces and theatres built to encourage by their magnificence an idea of greatness; to supply a demand which had hardly found time to grow into existence.

The troops were disappointed, because, in spite of appearances, the normal amenities of city life were lacking. Shops were scantily filled; cleanliness was only façade deep. Cheated, they tended to look upon Tripoli as a bombastic sham, and ignored achievement to point out defect. But the harbour at least was excellent. Although the R.A.F., the Royal Navy, and Rommel between them had destroyed and demolished most of it; although jutting, irregular, islands of metal marked the graveyard of ships and barges, the port was open by February 3rd. Convoys steamed in during the next week to ensure that the German and Italian armies would never return. 1,400 miles from their base, Allied forces were preparing for their next major offensive.

CHAPTER XX

THE OTHER SIDE OF NORTH AFRICA

ALAMEIN should never be considered as an isolated turning-point in the history of the war; it should be mentioned in the same breath with another far-distant battle—Stalingrad. There the Russians by incredible exertion had turned a town into a vast warren of death and destruction; there they were to reverse a verdict which seemed already to have been irrevocably declared; against the rock of that stubborn defence the German sword was to be decisively blunted.

The plan for German supremacy throughout the Mediterranean was crumbling to dust. The pincers which were to clasp Palestine, Iraq and Iran, and close in on Egypt from Abyssinia, Eritrea and the Sudan, were now locked at the northern end by the Russian stand. In the south they had already lost their power to grip by reason of the hurried decline of the Italian East African Empire. At Alamein they were robbed of the last remainder of their vigour. The war on two fronts, which Bismarck had been at pains to avoid, was a matter of present reality. There could be no increase in *Fliegerführer Afrika's* forces whilst Stalingrad remained unbeaten, yet at such a crucial moment *Luftflotte II* had been withdrawn from the Russian to reinforce the Mediterranean front.

From November 8th the Alamein-Stalingrad axis extended a spoke towards Algeria. If the Germans had specialized in pincers, the Allies were creating a wheel to encircle the Reich. The new landings in North Africa set in motion a new process.

Operation "Torch" planned to land men at focal points along the 400 mile coastline between Algiers and Casablanca. The Allied nature of the venture had at first to be concealed in American wrappings. French reactions could not be precisely prejudged, but considerable anti-British sentiment was known to exist.

The first convoy, escorted by 181 British and American warships, left Britain a fortnight before "D" day, *en route*, so the Germans thought, for Dakar. This modern armada needed all the air protection that could be devised; anti-submarine patrols in the Bay of Biscay took over from Iceland-based aircraft of Coastal Command to relieve 8th U.S.A.A.F. and Bomber Command.

The air component for the actual landings was split into three parts; the 12th Air Support Command, under Brigadier Joseph Cannon, was to go with Major-General Patton's Western Task Force; the 12th Air Force, under Brigadier-General Doolittle, was allotted to Major-General Fredendall's

Central Task Force at Oran; whilst the R.A.F. Eastern Command, under Air Marshal Sir William Welsh, was to support Major-General Ryder's Eastern Task Force at Algiers. Carrier-based aircraft of the Fleet Air Arm and the United States navy were also to share in the fighting at Port Lyautey and Algiers.

Not only were airfields unprepared, but reception committees were of uncertain temper. At Port Lyautey field, pitted with bomb craters, some aircraft of 12th A.S.C. ruined undercarriages on landing; at Tafaroui the Spitfires of the 31st Fighter Group, arriving during "D" afternoon, lost one aircraft for three French Dewoitines destroyed. Over the same field Dakotas of the 60th Troop-Carrier Group, carrying paratroops briefed for a friendly reception, had instead encountered flak. A Foreign Legion column had to be sent to relieve La Senia, where the airfield was under fire from French coastal batteries.

To help the situation, leaflets bearing Giraud's proclamation were showered in thousands over Oran and the other cities. By Tuesday the 10th the French air force had been captured, destroyed, or had surrendered. At Algiers, coastal batteries continued firing until silenced by sea and air bombardment. After some trouble with French tanks, Maison Blanche was captured and Blida fell shortly afterwards.

The way was now clear for 324 Wing; a contemporary report stated: "The only opposition was from a few anti-aircraft guns in harbour . . . next day (the 9th), 111 squadron went into action over Algiers, destroying a Ju. 88, one probable, and three damaged."

The light bombers were not far behind. The ground staff of 18 squadron had set sail on the 1st of the month from Glasgow; on the 11th eighteen Bisleys were detailed to fly from Portreath to Blida, and of these seventeen arrived by the end of the day. Seventeen hours later these aircraft were briefed for their first operation, but two developed technical trouble, and three failed to find the target, leaving one aircraft as the sole representative of the first British light bomber attack from Algerian soil.

Until the ground staffs arrived, servicing commandos and men of the R.A.F. Regiment filled the gaps in Maintenance and Supply to such effect that German aircraft attacking on the 9th were met by fighters in what had been considered a "safe" area. But six days later the Allied air forces were firmly in possession; Eastern Air Command was established at Maison Carrée, and after another five days Doolittle moved his 12th Air Force up to Algiers.

It is outside the scope of this chronicle to present more than a brief outline of events, but since 324 and 326 Wings, together with other squadrons, were later to be part of Desert Air Force, some idea of their background needs to be given in order to explain their particular virtues and defects. The air forces stemming from Algiers had to carry with them every single item of equipment from England. They had not the vast supply arsenal of the Delta at their back, nor were they well grounded in the lore of the country through which they were to fight. They had not paced the *Promenade des Anglais*; they had not seen small numbers grow from something relatively unimportant into a force united with the magnificence of 8th Army. Except by way of exercises in the United Kingdom, they had served no Desert apprenticeship in mobility and self-sufficiency. They could not well be expected to reproduce overnight an organization which in Desert Air Force had grown gradually during years of practical experience.

That winter in Algeria was the worst for many years. Mud was everywhere. Tents were like white mushrooms scattered over dark ooze; aircraft floundered through liquid brown glue to their dispersals. Intense cold ("Not my idea of Africa!" they complained) caught many unawares. Malaria and dysentery took toll of men who in the Desert would have been on their guard against, at worst, Desert sores. For the air forces and troops arrived in Algeria like pelicans, their bills stuffed with food, their feathers trimmed to last for a whole campaign—and a brief one at that.

Seen against such a background—one of phenomenal administrative problems and relative inexperience—the zeal and determination of the forces was remarkable. The paratroop operation whereby Bone was seized on the 12th by aircraft which had flown in to Maison Blanche on the 11th was only matched by the sequel. The battle for air superiority had not yet been fought; the Germans were able to pound the invaders from the air at their leisure. On the 13th anti-aircraft guns were rushed to the defenders to protect the town until paratroops could occupy Youks Les Bains airfield. Two days later the fall of Souk El Abra allowed the air force to settle in some strength in the area. From then on, troop carriers ran a ferry service, sometimes wholly without escort, right up to the front line. Allied air transport was approaching the German scale.

In November alone Ju. 52's had made over 1,200 trips to Bizerta from Sicilian bases only a short sea flight distant. Faced by slight opposition from the French, the German air transport service poured in troops and equipment from "D" day onwards. Bizerta and Tunis, Msus, Sfax and Gabes, and the surrounding airfields, were all occupied; within a fortnight of the Allied landings Axis forces in Tunisia numbered over 120,000. Sicily and Sardinia, previously robbed by Tripolitania, were now robbed of Messerschmitts by Tunisia.

During the winter, when military operations would be at a discount, the war of supplies could continue. Here the advantage lay with the Germans. They could operate from prepared runways in Tunis and Bizerta, flying in aircraft from Sicily whenever they wished.

The only good Allied field was Bone, in December 114 miles from the front. Two-thirds of the aircraft based on Souk El Abra, the most forward field, were put out of action as the surface progressively deteriorated.

2,000 tons of runway steel matting[1] (i.e. the entire capacity of the railway system) would be needed to construct a new advanced landing-ground. As Eisenhower has said, "It is logistics which control all campaigns and limit many".

Air superiority could not be contested so long as Spitfires could only carry enough petrol to stay over enemy lines for five minutes at a time. Hence, on December 3rd, German dive-bombers were able to operate with devastating results against 11th Brigade positions. Bad weather interfered with the only possible Allied reply—attacks on enemy landing-grounds by medium or heavy bombers from superior bases in the rear.

In these conditions the light bombers were in increasing demand; one incident in particular gleamed against a background of mud and cold. On December 4th the army put in an urgent request for air support over Chougui. Nine aircraft led by Wing-Commander Malcolm took off without escort, because no escort could be arranged in time. Whilst over the target the formation was attacked from all sides by Me. 109's. No aircraft returned to base. Flight-Lieut. Eller and his crew, one of whom was wounded, landed in enemy territory, and had to make their way back on foot to British lines, where they were joined by two other crews. These were the only survivors. Wing-Commander Malcolm was posthumously awarded the Victoria Cross.

February 14th initiated a thrust from Faid and Maknassi, to force the Kasserine pass, recapture Constantine, and drive on to Tunis. 12th A.S.C. upheld the standard of close support. Desert Air Force, from bases in Tripolitania, joined in the battle raging on the other side of Tunisia. The air forces of the Middle East and North Africa, which were already working together in practice, were linked officially a few days later. Tedder, in his capacity of C.-in-C. Mediterranean Air Command, took over command of all British, French and American air forces.

Under M.A.C. came North African Air Forces, a joint H.Q. commanded by Lieut.-General Spaatz with Air Vice-Marshal Robb as his deputy, controlling the Strategic Air Force under Doolittle and Tactical Air Force under Coningham. Desert Air Force, now a sub-division of T.A.F., was thus on an equal footing with 12th A.S.C., 242 Group and Tactical Bomber Force. Strategic and Tactical were thus withdrawn into specialized groups; Tactical was further divided into Tactical fighter and Tactical bomber. The quantity of Allied aircraft made such sub-division practical. "Penny packets of air" had aroused scorn in the past. "Pound packets" gave general satisfaction, especially since they were disbursed by an H.Q. where British and American officers formed a layer system of Allied command.

Reorganization of the German air command inevitably meant concentration of resources. *Fliegerführer Afrika* and *Fliegerführer Tunis* combined under Seidemann, leaving Harlinghausen free to take over the Sicilian-based

[1] Known as P.S.P. (pierced steel plate).

Fliegerkorps II from Loertzer. The latter, "Goering's inefficient favourite", was ousted from command, but not before he had succeeded in creating havoc and dismay, which Harlinghausen, painstaking and efficient, did his best to remedy. Training had come to a standstill; the supply organization had almost broken down; many crews had been lost during November and December. Nevertheless Harlinghausen was directed by Kesselring to apply his energies to shipping strikes.

The defence of ports and the maintenance of air transport were Seidemann's chief preoccupations. His units were either fresh, or had been back to Italy for a short period of rest. He could rely on von Maltzahn for fighter defence, on Hagen for close support, and on Kosch for the direction of long-range bombing, but, as the jam between two slices of a sandwich, his position was far from enviable.

CHAPTER XXI

CONSOLIDATION

ROMMEL'S "Staff appreciation of the situation", dated December 16th, enlarged on the lack of cohesion inherent in an Allied command, and drew attention to the weakness of French troops near Gabes. He therefore proposed to "hold the British 8th Army in Tripolitania, using the minimum force possible, and with the balance of my available forces to attack and cut the enemy lines of communication in Tunisia".

On February 17th, in the whole of the Mediterranean, there were about 1,570 Axis aircraft, 900 of which were German. In Tunisia itself there were perhaps 240 single-engine fighters and fighter-bombers, 50 dive-bombers, a few night-fighters and 25 reconnaissance aeroplanes. The Italian air force, now employed almost exclusively in defence, supplied a further 80 fighters. Serviceability was as low as ever, barely exceeding 50 per cent. Against this, R.A.F. Middle East alone, excluding the vast air forces in Malta, Algeria and Tunisia, could muster 966 aircraft, with an average serviceability of 75 per cent. Desert Air Force and 205 Group were still expanding.

Whilst Rommel withdrew to the Mareth Line, air activity on both sides decreased, the *Luftwaffe* adjusting itself to its buffer position, the Allied air forces constructing new airfields to supplement the heavily mined morasses which weather and the Germans had done their best to ruin. During February, Germans visited Tripoli almost nightly, their fervour diminishing gradually in face of concentrated anti-aircraft fire and night-fighters. That month the light bombers were brought out of retirement, 12th Bombardment Group moving to Castel Benito, whilst 232 Wing were *en route* from the Delta to Sirte, to join 3 S.A.A.F. Wing. Other arrivals included the Polish Combat team of sixteen experienced pilots who were to form another flight of 145 squadron. During this period, too, the 79th Fighter Group was on trek from Gazala to Castel Benito to start dive-bombing against the Mareth Line; this Group, from then onwards a loyal and efficient part of D.A.F., was to demonstrate with 239 Wing in July that complete Anglo-American air co-operation was not a problem, but a fact.

Meanwhile, all the other sections of D.A.F. were on the move to Tripoli. 12th Meteorological Detachment, which had never allowed the speed of the advance to interrupt forecasting, was extending its network. The Assistant Provost Marshal attached to Advanced H.Q. had responsibilities other than security and control of the men; his unit had to arrange guards for material left behind in the rush and see that the Maintenance units duly received anything capable of further use.

The medical authorities were improving the Mobile Field Hospital system, by which men were returned to their units when fit instead of being caught up in the time-absorbing machinery of evacuation to base. The Mobile Medical Inspection Rooms, first employed at Alamein, were gradually evolving from converted three-ton trucks. Air Evacuation, dealing with men of both services from February 17th to May 13th, handled 5,900 cases.

A subsidiary Welfare store was established in Tripoli to continue the work of providing sports gear, indoor games, musical instruments, gramophones and radios, whilst books, magazines and cigarettes were often distributed free. Station cinemas were constructed at Benina and Castel Benito; mobile cinemas competed with the R.A.F. "Mirthmakers" concert party. This, the fairy godmother side of Welfare, was equally as important as the Advice and Assistance Section, which could refer cases straight to the Directorate of Air Force Welfare at Air Ministry. Husbands serving overseas, separated from their families through no fault of their own, were often victims of inconstancy. Welfare was able to act as a mediator in many cases. Where the trouble was not domestic, but illness or financial distress, Welfare was also able to help. For anxiety crossed the Mediterranean in both directions; those at home worried about their men overseas; those out in the Desert heard news of the bombing of English towns with a disquiet which could only be allayed by letters. Welfare and the Postal Services alike contributed to the maintenance of morale.

All these sections, though not directly connected with Operations, were just as much part of a mobile force as the aircraft themselves. Their presence should be kept constantly in mind in order to offset the idea that an air force consists merely of the machines flown by a small percentage of its men.

Signals branches were more directly related to Operations. Together with the Air Formation Signals and A.M.E.S.,[1] they not only supplied telephone and radio communications, but looked after aircraft sets and staffed the Direction Finders and radar aids. V.H.F. (very high frequency radio) was coming to be used more and more in aircraft. During the coming months, also, V.H.F. equipment was to be fitted to an armoured car as an experiment in the front line control of "tank-busters".[2]

Equally closely connected, "the backbone of the Air Force", was the Repair and Maintenance organization. Constant references have been made to the extraordinary deficiencies in Axis maintenance, and their low serviceability percentage. This should not be dismissed as a propagandist attempt to denigrate any and every branch of enemy activity. The figures in this most important department were far too vital to tamper with. The assessments on which high-level decisions had to be taken were as accurate as prisoner-of-war

[1]Air Ministry Experimental Stations (Radar).

[2]At El Hamma an R.A.F. Liaison Officer was allowed to control aircraft by V.H.F. in direct close support. From this trial emerged "Rover"—a system which, for various reasons, was only fully developed in Italy in November 1943.

sources, captured enemy documents, Reconnaissance and Intelligence reports could make them. In contrast, Allied air successes in the Middle East appear to have been founded on Maintenance and Supply—in which Tedder, from the start, showed such a keen interest.

"Muddling through" was here displayed in what may indeed be its true form (hotly though the organizers themselves might deny it): as efficiency in planning coupled with the ability on all levels to improvise and alter. Latin disrespect for the overall plan and consequent chaos, or Teutonic adherence to the proper channels with consequent rigidity, illustrate clearly the Scylla and Charybdis which in the Desert campaign were avoided by the strategic planning of R.A.F. Middle East and the tactical improvisation of the forward Maintenance units and Air Stores Parks of the tactical Desert Air Force.

The Delta could no longer handle the far-flung units of the D.A.F. empire; technical and supply services on a large scale needed to be in the forward area. Thus a nucleus of the new 113 M.U. grew around Castel Benito. Workshops sprouted in Tripoli to deal with repairs to engines, air-frames and vehicles. From the Levant came both an Engine and an Aircraft Repair unit, whilst 136 M.U. at Benghazi was robbed to form a new Equipment Section. In April 159 M.U. was transplanted bodily from Ismalia to Mellaha, and to support these two another M.U. (114) found a site at Zavia near at hand. Their new buildings were not only damaged, but filthy; houses and hangars had to be cleaned and adapted by unit advance parties, whilst complete engine, aircraft and instrument shops were moving forward to take up their new positions. Most of the convoys had to come by road, for sea transport was at a premium; only goods carrying a high priority could come by air.

The most forward units of all were split. A rear party now shouldered part of the load which threatened to crush the more mobile A.S.P.s and R.S.U.s. The advanced R.S.U.s (Advanced Salvage Unit and Nos. 2, 3, 51, 53, 57, 59 and 61 R.S.U.s) and the Forward A.S.P.s (31, 33, 37 and 40) were then able to concentrate on work more within their scope.

D.A.F.'s high degree of mobility had been largely due to the services of the Supply and Transport columns. From railhead or port, from dump or depot, equipment or explosives could be rushed to wherever they were in short supply. Nos. 4, 5, 6 and 10 S. & T. columns, and Nos. 1 and 2 Bomber Maintenance Corps, were the arteries through which fresh blood for the Allied forces of D.A.F. flowed constantly.

Thus, during the short time elapsing between the capture of Tripoli and Rommel's withdrawal to the Mareth Line, R.A.F. Middle East had regrouped and rearranged its whole Maintenance and Supply organization. Desert Air Force was to be as well cared for in Tripoli as it had been in the Delta. When Rommel started his thrust "towards Algeria" on February 21st, Desert Air Force was not only capable of being redirected to support the 1st Army by the new Tactical Air Force H.Q., but was, thanks to these ground services, in fit enough state for sustained operations.

To distract German attention, 8th Army, though not quite ready to countenance a major offensive, was to stage a demonstration with the help of D.A.F. A mock softening-up process—visits to enemy forward fields followed by night attacks on lines of communication—contributed towards persuading the enemy that the usual offensive preparations were under way. 244 and 7 S.A.A.F. Wing moved up to Hazbub and Neffatia; the light bombers attacked dumps and concentrations in the Mareth area; the medium and heavy bombers of 205 Group concentrated on the town, airfield and approaches of Gabes. The feint succeeded; from the 27th, D.A.F. effort could safely diminish.

To repay the compliment, as it were, the Tunisian-based air forces now let loose their bombs on the Mareth Line. But a red rag had been waved at the bull; on March 3rd reconnaissance reports indicated that he was about to charge. On the 6th came attacks on Medenine from the west, supported by dive-bombers and fighter-bombers. F.W. 190's and Me. 210's used as bombers were new arrivals from Sicily; neither had been employed before so far south; they had been ordered especially for the action. This brief flowering of air activity was, however, fruitless; preceded by no systematic softening up, no sustained attacks were to follow. As the offensive petered out, the aircraft were to be switched back on to the northern Tunisian front. In contrast, though liable to some seasonal fluctuations in strength, D.A.F. had always been able to produce a record number of sorties for an important army manœuvre without promptly sinking to below average immediately after the attempt. Eight attacks at three squadron strength of Kittybombers, with Spitfire escort, made the 6th their best day; on the 7th low cloud blotted out enemy columns withdrawing through the passes towards Toujane.

There were those who said that the battle of Alam El Halfa had repeated itself, for there the enemy armour had been stopped by artillery fire from high ground, whilst air attacks had caused supplementary confusion. At Medenine, it was true, guns massed in the hills to the north-west again gave us command of the situation; but whereas at Alam El Halfa the weather had been good and the shuttle service had been fully occupied, now low cloud made it impossible to use anything other than the fighter-bomber.

The enemy offensive was over, but not before enemy ground forces had scandalized 244 Wing. Spitfires had been shelled out of Hazbub; on their return they were shelled again. Great indignation was caused; the 17-millimetre guns, after repeated visits from fighter-bombers, were only finally persuaded to retire by night patrols of the 4th Indian Division. The incident, in some curious way, brought ground and air forces closer to one another instead of having the opposite effect. It showed that D.A.F. could not be accused of lagging behind.

The next offensive during the March moon period was to be 8th Army's.

In the short lull, methods of rendezvous between bombers and escort were improved; the time taken to join the two parts of the striking force together was decreased.

Something, too, had to be done to reduce the bomber escort, in order to free aircraft for fighter-bombing. To deceive enemy radar, formations were directed to fly near the ground until the final climb over the target; if bombers were then only liable to be intercepted by enemy aircraft already airborne on patrol, large escorts would be unnecessary. "Wastage" of potential fighter-bombers was still a D.A.F. concern.

As though to strengthen their claims for such attention, the fighter-bombers meanwhile proved their value by adopting General Le Clerc's troops at Kasr Rhilane. The Fighting French Force, after moving northwards across the Sahara from Lake Chad, had established themselves within fifty miles of the front, to form a southern screen behind which 8th Army could prepare secret plans for outflanking the enemy. Though weak in artillery, anti-aircraft and anti-tank guns, this small but important bastion, essential to the success of the coming offensive, was political dynamite which the German commander would dearly have loved to ignite.

Tactical reconnaissance on March 10th confirmed French reports. The spark, a small force of armoured cars and vehicles, aided by five escorting formations of German fighter-bombers and fifteen dive-bombers, was even now travelling along the fuse. Caught in the open by 6 squadron tank-busters, at the end of half an hour twelve out of twenty of the vehicles were on fire, and the rest disorganized. Six more Hurricanes, arriving for a second attack, claimed an armoured car and a direct hit on a tank. In the afternoon two Kittyhawk squadrons started a chain of explosion involving an ammunition waggon and a petrol bowser of the relieving force.

There were six aircraft lost that day, but the spark was snuffed out; the venture was abandoned. General Le Clerc sent messages of appreciation to Desert Air Force. It was a singular coincidence that the squadrons which had flown in support of the Free French at Bir Hakim should now have had the chance to come to their aid a second time.

CHAPTER XXII

EL HAMMA

AFTER the Kasr Rhilane episode, Air Marshal Coningham, now the A.O.C. North African Tactical Air Force, convened a conference. The A.O.C. D.A.F., Broadhurst, was flanked by his Senior Air Staff Officer and his Air Officer Administration. The A.O.C. 242 Group and the Commanding General 12th Air Support Command were there, together with members of the N.A.T.A.F. staff.

Broadhurst had been working under Coningham for some time. He had been posted as Senior Air Staff Officer Desert Air Force in October 1942, and had at first been supernumary to Beamish (the champion of the shuttle service) until November. He had taken over D.A.F. during the reorganization just after the fall of Tripoli, and was to remain in command until March 1944. His expert hand was to guide D.A.F. throughout a period when his force under M.A.A.F. might well have lost its identity as a separate body.

At the conference, the Desert Air Force plan found favour. During the coming offensive, 242 Group and 12th A.S.C. were to divert attention and ensure air superiority by attacking enemy landing-grounds day and night. This would leave the whole of D.A.F. free to give full direct support to 8th Army. 285 Wing were required to make photo reconnaissance not only of the Mareth Line, but also of the area through which a wide outflanking movement was to take place. 8th Army envisaged a direct assault on the eastern flank, followed by a "roll-up" to the north.

Weather intervened; the bombers were not able to conduct their usual softening-up sonata. Not until March 20th could the first few notes be piped; the next day the shuttle service, ten formations of eighteen bombers, sounded a fuller chord; and the fighter-bombers, active against tanks and vehicles south of El Hamma, developed the theme in support of the New Zealanders. On the following day, whilst the enemy was digging in and whilst the flank was still weak, tank-busters of 6 squadron found their ideal target, claiming thirty-two hits.

When the frontal attack on the Mareth Line failed, the main armoured reserves of 8th Army were sent south to help exploit the success of the New Zealanders. Air support was accordingly switched to El Hamma and the Gabes gap. The 4th Indian and the 1st Armoured Divisions on their way south offered the German air force a tempting target from Medenine to Fuim Tattuin. There was no question but that the traffic jam many miles long was observed, for it was in clear view from enemy posts in the hills, but the battle for air superiority, in which lately D.A.F. had taken little part, had been won from the other side of Tunisia; troops and vehicles thronging the road went unmolested. The incident showed that in the air war, what the adversary was prevented from doing could have just as decisive an effect on the battle as the damage our own air forces could inflict on the enemy. Immunity from enemy air attack when troops were in transit gave the Allied Army Commanders a great advantage over their opponents.

El Hamma, the next objective, was a perfect funnel of defence—a valley commanded by hills, sown with mines—criss-crossed by dried-up beds of innumerable streams. Was the attacker to outflank (and give the enemy time to consolidate)? Or was he to make a direct thrust (and risk large casualties, if not failure)? In the predicament, Broadhurst dangled his bait, the Desert Air Force.

According to the plan, the army was to expect continuous Kittybomber attacks throughout a two-hour period at the density of two squadrons, starting half an hour before the ground attack. This was intended to disorganize the defence at the psychological moment and allow the fighter-bombers to continue supporting the assault during the most difficult period. Flak and enemy opposition might swell the air casualty list, but the risk was one worth taking. Both army and air commanders foresaw a sudden, dynamic success.

Every effort was to be made to perfect co-operation. Desert Air Force was given all possible information, and the ground forces prepared various schemes of identification. Red and blue smoke was to indicate the starting-point, whilst further forward trucks drawn up to form letters were to feed fighter-bombers towards the front, where lines of yellow smoke—the finishing tape—were to reveal the exact position of our troops.

Beyond in the enemy lines, smoke shells were to burst, each cottonwool cloud to act as a marker for our bombs.

But hardly had the outlines of this encouraging picture been sketched before fresh artists advanced with different canvases; the battle for air superiority threatened to brandish a blue pencil over the whole project. The situation in central and northern Tunisia appeared to demand a renewal of attacks on enemy aerodromes. D.A.F.'s effort might have to be diverted. This long-term benefit could only accrue at the expense of the immediate tactical plan. Desert Air Force claimed "with air superiority at last attained, now is the time to exploit it", and though the enemy air forces in turn might exploit immunity, the risk seemed more than offset by the advantages to be gained from a land victory. North African Tactical Air Force conceded the point. Operation "Supercharge" was to remain as first depicted.[1]

On the afternoon of the 26th light bombers started pattern bombing to dislocate telephone communications and to throw battery H.Q. into confusion.

[1] Here again the bomber *v.* fighter-bomber controversy reared its head. For Supercharge, the fighter-bomber was the chosen instrument; for action against enemy landing-grounds, light bombers were to have been escorted by Kittyhawks and provided with cover by Spitfires.

The preceding night the whole force had bombed by the light of the moon. The troops facing the Allied Divisions, already disgruntled by lack of sleep, were now discomforted by the prospect of having to repair this further damage. The final irritant was supplied before there was time to begin the routine work of clearing up after the R.A.F. The fighter-bombers started to bomb and strafe at low level, to turn dislocation into breakdown, confusion into chaos. Half an hour later, infantry attacked under cover of a creeping barrage, moving at the rate of 100 feet a minute, automatically defining the bomb line. As a result the armour broke through the "Valley of Death" without being forced to suffer the fate of the gallant six hundred.

One Italian General, whose Division was captured intact, said that the fighter-bombers had destroyed the whole of his divisional transport. But the most important aspect of the action was that for a short yet vital period enemy heads had been kept down. El Hamma did not, however, illustrate that an air force could blast a path of destruction along which those on the ground could pour pell-mell upon their enemies. El Hamma showed that widespread and temporary disorganization could be caused, which the ground could exploit provided that it did so in time. Later on at Cassino, in Italy—another ideal defensive position—air power was indeed to blast a path of destruction, and incidentally, in so doing, ruin the road to tactical success. El Hamma must be regarded as a classic of fighter-bomber employment. Its aim, "keeping their heads down", was limited, precise, and completely fulfilled.

CHAPTER XXIII

THE END IN NORTH AFRICA

After El Hamma, the N.A.T.A.F. plan was implemented as quickly as possible; direct support to the army was switched off and attacks on landing-grounds switched on, the air forces from either side of Tunisia working as a unit; Mitchells and Bostons from North-West African Air Forces joining with Desert Air Force to pound airfields at Sfax, La Fauconnerie and El Djem.

For the next operation ("Scipio"), D.A.F. went back to direct support, but not on the El Hamma scale; in Broadhurst's words: "The nature of the country and of the enemy defensive positions along the Wadi did not lend themselves to that form of attack"; nevertheless armoured reconnaissance by Kittyhawks and American Warhawks preceded bombardment of troop concentrations by the light bombers. That evening, vehicles moving slowly along the coastal road were strafed into ant-like action. During the day R.A.F. and S.A.A.F. Spitfires had patrolled overhead to split up what formations of Stukas cared to put in an appearance, and there had been several combats with enemy fighters. From then on the pursuit to Enfidaville gave D.A.F. a selectionof easy targets, for in six days 8th Army covered 150 miles. The retreating enemy, as before, forced to abandon forward airfields, could put up only faint opposition. "Intensive air operations continued. Formations of bombers and strong forces of fighter-bombers harried the enemy moving north-eastwards from Mezzouna and northwards from Mahares." During April 7th and 8th it was estimated that 130 enemy trucks were destroyed and more than 200 damaged. On April 8th alone, 11 attacks by 162 Allied bombers dovetailed with low-level strafing by 300 American, South African, English and Australian fighter-bombers. That night, Wellingtons of Strategic Air Force took up the tale. On the 10th, Marauders, Bostons and Mitchells joined with Hurricanes, Kittyhawks, Warhawks, Spitfires, Bisleys and French Leo 45's to rout the enemy columns. A dazzling constellation of international talent glittered over Tunisia as the star of German ascendancy faded from the sky.

As supply dumps exploded and flames from wrecked petrol bowsers illuminated the tired, desperate faces of some of the finest German Divisions on any front, fragmentation bombs were creating havoc not only at El Alouina and Bizerta, but at Borizzo, Palermo and Trapani, where Strategic Air Force extended its fingers to depress the arteries through which air supplies could flow.

From the time that German air transport had poured troops into Tunis and Bizerta just after the Allied landings in Algeria, traffic in Ju. 52's and heavy six-engined Me. 323's had increased to an average of well over 150 a day. Since the Ju. 52 could carry two-and-a-half tons and the Me. 323 over ten tons, their loads in aggregate supplied all the needs of German forces in Tunisia for one day in every three. If Rommel had complained at the time of El Alamein, "*Kesselring shickt mir kein' shprit*,"[1] von Arnim had no cause for dissatisfaction.

During January, February and March a plan to dislocate this phenomenal air traffic was carefully prepared. Reports as to numbers and points of departure of fighter escorts were plotted against routes, times of take-off and refuelling centres. By April the plan was ready to be put into practice. Whilst those already airborne were to be hunted by Lightnings, a crushing surprise blow was to be delivered against all their bases simultaneously. On the first day of "Pegasusdämmerung", April 5th, when the air effort was mainly American, reconnaissance showed that 161 aircraft had been destroyed on the ground in Tunisia and Sicily, whilst forty had been caught in the air; nine Allied aircraft were missing. During the 10th and 11th, when D.A.F. was helping to disorganize enemy troops rushing back to Enfidaville, aircraft from the "other side" struck a second blow against German air transport; seventy-one more Ju. 52's were claimed. Such tremendous losses made the massacre of Ju. 52's at the time of the retreat from Benghazi seem insignificant in comparison. If the Germans had been discouraged then, how much more were they to be dismayed by this second deadlier *débâcle!*

The *coup de grâce* was withheld; it was to be dealt by D.A.F. when plans for the final assault on Tunisia were maturing, when the fighter-bombers, of little use against an enemy in hilly wooded country, could be spared from close support. On April 18th four Warhawk squadrons of the American 57th Pursuit Group, with top cover of Spitfires from 92 squadron, came to grips with a hundred Ju. 52's near Cape Bon.

But what had led up to that moment? And why hadn't it arrived sooner? The backstage politics of that interception provide a good example of how the human element can affect a material situation. Desert Air Force, on the basis of its own Intelligence reports of enemy air transport, had decided how best to employ its aircraft. At certain times of the day at certain points in the Gulf of Tunis, they calculated, there was more likelihood of catching the Germans. But, on the other hand, these points were distant. Kittyhawks and Spitfires, operating at utmost range, would be able to remain in the selected area for only short intervals. Therefore a disheartening situation might arise; the patrolling aircraft might sight an air convoy only to find that, at that very moment, shortage of petrol might force them to turn and make for home. Weak patrols, fed into the air at chosen intervals, offered a tempting solution. But the Germans were short of aircraft; they preferred to despatch a few large convoys, needing in ratio less fighter protection than a number of smaller

[1] Dialect: "Kesselring ain't sending me gas."

ones. Weak patrols would have little chance of piercing the screen behind which the heavy, defenceless, transport monoplanes lumbered on their way to Tunisia, but large patrols might well be a waste of time and effort.

For the first few days this was alarmingly true. D.A.F. was out in strength, but nothing was sighted, though traffic was known to be running. Those were anxious days for the A.O.C. D.A.F., as for his men; the morale of air crew sent out on transport targets would obviously depend on sighting, if not on directly engaging, the enemy. But the Mediterranean sky continued to yield none of its secrets.

Doubts were expressed as to whether the air crew were carrying out every detail of their orders. Patrols were nominally stepped from sea level upwards, but pilots were sometimes disinclined to fly for long periods low over the sea. Yet it became increasingly clear that to escape detection this was precisely what the Germans were doing. On April 17th the A.O.C. was at pains to impress on all his squadron commanders the necessity for explaining the purpose of the sweeps exhaustively to all the pilots concerned. The carnage of the next day justified his words. The cumbersome formations of Ju. 52's were almost in view of Cape Bon when they met the British and American aeroplanes. They were too close to the sea to weave, and there was no time to gain height. They heaved slowly towards the coast, the machine-guns of the Warhawks tearing them apart one by one, petrol tanks exploding and fire racing all over their fuselage. Some tried to make land, some tried to turn back, and some were seen diving deliberately, unhit, into the sea. More than half the total were destroyed. The pilots of D.A.F., who had tried their hand at so many different tasks, were now thoroughly initiated into the mysteries of the new pursuit. The next day was the turn of the South African 7 Wing; one pilot was lost for fifteen out of eighteen enemy destroyed.

The Germans reacted swiftly; standing fighter patrols near Cape Bon took over from the escorting Me. 109's in a desperate attempt to allow the defenceless transports safe entry to the Tunisian front. Countering this move, 244 Wing Spitfires were sent against the standing patrols, leaving the Kittyhawks and the Warhawks free to venture over the sea. Before the *Luftwaffe* could evolve fresh counter tactics, 7 Wing, escorted by Spitfires, fell on a formation of the gigantic Me. 323's in the Gulf of Tunis and destroyed thirty. According to pilots' reports they were carrying petrol, for many burst into flames before hitting the sea.

That conflagration was the funeral pyre of the German daytime air transport supply services. There had been only some 250 Ju. 52's available for the journey from Sicily to Tunis, for possible reinforcements had gone to the Russian front. Magnificent as the work of these few had been, daily losses on such a scale could not be borne. From now on the transports tried to slip through by night, until this attempt, too, was thwarted by Beaufighters of 600 squadron and Hurricanes of 73 squadron. The troop-carriers were to be used once more to ferry out German air force specialists, some of the staff of *Fliegerführer Tunis*, and some sick and wounded. But this was a measure of desperation; air transport, had it been there, could have moved quantities of valuable equipment, which in fact had to be left behind.

The last card in the supply game had now been played. The German trump had been over-trumped, ships alone would have to supply the trapped armies of the Axis. Accordingly, during April the Royal Navy and the R.A.F. increased their attentions to the sole source of supply, the sea. Towards the end of the month Desert Air Force Kittyhawks and Warhawks adapted themselves to their fresh targets; their best day was the 30th, when they sank a destroyer, an escort vessel, a merchant vessel of 1,000 tons, a siebel ferry, an E-boat and an F-boat, besides damaging others. Desert Air Force, which even during a land battle had always been prepared to switch its effort onto convoy protection in the dark days when Malta was a besieged garrison, now showed equal *élan* when the tables had been turned and enemy shipping was running the gauntlet. As though to demonstrate their versatility, they were to return almost immediately to full direct support for the 8th Army's new push along the axis of the Medjez-Massicault-Tunis road.

In honour of the offensive, N.A.T.A.F. had convened a conference to decide how best to use its vast numbers. There was almost an *embarras de richesse*, for tactical air forces from all parts of Tunisia could join hands whenever and wherever they wished. Air supremacy was practically complete. The *Luftwaffe* could only spare aircraft to attack escorted bombers. The whole of N.A.T.A.F., for a short time at least, could be used for direct support. Deployed in such overwhelming strength, air power ensured that the enemy's last days in Tunisia was a disorganized rout without hope of withdrawal.

In direct offensive, air power blasted a way in the front of our troops, whilst concentrations to the rear were split up and disorganized. 2,500 sorties were flown on the first day of the advance; light bombers of Tactical Air Force—acting as part of the artillery barrage preceding the infantry—attacked the enemy positions at Bordj Fredj; aircraft of Tactical Bomber Force immobilized a convoy of a hundred trucks near St. Cyprien, whilst D.A.F. Kittyhawks and American Warhawks bombed and strafed traffic south and west of Tunis.

In direct defensive, air power threw a shield, as impenetrable as a smoke-screen, over Medjez. The 3,000-yard front and the one narrow bridge across which troops had to advance created a bottleneck, contrasted with which the El Hamma funnel was a wide causeway. All supplies for six divisions had to flow across this narrow ribbon; an army of robots could not have prevented traffic jams and congestion; yet, as at El Hamma, this ideal target begged in vain for the *Luftwaffe*.

By May 8th the enemy had only two aerodromes left in the Cape Bon peninsula. Throughout the day they could fly a mere sixty sorties over

Tunisia, and of these, some were sustained by Pantellaria-based fighters fitted with long-range tanks. The German air force was now concerned solely with the problem of extricating itself as best it could. The next day there were still fewer sorties; after that, none. By night the few surviving Ju. 52's tried to bring in stores, but their heroism went unrewarded, for they could do too little, too late.

Naval guns bombarded the remnants of troops left in the Cape Bon peninsula. Allied air forces bombed and strafed an army facing a Mediterranean Dunkirk. As though to maintain a parallel, a few small ships crossed the narrow Sicilian straits to try and rescue survivors, but this Dunkirk was the 1943 version; air power above matched sea power below to prevent any hope of escape. Desert Air Force was once more switched away from direct support, this time in order to be flung out over the little island of Pantellaria. Escorted Bostons, Baltimores and Mitchells attacked the airfields there to ensure that not only was the *Luftwaffe* to be driven out of North Africa, but that there were to be no floating aircraft-carriers, no Maltas, for it to turn to.

Switched back once more to direct support where the air was now alive with leaflets calling on the Germans to surrender, D.A.F. fighter-bombers continued to bomb and strafe whilst light and medium bombers found plentiful targets in the area between Zagouan and St. Marie du Zit.

There was little fight left in the enemy. On the 9th the 15th Panzer Division surrendered; by the 11th the armoured drive to Hammamet had sealed the peninsula. The veteran 90th Light Division, which it seemed that 8th Army were to be pursuing until the end of time, fought on, but Baltimores and Mitchells of Desert Air Force sought them out twice; these final blows, coupled with the exertions of the land forces, brought about their surrender. D.A.F. had attacked targets in North Africa for the last time.

. . . . .

It seemed somehow incredible, an appalling anti-climax to the past there years. When, on May 14th, the Tunisian campaign came to an end, Desert Air Force, flushed with victory, found itself dazed by the fact of its own prowess. What was to happen now? What was to follow? Now that the battle itself was over and won, the aim and object of the Desert Air Force seemed to be complete. The happy certainty of those days from Alamein onwards had disappeared; and in some ways there were few who could not but regret its passing.

For the airmen had steadily been drawing away from those great dusty areas where they had found a home for so long. Gambut, so distant now as to be the fragment of a dream, was behind them forever. The blue lagoon of Mersa Matruh, Benina with its little green trees, the lonely grandeur of Marble Arch, all were gone, never to return. Men were to go out into the blue no longer. In all these things there was sadness. Even the knowledge of a job well done could not displace the memory of those long, sand-filled days, when only the immediate problem mattered, and when the only reward was the sound of a friendly voice. That so many friends had gone forever did not bear reflection; even in the moment of victory their death still remained unavenged, as it would always remain. It was no consolation to know that the enemy, in the moment of defeat, shared the same feelings stripped of the elation of success.

Thus nostalgia, at the time perhaps unrealized, crept in, not to weaken, but to strengthen the bond already drawing all the members of Desert Air Force together in fellowship. For the Desert had brought its own recompense. In exchange for hardship it had given a kind of tough happiness, self-confidence, and comradeship. The sand had indeed entered into their souls, leaving them a little withered, but with an indefinable inner contentment.

Tunisia, bare and sandy though it could be in parts, was not Desert. Everywhere were evidences of rural if not urban civilization. Grapevines surrounded farmsteads where clustering trees were too small to conceal the vanes of an iron windmill; groves of olive, escorted by prickly pear, marched towards the coasts. In the battered capital, hotels still offered amenities, taps ran hot and cold, ice from refrigerators tinkled in glasses. In Tripoli there had been the theory but not the fact of urban comforts. But in Tunis the facts were there for all to see.

The men of Desert Air Force, like those of 8th Army, after spending so much time in primitive conditions, were once more back in familiar, though foreign, surroundings. They no longer had to deal with tiny scattered populations who took no part in the war, who existed, it seemed, solely in order to sell eggs and chickens. Benghazi had given hints of what was to come; Tripoli had shown them what had been rather than what was; Tunis was a city, and alive.

There the men of D.A.F. began to meet the men of other air forces, whilst 8th Army started to become acquainted with 1st and 5th Army. These strangers from the other side of North Africa had been working with them for some months; now here they were, face to face—two forces with different ideas, different ways of doing things, different traditions.

The Past had brought a way of life to splendid fruition; the Present dangled Tunis before their eyes; the Future carried prospects of a fusing of forces with men who had never known the Desert. Victory clearly possessed many facets.

There were many new adjustments to be made. Before a natural regret for the *Neiges D'Antan* had time to arise, it was overwhelmed by fresh preparations for fresh ventures. Air Marshal Tedder sent a message to all ranks of the Allied Air Forces:

> "By magnificent teamwork between nationalities, commands, units, officers and men from Teheran to Takoradi, from Morocco to the Indian

Ocean, you have, together with your comrades on land and sea, driven the enemy out of Africa. You have shown the world the unity and strength of air power. A grand job well finished. We face our next job with the knowledge that we have thrashed the enemy, and the determination to thrash him again."

Our next job . . . As most of D.A.F. accompanied units of 8th Army back to Tripoli, all knew that wherever 8th Army went, D.A.F. would go too. The partnership would continue.

CHAPTER XXIV

NORTH AFRICA . . . CONCLUSIONS

THIS account has consistently emphasized the increasingly decisive part played by air power in the North African campaigns. Full details have been given in order to show how, why, when and where. If the air has taken precedence over the land aspect of the campaign, this method of presentation has been intentional. Wars in the past have inevitably been seen through military or naval eyes, and the air point of view is so unfamiliar as to require unusual emphasis.

The Air Force, which in the early days in the Desert was mainly a useful irritant, later became an essential part of the whole war effort, capable of wrecking enemy supply lines and protecting its own by its own exertions.

The war in the Middle East was a war of supplies, which the Axis Command, in spite of starting with every advantage, lost and went on losing. Their superior air force was at first frittered away on purely tactical targets, and devoted almost entirely to shipping protection. They were blamed for having lost an air war which they had hardly ever been allowed to fight. Their maintenance was unimpressive throughout. They had not won sufficient bargaining power to get their fair share of supplies in competition with the land forces. Thus, though they had spectacular success when present in overwhelming numbers, they could not rescue the German army in defeat. Their air transport, which with air superiority had waved a magic wand over problems of supply, was blown out of the sky by Allied fighters.

It must, however, be appreciated that the Germans developed a fine system of direct support whilst they possessed air superiority, and that they had the foresight to create an air transport system long before we did. They were organized to win a quick war which in itself prevented them from building up an air force by long-distance planning.

Before the start of Crusader, Tedder was able to guarantee air parity at least. Generally speaking, from then onwards the German air force was in decline. It might therefore be considered that in view of the handicaps of organization and maintenance during the next year, the *Luftwaffe* put up a remarkably stubborn fight.

This serves to emphasize the excellent achievement of R.A.F. Middle East; enhances the reputation of those responsible for creating such a force; for R.A.F. Middle East went from weakness to strength with D.A.F. constantly reshuffled and reorganized in order to arrive at the best method of air/army co-operation.

The air side of the victory had been a triumph of administration, and of maintenance, shared by the Orderly Room Corporal, the Fitter, the Staff Officer, and the Technical Expert alike. Air crew, the operational spearhead, represented the final point of a long durable shaft, supple to bend, unable to break.

The Prime Minister's pronouncement after operation Battleaxe, as to how air power was *not* to be used, stopped any tendency to look upon D.A.F. as a convenient piece of specialized artillery. As a result, the air battle could be fought first, and then the army could be given the most effective help. In the retreat to Alamein the air alone could sound the offensive note; at El Hamma, the army followed on the heels of a concentrated air attack which achieved what it set out to do; at the start of the final break-through, the air was able to guarantee complete protection from the *Luftwaffe*. During the last days of the Tunisian campaign, air power spread confusion and dismay, joining with the Royal Navy in preventing a German Dunkirk. To quote Montgomery at Tripoli:

> "On your behalf I have sent a special message to the Allied Air Forces that have co-operated with us. I don't suppose that any army has ever been supported by such a magnificent air striking force. I have always maintained that the 8th Army and the R.A.F. in the Western Desert together constitute one fighting machine, and therein lies our great strength."

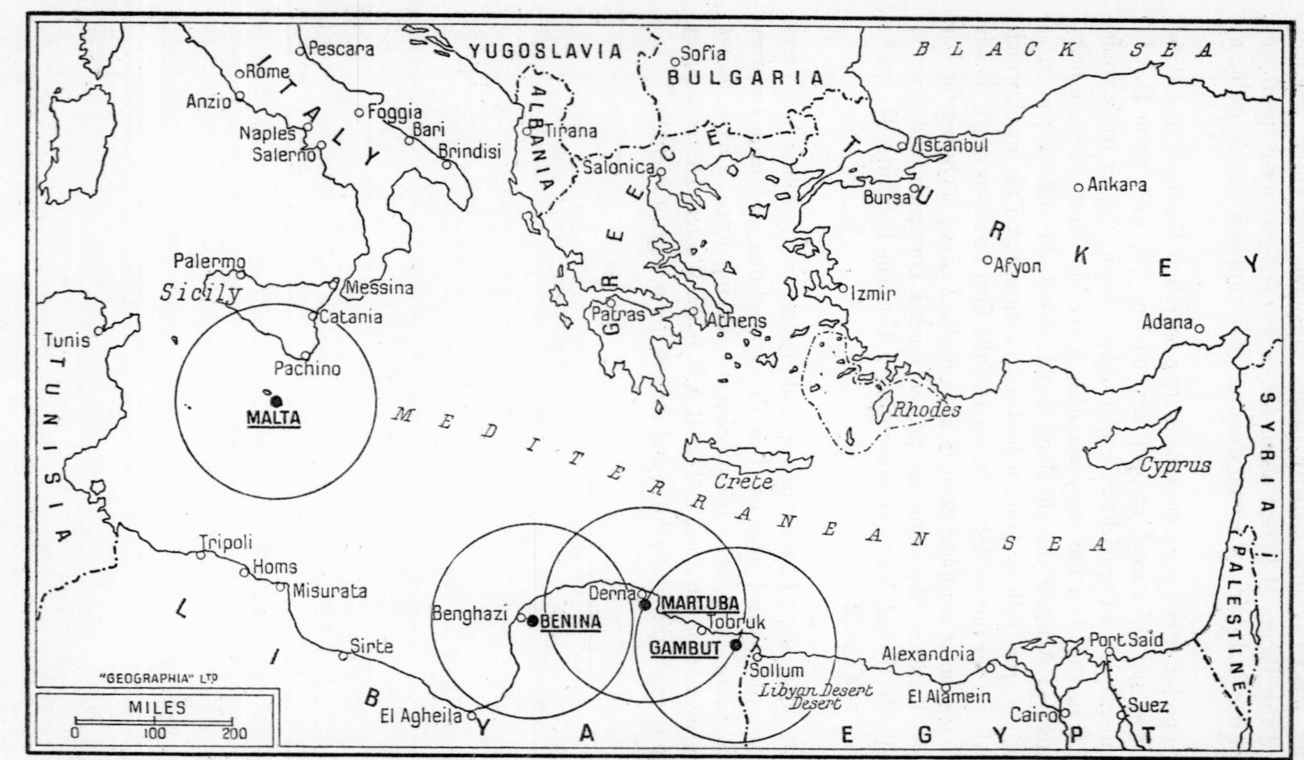

Map showing the importance of Gambut, Martuba, and Benina Airfields, in terms of Fighter protection. With the German Air Force established in Crete, these airfields on the Libyan shore had to be in British hands if the convoys running between Alexandria and Malta were to be given adequate air cover.

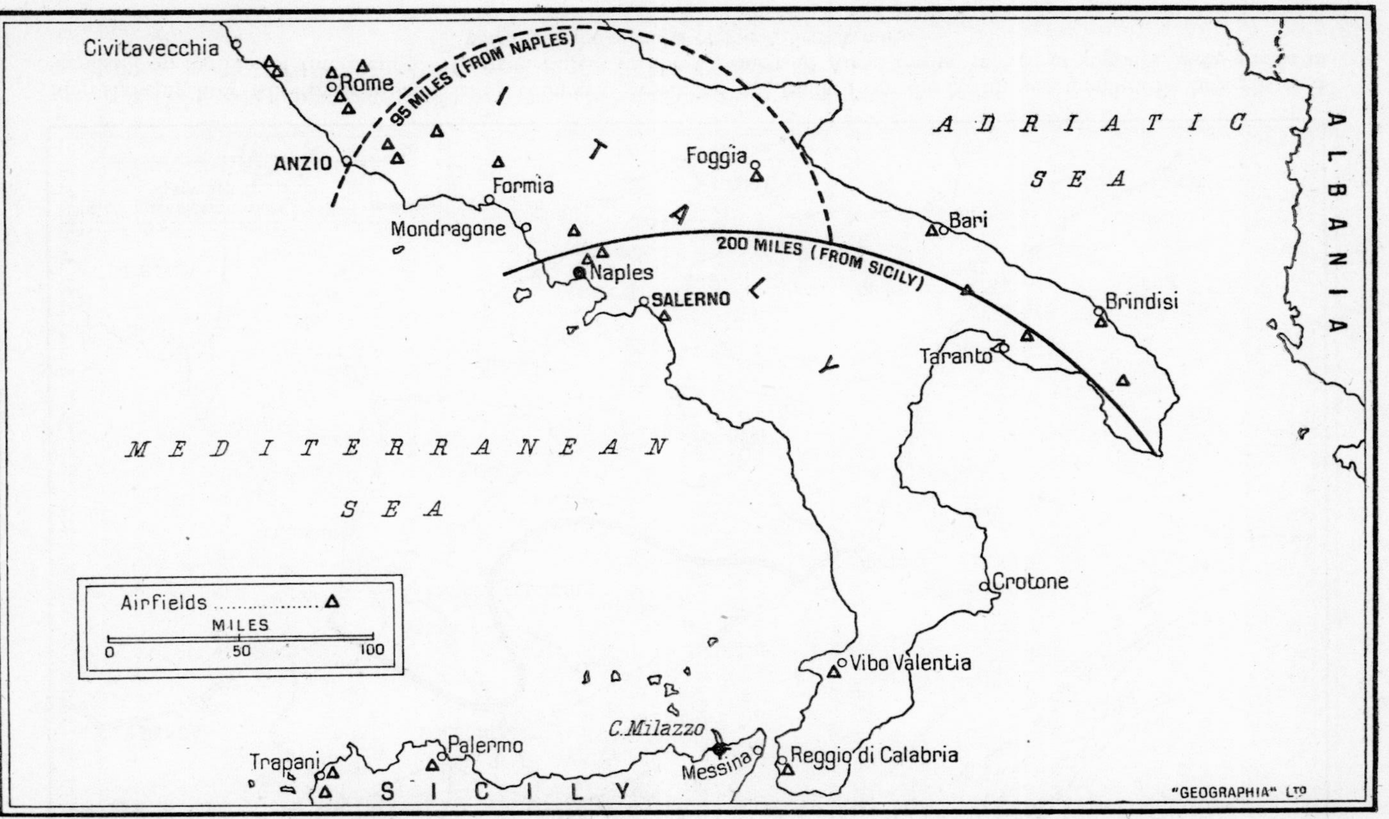

Map showing the inevitability of the landings at Salerno. Effective air coverage from Sicily extended to points only a few miles north of Naples.

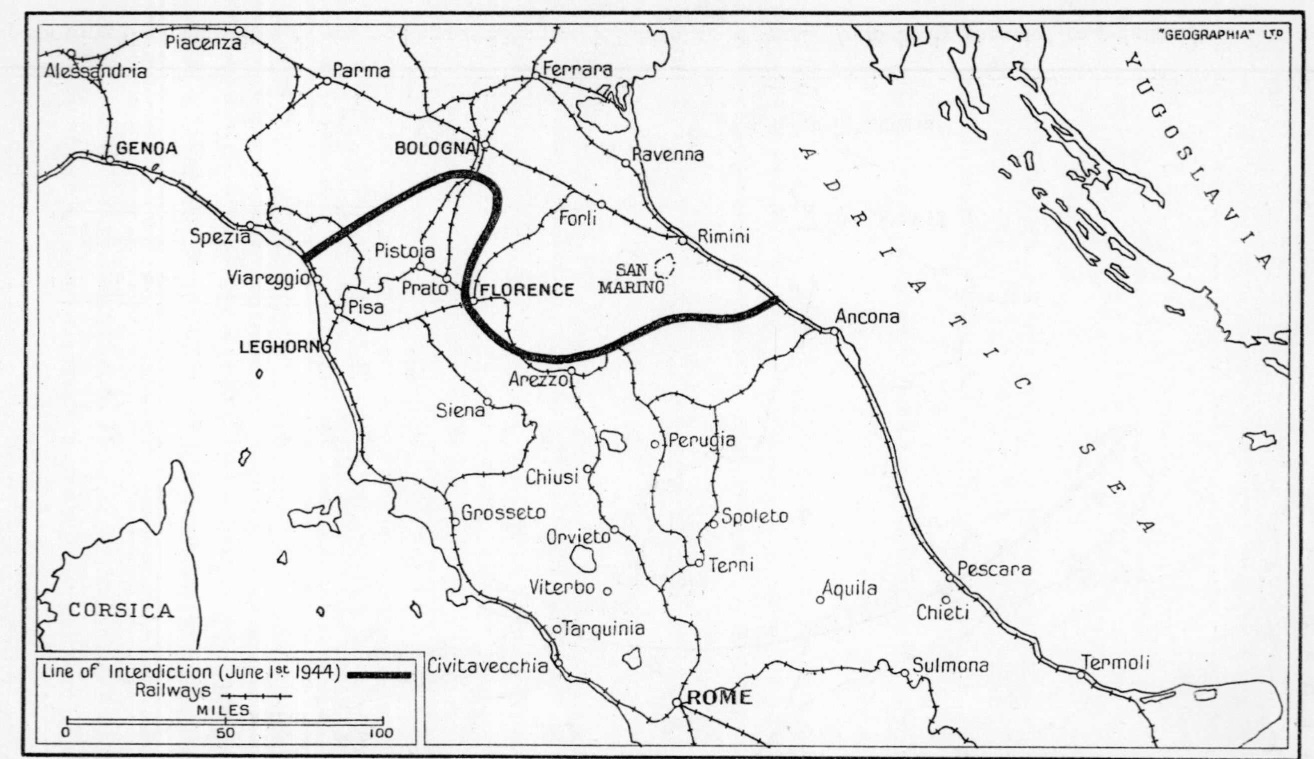

Map showing how Air Power isolated half a country. Road and rail traffic from the North was temporarily brought to a standstill on the line of Interdiction. German Forces on the Cassino and Anzio fronts, starved of supplies, were unable to withstand the assaults of the Allied Armies.

BOOK II

CHAPTER XXV

PREPARATIONS FOR SICILY

WHILST the German radio dilated on "the wave of terror which has now begun in Tunisia", Japanese forces in the Aleutians were withdrawing to Chicago Bay. In Burma, the British Long Range Penetration Group had returned to base after crossing 250 miles of enemy-held territory, with the destruction of the Mandalay railway at seventy-five places to its credit. In Russia, attack and counter-attack south of Lake Ilmen and north of the Orel salient matched the same semi-static conditions in the Veliki Luki area and the region south-west of Krimskaya.

The world war seemed to be passing through one of those less decisive phases which by comparison with more stirring times appeared uneventful, and, in a purely relative sense, peaceful.

Appearances were deceptive; for though there were no more final battles or completed campaigns, less dramatic preparations, which each side fervently hoped would bring victory, were in progress as before. Factories in London and Birmingham, Berlin and Cologne, Moscow, Milan, Tokyo and Pittsburg supplied the fighting services as before; reorganization and redistribution went on as before; plans were being made, modified, or rejected as before. Against this setting Allied air power glittered like a small brilliant diamond. Bombers were over Wilhelmshaven and Emden to destroy the U-boat pens, over coke ovens at Zeebrugge, over Lorient, over Bordeaux, whilst in Sicily and southern Italy railway junctions at Catania, Messina, San Giovanni and Reggio were in constant jeopardy. The effects of air power were often startling; the destruction that could be dealt to areas "behind the lines" usurped a place in the public imagination which had formerly been occupied by saboteurs.

To describe D.A.F. merely as one of the smaller facets of that diamond would, however, hardly be adequate. Even though it was now part of T.A.F., itself under N.W.A.A.F., it had the record, traditions and integrity of a special (though not separate) air force. Its importance had not diminished because there were now so many other air forces in the field, for there were now so many more functions which air power was called upon and was able to perform.

To 8th Army in particular, D.A.F. was *the* air force. Months of personal contact had given them complete confidence in it. The fact that they were liable to regard all other air forces with suspicion had to be taken into account during the planning for landings in Sicily (Operation "Husky").

Pending this, D.A.F. withdrew to the Tripoli area for rest, recovery, and training, shedding as it did so some of its units to Tactical Bomber Force. During the next month still more were to be detached—this time to Malta. But in Sicily most of these were once more to be welcomed back into the flock; and in Italy D.A.F. was to represent the British, as 12th A.S.C. the American, contribution to direct support.

Tactical Bomber Force, which at first swallowed and later disgorged parts of D.A.F., had arisen in March to co-ordinate and direct the activities of the light bombers; the advantages of such specialization being that targets could be selected more quickly and be more heavily pounded at shorter notice than by any other means.

There were, however, various disadvantages which finally outweighed the points in favour and led to the disbandment of the British part of T.B.F.; not, it was true, directly after the defeat of the Axis forces in North Africa (which T.B.F. had been expressly designed to hasten), but after a period of juggling for control of units which from the D.A.F. point of view should never have been in its hands. For the establishment of a separate tactical H.Q. implied that other formations would lose control of their tactical bombers. Neither D.A.F. nor 8th Army could welcome this if it meant that requests for that type of close support would have to be made to an agency "outside the firm". Nor was there much solace to be derived from the assurance that "bigger and better close support" would result.

This partisan standpoint, wrong from one angle, right from another, was nevertheless a very definite factor in destroying first the power and then the R.A.F. establishment of T.B.F. The episode well illustrated the only defect from which a loyal and compact force like D.A.F. or 8th Army could suffer—suspicion of the outsider who played the game according to new rules.

Two squadrons of the American 12th Bombardment Group flew to T.B.F. immediately, but the Group at that time had no ground staff and little equipment. The brunt of maintenance fell on the British Servicing Commandos; spares had to come from American units of the 12th Air Force. On the other hand, 18 and 114 squadrons, scheduled to convert from Bisleys to Bostons, borrowed two A. 20's from the American 47th Bombardment Group. The *quid* was *pro quo*. T.B.F. performed further feats of Anglo/American co-operation when the most experienced navigators of 18 and 114 squadrons were lent to the 47th Bombardment Group to act as leading bombardiers on daylight missions. T.B.F. was also successful in liaising with the 8th Groupement Free French air force; a flarepath for diversionary landings was laid and maintained by 326 Wing; a signals channel was opened between Oulmene and Biskra.

By the end of the Tunisian campaign T.B.F. had been operating for fifty-three days (forty-one flying days), in which it had averaged seventy-seven sorties per day. This, added to its night effort, made an impressive total, for apart from the fact that the two Mitchell squadrons had no ground crews and that men had to be lent to the 47th Group, Bisleys were only suitable for night-flying and Boston replacement was slow.

Here is an example:

18 squadron had its first Boston on loan from the Americans on February 9th. Flying practice started on the 14th, when General Eisenhower visited the aerodrome. On March 7th the Boston was returned (total none), but four days later another was borrowed for further training (total one). On the 21st the first three Bostons arrived from Egnland and another was received on loan from the Americans on the 27th (total five). Another Boston arrived on the 31st and from then until April 20th another ten Bostons were received and the American one returned (total fifteen). Two days later one Boston crashed at the new aerodrome, Kings Cross (total fourteen). One aircraft was lost the next day; and on the 25th a further aircraft and its crew were lost after attacking an enemy strongpoint; then two aircraft collided after rendezvous with fighter escort (total ten); the following day two replacements arrived (total twelve), on the 27th one more, one on the 28th, and one on the 30th (total fifteen).

Fresh aircraft brought fresh problems. A report on July 11th sounded a note of desperation. Spares for Bostons were in illogically short supply; about 26 per cent of the aircraft were due for Major Inspections within forty flying hours; serviceability was only being maintained by cannibalization, that disastrous long-term policy; absence of wing jacks and other special equipment had to be overcome by the initiative of the men on the units, who had meanwhile still to maintain the old Bisleys.

The replacements, welcome though they were, were neither the latest nor the most efficient light bombers available in 1943. Bostons, which had appeared in the Middle East in 1941, were to be in service right up to the end of the war in Italy. D.A.F.'s further contribution to the science of light bomber employment was to be made with aircraft which 2nd Tactical Air Force in Normandy would have considered outmoded.

Having shown that it could work well under handicaps, T.B.F. started to swell with phenomenal rapidity. As from May 16th some of the best-loved D.A.F. units came under the hammer and were transferred to the new command; 232 Wing, controlling 223 and 55 squadrons (which had opened the campaign in 1940 by interrupting the Italian Commander at El Adem), 3 S.A.A.F. (the first light-bomber wing in the Desert), and the other two squadrons, 83 and 434, of the 12th Bombardment Group (the first American Bomb Group to start operations in Middle East). And in the train of these long-established D.A.F. pioneers followed the Maintenance and Supply Services, 51 R.S.U. and 31 A.S.P. 121 M.U. and 10 S. & T., scheduled to go too, never finally went.

Administrative control still remained with D.A.F. It was clear that the units were regarded as lent only for a particular operational purpose and that they were still part of their traditional parent body.

Being lent to T.B.F., however, gave D.A.F. a share in the bombardment of Pantellaria, just as later, being lent to the American 12th T.A.F., was to allow them to claim a share in the landings at Salerno and Anzio. As in the Desert, so in Sicily, Italy, France, Yugoslavia, and Austria, D.A.F. units were to have fingers in every pie.

Pantellaria was the Italian equivalent of Heligoland; a forbidden zone since 1926, a volcanic rock pockmarked by a hundred or so gun emplacements, supporting an aerodrome with underground hangars and powerful radar apparatus. To declare, as Mussolini did, that it was impregnable, was, in an air age, nonsense. However, its forty-two-and-a-half square miles were defended by some 10,000 men, well provisioned, with sufficient though not ample supplies of water.

The island functioned chiefly as a gigantic spying glass to keep Rome informed of every movement in the narrow straits, on the North African coast, and in the air above. To mount an invasion of Sicily without first knocking out Pantellaria was to enable the enemy to give a running commentary of top-secret news. To leave its eighty aircraft unmolested was to invite attacks on formations bombing in support of the landings at Gela.

Since the island had to be reduced it was decided to make the assault a laboratory experiment. Professor Zuckermann was called in to advise on the quantity of thousand-pound bombs needed to give an even chance of silencing two of the six guns in each battery and of neutralizing four by other means (such as the dislocation of communications, lowering of morale of the gun crews, etc.).

Though the island guinea pig would absorb engine hours, time, and effort which might be employed to advantage over Sicily, there might never be another chance to study the effect of bombs on heavily fortified, heavily defended, emplacements.

T.B.F.'s sortie rate rose from 72 on June 6th to 131 the next day, to 167 and on the 9th to 240. But to give some idea of the overall picture, of the 4,656 tons dropped on the island between the 6th and its surrender, only 170 were dropped by T.B.F. Bombardment on June 8th in particular, by naval cruisers, synchronized with heavy attacks by Flying Fortresses. Strategic Air Force had joined in the fray.

Assault forces embarked to capture the island, but before their craft arrived a white cross of surrender lay out on the airfield and a white flag flew from the Commander's Headquarters. Although there was opposition to the landings from part of the garrison out of the Governor's control, it was clear that sheer weight of bombs had reduced a floating blockhouse and broken the spirit of its defenders.

Just before this scientific unleashing of destruction 326 Wing with 18 and 114 squadrons had moved to the grassy plain of Grombalia. The prelude to Pantellaria was a descent on the landing-ground of a galaxy of V.I.P.'s[1]—the Prime Minister, the Foreign Secretary, the Chief of Imperial General Staff, Tedder, and Coningham. On the day that the island surrendered Lord Trenchard, that protagonist of air power, arrived. By the time that His Majesty the King visited the aerodrome a week later, Lampedusa had fallen within a day after bombardment by naval guns and by medium and light bombers; American units of 12th A.S.C. were already installed in their new bases; obstacles barring the invasion of Sicily had all been removed.

Whilst the bombers of T.B.F. were fully employed, Desert Air Force was already *en route* for Malta.

244 Wing was the first to go. Preparations continued feverishly. New establishments and new scales of equipment had been received; men and equipment were being sorted out to conform with them. The aerodrome construction sappers built them a ramp from the jetty from which drivers could be exercised in driving off landing craft through the water. By the 8th about half of the vehicles and the whole of the Wing signals section were at the assembly area. On the 14th the aircraft of 1 S.A.A.F., 92, and 145 squadrons took off for Malta, to be followed the next day by 601 and 417 squadrons.

Aircraft of 244 Wing crowded into shelter pens in three dispersal areas. The equipment and vehicles had to be stored in quarries pending embarkation for Sicily; waterproofing arrangements had to be completed. If stowing the machines brought special problems, disposing of the men was even more difficult. The island was filling up rapidly with army and R.A.F. Conditions described by the vanguard as "cramped" were, in the opinion of later arrivals, palatial. The officers of 244 Wing found accommodation in the Modern Imperial Hotel, Sliema; other ranks in a specially prepared tented camp outside the station perimeter. Buses ran to and fro with air crew; and though the arrangement was not ideal, it worked satisfactorily.

That Malta could handle and supply so many new units after enduring such a long siege was in itself an amazing commentary on the efficiency of the supply system. The island was turning into a vast arsenal for the coming offensive. Hollows in the rock which had sheltered the population during German bombardment now became storage chambers. From January to June, Malta airfields had been improved and extended, their capacity stretched to operate twenty-six fighter squadrons. A Combined War Room next door to the Army Support Control guaranteed liaison between the services. By D minus 7 (seven days before the invasion of Sicily) there were twenty Spitfire squadrons, five night-fighter squadrons, four flights of mixed ground recon-

[1] Very Important Personages.

naissance aircraft, and the ground crews of three fighter-bomber Wings whose aircraft, as the report put it, were "still on the mainland almost literally awaiting space to set down". A giant aircraft-carrier, moored at a strategic point in the Mediterranean, Malta was now ready to play the part for which it had been nursed during the dark days of 1940, 1941 and 1942.

Towards the end of the month 244 Wing were carrying out offensive sweeps over southern Italy. July 4th sponsored the softening-up process; 601 and 1 S.A.A.F., together with Spitfires of 152 and 249 squadrons, gave close support to forty-eight Mitchell bombers over Comiso; later in the same day 92 and 145 squadrons provided high cover for Mitchells and Marauders attacking Gerbini.

At Malta, Advanced H.Q. D.A.F. shared a joint Headquarters with 8th Army, but for the moment control of operations rested with the Air Officer Commanding Malta, who also controlled the American units on Gozo and Pantellaria. Immediately the landing had been completed and the bridgehead enlarged the 57th and 79th U.S.A.A.F. Groups and 239 Wing R.A.F. all moved into Malta, whilst the light bomber units stayed on the Tunisian mainland.

Softening up, for Tactical Air Force, started with the central Sicilian airfields (for which Malta provided escort), and the western airfields (for which escort was provided by units from Tunisia and Pantellaria). In the main, the great Gerbini/Catania group of airfields was left to the Strategic Air Force, whose efforts since June 20th were constant, and whose steadily mounting harvest of destruction was a sure sign that there would not and could not be any last-minute enemy air counter-offensive.

Opposition was described as "patchy". The *Luftwaffe* could only afford to intercept a few raids; hence, of the formations visiting the same locality at half-hour intervals, one might be attacked and the other go free. Over the period of the invasion, if an aircraft was seen overhead the chances were only one in thirty that it would be enemy.

At the outset, however, Tactical Bomber Force came up against some stiff enemy opposition, but this fell off towards the 9th, when only the two airfields of Sciacca and Milo in the western sector were serviceable, and when Comiso and Gerbini could only be used intermittently. As the amount of landing-grounds which the enemy could put into use decreased, so those that were left were more heavily defended by a stronger concentration of flak—virtually every raid suffered flak casualties.

By the eve of the invasion, comparative air strengths showed that an enormous advantage lay with the Allies. 4,000 aircraft were available for operations directly connected with the new campaign; in addition there was the large American glider force. In broad outline, the R.A.F. supplied the fighters, fighter-bombers, and coastal aircraft, whilst the bomber and transport forces were American. But exceptions, the American units which had been with

D.A.F., and 12th Air Support Command, were many. The heavy night-bombers were mainly R.A.F., whilst the light bombers could almost be called hybrid.

Against this total, the Axis in Sicily, Italy, Sardinia, and southern France could muster 1,800 to 1,900. Of these in Sicily and southern Italy immediately available for operations there were only 260 German and 200 Italian fighters and fighter-bombers. The German twin-engined fighters (75 in all) were half in Sicily and northern Italy and half in central and southern Italy. There were also fifty Ju. 88's in Sicily, the rest of the German long-range bomber force being in Italy and southern France.

Small wonder, then, that Allied air power on the eve of the assault had achieved all its aims. The inferior enemy air forces had been scattered; unable to cohere so long as the bombing continued, they were not only driven from one airfield to another, but even pushed back onto airfields in Italy. German fighters were already defeated before the land battle began. July 5th was the last day on which any serious German intervention was encountered; and from then on their activity was negligible. Only a few night attacks hindered the assembly and dispatch of the invasion forces from their ports in North Africa; only one enemy attack disturbed the smooth progress of the vast seaborne armada. Allied naval authorities had been prepared to lose 300 ships; but in three days, on the British side, three motor-boats and one specially illuminated hospital ship were sunk; and the Americans lost two destroyers, two submarine chasers, and six landing craft. Other ships were damaged, though not seriously. Of eighty-nine *Luftwaffe* raids, twenty-six were intercepted before reaching their target.

Incessant pounding of the Messina ferry was meanwhile hindering the flow of Axis supplies into Sicily, shortening the struggle in advance.

Thus, before the opening blow had apparently been struck, before the general public realized that there was a new campaign afoot, in fact a great part of the battle had already been fought by Allied air power.

CHAPTER XXVI

INVASION OF SICILY

THE plan for such a tremendous air/amphibious invasion had preceded the bombing, preceded even the rout of German armies in Tunisia. It had crystallized during April after the selection of "D" day in July, when the moon would be at its most favourable.[1]

There was little choice of a flashpoint. Messina, the link to the Italian mainland, was the train ferry centre from which men and material poured into the island from Italy. Messina, alas, could not be captured by direct assault, for those narrow straits were closed to Allied shipping and beyond the range of Allied fighters.

If the attack could only come at a place where beaches could be protected by fighters, the other necessity, a port, did not coincide. Between Avola and Gela in the south-east and between Sciacca and Marinella in the south-west there were no major harbours. The first troops to land would have to be concerned mainly with the capture of Syracuse and Catania in the east or of Palermo in the west.

An initial assault in the east would possibly achieve more surprise and would help to draw off forces from the west. Hence the first plan provided for a series of staggered landings in the east and then in the west—paratroops were to hold certain vital positions to diminish the risk for the main forces coming in by daylight under naval protection with fighter cover.

But modification acted as a simplifier. The final plan, which Eisenhower described as "a series of simultaneous seaborne assaults, assisted by airborne landings, to seize the ports of Syracuse and Licata and the airfields within striking distance of the south-eastern coastline between these two ports in order to establish a firm base for operations against Augusta, Catania and Gerbini airfields", showed that the idea of capturing Syracuse and Palermo simultaneously had been jettisoned. The less risky course (concentration in the south) was to be followed.

Now that both armies were to attempt landings in adjacent areas, the first airborne assault was re-tailored to fit the new plan. American paratroopers, who were to have landed and neutralized beach defences, were now to share in holding inland strongpoints. After a sea route of 400 miles, 350 aircraft and 130 gliders were to drop some 5,000 men in selected areas. The first lot (British) were to land near Syracuse, where some were to hold the canal bridge and the

[1] I.e. a time when the moon was at its second quarter; when it would be light enough up to midnight for an airborne invasion, but dark enough after moonset to allow the approach of naval forces. The 10th was the best date for the month of July.

railway whilst others entered the western suburbs. The second lot (American) were to be dropped six miles east of Gela, to capture and hold the high ground dominating the roads from the beaches.

Apart from the fact that this was the first time that the Allies had attempted airborne assault on such a scale and that there had been little time to train, a high wind sprang up which, far from losing force after twilight, increased to forty miles an hour at the dropping height. Gliders were released too far from the shore; the Navy reported "the depressing sight of large numbers of gliders floating in the water". Twelve only landed in the right area, seventy-five in widely dispersed parts of southern Sicily, the remainder coming to rest on the sea.

Nevertheless, where plan had failed gallantry succeeded. Of the eight officers and sixty-five men who reached the bridge at Syracuse, four officers and fifteen men were found holding their own against an entire battalion supported by field artillery. The relieving patrols, arriving just as they were being forced to withdraw, recaptured the bridge intact.

Outside Gela, the Americans, though surrounded by tanks, succeeded in preventing enemy reinforcements from reaching the beaches. According to Eisenhower: "The operation had a decisive effect on the successful landing and is estimated to have speeded up the inland advance by at least forty-eight hours."

One curious result of the scattering of airborne forces was that the enemy was unnerved to a much greater extent than could have been foreseen, Italian prisoners giving it as their opinion that anything from 20,000 to 30,000 paratroopers had been dropped.

If the first part of the programme had revealed many unlikely and unforeseen corrigenda, the main landings showed less. The high wind blowing from the previous night had not entirely spent its force; on "D" day the state of the sea hampered the landing of supplies quite as much as the lack of sufficient men hindered their unloading. But the new Amphibian D.U.K.W.s (Ducks), which could carry their load to dumps beyond the immediate beachhead area, now proved invaluable. In under two days 15th Army Group landed 80,000 men, 7,000 vehicles, 300 tanks and 900 guns. During that time not only were Syracuse and Licata captured but the ports were in use almost immediately—Licata on the day of entry, Syracuse forty-eight hours later.

Overhead, with many others, patrolled the Spitfires of 244 Wing. On "D" day they had been on continuous patrol, but the invasion had not provided the excitement which had been anticipated. In the early morning 145 squadron sighted eight Me. 109's flying north, but the chase yielded no definite results. At midday some F.W. 190's dived and climbed away too quickly for interception; in the afternoon twenty-two Me. 109's and two Mc. 202's were engaged, but almost immediately afterwards anti-aircraft bursts indicated another six Ju. 88's near Avola; of the latter, one was damaged and one destroyed for the loss of two of our aircraft. No other enemy aeroplanes were sighted during the day.

The ground party of the Wing was meanwhile at sea. On the 9th L.C.T. 411 weighed anchor at dawn and set sail for Sicily by the invasion route, in convoy with some two dozen other landing craft. In the early afternoon the tall Signals' vehicles proved difficult to secure as the craft rolled in the riding sea, but the day passed uneventfully; a mass of ships, compared by an observer to a "moving Spithead Review", thronging all round; a big convoy from England overtaking the party during the afternoon.

There was the usual seasickness, but this on "D" day mostly abated; and the Station Commander's party was astir early. At dawn the convoy seemed lost, but by 10 o'clock L.C.T. 411 was reporting to the Headquarters ship off "Bark East Beach" (Mazarmemi).

By then it was flat calm, with a burning sun, no enemy air activity, and only spasmodic sounds of fighting on land. At 11.30 the L.C.T. beached; all the vehicles would have been ashore within ten minutes but for the fact that inexperience led to mishandling.

As soon as the trucks were de-waterproofed and hunger and thirst satisfied with captured fresh tomatoes, contact was made with the senior R.A.F. officer in the "Beach Brick". It was learnt that the army were "definitely not going to meet their commitment", to provide vehicles to carry operational supplies from the beach dump to the landing-ground, and that, anyway, no operational supplies were ashore. The Servicing Commandos and an R.A.F. Anti-Aircraft unit had been put ashore without transport—a grave error which showed no signs of being rectified.

A visit to Pachino aerodrome disclosed C.R.E. 15th Airfield Construction Group, without their full equipment, busy on its ploughed surface. The engineers guaranteed that the field would be ready on the 13th. By then it was near nightfall; and the men slept by the beach in the lee of a quarry wall.

Throughout the next day the Wing aircraft from Malta destroyed four Ju. 88's and damaged two for the loss of one. Meanwhile, in the early morning, the ground party had moved to Pachino and were there choosing sites for squadron dispersals, for the Wing hospital, and for the Air Evacuation Centre. Two R.A.F. Regiment Anti-Aircraft units arrived, still without their transport, followed by the Air Formation Signals Detachment No. 1 M.P.R.U., and No. 3 Advance Landing-Ground Signals Section.

At ten o'clock General Montgomery appeared in a "Duck", ordering that the landing-ground was to be ready by the next day. But the engineers' plant had not yet arrived and did not get through until the late afternoon.

In the hectic rush that followed the General's order, still more efforts were made to bring ashore transport for the Servicing Commandos; a couple of lorries borrowed from the Station Commander's party were hard at work ferrying aviation fuel. There was still virtually no 20-mm. ammunition on dry land; "Beach Brick" was prodded strenuously for supplies.

At midday, one of the Wing pilots force-landed on the half-levelled surface of the airfield, refuelled, but preferred to take-off again from the road. During the afternoon two more Spitfires landed and were strafed by six Me. 109's before taking off again for Malta. By nightfall the Servicing Commandos had obtained their transport and were now ready for work.

Next day the Engineer Officer and eighteen of the ground crew arrived from Malta, to settle without means of cooking or bivouacs in the squadron area. The ground crew came ahead of schedule because it was expected that the Servicing Commandos might never have seen Mk. IX Spitfires. This surmise proved correct.

Meanwhile the Wing was worried about the anti-aircraft defences. Anti-aircraft batteries moved in and out with bewildering rapidity; and those detailed to defend the beach area overflowed on to the landing-ground. There was no A.A.D.C.[1] and the Gun Operations Room was not connected to any sites or warning set. It was therefore not surprising that no fire had been opened on the six Me. 109's the previous evening until they had actually started strafing, or that a Spitfire landing at dawn was heavily engaged, fortunately without result.

Assorted ammunition and petrol was, however, streaming in from the beach; but since the loads were put direct from the ships into the Ducks, the R.A.F. spotter at "Beach Brick" had been unable to check each cargo; "and," stated the report, "it was distressing to see 4·7 mortar shells and army tank fuel being delivered for use in aircraft".

Before the end of the day the A.O.C. D.A.F. landed in his Spitfire to announce that three squadrons would be flying in by first light the next morning. By then No. 2 Mobile Plotting Room Unit was ready to control their approach, and a skeleton Wing Operations Room housed in a three-ton truck was able to give them landing and disperal orders. With the arrival of the Signals section complete with transport, No. 3 Advance Landing-Ground section was relieved of responsibility. The airfield was operationally ready; six aircraft stood by for local defence but they were not called out. As Augusta fell, the spearhead wing at Pachino earned the distinction of directing the first Allied squadron to operate from European territory since the fall of France.[2]

They were established, however, only to move again almost immediately to Cassibile; bulldozers still at work on the dispersals had hacked a landing-strip out of the surrounding almond groves in a surprisingly short space of time. To Pachino then came 239 Wing, shadowed by 285 Wing, whose detached squadron, 40 S.A.A.F., was already at 244 Wing's new landing-ground.

The light bombers of T.B.F stood aside from these pioneer activities.

[1] Anti-Aircraft Defence Control.

[2] Unless Europe, as it has been claimed, starts north of Rome.

There was no room for them; they were able to operate from the Tunisian mainland and from Malta until a large part of Sicily was firmly in Allied hands. The squadrons of 326 and 232 Wings had turned over to night bombing; for 232 Wing this was an acquired taste, shortly to be abandoned; for 326 Wing it was to become staple fare.

As 244 Wing were moving into Cassibile some units of T.B.F. were detailed to proceed to Malta: 232 Wing squadrons, flying into Halfar, transferring almost immediately to Lûqa, where on the 20th they were joined by the squadrons of 3 S.A.A.F. Wing. Three days later, after advanced T.B.F. was already installed, 921 men of the 47th Group were flown over in eighty-one Dakotas.

T.B.F. shed some of its power *en route*. Personnel administration of all its units, both operational and ancillary, was transferred to Middle East Command; the next day operational control of its light bombers was handed over to A.O.C. D.A.F., who had contended that it was essential for him to have a specific number of aircraft at his sole disposal so that he could plan ahead in conjunction with the G.O.C. 8th Army. Thus the light bombers working under T.B.F. (Advance) were now placed under his direction, whilst 12th A.S.C. took over one of the medium groups working under T.B.F. (Main). T.B.F. was still, however, the Headquarters through which the A.O.C. D.A.F. or the Commanding General 12th A.S.C. passed requests for "loans".

The whittling away process continued. Advance parties of T.B.F. H.Q., 326 Wing and units, 31 A.S.P., 12th Bombardment Group, 340th Bombardment Group, and 306 Service Group, disembarked at Gela on August 1st and assembled at a staging area a mile north of the town before spreading out over Comiso, Monte Lunga, and Ponte Olivo. During the next weeks the ground staffs of the Wings which had gone to Malta moved over into Sicily. Desert Air Force now welcomed back 3 S.A.A.F. and 232 Wings, together with 51 R.S.U. and 31 A.S.P., once more under D.A.F.'s administrative control.

A week later T.B.F. as a whole came under operational control of D.A.F., 12th A.S.C. putting their calls for support to the Headquarters. The D.A.F. contention remained fixed and immutable:

> "One thing is certain. It is impossible to give timely and accurate close support with light and medium bombers unless, together with fighters and fighter-bombers, they are under the direct operational control of the R.A.F. commander working with the army concerned. Bombers worked on the Daimler Hire System do not give the best results in close support."

The attitude of D.A.F. was that it would have been better to have split the light bomber force right from the start, some put under D.A.F., the rest put under 12 A.S.C., leaving the two Headquarters to make mutual arrangements for loans whenever necessary.

It is not here proposed to judge either the efforts of D.A.F. to be the sole body in control or the efforts of T.B.F. to carry out its charter. The struggle in any case had little immediate effect on operations, for at no time would either "side" let administrative differences hinder the air war. But this brief survey of D.A.F.'s relations with other parts of the air command may help to give some idea of the strength and persistance of Desert tradition.

Within itself, D.A.F. had special difficulties enough. It was obvious that a combined operation would bring to light any number of apparently insoluble problems. Some, after low-level bickering, would be solved at a higher level over a cup of tea or a bottle of wine. Others would fade away and be forgotten as the conditions which gave them birth were never to be repeated.

There were those who in retrospect pointed out blunders. They considered that the Servicing Commandos had shown too much commando and not enough servicing spirit; that the Airfield Construction Liaison Officers had been inexperienced; that too much use had been made of fresh units from England when toughened veterans from the Middle East were ready and willing. But success robbed complaint of bitterness; the decision "to do better next time" was born not of desperation but of self-confidence.

In retrospect the smoothest cog in the whole machine appeared to be the Malta ferry. A ferry control had been formed by 8th Army, the R.A.F. being represented by the A.O.C. and Movements Section of Desert Air Force. At the outset the Chief of Staff, 8th Army, ruled that R.A.F. requirements were to be granted priority No. 1. The R.A.F. controlled their own movements, making a bid each morning for a number of craft which were then loaded on the R.A.F. priority system, lists being supplied daily, sometimes hourly, to Malta Movements.

The report commented:

> "Relations between the 8th Army and Desert Air Force are very close and the army fully appreciate their responsibilities as regards the provision of labour and transport for the handling of R.A.F. supplies."

In contrast, claims were made that these matters were not clearly understood by units fresh to 8th Army.

Those who criticized D.A.F. on the grounds that its attitude was too partisan and its outlook too narrow had in fairness to admit that such a high standard of co-operation between land and air forces was well worth the small price exacted. "Go thou and do likewise!" was D.A.F.'s unanswerable reply to its competitors.

CHAPTER XXVII

THE PELL-MELL CAMPAIGN

By August 5th Catania, and all the island apart from the north-eastern tip, was in our hands. About 131,000 prisoners had been taken. From then on only Messina was outstanding; and over the port from which the German troops were disembarking flak in such concentration as had never been seen in the Desert or North Africa protected the withdrawal of enemy supplies. By the 17th, forward troops entered this Mediterranean "Happy Valley"; Sicily had fallen.

July 13th was the last day on which the enemy put up any real show of resistance in the air. So weak had his position become that twelve Ju. 88's were sent out unescorted; they fell prey to 243 squadron, five being shot down and the remainder damaged. Enemy radar, sited mainly in the south, had been overrun during the first days of the invasion. A report described their coverage as "spotty". But it made little difference.

In contrast our own radar arrangements were "over-generous". No stations were lost in the assault; there was enough equipment to allow for ample coverage as the army advanced up the eastern coast. There was only one disturbing factor: Mount Etna's "all-time record for permanent echoes" compelled light warning stations to be sited with some care to the south-west, for enemy night-bombers were wont to approach the ports on the east coast from round the west side of the volcano.

The assault had not produced the expected casualties, but important units from England might well have considered that the defeat of the German air force was a propagandist's fiction. No. 1 Mobile Air Reporting unit and No. 1 Mobile Operations Reporting unit, arriving to take over the static defence of the Catania-Gerbini group of airfields, were in Augusta harbour for the most successful German air effort of the short campaign. M.A.R.U. lost all its equipment. M.O.R.U., missed during disembarkation by three Macchi 202's, was less unlucky, though the arrangements for its reception had gone astray; for Catania had not yet fallen. An ammunition ship, hit on the night of the 19th, blew up in harbour next day. A midnight raid followed; and by the 23rd reference was made to "the usual air raid" at 3.30 in the morning. The unit diary of the period reads more like an excerpt from 204 Group's operational record book of 1941.

At first M.O.R.U. controlled the aircraft of 600 squadron which came from Malta for night interception duties. It then took over 284 Air-Sea Rescue squadron, besides controlling the standing patrols over Augusta and Syracuse in the daytime. After the end of the campaign it changed places with 211 Group, to be thenceforth D.A.F.'s forward control.

The inauspicious start of the M.O.R.U. officers and men was the subject of joking among the more experienced, for besides losing equipment they could not get their hands on what remained. Their transport, on another ship, was loaded with the emergency "compo" rations. Hence, as they had no vehicles, so they had nothing to eat; they had to spin out the forty-eight-hour issue as best they could with dubious local purchases.

Sicily was highly malarial, especially in the low-lying coastal areas. Comment took the form of understatement: "We ought to have been issued with mosquito nets but we were not; there seemed to be quite a lot of mosquitos about."

Lastly, many other units had never heard of No. 1 M.O.R.U. "What do those letters stand for?" was a question repeated over the hastily improvised telephone exchange several times a day.

Air-Sea Rescue activities soon broadcast the fact of M.O.R.U.'s existence throughout Sicily. On August 4th a pilot was picked out of the sea about six miles east of Catania. At midday the Walrus was sent off again for another rescue when news was received of yet another man "in the drink".[1] The Walrus pilot went to collect the third victim, only to discover that he could not become airborne. A damaged float made it difficult for him to taxi home across the waves and so a high-speed launch put out from Syracuse to take aboard rescuer and rescued.

That day had been full of activity for D.A.F. fighter-bombers. Four Kittyhawks had taken off every fifteen minutes to bomb and strafe roads north of Catania. The light bombers had attacked anything they could find north of the bomb line, whilst twelve Spitfires had patrolled constantly overhead to the east and west of Etna.

Mussolini's resignation, bursting like an over-ripe tomato on the heads of a German army retreating into the north-west corner of the island, caused embarrassment rather than dismay. Catania was turned into a rearguard stronghold for the protection of troops making their way back to the mainland of Italy. Allied air effort centred almost entirely on measures necessary to pierce that enemy screen. Spitfires swept the area whilst A. 36's concentrated on smashing reinforcement columns moving to the battle zone from north and west. Strategical heavy bombers by day and night destroyed every Italian road and rail centre leading to the south, to start the process of restricting the flow of possible reinforcements to the island. Drawing nearer the battlefield, the tactical air forces helped to strangle all movement on the coastal road from Cape Orlando to Messina, without ceasing to attack Milazzo, Troina, Stefano, Regalbuto, and Randazzo.

Axis air effort was described as "sporadic and unpredictable", but losses

[1] Jargon: "In the sea."

were constant and proven: 750 aircraft since the start of the campaign.

It was not helpful, in face of this disaster, to have *Reichsmarschal* Goering say in his Order of the Day:

> "Together with the fighter pilots in France, Norway, and Russia, I can only regard you with contempt. If an immediate improvement is not forthcoming, flying personnel from the *Kommodore* downwards must expect to be reduced to the ranks and transferred to the Eastern front to serve on the ground."

Catania provided the first example on any scale of "interdiction"—the isolation of an area by systematic interference from the air with all rail and road communications. The noose, already round the neck of the city, was finally drawn tight when the 78th Division seized the heights of Centuripe, nearly twenty miles away, from which it could control the road from Catania to the west of Mount Etna. When, on August 5th, our forces entered the city gates not a shot was fired. A notice handed to the Commanding Officer read: "The authorities and functionaries of the city of Catania are in the Carabinieri Caserma at Piazza Giovanni Virga, awaiting orders."

Whilst the civil population, as though to indicate that the assumption of the army command by the King of Italy was an empty gesture, were welcoming our troops with handshakes, flowers, and requests for food, D.A.F. was preparing to move forward to the Gerbini group of airfields whence it could control road and rail movements in southern Italy. This, the first European system of aerodromes, could be called the air key to the invasion of Italy. Low-lying and malarial, the plain was well irrigated, supporting uniform small farmsteads of a land settlement scheme. The ground surface, baked by the sun, was hard; the top soil firm. So long as there was no rain, landing-strips, sited to dodge both houses and ditches, could support any aircraft that flew.

Messina was now within easy reach; the fighter-bombers turned their attention to shipping in the Straits, after first pausing to attack enemy lorries moving away from Catania. Barges, siebel ferries and smaller ships were either damaged or sunk. Spitfires escorted the light bombers raiding Randazzo, the town which contained the last road junction between Axis positions in the north and those on the east coast. Randazzo was "worked over until it was untenable". The threat to the town provoked a German reaction which took the form of a low-level attack on 244 Wing's aerodrome by thirty Ju. 88's, operating with the help of a bright moon. One of the first bombs hit an ammunition dump close by 417 squadron's dispersal, illuminating the target for succesive waves. A direct hit on Wing Operations, and two 1,000-kilo bombs on the runway, delayed take-offs until twelve o'clock the next day; two delayed-action bombs exploded in the early hours of the morning, damaging three aircraft. Further raids, which might have seriously interfered with the efficiency of the field, were not forthcoming. Randazzo continued to suffer.

Landings by sea and air behind the enemy lines at St. Agata were followed by other (7th Army) assaults east of Cape Orlando. Randazzo fell, the Americans capturing Patti and entering the town whilst 8th Army was about to come in from the south. With its fall on August 13th, Messina lay open to direct land assault; it was clear that the campaign was swiftly drawing to a close.

On the 14th, Bostons of T.B.F. showered fragmentation bombs over Nicola and Gesso, whilst Mitchells and Baltimores went for the lines of communication in southern Italy; by night Bostons continued armed reconnaissance, Wellingtons of Strategic Air Force worked the "milk run" to the beaches. Throughout the 15th, 16th and 17th, D.A.F., 12 A.S.C., and T.B.F. crowded the air over the straits in spite of the intense flak. And though another Cape Bon was out of the question, scores of craft, forging laden with Germans slowly across the narrow strip of water to the mainland, had to face a hail of bombs and cannon-fire.

Thus, after thirty-eight days, the campaign had rushed pell-mell to an end. The Mediterranean was now an Allied sea lane safer than any in the world. The German air force was almost completely defeated, the final count of casualties being over 1,100. The springboard for the invasion of Italy was underfoot.

That the enemy had managed to move so much material away was not surprising in view of the narrowness of the straits. Early in August they had begun to withdraw heavy equipment, which was in any case of little use in hilly country. Tanks had been the first to go, followed by vehicles and non-combatant troops. There had been nothing hurried about these movements; the defence of Catania had given them all the time they needed. The high standard of German morale was not therefore difficult to explain.

There were some lessons in the use of air power to be learned. Glider operations at the start had been disappointing, but experience gained in Sicily was the cornerstone of success in Normandy.

Employment of light and fighter-bombers had been satisfactory. Though olive groves concealed targets, D.A.F. had proved able to adapt itself to changing conditions of warfare; the theory of interdiction had been well mastered by a force which had enjoyed its whole experience in the Desert, where bottlenecks hardly existed, where flat surfaces had usually robbed roads of importance and denied to railways pre-eminence in the sphere of communication and supply. General Alexander, three days before the capture of Catania, reported that the air effort of the previous three days against the Germans had been very heavy, that 8th Army was "well satisfied" with Allied air support; and at Troina, General Patton emphasized how helpful the dive-bombers had been in contributing to the final capture of the town by the 1st Division.

Political repercussions from the collapse of Sicily were all that could have been hoped for and more. General Eisenhower commented: "The shock of the invasion, accompanied by the heavy bombing of keypoints on the Italian mainland, culminating in the bombardment of the marshalling yards in the Rome area, exposed the bankruptcy of the Fascist régime and led directly to its overthrow."

Badoglio was the intermediate rung on a ladder of defeat which Italy was ready and willing to descend. The Rome–Berlin Axis, on which the New Order was to have revolved for a thousand years, was about to disintegrate; not even the contemporary German jokes that Italy was more effective as an Ally when she was one no longer could disguise the fact that German responsibilities would have now to include Sardinia, Corsica, southern France, and the Balkans.

Though pretending to find advantages in the new situation, Goebbels was not slow to quote the Italian defection to excuse defeat in Russia. But the Armistice, signed on September 3rd, kept secret until the eve of the invasion of the mainland, was a pill which no amount of sugaring could render palatable. The two irreconcilables who had come together on purely idealogical grounds had returned to their two traditionally separate camps. An historical pattern of longer standing was to be reaffirmed.

CHAPTER XXVIII

MEN AND MANNERS

THOSE who could be released were encouraged to take a few days' leave. The pilots and ground crews alike made the most of a short stay at Taormina, from which Kesselring's headquarters had so lately been driven. Before the war, Taormina had been world-famous as a place of exceptional beauty, where the flat, inhospitable plain of Catania gave way suddenly to soaring cliffs and gently shelving sand. Apart from unusual scenery, Taormina boasted large hotels of a type quite alien to the battered caravanserais of southern Sicily.

The inhabitants, quick to sense a return to the old tourist days, collaborated quite frankly from the start in an effort to make the newcomers feel at home and to relieve them of their spare *lire*. And if the visitors showed little inclination to visit the ruins of the amphitheatre on the slopes, the taverns and shops below felt the benefit.

Thus far, the men of Desert Air Force had seen very little of the country. Those who flew had viewed the crumpling hills and the olive groves as a coloured, three-dimensional map, too close to which wind currents or flak made flying dangerous. Those who never left the ground had lived in tents and bivouacs—in worse conditions, they sometimes considered, than even the natives themselves—too absorbed in the job on hand to stray into the villages or towns, many of which in any case were out of bounds.

The aerodromes, inevitably on flat plains near the coast, resembled one another and were uniformly uninteresting. After the first shock of Gela, where mud-packed streets and pockmarked houses suggested an African, rather than a European, village, Comiso, Vittorio and Lentini brought few fresh surprises. (Few of the ancient towns hyperboled by *Baedeker* were in Desert Air Force territory.) Finally Gerbini plain, its marshes and mosquitos, its baked earth and stunted trees, its hot sun and hovels, confirmed the airmen in a dislike of the island which nothing would ever eradicate.

Catania, industrial, shattered, was the only city in Sicily that many D.A.F. airmen were to see; to reach even this meant a long journey over rough tracks to the plain where improvised crosses and abandoned gliders converged on the red death's-head-surmounted warnings—"*Minen!*"

For those of the Allied forces who had discovered relatives in Sicily the country had assumed a different aspect from the start; but there were few English to whom this applied. Contact with the native inhabitants, in the towns, was mostly limited to the shops and bars; and in the countryside to the peasants with eggs and fruit for sale. Although a few words of the strange tongue were pressed into service, Anglo-Italian fraternization did not on the whole develop until D.A.F. reached the mainland.

Unlike the Carthaginian hordes, the Allies carried everything with them. The aerodrome became a sealed camp supplied almost entirely through Service channels. There were many who could say in all truth that they had never been outside the magic circle of squadron life except to move to a fresh locality; many who left the island with little more knowledge of it than if it had been Timbuctoo; for even in transit their view was obscured by canvas flapping over the back of a three-ton truck.

For the fortunate, however, Taormina supplied some information as to local conditions; but being a tourist centre it gave a false impression of the amenities of an impoverished island. Taormina's luxuries contrasted illogically with the near-primitive conditions of the general run of inhabitants.

But the visitors, after all, were not the old-style tourists; if anything they were unwilling tourists, phenomena unknown hitherto in Sicily, as in Italy. They had come to seek neither cultural nor architectural refreshment; few of them had sketch-books, even fewer wished to "go native" or "lead the simple life". They were men on rest from a hazardous campaign, notable for overwork rather than for the traditional thrills of battle—thrills which for the majority of an air force are bound to be non-existent. D.A.F. commanders, vying with each other to secure the best allocations of hotel space, were concerned mainly with giving their men a refreshing holiday to tide them over until the invasion of Italy could put at their disposal other rest camps with even finer amenities.

The reaction of the Sicilians towards their invaders was so extraordinary as almost to constitute a separate problem in itself. Sicily had been a bone of contention between the Phœnicians and the Greeks, the Carthaginians and the Romans, the Saracens and the Normans, the Spaniards, the Germans, the French, and the Italians. Historically prepared for liberators, the islanders were immune to lasting enthusiasms for this or that country or régime, but expert at creating a false impression of complaisance. Therefore, far from being greeted with poisoned wine and daggers, Allied troops who broke fresh ground were astonished by cheers and flowers. Those following were disconcerted by the insistent requests for food and materials, things which the islanders evidently considered their due.

If, as Eisenhower remarked, "Italy had been for all practical purposes out of the war since the invasion," this new status seemed to have the vociferous backing of the vast majority of the civil population. The more prominent citizens vied with the peasants in claiming that, whilst others had followed the wicked Duce, they alone had drawn skirts aside in horror. Those who in view of their office or known beliefs could not make such bland denials convincing informed all who would listen that they had joined the Party under duress in order to keep their jobs, or that they had been secretly conspiring against the régime throughout. In a land gridded with secret societies, many of these claims were likely to be genuine; how then to sort out one from the other? Accusations and counter-accusations flew thick in the air; citizens indicted each other as freely as in some topical comic opera; it was sometimes hard to remember that this was no farce and that the actors were as real as the plots in which they were involved.

No airman was unduly surprised on hearing that Italy as a whole had withdrawn from the war. For what else was to be expected? But few were immediately able to grasp what the consequences would be. The more optimistic imagined a general uprising throughout Italy; they saw themselves strolling alongside the Tiber in a matter of days. Others thought that the Germans would now retreat into northern Italy, there to dig themselves in, waiting for the Allies to catch up. There was some surprise among the men of the units because bombing operations continued as before. Directifs from higher quarters were guarded. Italy might be out of the war, but Allied troops were not yet occupying her territory; therefore the war continued. The military attitude towards the civil population was to remain the same as before—strict, fair; only when the Service situation demanded it was there to be contact with the Italians.

As far back as the fall of Tunis, Allied propaganda had been easing off Italy and had been devoted to an "*Ici l'Enemi*" campaign to show that Germany was the real enemy. There was now no need for a sudden change in the official viewpoint. But Italy's surrender could not swing opinion at once. The Allies had fought too long and too bitterly against the country which was now ready to woo their favour. The word "co-belligerent", which many at the time considered a statement of wish rather than of fact, covered the interim period during which Italy advanced towards a passive and finally an active state of co-operation.

The armed revolts in the great industrial towns of the north, the sudden increase in the numbers of Partisans, particularly in the mountain districts, the surrender of that part of the Italian Fleet which managed to escape, all were welcome straws in the wind. Desert Air Force units were told to be on the look-out for Italian aircraft coming in to fight on our side, but few appeared. After a while the former optimists became the greater pessimists. "It has made no difference after all; we're still here, and the war's still on."

In an attempt to give a brief resumé of the human, as opposed to the mechanical, side of the war in Sicily, much must be omitted. Shades of opinion were as numerous as their holders. Many airmen, for instance those who manned D.A.F. outposts, were in isolated units in daily contact with the Sicilians after hours of duty. Others, for example those concerned with Intelligence on the Wings, could garner an accurate picture of the progress of the war from documents passing through their hands. Some could talk the new language fluently, whilst others could predict with fair accuracy the next moves in the Allied game; but the majority accepted new conditions as being in the natural order of things and made the best of what lay at hand.

If the crowded streets of Tunis had been surprising after the emptiness of the Desert, Sicily was the first gateway to European civilization. Taormina showed what might lie in store in Italy; the welcome from the inhabitants of one tourist centre was some indication of the reception to be expected in "The Garden of Europe".

In such an enervating atmosphere of adulation, considerations of war strategy might well have assumed some indolent, southern aspect; but planning for the invasion of Italy took place from far-off Tunisia. Not until after the capture of Naples did Headquarters Mediterranean Allied Air Forces move to the Royal Palace at Caserta, where lofty halls and dim unapproachable attics suggested grandeur in decline, masking plots, incarcerations and assassinations. Yet, even there, the huge Headquarters staff was later to show a spirit of stubborn resistance to foreign influences. In the past they had not succumbed to "the harsh meridional ecstasy of Algiers".[1] In the future, isolated in splendour and discomfort, they intended to remain deaf to the blandishment of "*Dolce far niente*".

[1] Conolly.

CHAPTER XXIX

PLANS AND PREPARATIONS FOR THE INVASION OF ITALY

CHILDREN are usually eager to compare Italy to a spurred boot kicking Sicily towards the continent of Africa. In order to understand the communications system this simile might be expanded to include the mountain ranges running down the length of the country (the bones); the coastal plains (part muscle, part sinew, and part fat); and the railways and roads (the arteries and veins).

The Toe and Heel, at the end, as it were, of the line, in Italy as in the body, would then be the first to feel the effect of constriction or blockage higher up.

To instigate this process the bombers of Strategic Air Force were, in the brief space between the two campaigns, mainly employed in the smashing of vital junctions, road or rail, in the north. Starved of blood, the Toe and Heel might then grow stiff and cold.

Air interdiction of Catania provided a model. In Italy the task was bigger, nothing other than the slow starvation of a whole country.

The marshalling yards were selected as the primary targets. A study of the map will explain why, for instance, the little University town of Bologna was doomed to a pounding from the air which its mediæval school of law had done nothing to deserve, and why Rome, for all her status as the great city of Christendom, could not escape the consequences of her spider-like hold on both northern and southern approaches. The campaign in Italy was dominated by geography and communications. Immunity or destruction of this town or that could be to some extent assessed in advance.

95 per cent of Italy's oil, 80 per cent of its coal, and a wide range of other products had to be coaxed into the country from the north. The Brenner Pass, the traditional key to invasion, forwarded about 50 per cent of the total, whilst about 38 per cent came via the Swiss lines, St. Gothard and Simplon. The eastern routes, via Tarvisio and Postumia, carried much of the remainder. Thus the first strategical interdiction targets were the northern termini: Verona for the Brenner; Milan for the Simplon and St. Gothard; Turin for the French Riviera; Trieste and Fiume for the Balkan traffic (which included some two-thirds of the oil). Sea traffic could be discounted, for the Mediterranean was no longer *Mare nostrum*.

Once material was within the country it might be trapped on its way to the fighting front. From the north to the south there was a choice of only three main routes: one on the west coast having the lowest capacity; one on the east coast; and one which rode high above the bony ridges of the Apennines to link Bologna with Rome. The three vital bottlenecks were Rome, Naples, and Foggia; but there were five of lesser importance at Bologna, Genoa, Pisa, Florence, and Rimini.

Drawing closer to the battlefield the harassed goods could take the electric train from Rome via Littoria to Naples, or could travel more sedately on the older steam track (Rome–Frosinone–Caserta–Cancello–Naples). Or there was a choice of two main roads, one running through Cisterna, Littoria and Formia, the other winding inland through Frosinone and Caserta.

Interdiction points in the immediate tactical area, the Toe, were plentiful. There were two invitingly narrow necks of land; one between the Gulf of Squillace and the Gulf of Santa Euphemia; and one further north between Villapiana and Scalea. Then there were the bridges near the River Leo, the Castravillari defiles, and Sibari junction. In the Toe as a whole, so tortuous were the roads and so constricted the average village—designed originally for defence rather than for access—that hardly a bomb could fall without blocking something.

The air war against Italian communications started before the end of the Sicilian campaign. A series of blows at Marina di Catanzaro and Angitola were deflected from August 19th north of the line Sapri to Trebissacce and were switched again after the 23rd to Caserta, Cancello, Battipaglia and Salerno. Sulmona and Terni near Rome, Bologna and Pisa more northerly, were other victims. The 9th Air Force meanwhile operated against Foggia, Benevento and Potenza.

General Doolittle's appreciation of the work of the night-flying Wellingtons really applied to all branches of Strategic Air Force: "The targets to which your organization was assigned could not at first glance be interpreted as contributing greatly to the ground force's efforts. This, however, is not the case."

It was inadvisable to give more details. The air forces' purpose could not be fully explained without revealing the plan of invasion.

To maintain such a long-range policy successfully required that the *Luftwaffe* should be given no chance of resurrection. In attacks on the vast Foggia complex of airfields on the 25th, 135 Fortresses completed the work started by 140 Lightnings, dismayed but not hindered by sixty enemy fighters which tried hard to split up the steady formations by aerial bombardment and rockets reminiscent of a firework display.

Its novelties momentarily exhausted, the *Luftwaffe* sent its bomber units north. Once again Allied air power had removed, in advance of the actual land battle, a hazard which might well have embarrassed both the troops and the convoys bringing reinforcements. On the following day, in order to drive the lesson home, the airfields around Naples—with the exception of Monte Corvino, earmarked for Allied occupation in the near future—were similarly treated.

A bald statement of the numbers of enemy aircraft destroyed on the ground, eked out by quotation from diaries of the more neurotic prisoners of war, cannot here serve to give much idea of the damage dealt from the air. The effect was significant because cumulative. Wrecked hangars, on one field only, of themselves meant little; but when at the same time another landing-ground was cratered to the consistency of Gruyère cheese, and when simultaneously workshops and repair rooms on yet another were out of action, then disorganization could indeed be called almost complete. In the same way the reduction of one marshalling yard to a mass of burnt-out rolling stock and twisted rails by itself meant little, for such things were not impossible to repair in a matter of days, if not of hours. But when all the major arteries were simultaneously depressed, then the whole body of Italy groaned. The Allies had accumulated an enormous air bank-balance; they were bent on seeing that interest on these assets was compound.

To these pre-invasion credits D.A.F. could not, in the nature of things, contribute very much. Its light bombers on loan from T.B.F. could add their mite to the profusion of Strategic Air Force effort. Bostons, Baltimores and Mitchells adopted several towns, such as Limezia, Cozenza and Catanzaro, whilst by night Bostons on road reconnaissance contributed to the general unrest in the German lines. 65 per cent of fighter-bomber sorties were flown against enemy lines of communication, against bridges, vehicles and barracks in the Toe, the American share being the lion's.

Compared to the air armada massed in the skies of Italy, D.A.F. might appear a very small speck. But D.A.F. for the 8th, and 12th A.S.C. for the 5th Army, were the only "tangible" representatives of air power; and D.A.F. with its well-tried technique of Army Co-operation lost no prestige in spite of the fact that it was now a minnow contrasted with the triton of Strategic Air Force.

The overall result of co-ordinating all branches of the Allied Air Forces towards one purpose—wrecking the traffic—was that reconnaissance aircraft were able to report on the eve of the invasion that at Pisa, Sulmona, Cancello, Aversa, Benevento, Foggia, Salerno, Paola, and Catanzaro the lines were blocked and all railway activity had ceased; Littoria and Battipaglia were slowly recovering from the blows.

It seemed that a third lesson of air superiority was being taught. At El Hamma, air power had "kept their heads down"; at Catania, air power had restricted but not stopped traffic on all the roads leading from the city. Now, on a still larger scale, air power had temporarily strangled rail communications of an entire country from north to south. There was a common factor of these three actions; for a brief period the air had called a halt to enemy activity. There was a rider, too; such a lull was short-lived and had to be utilized at once.

A shrewd officer at Kesselring's Headquarters might well have rung the alarm; for the simultaneous blocking of all these junctions could be interpreted in only one way. Invasion was imminent.

• • • • •

A feature of the invasion plan was that there could be little or no hope of preserving secrecy. Not because of Anglo-Sicilian fraternization, nor because security was bad, nor because regulations were being improperly flouted, but because, apart from the inferences to be drawn from the air bombardment, it was obvious that troops would not be prevented by the narrow straits of Messina from landing in the Toe of Italy. To defend such bony extremities was impracticable. The Germans would clearly have to abandon the unproductive Toe and Heel and pick their ground elsewhere.

But apart from the Toe, the other point of impact could be predicted. An intelligent German with a pair of dividers and a knowledge of the respective range of Spitfires, Seafires, and Lightnings could have proved that the assault must fall somewhere south of the latitude of Rome; for the Allies, having gone to such trouble to attain air supremacy, were not likely to let a valuable weapon rust in their hands.

Failing a Mulberry,[1] the immediate aim of any assault would be a port for supplies and reinforcements. Naples was the one and only. If to assault the heavily defended port direct was to court disaster, the choice of landing areas was now whittled down to three. The beaches of Gaeta, Mondragone, and Salerno.

At Gaeta an open plain seemed to counteract the disadvantage of an indifferent beach, but it was furthest from Naples and beyond the range of single-engined fighter cover. Thus there were finally but two alternatives. Aeneas the Greek, founding the colony of Parthenope, had landed near Cumae, considerably nearer modern Naples than Mondragone; but his problems were scarcely relevant to more "progressive" conditions of warfare, for the Allies had to expect not a few possibly hostile tribes, but an organized defence. The voice of the Sibyl had long ceased to "resound through the cave of a hundred corridors". There was no inducement to follow a classical pattern. Mondragone lay on the other side of the broad Volturno river. The nearest airfield, Capua, was fifteen miles away; the beach gradients were not well suited to twentieth-century landing-craft.

The crescent of fertility surrounding Naples, though interrupted to the south by the hilly Sorrento peninsula, offered the flat plain of Salerno, a grassy triangle twenty-one miles along the shore, penetrating eight miles inland at the centre. The small river Sele, the only water obstacle, ran beneath the first towering outpost of the Apennines to create a splendid defensive position for German troops; but on the other hand the heights, if captured sufficiently early on in the campaign, would throw a strong arm around the invaders behind which enough supplies could be landed for a wholehearted assault upon Naples. If the army could envisage their armoured fighting vehicles navigating the Sele with less difficulty than the Volturno, the navy visualized a string of small harbours from Salerno to Torre del Greco, capable of absorbing many thousand tons of supplies, falling into their hands. From

[1] A prefabricated harbour used for the landings in Normandy.

Mondragone southwards, Pozzuoli and Bagnoli offered nothing comparable. The R.A.F., whose fighters would be easily within instead of at the limit of their range, had their eyes on the airfield at Monte Corvino, a bare three miles from the beachhead. They were already assessing the relative merits of other landing-strips in the area.

So loudly did Salerno call for a landing that Rommel, during August, held a full dress rehearsal of an invasion on its beaches. Since neither intent nor even tactics could be masked, the new assault could clearly not be on the Algerian or Sicilian pattern.

• • •

Operation "Avalanche" (Salerno) only assumed priority from August 17th. The plan for operation "Buttress", with its smaller brother, operation "Baytown" (landings in the toe and heel to establish Allied troops on Italian soil), was of older standing. But the arrival of General Castellani by submarine from Portugal and discussions on the "Short Instrument of Surrender" reshaped decisions originally taken at the Casablanca conference. Now even an airborne descent on Rome seemed feasible. Buttress rode side by side with Avalanche for some days before dropping out of the race, leaving the field clear for Baytown to be carried out by 8th Army and D.A.F. on September 3rd. Avalanche was to be set in motion by 5th Army and 12th A.S.C. on September 8th.

Baytown should be judged simply as a manœuvre to "break the ice"; to contain German forces capable of playing a part in the defence of Naples; and to open the Messina straits to ships supplying Avalanche. As it happened, Baytown met with such success that the capture of Taranto (operation "Slapstick"), could be achieved inexpensively, whereas Avalanche exacted a high price for Naples.

An hour before first light on September 3rd the navy was to land 13 Corps north of Reggio de Calabria, and subsequently further troops at Bagnara and Pizzo. Later developments were to be based largely on fresh assessments of the situation. The air forces were to neutralize the airfields of Reggio, Vibo Valentia, Crotone, and Botricello, in order to reduce the risk of German air interference. They were then to occupy the fields themselves as soon as possible.

Just as Baytown was ancillary to Avalanche, so D.A.F.'s work was merely part of the air policy whereby enemy movement was to be restricted and our own protected. D.A.F.'s actual brief was, firstly, direct support for the troops; secondly, the air defence of north-eastern Sicily, including the coastal waters, their hunting-ground being north and east of a line drawn through Cap Orlando–Caltigirone–Cap St. Croce. Thirdly, the A.O.C. D.A.F. was charged with the responsibility for calling transport aircraft into the forward operational areas and for providing them with bases—a duty which promised air-lifts and other benefits.

It was impossible to contrast Allied and German air strength on a sectional basis; to say that as against D.A.F.'s X the Germans could array Z. Allied air power was by now a Hydra whose necks could crane outwards over southern Germany and southern France or dart at close quarters at the troops in contact with the army. The overall number of aircraft, not including transport types, for operations from October 1st consisted of 39 Groups of the U.S.A.A.F. (about 2,300) and 84 squadrons of the R.A.F. (about 1,400). To break down these figures into what was actually available for Avalanche alone shows once more the gap between paper and working totals which the previous campaign in the Middle East had constantly revealed.[1]

The Outline Air Plan specified 350 heavy day bombers (but of these, in the event, 95 Liberators were not forthcoming), 650 medium and light bombers, 320 single-engined fighters, 110 carrier-borne Seafires, about 160 fighter-bombers, 32 night-fighters, 40 tactical reconnaissance. These aircraft were as usual about 75 per cent serviceable. It should be remembered that these figures do not take into account the aircraft of Desert Air Force available for Baytown, the reconnaissance Spitfires of 285 Wing, P. 40's of 239 Wing, the American 57th and 79th Fighter Group, the two Spitfire Wings, 244 and 7 S.A.A.F., the 47th Bombardment Group, and 232 Light Bomber Wing.

What, then, of the *Luftwaffe*? Overall figures misleadingly topped the thousand mark; but the Coastal Air Force estimate on September 3rd mentioned 220 long-range and torpedo-bombers, 50 reconnaissance bombers and 260 fighters and fighter-bombers in Italy and Sardinia. Their serviceability, it was assumed, hovered as before at 50 per cent. The latter totals then could be halved. The Air Ministry Intelligence Forecast predicted opposition from 105 to 110 fighters and fighter-bombers and 70 long-range bombers, which might possibly be increased to 120. And the Italian air force? Overall figures had never sunk far below 1,500. But their performances, torpedo-bombers excepted, so long confined to backstage, were shortly to be given under fresh management. In time, enough Italian pilots and aircraft joined the Allied cause for a force of some 300 to be fashioned. Others, however, were to find an outlet for their talents by withdrawing northwards with the Germans in the newly formed Fascist Republican Group. Over the period of the invasion the *Regia Aeronautica*, which had fought with real if misguided skill far from the shores of its country, was at this crucial moment *hors de combat*. Its contribution to the Allies, though negative, had at least the advantage of not being positively detrimental.

Allied air power was a giant to the German pigmy as, in the early hours of September 3rd, under cover of naval bombardment and heavy artillery fire from the Sicilian coast, British and Canadian troops of the 8th Army crossed Messina Straits to the Calabrian shore.

[1] There must have been more confusion in the public mind over numbers than over any other aspect of the air war. It cannot be too strongly emphasized that totals mean little or nothing. Aircraft have to be available at the right time, in the right place and in a fit state for operations.

CHAPTER XXX

SALERNO

AVALANCHE cast a long shadow over the first landings in Italy. 322 and 324 Wings were to be under 12th A.S.C. from the start; arrangements for the control of fighters were to be based on the interchangeability of the Fighter Wings between 12th A.S.C. and D.A.F. Up to "D" day all fighters in north-eastern Sicily were to be controlled by one central operations room (No. 1 M.O.R.U.), where two American liaison officers watched the interests of the American squadrons. From "D" day onwards, 12th A.S.C.'s 64th Fighter Wing was to take over, at first from the Headquarters ship and later from land, with D.A.F. liaison officers in attendance. Such parts of T.B.F. as were not already controlled by D.A.F. were allotted to 12th A.S.C.; liaison sections attached to both Headquarters maintained the somewhat fragile theme of T.B.F. as a separate entity.

Baytown was therefore left with a fraction of a fraction; there was little at first for even this reduced force to do. Standing patrols over Messina straits and Catania–Augusta tempted, but did not draw, the *Luftwaffe*. One reconnaissance Ju. 88 and one Me. 109 were shot down, but there was a general atmosphere of anti-climax about the whole invasion which showed only too clearly that the Germans were waiting for the action at Salerno to begin. On the ground Italian coastal troops put up a token show of resistance, but there were neither mines nor extensive demolitions; the submarine cable was intact; our troops made no contact with the Germans. A report commented, "Air support was given all day but the chief difficulty was to find targets." A quantity of vehicles, discovered by Warhawks on early armed reconnaissance, dispersed by the time that Kittyhawks could reach the area. Even as late as September 6th and 7th "the day was dull in the extreme" . . . "in the air we had a very dull day except for a Kittybomber raid in the evening which destroyed some M.T. There were no air combats at all." On the other hand, the light bombers on September 3rd had attacked Cozenza marshalling yards, the road, and near-by bridges, with some success. "D" day was not wholly uneventful. On the 4th two events had not been dull. A cackle of enemy activity over the landing beach was soon silenced, Spitfires accounting for six Macchi 200's and one F.W. 190. The light bombers were again out in strength, co-ordinating a raid on San Stefano with the successful ground assault. Photo-coverage revealed that the enemy had evacuated all airfields from which his fighters could operate against our slowly advancing ground forces.

The writing appeared on the wall; the days of fighter interception over the front line were numbered. But as if to replace the old, a new enemy was appearing on the horizon. The weather. After a summer of blazing heat ("No hotter than the Desert," said the veterans), the sky began to hint belatedly at European rather than African origins. During the actual assault the weather had remained fair with light westerly winds and good visibility, though haze had developed in the afternoons. All too soon, however, low cloud was spoiling the bombing raids on Cozenza; and photo-reconnaissance aircraft were unable to cover several airfields singled out for attack. On the 6th, 12th Meteorological unit sent out thunderstorm warnings which persuaded D.A.F. to move some aircraft from Milazzo back to Catania and Gerbini; yet as the ground forces thrusting towards Cittanova took Gioia and Palmi, the evening, calm and cool, dissolved into summery night.

From then onwards weather was to lead the air forces a perpetual dance. The Apennines produced Jekyll-and-Hyde conditions, scudding clouds to the east could mask a blue sky to the west. There were few means of disseminating fresh meteorological information, or of arranging for diversions of aircraft in flight. Flying Control, which in England could handle several hundred bombers at a time, come fair, come foul, was a *parvenu* to Desert Air Force. The rules and regulations of Aircraft Safety were unpopular with pilots who had done without irksome restrictions in the Desert and Sicily. Although, later, there were to be some chaotic cloud-capped moments, there was then no general desire to take inconvenient precautions.

Tendencies in Italian weather were of course well known, but such data formed a guide rather than a forecast. Occasional rain and fog were to be expected even in the halcyon days, the two-thirds of the year during which sunny Italy lives up to its name. But in the remaining one-third every variation of the English climate could be produced at a moment's notice. Thus there was to be the novel problem of airfields becoming unfit[1] very suddenly; flying conditions could deteriorate so much in so short a space of time that a closely knit system of homings, diversions, and recalls to aircraft in the air was going to be needed.

Arising from the weather was another problem which D.A.F. was soon to face. Airfields which in the Desert had been sited practically at will and which in Sicily had been hacked out of olive groves or spread on compacted earth, in Italy, especially in the winter, would have to be made wholly of P.S.P. if they were to be used under all conditions. P.S.P., which occupied an unconscionable amount of space in ship, train, or truck, was in short supply. Runways had to be the narrowest, taxi tracks the shortest possible. Hence rigid control of aircraft landing or taking-off was the only sure way of preventing ground accidents. This, too, was a matter for the flying control section, but in D.A.F. the organization hardly existed. M.O.R.U. fulfilled the function of

[1] "Unfit" means unfit for use due to weather; as opposed to "unserviceable", which means unfit for use due to any other cause.

Central (Regional) Flying Control; a few officers on the Wings attempting Aerodrome Control.

If untried Aircraft Safety found few patrons, Air-Sea Rescue, Desert-tested, was promoted with zeal and energy. According to the 244 Wing diarist:

> "We should have considered this invasion business a dull performance had not Lieut. Bolitho of 145 been forced to bale out owing to engine trouble, for his rescue accounted for the majority of today's sorties."

Whilst the squadrons were "de-lousing"[1] the Vaticano area, the Lieutenant developed engine trouble. Spitfire VIIIs covered him down; Spitfire Vs jettisoned their long-range tanks and climbed; a Walrus was escorted over the pilot afloat in a dinghy, but the sea was too rough to land. In the meantime an Air-Sea Rescue launch got under way. Unfortunately a pilot from 1 S.A.A.F. crashed into the sea and the launch was directed to search for him, too, but only debris could be found. The launch was finally able to rescue the Lieutenant; the Spitfires could cease their escort activities.

Air-Sea Rescue was demonstrably efficient; the morale of air crew on flights over the sea remained high. Operations, however, continued to be for the moment "dull". The enemy was ploughing up the Crotone landing-grounds, still clearly awaiting the battle for Naples.

But if the Germans were trying to keep aircraft in reserve, Strategic Air Force was intent on denying them the fields from which to fly. A Wellington blitz on Capua and Capodichino was followed up by American Fortresses and Lightnings on Terracina and Grazzianise. American Mitchells and Marauders over Grazzianise satellite, on the same day that ninety-nine American Fortresses visited Viterbo, spread fragmentation bombs far and wide. The final onslaught on the 6th against fighter bases (Pomigliano, Capodichino, and Grazzianise) stencilled the Stars and Stripes over the entire Naples area. Monte Corvino, by deliberate intent, alone survived. Of the others, nothing but small strips remained in use. From then on, Strategic Air Force resumed interdiction of the proposed battlefield by attacking marshalling yards. The principle of interdiction was even applied to high-ranking German officers; for on the 8th, Strategic Air Force bombed Kesselring's Headquarters at Frascati.

Laurels had thus been plucked, formed into a wreath, and already fitted to the head of the air forces by the time that the invasion fleet arrived in the Gulf of Salerno on the night of September 8th/9th. British and American naval units screened, whilst carrier-borne fighters and squadrons of coastal and Tactical Air Forces held an air umbrella over, the convoy, to such purpose that only one ship was sunk (and that by torpedo) before the assault began.

The presence of the convoy off the shores of Italy provoked the only

[1] The expression in current use at that time.

possible German reaction, an attack from the air that night. But patrolling Beaufighters were lying in wait: the Germans lost seven aircraft.

In the early hours of September 9th, 6 (American) Corps on the right, and 10 (British) Corps on the left, landed at Salerno. The first bridgehead was established in spite of fierce opposition, while Commandos occupied the western half of the town and United States Rangers secured the mountain pass at Nocera. Ship-controlled fighters of 12th A.S.C. and carrier-borne Seafires, patrolling overhead, engaged F.W. 190's which appeared in the late afternoon. As a result, few bombs were dropped on Allied forces, and four aircraft were destroyed for the loss of two.

Whilst still at sea, the men in the invasion armada had been heartened by the announcement of the Italian surrender, but they little knew of the anxious moments which those at Allied Force Headquarters had endured. Apprehensive of strong German forces near Rome, Badoglio sent a sudden message that he could not now guarantee the three airfields on which the men of the 82nd Airborne Division were to land. His last-minute representation was accepted; the airborne operation was cancelled. But the other Italian request, namely for a postponement of the announcement of the Armistice, smacked of indecision; and a reply blending menace with an appeal to good faith was sent swiftly back. For some fateful hours it appeared to have had no effect. At the moment when General Eisenhower was broadcasting the Armistice from Algiers, Arab listeners, tuned in to an Italian station, were being regaled with the news that the Italians were determined to fight to the bitter end "despite lying propaganda to the contrary". Three-quarters of an hour later Badoglio's voice was heard and anxiety was at an end.

Relief was general. No. 1 M.O.R.U. commented:

> "It was fortunate that the news coincided with a N.A.A.F.I. issue of gin and whiskey, the first for some weeks, as well as the purchase in the morning of ninety-four litres of *vino bianco.* It was accordingly possible to celebrate the news in due form and with proper ceremony."

As the landings were taking place at Salerno, the 1st British Airborne Division was put ashore at Taranto, the naval units involved being escorted by the fighters of D.A.F. working at extreme range. There were few Germans and so there was virtually no opposition; for the "Short Instrument of Surrender" (Clause 7) guaranteed "free use by the Allies of all airfields and naval ports in Italian territory regardless of the rate of evacuation of the Italian territory by the German forces". Ground patrols occupied Brindisi on September 11th, Bari on the 14th, to set the Heel, with its airfields, under Allied control.

Events, encouraging enough on the eastern side, gave less cause for satisfaction in the Avalanche area. For though 10 Corps captured Monte

Corvino airfield on the 10th, the prospective tenants were baffled by enemy gunfire. Even when Monte Corvino was retaken it proved to be too unsafe to use until the 20th. The carrier-borne Seafires soon found that they would be required for longer than the two days as originally planned.

American engineers were therefore busy making landing-strips in the relatively safer areas. Whilst 324 Wing moved into Tusciano, at Paestum the ancient temple found itself suddenly confronted by Seafires on the 12th and by Warhawks of the 33rd Fighter Group on the 14th. Other dry-weather strips varying from 650 to 1,400 yards long by 50 to 100 yards wide were constructed near the Sele river, Asa, and Capaccio. Each could accommodate three squadrons, but all were dustbowls eager to veil and trap the unwary.

The Germans, in strength on the hills commanding Monte Corvino, could not exploit their advantage, but their counter-attack, launched on the 13th to exploit our weakness in the Sele river area (where the two army corps joined), carried them almost to the sea. Hence practically the whole of 6 Corps had to be moved north of the Sele towards Battipaglia, leaving the mountain passes to the south and south-east to be protected only by engineers and other non-combatant troops. To avoid being caught by German pincers, the Allies urgently needed to stage a diversion; the 82nd Airborne Division, which had so narrowly escaped being dropped on Rome, was called into battle behind our own lines where the men assumed positions most likely to be threatened.

During those critical days the entire available forces, land, sea, and air, concentrated on maintaining the bridgehead. British and American ships bombarded enemy positions—on the 14th they succeeded in breaking up a tank formation—whilst T.A.F. sponsored 700 sorties as against a German 100.

On the 13th, the bombers of N.W.A.A.F., which had up to then been used indirectly against road junctions and bridges, were switched wholly on to support for the besieged bridgehead. Photo-reconnaissance showed that they had already destroyed the Castel Nuova road junction, cut the Formia road in three places to the north-east of the town, blocked Benevento bridge, and cratered all the approaches to Ariano.[1] Now they were to depress the arteries nearer the battlefield where, for the few vital days, they could exercise a decisive strangulation of German supplies. The enemy was using what strength he could muster against our army and ships; his troops and communications, protected only by flak, lay at the mercy of an air force which had already won its air battle before the start of the action.

As the German counter-attack threatened to drive the Allies into the sea, British and American heavy, medium, and light bombers spread a carpet of destruction over Battipaglia and Eboli, on the roads leading northwards from Salerno to Avellino and southwards to Auletta. "One must admit they were thorough," commented an Italian. "When they bombed Pompeii, it wasn't even safe in the ruins!" That night the Wellingtons, rising to the occasion,

[1] The reader is advised to study a map. Interdiction is best explained visually.

hammered Battipaglia and Eboli; American Mitchells were led by Boston pathfinders over Auletta and Controne and followed by night-intruder bombers of T.B.F. Photo-reconnaissance reported:

> "The railway lines to Castellamare, Salerno, Naples, and Cancello, are all cut by direct hits. The highway to Naples north-west of the town is blocked, and the roads to Castellamare and Naples are severely damaged. Around Battipaglia, the Naples, Metaponto and Reggio lines are still cut. The roads to Naples and Rutino are cut and the bridge destroyed, whilst the road to Metaponto is severely damaged."

No band of fifth columnists could have produced more far-reaching results than these. No Olga Polovska could have achieved half as much in twice the time as the massed squadrons of the Allied air forces. At the close of September 15th, although there were no great changes in the battle line, the enemy was already showing signs of passing from offensive to defensive. The reinforced 5th Army had already consolidated its positions and regained the initiative. A very dangerous moment had passed.

General Alexander wrote:

> "The tremendous air attacks added greatly to the morale of the ground and naval forces and in addition have inflicted on the enemy heavy losses in men and equipment. They have seriously interfered with his movements, interrupted his communications, and prevented his concentration of the necessary forces to launch large-scale attacks."

Once again air power had demonstrated exactly what it could and could not do. It had restricted drastically but not strangled completely. It had damaged, but not irrevocably. It had "kept their heads down", and had attenuated German supplies at the moment when our naval and land forces needed precisely these conditions.

Not only had D.A.F. maintained patrols over the actual bridgehead, but its fighter-bombers had contributed indirectly to Avalanche by harassing vehicles and troops on their way to Salerno. On the 15th, Kittyhawks, from their new base at Grottaglie near Taranto, joined in the fray, able to operate from Italian soil at such an early stage in the campaign because of a remarkable air-lift on the "Marble Arch" pattern.

The continuity of Desert Air Force experience was perhaps even more remarkable than the action itself. On every fresh occasion, it seemed, the veteran could say, "This has all happened before, under 'Collie' or 'Mary'."[1]

[1] Collishaw and Coningham.

A conference convened by Broadhurst on the 12th outlined plans for the move. 239 Wing, to be followed by 244 Wing, were to be transplanted in working order to Italy. The next day the Officer Commanding 239 Wing passed instructions received from D.A.F. Headquarters to the Commanding Officers of 3 R.A.A.F. and 112 squadrons; at two o'clock that afternoon the Station Commander's party was to set off by air for Grottaglie. Accordingly, only ten minutes behind time, three Dakotas took off from Agnone in Sicily. Some two hours later the party arrived over the airfield to find flak going up from Taranto.

On landing, the Group-Captain introduced himself to the *Chef d'Aeroporto*, an Italian air force *Colonello*, who gave him to understand that little or no support could be expected from the *Regia Aeronautica*, as the Germans had taken all the trucks and had destroyed everything which had not already been blasted by Allied bombs. This, though disappointing, was only to be expected. Other matters crowded out regrets; for the Mobile Operations Room site had to be selected and the Signals Section had to be put into working order as soon as possible. Whilst the Group-Captain was paying calls on Navy House and on H.Q. No. 6 Sub Area in Taranto, the Air Formations Signals party were laying telephone lines, and the little mobile radar, "Mickey", was being installed (amidst head-noddings from those who had been air-lifted to Marble Arch). Billets in the town were then found for the officers, who were meanwhile to eat in the Italian mess.

The 13th was liaison day. Italian officers discussed the aerodrome and its facilities with their English counterparts. A visit from Air Vice-Marshal Broadhurst put the official seal on individual arrangements. The Wing Headquarters settled in what was left of the control tower; messes for all ranks sprouted at the back of each squadron dispersal. All was now ready for the fifty-two Dakotas to fly in supplies, including jeeps, for the Wing.

Operations, of course, were already in progress, since moving and operating the same day was a matter of principle with D.A.F. units. An early tactical reconnaissance revealed little; morning mists made visibility poor. Later in the day lorries packed nose to tail between Potenza and Postiglione were damaged from low-level and then strafed. During the next few days 244 Wing arrived by air and operations increased, though various side activities distracted the ground staff. A phenomenal number of important military and naval visitors descended on the field, requiring in practically every case motor-cars to take them on to Taranto or Brindisi. These the Wings would have been unable to supply even had their full complement of transport arrived. Regrets, with constant repetition, grew blunt.

The visitors included, it seemed, the entire Higher Command. The A.O.C. was often there; on the 21st he met Tedder and Coningham at the airfield and the party went on a tour of the squadrons. The next day he met Montgomery and Alfrey. Two days later, Coningham and Alexander pursued 239 Wing to Bari airfield, its new base.

244 Wing, too, had not stayed long at Taranto; after a few days it was *en route* for Gioia, where the Officers' Mess was for the first time within memory installed in a house. There it was joined by 285 Wing and some undefined parts of 225 squadron and 1437 strategic reconnaissance flight; and finally by war correspondents representing practically every newspaper.

Those were strange days for the airmen. Each aerodrome they occupied had barely been cleared of Germans by the Airborne Division. Italians, so lately enemies, were not only ubiquitous but were still in positions of responsibility. The situation appeared to be growing daily more surrealist; the unpredictable was becoming the ordinary; the humdrum would have seemed fantastic.

They could perhaps have had no better introduction to a country through which they were to fight for so much longer than they had ever imagined.

CHAPTER XXXI

THE FIRST FRUITS OF THE INVASION OF ITALY

On the other side of Italy, slow but sure Allied gains contrasted with the rapid accumulation of thinly defended territory in the Heel. 6 Corps occupied Contursi and Campagna and advanced towards Acerna and the high ground ten miles north-west of Eboli, nearing targets already well known to Allied air crews. On the 28th, armed units of 5th Army pushed through the pass of Pagani and entered the Naples plain to occupy Pompeii and Castellamare. Nothing now stood between them and Naples. The days of anxiety for Salerno were over.

8th Army, a day earlier, had quietly achieved one of the principal strategic aims of the war in the Mediterranean. An armed thrust from Cerignola overwhelmed Foggia. By the close of the next day the whole of the Gargano promontory was under their control.

As September drew to a close the invasion seemed to have yielded its most precious fruits, for Naples, too, was in our hands. Troops were converging on the airfields of Pomigliano and Capodichino, where wrecked gliders and burnt-out shells of German aircraft were hardly discernible amidst the chaos of smashed hangars and cratered workshops.

Before abandoning the city the Germans had carried out thorough demolitions; cranes were destroyed and ships deliberately sunk in awkward places. Within a week, however, five berths were ready and the harbour was clearing upwards of 2,500 tons daily. But German engineers had been busy elsewhere, for in the Post Office nestled a time-bomb.

Lurid reports had come over the German radio; the city was said to be in the grip of disease on an epidemic scale; the population famished and rioting; the city in ruins after the terror bombing of residential areas, for which the Americans were particularly blamed. But though German troops had looted extensively before retreat, and though the Allied troops with their paper *lire* rapidly started to buy what had not already been stolen, the doctrine of "*Dolce far niente*" spread beneficent wings over the town; and the civil population was officially described as "orderly".

The retreating Germans were literally swathed in cloud. T.B.F. could attack Benevento, and Warhawks sprayed road junctions north of Naples, but many missions had to be cancelled. Night operations were discontinued, D.A.F. Spitfires were able to patrol from Bari to Termoli, but their advanced ground parties, *en route* for a somewhat ambiguous location in the Foggia area, found themselves forced to take cover in the buildings of a technical college; there they crouched, their aerodrome unserviceable, their hopes low, whilst the rear party at Gioia welcomed the advanced road section of 7 S.A.A.F. Wing arriving, covered in grey dust, from Sicily. The meteorological officers at D.A.F. Headquarters were clearly to have no sinecure.

Foggia, the bare bleak plain, the spur on the boot of Italy, was to afford temporary harbour to D.A.F. units before they could move on northwards. It was then to be given over entirely to Strategic Air Force, for whose benefit the area seemed expressly designed. With the capture of that group of airfields the Allied wheel of air encirclement was nearly complete. Whole sections of Southern Europe and the Balkans, formerly relatively safe—the industrial parts of Silesia, the factories of Czechoslovakia, the oilfields of Roumania—all were now within range of escorted bombers. From Lincolnshire and Foggia spokes radiated outwards to cross every part of Hitler's empire except, ironically enough, Danzig.

Possibilities fought for attention. Bombers escorted over southern France and the mounting of yet another invasion; a shuttle service between England and Italy, aircraft taking-off from one country, dropping their bombs on the Reich, and landing in another; air contact between Italy and the U.S.S.R.; supply running to the Partisans of Yugoslavia. If Naples held the key to a successful invasion of Italy, Foggia seemed to many to be the threshold of Europe.

D.A.F. units, the first to arrive, could scarcely share such a view. For them the threshold was brightened by no strategical considerations. Each flat stretch of earth was but one more forward field destined to be too long underfoot for their liking. The drab windswept plain grew little but corn, and had in the past been renowned as a place where horses ran almost wild to gain strength and sinew for a military future. Trees, bent by the prevailing wind, were stunted and unlovely. Villages, scattered like clumps of peeling mushrooms in uninteresting paddocks, were relieved by no sudden touches of beauty or civilization. Gerbini was here repeated, a Gerbini less arid, less primitive, but with the same uniform farmhouses of a land settlement scheme and the same purely rural aspect.

Whilst the forward fighting units were moving up to this ill-favoured Canaan the light bomber ground staffs were on the road from Gerbini to Brindisi. On September 21st, T.B.F. ordered the A parties of 232 Wing to proceed to Messina marshalling yards preparatory to embarkation for Italy. The first convoy (25 officers, 380 other ranks, 72 prime movers and 22 trailers) arrived at Brindisi on the 29th, a day after their aircraft. The second party (24 officers, 383 other ranks, 72 prime movers and 22 trailers) left Gerbini on the 5th and arrived on the 13th. When 326 Wing was also preparing to move it seemed that the order had not come a moment too soon; a thunderstorm had already torn tentage to shreds and soaked the dark-brown earth; the day of uprooting produced a second storm which drenched much of the excitement of travel.

There were few regrets at the prospect of leaving Sicily. Mosquitos, dust, rough landing-strips and even rougher roads, these were hardly happy memories for air or ground crew. Even Taormina, forever climbing its rocky cliff, could fade into the distance without claiming more than a turn of the head. Etna receded as the convoy reached Messina, the ferry terminal which war had damaged more than the great earthquake of 1908.

The last night spent by the Wing on Sicilian soil renewed hopes that Italy might have something different to offer. Drawn up on a leaguering ground outside Messina, the trucks disgorged their damp cargoes, whose first aim was to swallow the hot food prepared by the captured German Mobile Cookhouse. A throng of men, women and children from the town, permanently stationed near at hand, eagerly grasped for scraps. What could not be begged was, if possible, stolen; and what could not be stolen was regarded with envious curiosity coming close to hatred. Well-fed airmen and ragged, under-nourished children did not make a happy contrast. Much was given away that ought, strictly speaking, to have been retained. Maddened finally by the insistence of the appeals to their generosity, the airmen hardened their hearts and would supply no more. But few escaped the feeling of unease at a situation for which they were indirectly responsible, yet for which they saw no remedy.

Reggio di Calabria next day sparkled across the straits in the sunshine; and though closer acquaintance revealed little that was unlike Sicily, greener fields and taller trees soon contrived those small modifications in scenery which mark the transition from insular to European.

On the road at the same time, engaged in what appeared to be an unending "moonlight flit", were thousands of Italian army soldiers making their way back on foot to their homes. Some were in uniform, some partly clad in civilian clothes, some carrying bags of different shapes and sizes in which all their possessions were packed. If the trucks of 236 Wing sagged under an assortment of freight far in excess of what had originally been specified by the manufacturers, the few Italian lorries were even more drastically overburdened, their human contents surmounting a pile of luggage that whole charabancs might well have refused.

Evidences of Italian defeat were ever-present. There had been the ruined towns and the ragged population; now there was the beaten army, disorganized, rootless, without equipment or centralized control, splitting up once more to return to the only unit still maintaining any signs of cohesion—the family group.

The convoys moved slowly, roaring in low gear up tortuous mountain roads, bumping amidst clouds of dust over diversion tracks, descending carefully through chestnut groves towards smiling valleys, emerging once more on to flat plains, perpetually overtaking remnants of the Italian army.

When the last units of 326 Wing finally arrived at their destination, to find that 232 Wing had already taken over the choicer offices on the waterfront, there were only some wooden huts erected for the Italians and some of the less inviting buildings left for them to commandeer. On the water bobbed a few Italian hydroplanes; on the field itself Italian aircraft competed for hangar space and required to be fitted into the pattern of take-off and landing. Both the men and the aeroplanes of D.A.F. appeared to be interlopers. T.B.F. Advanced Party, the last arrivals, completed the complement. Brindisi, which had known busy days before the war, was astonished by the continuous stream of aircraft which now took off from, or landed on, its smooth prepared surface.

The two Wings, 326 and 232, the one with night-flying Bostons, the other with day-flying Baltimores, seemed at Brindisi to grow together almost by common consent. In order to avoid duplication the ground sections pooled resources to provide night and day services. It was not long before rumour, adding one and one together in prophetic arithmetic, made one; because the position so obviously called for amalgamation. In fact, by the end of the month 326 Wing was officially disbanded, the officers and men in most cases rejoining their sister Wing, the squadrons transferring complete.

The fusion was not accomplished without arousing a conflict of emotions; for whilst 232 Wing had been in the Desert, 326 had known the Algerian side of North Africa. Both wings were fully conscious of the splendours of their past. If 326, the newcomers, seemed inexperienced, 232, the Desert bloc, were quite sure that theirs was the only possible background and that their methods were the only possible methods. Resentment was sometimes caused by the Desert assumption of superiority; for the "Desert Types", now reduced in numbers and surrounded even in their own Wing by new faces, insisted even more strongly on the ties of brotherhood which had first bound them together during advance and retreat across the sands of Libya.

The clash of loyalties revived all the old arguments and evoked the familiar recitals of past hardships. "The sand and sun of the Desert" countered "the mud and misery of Algeria". It needed a winter in Italy to knit these factions together in opposition to discomfort eventually shared.

. . . . .

Whilst the two Wings were discussing ways and means at Brindisi, 3 S.A.A.F. Wing were still in Sicily. 21 squadron, after flying some 217 sorties from Cuticci, moved, together with the rest of the Wing, to the Italian mainland on October 16th to settle down at Tortorella (Foggia). There for the next four months the Wing remained, like most of D.A.F., resenting the weather and the mud almost more than the war itself.

A pilot of 21 squadron, the next month, was to give a splendid demonstration of perseverance which showed that the Desert spirit of D.A.F.'s first bomber Wing had survived the change of conditions. After a raid on the junction at Castel Fentano, the Baltimores ran into intense and heavy anti-aircraft fire. In one aircraft two members of the crew were killed outright; the gunner bleeding profusely, the pilot suffering from wounds in the legs, thigh and hands. The machine itself, riddled with bullets, barely kept together; one engine stopped and the air-speed indicator failed. Since the intercommunication wires had already been severed, the pilot was no longer in touch with his crew. Back over the base the pilot found that his wheels would not come down and that he would have to make a belly-landing. This he managed successfully in spite of his wounds, ploughing alongside the runway, leaving the field clear for other operations.

Incidents of this type, which called for a display of sustained bravery, were exceptional, but might occur at any moment; they were inherent in aerial warfare. For both Allied air crew and their German counterparts these dangers lurked in the background, adding hazards to the already risky business of flying in field conditions. Air crew might at any moment be killed, burnt, blinded, deafened, or broken in mind and body. Incidents could not always end successfully. From each new landing-ground there were some who took-off never to return.

The relatively slow advance of the army up Italy meant that there were, for the time being, no new bases for D.A.F. Operations were as usual closely related to the ground situation. The number of air sorties rose and fell as usual according to the urgency of the tactical situation. Small formations of F.W. 190's caused a few casualties to D.A.F. Spitfires patrolling over Termoli during the assault by 8th Army Commandos, but the enemy had evidently no intention of withdrawing entirely from the area except under continual pressure. Counter-attacks brought the Germans to a line west of Termoli–Larino, but the next day they started to evacuate their positions, demolishing skilfully as they went.

Demolitions, however, slowed down 8th Army less than the weather. Air force support was dependent more than ever on the findings of 12th Meteorological Section at D.A.F. H.Q.

Fortunately, on the critical October 6th, the weather allowed nearly 500 Kittyhawks and American Warhawks to spread confusion over the roads from Termoli, Isernia, and Chieti (84 vehicles destroyed, 113 damaged), whilst Spitfires forced a box of ten F.W. 190's to jettison bombs and seek cloud cover. The losses of the day, two Kittyhawks and one Spitfire, were described as "slight considering our scale of effort and the success of the attacks".

That evening the army sent through a message: "Many thanks for the terrific effort you have put up today. Jolly good show!" The Germans were known to be short of vehicles; D.A.F.'s bill of destruction discounted reinforcements for some days to come.

The drag-net across Italy no longer tended to sag at the centre. Allied troops now extended their sway to a line running from east of Termoli between Palata and Palena, through Ielsi and Circello, to a few miles north-west of Benevento and then along the rivers Calore and Volturno. Foggia was safe. Naples was safe. The most precious fruits of the invasion of Italy could be enjoyed to the full.

CHAPTER XXXII

TRIGNO AND ROVER

"HAVING secured the Foggia airfields," stated General Montgomery, "8th Army was given the task of advancing to the Rome Line, which was the name given to the lateral road Pescara–Avezzano–Rome." There were two barriers of water to cross before coming within reach of Pescaro, the rivers Trigno and Sangro. Of these the enemy had chosen the latter as the bulwark of his winter line, and for good reasons; on the south side of the river there was an escarpment; on the north a steep ridge frowned across a shallow plain.

"Winter Line" is descriptive. Armies in the day of Hannibal went into winter quarters—sometimes by mutual arrangement. In 1943 there were those that agreed with the verdict of the Ancients. The river Sangro could be relied upon to be in flood. An offensive was indeed a bleak prospect.

Whilst preparations for the Trigno assault were maturing, D.A.F., never sure from day to day whether the Foggia system would remain serviceable or not, attacked trains north of Pescara, reverting to tanks and gun positions west of Termoli in support of the Canadian push towards Campobasso.

Enemy air activity could hardly even be described as slight. On October 10th a Do. 217 was shot down and a reconnaissance Ju. 88 damaged for the loss of one Spitfire. A week later there were small-scale raids on Termoli harbour and Foggia. Bostons, night-intruding over the roads and railways from Vasco to Pescara, were rarely challenged.

8th Army neared the lower reaches of the Trigno on the 21st, to establish a bridgehead after two days of attack and counter-attack. Then the Canadians started a thrust towards Isernia, the important junction on the Vasco–Naples lateral. Until the 27th, the weather was fine and warm. D.A.F. Spitfires flew offensive sweeps, patrolled over Foggia and Manfredonia, flew strafing missions along the east coast up to Ancona in company with the fighter-bombers, and escorted light bombers to close-support targets. From the 18th, Boiano in the southern sector was the scene of the most consistent close-support activities. Light bombers followed the fighter-bombers, their work, according to army reports, being in all cases excellent.

Air operations tended to become repetitive. Effort remained constant; only the place-names changed. Sometimes it would be the turn of Bostons and Baltimores, sometimes of fighter-bombers. The victims, the San Salvo batteries, the bridges across the Sangro, the road convoys by night, were all direct army targets.

D.A.F. was becoming more and more parochial. Strategic Air Force carried the main burden not only of air interdiction, but also of attacks on town centres.

From time to time the larger air war revealed its existence. On the 24th a huge number of Liberators and Fortresses escorted by Lightnings passed over M.O.R.U. Headquarters on their way to the Messerschmitt works at Wiener Neustadt. Nine days later they passed over again.

D.A.F.'s parish, however, was thriving. Numbers were increasing, 322 Wing had returned from 12th A.S.C. and was now at Gioia; 324 Wing was expected shortly. The 79th Group was joined by the 99th (coloured) squadron. But rain and mud drowned the increase, bringing about an almost complete standstill on the 27th. The next day, when weather was even worse, only twelve aircraft took off, and of these, two of 92 squadron vanished. It might have been an unfortunate omen for the main thrust across the Trigno, but this, equally swamped, did not take place until the night of November 2nd. By the time that 5 Corps poured forward to the accompaniment of aerial and naval gunfire the skies favoured 326 sorties against eight different army targets.

One very successful fighter-bomber attack was, in fact, an inspired mistake. Our troops were both behind and in front of Tufillo when D.A.F., the *deus ex machina*, dropped bombs in the centre; the village was then captured. The real target, Palmoli, two miles to the north-east, escaped.

As 8th Army left flank was occupying Isernia, the Americans on 5th Army right front closed in on the Venafro–Isernia highway, one of the roads to Rome. The Germans retaliated by flooding the Pontine marshes and by demolishing all the rail and most of the road bridges over the lower Garigliano river. When Mignano was knocked flat in order to make way for defences, the other part of the Winter Line revealed itself as a bottleneck barring access to the Cassino plain. Such measures ensured that the march to the capital would be more in the nature of an obstacle race.

. . . . .

After the Trigno crossing, a new experiment in ground control paraded on the 8th Army front: "Rover David Cab-rank".

Before explaining the meaning of this cryptic phrase, a few words need to be said about the usual system of delineating close-support targets. The methods had changed very little since Desert days, although Air Liaison Officers were now better equipped with larger staffs.

In principle, then, the forward Tentacles broadcast a series of code-numbered targets to Air Liaison Sections at D.A.F. H.Q., M.O.R.U. and at all Wings or Groups. No action could be taken until the Army H.Q. had consulted D.A.F. H.Q., and accepted or rejected specific targets. Then D.A.F. H.Q. only needed to send out a message, "Signal code No. —— accept", and M.O.R.U. would allot the task to one of the Wings. The Wing Air Liaiso

Officer, who would by then have prepared his maps and charts in the light of the broadcast, was ready to brief the squadron chosen to carry out operations by the Wing. That, then, was the usual method.

"Rover David Cab-rank" approached the problem of air support from quite another angle. In essence, a mobile Army/Air Observation Post briefed aircraft flying overhead to attack targets new to both ground and air. The key to briefing was a grid superimposed on a photograph, copies of which were carried by both the ground controller and the pilot.

The first Rover party was organized by Heysham, the Wing-Commander Operations at D.A.F. H.Q. His Christian name, the call-sign for the first experiment, stayed in that capacity until novelty became accepted practice. Cab-rank is self-explanatory; aircraft patrolled overhead until whistled out of the line by the ground controller.

At first, Rover David consisted of armoured cars, fitted, whilst D.A.F. H.Q. was at Vasto, with V.H.F. radio. Finally the section carried on its strength a truck, a jeep and trailer, two army and R.A.F. wireless operators, and a mechanic.

The workings of Rover are best illustrated by a reconstruction. The time is six o'clock; the place is Air Commodore Pike's caravan at D.A.F. Headquarters. The conference—though that is perhaps too formal a word to describe a friendly meeting—is due to begin. The R.A.F. are represented by the Senior Air Staff Officer, the Group-Captain Operations, the Wing-Commander Operations, and the Wing-Commander Intelligence. On the army side sit the Brigadier-General Staff, G.I.[1] Intelligence, G.I. Operations, and the G.I Air.

The army outline what they have done during the day. The R.A.F. then give a résumé of their work. The army say what they propose to do the next day. The R.A.F. then consult amongst themselves and decide what they can do to help. For instance, the army might say, "Can we have Rover control from ten to twelve o'clock in XY area?" The R.A.F. would answer: "Yes. What sort of targets?" . . . "Various buildings we have our eye on."

After the conference, the directif for the next day's operations will be sent to M.O.R.U. which will then normally allot Wings. At Wing, one of the squadron Intelligence Officers will be warned of what is in store for tomorrow. Briefing will be simple, since the aircraft are to fly to some easily distinguishable landmark and orbit overhead for twenty minutes, or until given further instructions from the ground.

From nine o'clock next day all sorts of requests will be sent to the Rover control post; and if telephone communication is good, the army representative can check the priority of the targets by direct consultation. If, for some reason, this cannot be done, then he will have to draw upon his military experience to decide which to accept. The Rover staff, all of them officers, were capable of

[1] General Staff Officer Number One.

assuming complete responsibility whenever necessary without further sanction from Higher Authority.

Imagine, then, a battered hut with peeling walls set on a slight eminence—possibly, though not necessarily, within sight of the battle area. Imagine, if you wish, the noise of gunfire, the crackle of radio, the difficulties with the telephone, the coarse jokes, in short the undramatic setting and undramatic behaviour of men who find themselves doing a particular job in circumstances sometimes dangerous, but whose conversation is neither high-flown nor terse, nor preoccupied with any other than everyday matters. Hysteria and the crusading spirit alike, both are at a discount here.

As though to insist on individuality, dress is anything but uniform. One has a sheepskin coat; another has corduroy trousers—in fact they are typical, in their diversity of appearance, of all the men of Desert Air Force.

The moment for which they were waiting has arrived; the Kittybombers will soon be overhead. By the time that the aircraft are in the cab-rank the R.A.F. controller will have marked the first target on his map and discovered the grid reference.

The German wireless interceptor would hear something like this:

"Hello Rover David: Shabby Leader calling."

"Hello Shabby Leader: Rover David."

"Have you a map of the Sangro north?"

Call-signs will be repeated each time; as also any instructions given.

The conversation continues:

"Look at Square B15 . . . have you got it?

"At the top right-hand corner you will see a bend in the river turning sharply to the west . . . just in the north of the bend there are two houses side by side . . . take the left-hand one, the west one, that is your target."

Shabby Leader then repeats the instructions and checks with each of his aircraft in turn to make sure that all have seen it. The final words may be:

"O.K. One more circuit and down we go!"

When the formation leader repeats the target instructions he may add one or two more details as to the colour or type of country—ploughed field, line of green trees, etc. For he can see his target clearly, whereas Rover David might well be sited out of view. Rover briefing could be carried out at some distance from the battle, even from behind a hill; for the object of Rover was not to see the target he was describing but to act as an agent for immediate air support.

Theoretically a target could be attacked very shortly after request, the only time-lag being the actual passing of close-support calls from Brigade via Rover to the aircraft overhead. The system was particularly effective against enemy guns liable to change sites overnight. The latest analysis of the Army Counter-battery Officer could be flashed via Rover to the waiting squadron. There was less chance of wasting bombs on vanished foes.

The success of Rover David proved infectious. Other Christian names soon crowded the lists—Jimmy, Frank, Joe, Pete and Paddy. Experiments helped to perfect the system; keeping up with the battle had caused difficulties, so mobile Rovers were installed in four Sherman tanks in December 1944. Owing to technical troubles the experiment was a failure; but in 1945 a series of trials lasting three days were held near the River Ronco, an armoured regiment out of the line taking part in a mock battle, one aircraft representing a cab-rank. The Americans, developing the idea still further, linked Rover with a Cub aeroplane working on the same radio frequency as the fighter-bomber and the ground controller, the crew of the Cub consisting of a pilot from 22 T.A.C. and an artillery officer from one of the 5th Army Divisions. Aircraft then became in effect flying guns. This, known as Horsefly, produced swift results, but was regarded with disfavour by the R.A.F. as being uneconomical in air support resources.

One obvious question remains to be answered. Why wasn't Rover developed earlier? There had been experiments at El Hamma (that breeding-ground of innovation), with a flight-lieutenant in an armoured car. Might not the gridded photographic maps, the wireless sets, the army/air combination, have started work sooner than November 1943?

It might have been possible to arrange for all the Rover facilities in Sicily. But an amphibious operation followed by rapid advances did not provide many suitable opportunities for trying out experiments in air support; nor, during the period of fluidity in Italy, was Rover likely to be given the leisure to emerge. Chiefly, Rover David Cab-rank was the by-product of unchallenged air superiority. Fighter-bombers could never have patrolled over set areas waiting for instructions from the ground had there been even the remote chance of enemy opposition. Solely because the *Luftwaffe* was not only defeated, but by that time practically non-existent, could D.A.F. take such liberties with the air crew.

The Rover system had evolved in answer to the logic of the situation, as all the tenets of D.A.F. had in the past evolved. The spirit of improvisation which had carried D.A.F. successfully through the Desert was by now a tradition so deeply embedded that changing conditions simply gave fresh scope for the show of initiative. The swing of the pendulum in the Desert, the scramble through Sicily, the upheaval in Italy; air warfare against an enemy first waxing and then waning in strength; winter stalemate amidst mud and thunder of the Sangro; summer lull amidst sand and stones of Alamein; all was grist to the Desert Air Force mill.

. . . .

On December 1st a few flakes of snow drifted down over the Foggia plain; yet on the 2nd Tactical Air Force was able to establish a record, flying 1,200 sorties, more than had been flown in any one day since the start of the

Tunisian campaign. Of that total, D.A.F. Spitfires, Kittyhawks and Warhawks contributed 340 for the 8th Army and 70 over Yugoslavia. Forty Mitchells flew four missions against a bridge over the Pescara river in order to hinder the enemy from reinforcing his sector north of the Sangro now menaced by the 8th Army.

Three days later, Thunderbolts made their début when the 79th Group provided area cover for Mitchells attacking Split. Pilots of the 57th Group, also soon equipped with the new Thunderbolts, were to be seen mainly over targets in Yugoslavia until moved across to the other side of Italy for the Nettuno–Anzio landings.

Few references can be made to the *Luftwaffe*. It was increasingly inactive, and only once effective. A freak raid on the night of December 2nd/3rd by Ju. 88's transferred from Milan to forward bases at Rimini caused widespread destruction in Bari harbour. The thirty aircraft carrying bombs and mines were preceded by others dropping "Window" (tinfoil to jam our radar). The harbour was crammed with vessels newly arrived; a hit on two ammunition ships brought about a holocaust. The entire town resounded with the noise of the explosions, the port capacity was seriously reduced for some time to come, casualties were high. Had the Germans been able to maintain such an effort on a nightly basis, dislocation could have been made permanent; and yet even then there would have been no clear comparison between the scope of the *Luftwaffe* and that of the Allied Air Forces. But this was an isolated raid. It was not to be repeated.

And thus the year which had promoted such stirring events in the Mediterranean ended; "not with a bang but a whimper".[1] Swollen rivers, blocked roads, ruined railways, demolitions, a stubborn enemy determined to defend the southern approaches to the Fatherland—all these barred the road to Rome. But on all fronts the Allies were slowly advancing; with the occupation of more and more Italian airfields the air forces were able to strike progressively further into the hitherto inaccessible parts of Hitler's Europe.

Nevertheless the phrase, "Soft underbelly of Europe", seemed to the ground and air forces in front of the Winter Line to be not merely understatement but purest fantasy.

[1] T. S. Eliot.

CHAPTER XXXIII

WINTER PROBLEMS

MORNING of the new year, which should, according to the poet, have dawned bright and clear, ushered in a day of damp and misery. M.O.R.U. at Penna Point were in a particularly exposed position. The Unit Diary gives a most human account of their sufferings:

> "Daylight found the site an indescribable scene of desolation. In the small hours, probably between 0300 and 0400, the abominable gale returned, accompanied by very heavy rain. One and all suffered; the Orderly Room was flattened and draped half across the road, and the officers' tents on the old site all collapsed except for the one which was moved on the leeward side of a technical vehicle. Certain of our Scots were difficult to arouse from a slumber induced by a traditional celebration of Hogmanay, but eventually, one and all, except for the one tent which was anchored, found their way into the mess in varying degrees of dampness. The plight of the few airmen accommodated in tents was no better. Practically every tent was torn and there was no hope of them being used again until either they were replaced or extensively repaired. Airmen were all squeezed somehow into buildings, and there remained the question of accommodating seven officers. The only available building was the chapel of Santa Maria Della Penna, so the pews were removed and stacked in the chancel and the seven officers installed themselves. The verger or caretaker came in and lent a hand and then produced a vast bottle of *Vino Rosso*, and made us all drink to *Capo d'Anno*. No flying was possible; 7 S.A.A.F. Wing on the beach at Trigno were literally washed out, the sea being forced up on to the beach by the strong northerly gale."

In 1942, 244 Wing, waiting to go for the first time into the Western Desert, had been victims of a storm at Amriya. Then "the canvas-covered holes in the ground where the airmen slept were super swimming pools and airmen could be seen fishing disconsolately for treasured boots and socks". Since then the Wing had travelled many miles, to find past history awaiting it far across the Mediterranean.

The Meteorological forecast stated that no improvement in the weather was to be expected next day, but in the Country of Surprises the sun shone brightly and a fresh north-west breeze encouraged flying. The after-effects of the storm prevented the most being made of the opportunity. 7 S.A.A.F. Wing was emerging like some buried city from the waves; 57 Group and the forward party of 239 Wing were out of action. Other D.A.F. units, however, put up 252 sorties. German trucks snowbound near Avezzano and Manopello were attacked to some effect; 130 were claimed, destroyed or damaged. The A.O.C. sent his congratulations to all the Wings concerned, adding that he hoped they would finish off their work. This they attempted on the next day, claiming another 120.

3 S.A.A.F. and 232 Wings were meanwhile directed against the enemy's strongpoint at Palena, in the centre of the eastern defence line; and to a lesser extent against St. Donata, to the west of our left flank.

The storms of the last few days had not, as might have been expected, put the heavier aircraft completely *hors de combat.* Celone (Foggia), which before Christmas had been a morass, had been given a lease of semi-permanent life by British and American Airfield Construction Companies. A runway of pierced steel plate was ready, taxi tracks and dispersals like elongated steel waffles were gradually laid during the month. Celone, within a few days, had become "all weather".

Unlike the British wire mesh which had been used in the past, the American P.S.P. did not adapt itself immediately to the bumps and holes in the ground, but formed a causeway rigid and enduring. With P.S.P., airfields could be constructed wherever there was a stretch of flat land. Bulldozers crashed across fields and ditches; gravel was smoothed in their wake; the P.S.P. was clipped together; and a new airfield was ready for use. The army was at last being freed from the need to make the capture of permanent aerodromes part of the tactical plan. Flat country near the sea offered plenty of excellent sites for the new type of landing-grounds. P.S.P., like Bailey bridges, took up shipping space. Like Bailey bridges, too, P.S.P. had to be transplanted and used again as the battle passed onwards up Italy. So precious was each sheet of perforated metal that there could be no question of making aerodromes on the usual pattern with two or more runways. Enough for one strip only could be spared; pilots had to adapt themselves to new conditions. In England, Flying Control Officers who allowed aircraft to land in a cross-wind were courting trouble; a cross-wind of over 25 miles an hour debarred flying. In Italy cross-winds were the order of the day. Pilots had to land on a narrow strip with the certainty of crashing into rough muddy ground if they swung off the runway.

As aircraft crowded on to the new all-weather surfaces, control of their movements whilst still on the ground became more and more difficult. Taxi tracks were too narrow to allow aircraft to pass one another; ideally, therefore, there should have been a one-way traffic system. But squadron dispersals, leading off the track, had to be as near as possible to the runway and use a minimum of P.S.P. Getting a squadron in position for take-off via a one-way system might mean that the aircraft would have to taxi almost the whole way round a large airfield. Overheated engines and accidents would result. Therefore they had to proceed by the shortest route.

On the other hand, aircraft would meanwhile be landing. Each one had to clear the runway rapidly, to avoid being run into by those behind. These, too, had to pass along the taxi track to their dispersal, possibly hindering those wanting to take-off.

The problem, had it ended here, would have been awkward enough. But there were other points to consider. Marcianise, to which 18 squadron moved in February, was further blessed by detachments of 114 squadron, some Tactical Reconnaissance aircraft of 40 S.A.A.F. squadron, all the Spitfires of 244 Wing, and the Beaufighters of 600 squadron. So congested grew the air over the two-thousand-yard landing-strip that aircraft were sometimes in danger of running out of petrol simply because too much was happening on the ground for them to land for periods upwards of half an hour from the time of first entering the circuit.

To ease this situation, aircraft were often to be seen taking-off in one direction and landing in another, even with a down-wind of anything up to twenty-five miles an hour.

To have aeroplanes orbiting the fields in exasperated circles, to have one aircraft preparing to land one way as another was taking-off from the opposite end—such an arrangement should have invited head-on collisions in mid-air and consequent disaster. But the P.S.P. strips had already taught squadrons to pay the closest attention to orders from the ground. One more innovation passed without comment.

Whilst D.A.F. was at Marcianise there was not a single collision, but there were several "near-misses". Light communications aircraft, the Austers, the Piper-cubs, were often not fitted with radio. These had to be controlled by the uncertain and unsatisfactory means of the signalling lamp. The R.A.F. lamp, though visible at night, could be seen only with difficulty during the day. The larger, more powerful, American pattern was borrowed whenever possible, but even so, red flares floated upwards in dazzling profusion from the Control Tower to indicate that accidents were being narrowly avoided. All-weather temporary airfields could have their disadvantages.

Weather intervened with untiring persistence in all air activities. 55 squadron's aircraft were delayed from taking-off on the first stage of their journey to Kabrit to join ground crew who had left D.A.F. in December.

As the weather grew colder, new technical problems arose. In tropical conditions, carburettor de-icing and oil dilution had been unnecessary; now, however, the air filter on Baltimore intakes tended to ice up rapidly, particularly at night. Snow guards even had to be improvised for the Baltimores. Times had indeed suffered an air-change.

CHAPTER XXXIV

ANZIO AND CASSINO

THE presence of D.A.F. squadrons on "the other side", away from the D.A.F. area, under the operational control of 12th A.S.C., was a sign that the eastern flank was to act as a holding line and that a fresh offensive would be started by the forces in the west. 244 Wing and the 79th Fighter Group had left their aerodromes at Termoli and Madna; 324 Wing were installed at Lago, hard by the Volturno river; 114 and 18, bereft of their parent Wing, came temporarily under the scrutiny of Saville, the Commanding General of 12 T.A.C. Though Tedder had now left his command for promotion as Second in Command to Eisenhower, in spirit he continued to pervade the Allied air forces. Under his guidance American units had been absorbed into D.A.F.; similarly, to have British units under American control was now an accepted practice presenting few new problems.

600 squadron had been on the 5th Army front for some time past. The night-flying Beaufighters had come to D.A.F. in June '43, but from the moment that they had occupied Monte Corvino there had been little but the few patrols from Brindisi and Foggia to show that they were from D.A.F. rather than from 12th A.S.C. By the time that the squadron moved to Marcianise, from which they could intrude by night over Anzio, their record was unusually impressive—101 enemy aircraft destroyed for the loss of only two crews. A few weeks later, although another twenty aircraft had been shot down, 600 had lost a further six crews. They complained that "the run of good luck seemed to have run out". With this comment, however, the *Luftwaffe* would no doubt have disagreed.

Rumours about the projected bridgehead at Nettuno-Anzio were soon being discussed by all the units which had moved over to implement the new landings. The prophets predicted another Salerno, accompanied by an intensification of air support and a break-through to Rome. Few would have cared to discuss the prospects of the troops nearing Cassino, for that battleground was the Italian General Staff's idea of an impregnable defensive position.

Whilst those parts of D.A.F. remaining on the east coast continued to support the 8th Army and the Partisans in Yugoslavia and helped to prevent the transfer of German troops from coast to coast, Tactical and Strategical Air Forces joined hands for the softening-up process which in the Desert had inevitably heralded an offensive, and which in Italy, though differing in form, was the same in intent.

Softening-up implied attacks on central railway junctions, followed by a decoy bombardment of Civitavecchia, intended to persuade the enemy that the assault was planned to take place at a point north of Rome. During the second phase, from January 14th to the 21st, the bombers were to interdict the battle area and the area immediately north of Rome. During the third phase, after the assault had started, they were to isolate the battleground.

One of the air weapons to be used was Tactical Bomber Force, now a reformed character. A wholly American force under 12th Bomber Command, though still under the general direction of T.A.F., it now contained six groups of Mitchells and Marauders. No longer in the position of growing only at the expense of D.A.F., T.B.F. was at last able to carry out the terms of its charter to the full, to provide tactical bombardment, whenever and wherever needed, through its own separate Headquarters.

The mammoth Allied air forces immediately available for operations—those in fact located either in southern Italy or in Sardinia and Sicily—numbered well over 2,500, 45 per cent being in the west. In contrast the *Luftwaffe* was a flea. The wonder was not that it could hop so little but that it could hop at all. German aerodromes were showered with fragmentation bombs; their fighters could have been fully occupied in trying to defend the industrial towns of the north from attacks by heavily escorted formations of Liberators and Fortresses. Their total fighter strength—200 Me. 109's, and 30 F.W. 190's—was mainly deployed in northern Italy; only about one-third of the Me. 109's and the 30 F.W. 190's remained on aerodromes near Rome until forced out by the Allied air assault. Almost all the long-range bombers had left the eastern Mediterranean; but there were a few Ju. 88's and torpedo-bombers in Greece, Crete, and the south of France. The only bomber units remaining in Italy were two *Gruppen* at Aviano and Villafranca, near the Yugoslav border.

In spite of this unenviable disparity, the German air force during the autumn started to construct *Luftwaffen festungen.* These fortresses, built by the *Todt* organization in mimicry of the interlocking Malta system, looked from the air like vast super-airfields. Concrete runways joined by innumerable taxi tracks and sub-taxi tracks allowed aircraft to be moved at will from one field to another, or to be dispersed at distance from bomb dumps and workshops.

The 850 Allied aircraft jammed cheek by jowl on the airfields of Naples demonstrated once more the air equivalent of Montgomery's "Once a commander defeats his enemy in battle everything else will be added unto him." Air superiority made elaborate plans of construction unnecessary. So long as there was no risk of enemy bombs, aircraft could be parked like motor-cars at a gymkhana. At the time of Alamein, landing-grounds on either side of the Alexandria–Cairo road had been guilty of not "assuming a layout more in consonance with front line activities", because at least three squadrons had been together on one field. Such voices from the past echoed strangely through the serried lines of aircraft standing at readiness for the Anzio adventure.

The invasion fleet was to be well screened. Coastal Air Force was responsible for providing air protection from Naples to the little island of Ponza.

12th A.S.C. took over from then onwards, employing aircraft stepped up in layers. Four Spitfire patrols at 20,000 to 25,000 feet over the beachhead and convoy; twelve Spitfires at 16,000 to 18,000 feet (eight over the beachhead and four over the convoy); sixteen United States Warhawks (half over the beachhead and half over the convoy). 64th Fighter Wing in Naples, a control ship off the assault beach, and finally a control post on the beachhead, directed the activities of the close-support fighter-bombers.

Taking off in the pallid glow of a waning moon, 92 squadron were on patrol before first light on the 22nd. Below, the troops were already disembarking; a British infantry division with supporting artillery and tanks on the left, five miles north-west of Anzio, and an American Corps consisting of infantry, rangers, artillery, tanks, and other units, on the right near Nettuno. By nightfall the ports of Anzio and Nettuno were in our hands, whilst inland, with little enemy opposition, the bridgehead was rapidly extending.

Further on up the coast, above Rome, the navy bombarded Civitavecchia to create a diversion. If the assault on Salerno could have been prophesied by any intelligent German with a pair of compasses and a knowledge of the range of fighters, the landings at Anzio scorned prediction. The remaining inhabitants of Civitavecchia, the only port of deep draught near Rome, were convinced that the Allied convoy would appear any moment off the horizon. The German command, its eyes temporarily blinded by a raid on Perugia, which had destroyed reconnaissance aircraft, had little more reliable intelligence.[1]

The first four F.W. 190's appeared at 6.30 in the morning; one was shot down. At 11.30 another eight turned away before contact could be made, but at twelve o'clock forty Kittyhawks claimed six destroyed, one probable, and one damaged. The Spitfire pilots complained: "We are being made to fly too high for effective interception. The four who remain at 20,000 feet will never have any joy."

In the eastern battle area, D.A.F. pounced on the 26th Panzer Division en route for the bridgehead. Baltimores helped to block roads at Popoli, a town on the Chieti–Avezzano road. Both Tactical and Strategical Air Forces did their utmost to delay the enemy by wrecking communications, road and rail, whilst the Royal Navy bombarded coastal routes. Hence the Germans, in spite of recovering quickly from the surprise of the landings, could not muster up enough supplies to become aggressive until the start of February. They could not counter-attack until February 16th. Air power had created the customary breathing space.

This lull, said the critics, was/was not exploited fast enough. The Germans

[1] Why, it might be asked, in that case, did the landings not take place at Civitavecchia? Without entering into detail there were the following obvious considerations: although air cover at the limit of range could have been provided, strong German forces were at hand. There were no suitable beaches nearby. Even though the port could take big ships, contrary winds could make the manœuvring of tugs extremely difficult. Once stores had been landed the narrow streets hindered them from being carried rapidly elsewhere.

reacted with expected/unexpected spirit. As the Allied build-up in the Anzio area was continuing slowly, the Americans were attacking towards Cisterna, the British and Americans pressing towards Campoleone. Enemy tanks and self-propelled guns appeared in force to block both manœuvres.

The *Luftwaffe* meanwhile hopped this way and that; but there was per day, on average, five to six times as many 12th A.S.C. fighters and fighter-bombers as enemy aircraft operating. From January 23rd to February 1st fifty aircraft were claimed destroyed, with forty probables. On the 27th in particular, claims mounted to twenty-five destroyed, three probables, and twelve damaged. Allied losses, approximately one-third of the enemy, could hardly be called serious. When Allied anti-aircraft gunners claimed another twenty-five victims, the total for that week represented a substantial percentage of the entire enemy air force in the Mediterranean.

The Germans did, however, achieve some results. The new radio-controlled bombs showed that ingenuity could sometimes triumph over deficiency. Two destroyers and a hospital ship were sunk, a Liberty ship beached, and three destroyers, two hospital ships, and several other vessels damaged. Once again, as at Bari, the implications shouted their message aloud. If such slight air effort could produce such alarming results, what must be happening on the other side of the line where air attack was heavy, sustained, and intensive? The strategic bombers were still carrying on their work of interdiction unabated. Enemy road and railway junctions in one day were receiving more attention than the German air force could give to the bridgehead during all the weeks of its existence. Not only the junctions, but the industrial towns of the north and the ports were seldom for long undisturbed by the steady drone of four-engined bombers. Allied air power, now more than ever, remained a Hydra, darting out heads to protect not only our troops but our lines of communications, our ports, and our base towns, whilst German-held Italy was never allowed to be free of the all-seeing eyes, the tongues of fire, and the breath of destruction.

. . . . .

Although Anzio claimed most of the Allied effort, the 5th Army offensive was given a full quota of close support. But since there were now three fronts all marching simultaneously, to promote success on one was the surest way of helping another. Anzio drew off all the available strength of the *Luftwaffe*. D.A.F. on the eastern front prevented troops and reinforcements from flowing across Italy to join in the western fray.

D.A.F. continued to interfere with movements on the roads by day and by night; Baltimores battered Popoli (a target which for some reason they found difficult); the fighter-bombers strafed the town approaches. Monte Silvano station failed to survive a particularly intensive attack by Baltimores and Thunderbolts, whilst further up the coast the line was cut at San Benedetto. Each night, weather permitting, Bostons flew over the mountains to attack vehicles moving with dimmed lights along the Frosinone–Rome highway. To extend the field of destruction, Italian Mc. 205's were directed against enemy shipping in Yugoslav coastal waters.

Near Cassino, fighting had assumed curious proportions, as though designed to give the German Command more cause for confidence in the pre-war opinions of the Italian General Staff. American troops from high positions to the north and north-west pressed southwards into a town where every house was fortified, linked to its neighbours by underground passages—some of considerable antiquity—to create a formidable warren. Attacks on Abbey Hill and on Hill 593 had to be called off.

Against fortified emplacements set in the sides of hills, fighter-bombers could have very little effect. The Germans could go to earth and emerge after the danger had passed. Heads already down but still in control of guns could resist attack as fiercely as before. D.A.F., operating against enemy vehicles, did possibly the most useful form of damage when, on February 7th, 92 Spitfires, 49 Kittyhawks and 12 Thunderbolts caught enemy transport, *en route* to Cassino, snowbound at Sora; 46 vehicles were destroyed and 50 damaged. The most consistent close support by United States Invaders, though causing destruction above ground, failed to root out troops envisored in steel and concrete shells; only the hand-grenade or the bayonet sufficed.

As at Petra, in far-off Transjordania, the Nabataeans had been able to defend the narrow defile leading to their capital against all-comers, so at Cassino the Germans could close the road to Rome. And though, in Italy, perched high upon a dizzy cliff was no city rich with promise of loot, yet the highway below would only be clear when all the surrounding heights were in our hands. Rising from the most prominent and commanding of all the hills was the monastery. Even if it was thought to harbour no more than an observation post and some Italian civilians, potentially it could be the strongest of all strongpoints.

The cultural significance of destroying that monumental foundation of the Benedictine Order will no doubt occupy the minds of sensible people of all nations for some time to come. Such considerations had guaranteed its immunity in the past months, but were, in February, declared to be no longer tenable. Apart from the fact that the troops in the plain had already begun to feel "watched" from the rectangular windows of the grey stone building, the monastery had become identified with the delay and disillusionment of the entire Italian campaign. A symbol of German resistance visibly exploded by air bombardment would, for the ground forces besieging the town, become an augury of German defeat. Actually and potentially, by its physical and its symbolic presence, Monte Cassino menaced the march on Rome.

Air power unrolled a carpet of destruction; Indians, during one of their attacks, actually entered the ruins; but the hill itself, bristling with defences which offered aeroplanes no targets, was furthermore defended by German troops, whose determination could not be explained away by the word "fanaticism". As the sun went down, the ruins were still in German hands, as though expressly to deny the Allies the chance of pleading expediency for a wanton act.[1]

That midnight, at Anzio, the enemy opened up an artillery barrage against American troops who had just relieved a British Division on the left of the bridgehead front, two waves of long-range bombers backing up the attack. The next day the German *putsch* continued down the Anzio road. Tanks and infantry intended, as at Salerno, to split the defence and to drive the Allied forces into the sea.

Although raids on Udine at the end of January had claimed 161 enemy aircraft destroyed or damaged, the *Luftwaffe* had somehow managed to produce over 100 sorties on February 16th; and although on that day ten were destroyed and one or two damaged, the next day the *Luftwaffe* contrived 170 sorties and the next day 150. These, as nothing compared to the heavy, medium, light-bomber, fighter-bomber and fighter sorties flown as a daily rule by the Allies, slackened off when the German land drive came to a halt.

Once again, as at Salerno, Strategic and Tactical Air Forces were called in to help 12th A.S.C. This time bombing was planned to disrupt communications and interdict road and rail traffic in the Colli–Laziali area; this time, on February 17th, Allied aircraft dropped the heaviest weight of bombs in support of the ground forces ever recorded in the Mediterranean—952 tons. D.A.F. Baltimores from the other side of Italy even crossed the Apennines to contribute 27 tons.

To the enemy's next bridgehead offensive the air answer was similar. Although bad weather limited flying on March 1st, on the 2nd over 600 tons of bombs cratered the German assembly areas. By the 3rd, the last attempt to drive the Allies into the sea had failed.

In a simplified account such as this, much has to be omitted. Emphasis has been laid on air support and not on army operations. Tactical air support was, however, the means to an end, namely a successful outcome to the land battle. The air contribution at Anzio was impressive, possibly decisive, but it remained a contribution.

The next outstanding example of the use—or as critics have claimed, misuse—of air power was the bombardment of Cassino town as a prelude to land assault. Fighter-bombers of D.A.F. operated on the fringes of this exploit, silencing guns to the north of Aquino, whilst Spitfires joined with American Lightnings to patrol the battle areas, and Thunderbolts swept Viterbo–Canino to stem any enemy fighter opposition at source. The main

[1] This is the writer's personal opinion.

air blitz, by eleven Groups of Strategic Air Force American bombers and five American medium bomber Groups of Tactical Air Force, was to begin at 8.30 and continue at ten- to fifteen-minute intervals until noon. Cassino, as a result, was reduced to a mass of rubble. Allied artillery bombardment followed air attack as New Zealand infantry and tanks made their assault from the north. But Cassino was not El Hamma. The Germans crept out of the underground beehive to take up fresh positions in the ruins. Craters blocked all the roads. A team of bulldozers would have been the most useful contribution to the Allied cause for the next forty-eight hours. For although the New Zealanders and the Indians succeeded in occupying most of the wrecked heaps which had once been buildings, behind and in their midst reappeared the paratroops. The Cassino stalemate continued.

At Stalingrad, German efforts had created a warren of defence within which the Russians had held out indefinitely. At Cassino, too, wreckage had been over-thorough. It was demonstrated that, against a certain type of defended position, air attack could not only beget insuperable land obstacles, but could even help the defenders by providing new coigns of vantage from which to infiltrate amongst their opponents.

Such lessons of air superiority were refreshing to learn. For in the future there was to be every chance of applying improved tactics.

CHAPTER XXXV

ADJUSTMENTS, APRIL FOOL, TITO AND ROME

TOWARDS the end of March 1944 there was a change of command in D.A.F. Broadhurst left, Air Vice-Marshal Dickson took his place. It was fitting that the departing commander had gone on to other things on the anniversary of his greatest success. Exactly a year before, El Hamma had demonstrated the potentialities of the fighter-bomber when used with expert understanding. Since then Broadhurst had kept his units loyal and efficient, and had steered D.A.F. unscathed through the intricate whirlpools of centralization. In the vast complex of air forces under M.A.A.F., D.A.F. still retained its individuality and defied absorption.

The new A.O.C. took over a force that was a going concern. There were few corners for the new broom to sweep. It so happened that Dickson was familiar with events leading up to El Hamma; for at that time he had been touring the D.A.F. units in company with Air Marshal Leigh-Mallory, the Commander in Chief Fighter Command. The visitors had taken notes on D.A.F.'s organization and tactics and returned to England. Thus, under Dickson's guidance, 83 Group, the spearhead for the Normandy landings, had imbibed the savour of Gambut and El Alamein without being forced to swallow the bitter draught of actual experience.

The reshuffling of appointments in March 1944—Coningham in command of 2nd Tactical Air Force, Broadhurst at 83 Group—preserved the Desert pattern intact for Montgomery when the Second Front opened.

D.A.F.'s new commander not only understood his force, but was, as it were, one step ahead of it. 83 Group had been given the equipment and aircraft which represented the D.A.F. ideal, whilst D.A.F. itself still maintained trailers from the Desert, the ancient Baltimores, the almost obsolescent Bostons, the out-moded Kittyhawks, only able to be employed because there was scarcely any enemy opposition.

Broadhurst had recognized the capabilities of the fighter-bombers. Dickson extended D.A.F.'s night-flying capacity, encouraging 232 Wing to exchange the remaining two Baltimore squadrons over to night-intruder work. He also continued the process of converting fighters to fighter-bombers.

"Killer" Caldwell had dropped the first bomb from a Kittyhawk in March 1942. Since then, aircraft originally designed as fighters had been carrying greater and greater bomb loads. Colonel Wilmot on January 12th, 1944, had taken-off from Cutella to attack a town near Orsogna with one 1,000-pound bomb under the belly and two 500-pounders under the wings of his Kittyhawk.

Three months later he had tried a Mustang of 260 squadron with two 1,000-pounders; and though on landing the undercarriage was slightly bent, the rest of the squadron was soon in his company. Thunderbolts at Amendola in the new year had carried two 1,000-pounders; the verdict of the American Group-Leader being "Never again!" But soon this, too, became routine. The Spitfires of 7 Wing in October 1943 had carried two 250-pound bombs. In May they were to carry a 500-pounder.

With the whole force dropping bombs of different sizes, D.A.F. had now almost ceased to exist in its original form. Dog-fight victories had become increasingly rarer and were soon to become almost unknown. The eight days between May 13th and 21st provided exceptions to this rule, for Squadron-Leader Duke's squadron destroyed sixteen aircraft and damaged eight, whilst on the 21st Spitfires encountered twenty F.W. 190's and shot down eight, to make Duke's personal score twenty-eight. But the point of emphasis had been slowly shifting for some time past from the individual fighter-pilot to the group work of a formation. Air superiority meant that there would no longer be "One against the World".

Tendencies in air support had also altered. The Rover system, a luxury which earlier air forces could not have afforded, brought close support closer still. As though in compensation, other types of close support drew further away from the battlefield; fighter-bombers came to be used at more of a distance behind the enemy's front line as agents of the larger policy—air interdiction. Higher up the scale, interdiction itself was being reinterpreted M.A.T.A.F. Bombing Directive No. 2 politely reversed Directive No. 1. Marshalling yards were no longer to be the main targets for heavy bombardment; instead, bridges were to be cut. Road and rail traffic was not to be destroyed at a few heavily defended points of concentration, but was to be prevented, whilst in transit, from reaching the battlefield. To simplify the issue, the air war was now to be directed against movement rather than against centres. The supporters of the earlier theory had enjoyed a run of success. Now their work was to be implemented by a reinterpretation of the aims of interdiction.

The last days of March went out, not like a lamb, but a dragon. A pall of smoke hung over the aeroplanes crowded on to the Naples plain as Vesuvius, after warning rumbles, erupted with a violence unparalleled since 1906. Great fingers of molten fire splayed with a portentous hissing down the slopes, crushing several small villages accidentally obstructing the flow. Those who, during the Salerno days, had advocated dropping a bomb in the crater in romantic hopes of inspiring an eruption were now to see what the mountain could do without their help.

The air forces were drastically affected. One aerodrome, nestling against the leeside of the volcano, suffered the fate of ancient Pompeii. Hot ash floated down in ever-thickening layers to burn every scrap of fabric off eighty aircraft caught before they could be moved. A composite party of 18th Airfield Construction Group, with the help of 815 Aviation Engineer Battalion, cut a way through to the military service road, linking the trail to Vesuvio aerodrome some seven miles distant. Aircraft were towed to safety whilst burning cinder was falling like thick snow.

Marcianise aerodrome, already supporting more than its fair quota and sustaining a flow of air traffic for the new M.A.A.F. H.Q. at Caserta, was embarrassed by dislodged squadrons whose aircraft had to park at the edge of the narrow strip of P.S.P., defying all regulations of Aircraft Safety simply because they could be fitted in nowhere else. A few Ju. 88's might have set the airfield ablaze from end to end, could they have penetrated the defences and dived on the improvised dispersals.

Units on the other side of Italy had evidence of the upheaval; for dust, which had first floated out over the sea to descend on Capri, later became prey to the fickleness of upper winds. Powdery fragments were carried across the Apennines to Bari, Brindisi, and Foggia, then upwards to Termoli, to blow faint trails of grit over the Baltimores of 232 Wing, the new Marauders of 3 S.A.A.F. Wing, the Spitfires of 7 S.A.A.F. Wing, the tents and caravans of M.O.R.U. and D.A.F. Headquarters, before disappearing over enemy lines.

The start of another month gave an excuse for exercising an age-old prerogative. The weather on that All Fools' Day was exceptionally disheartening. If the inventive found their talents operationally unemployed, faked signals helped to eke out the hours when only fourteen sorties could be flown. D.A.F. Headquarters unbent so far as to instigate the first message. Their All Fools' Directif ran:

> "Spitfires: 13 aircraft offensive patrol Penna Point and Vasto, particular attention to low strafe of M.O.R.U. and Advanced Air Headquarters. 7 aircraft strafe anti-aircraft positions bridgehead area.[1]
>
> "Kittyhawks: 1 squadron fighter sweep Termoli, Foggia, Naples, Campobasso. Aircraft with stars only to be attached.[2] 1 squadron to attack buildings of cultural and historic value.
>
> "Baltimores: 3 squadrons to attack Air Ministry. Remainder to stand by and ferry personnel to England for accelerated promotion.
>
> "Italian Air Force: 12 aircraft to attack Vatican City."

When the weather cleared, the war once again intervened. From April 4th, D.A.F. was directed to give bridges first priority. Enemy traffic had now been almost driven off the roads during the day; movements were tending to take place at night.

Aid to the Partisans, mainly shipping strikes off the Dalmatian coast

[1] Not an ideal target. [2] I.e. Americans.

or supply dropping, intensified when on the 7th Nicsic was visited by forty-eight Kittyhawks, and on the 11th Zemonica by seventy-six Spitfires. The raid on Banja Luka by Spitfires of 7 S.A.A.F. Wing was the most outstanding. Early in April, reconnaissance confirmed Intelligence reports that the Germans, in an attempt to harass Marshal Tito's supply lines, had assembled forty-three aircraft of different types on the airfield in central Yugoslavia. A raid planned the week before had gone awry because the Spitfires had not had enough petrol to make detours to escape bad weather. Even in ideal conditions the flight—nearly 500 miles from Trigno to the target—called for extra-large jettisonable fuel tanks.

The first aircraft took off at five minutes past ten; soon the formations, 2 squadron carrying two 250-pounders, 4 squadron providing medium cover, 1 squadron top cover, were airborne. For some time after crossing the Dalmatian coast navigation was extremely difficult; the whole countryside was snowbound; the aircraft had to hug the ground in order to discountenance enemy radar. Thirteen miles from the target the formation split up. Dive-bombing, followed by low-level strafing in successive waves, was the plan of action.

A direct hit on the hangar caused consternation on the ground, for as 4 squadron fanned across the aerodrome at low-level, guns blazing, men were still running out of the hangars, not to escape below ground but to peer up at the invaders. Wave after wave chopped across the field, first from one direction, then from another. Within a quarter of an hour three German fighters, two bombers, some light craft and some dozen Italian-type fighters were all ablaze; the Control Tower was out of action; an ammunition dump exploded. One Spitfire was slightly damaged by anti-aircraft fire and one by flying too low over the scene of destruction. Otherwise there were no casualties.

This was but one instance of the ever-increasing assistance to the Partisans, of which the air forces were never sparing. Towards the end of the last week in May, whilst the Germans were on the offensive in western Bosnia, M.A.A.F. aircraft flew 415 heavy-bomber, 118 Baltimore, 42 Marauder, 327 Lightning, 55 Spitfire, and 15 Hurricane sorties over Knin, Zagreb, Kutlovec and Bihac. Messages received from Tito on May 31st and June 3rd showed that such efforts were fully appreciated:

> "British and American aircraft have driven the *Luftwaffe* from Yugoslavian skies, and considerable damage has been inflicted on German forces. As a result Partisan morale and Anglo/American prestige have soared."

Just over a year before, Mr. Eden had said in America:

> "If there is one lesson we should have learned from the distresses of these years it is surely this, that we should not close our windows, draw

our curtains, and be careless of what is happening next door or on the other side of the street, for no nation can hope to close its frontiers and hope to live secure."

A year later the window facing Yugoslavia was permanently jammed open as Coastal, Strategic and Tactical Air Forces alike, in spite of heavy casualties, were switched to Tito's aid.

For a brief period in April, 232 Wing presented the extraordinary appearance of a Wing divided into three parts. 223 squadron had gone to Campomarino (Biferno) to be joined by 55 squadron, and by 13 squadron from Kabrit. 18 squadron was at Marcianise near Naples. 114 squadron, based on Celone (Foggia), flew daily over the Apennines to operate from Pomigliano. The Wing Headquarters staff spread out over Italy in Advanced, Rear, and Main parties, attempting to knit these sections together into a whole.

The crews of the night-flying Bostons, the Pippos,[1] were the men of the hour. Air Marshal Slessor paid a visit to congratulate the squadrons on their useful work. Having suffered somewhat of an eclipse when fighters converted to fighter-bombers and started to carry an equal bomb load, the Bostons had now come into their own in the war against enemy movements, for the night was the weak link in the chain of air interdiction. Now it seemed there could not be enough Bostons, that one night-intruder was worth a whole formation of daytime light bombers. The Commanding Officer of 232 Wing flew each day to the Headquarters of 12th Tactical Air Command[2] to receive a personal account of the situation and to obtain briefing instructions for the night's operations from General Saville.

Changing conditions constantly altered the relative value of one type of aircraft as against another. By clinging to its bombers in the teeth of T.B.F. proposals, by refusing to become a specialized fighter force, D.A.F. had ensured that, whatever the changes, it would be ready for anything. Each fresh display of adaptability toughened tradition and strengthened D.A.F.'s claims to be regarded as a phenomenon requiring special appreciation, rather than as an ordinary collection of air force units.

During April, in a breathing-space as uneasy as the lull before Alamein, the armies in Italy had taken advantage of their air umbrella to move units across the Apennines. The control of the Adriatic sector was now vested in 5 Corps; 8th Army grouped itself beside 5th Army in front of Cassino.

Tactical Air Force was meanwhile concerned with operation "Strangle" —the name given to the process of interdicting Rome and isolating the western battlefield. Coastal and strategic air forces were called in. Desert Air Force Kittyhawks contributed to a lesser degree by bombing bridges at Bastia and Marsciano. Whilst American fighter-bombers carried out attacks

[1] Shortened form of "Pipistrello", a bat. Pippo is a comic character—*cf.* "batty".
[2] 12th A.S.C. renamed.

on tracks, overpasses and tunnels, D.A.F. Kittyhawks, Mustangs, Baltimores, and Spitbombers continued to attack bridges in central and eastern areas. During this period, D.A.F. was allotted the Terni–Perugia line and the Terni–Sulmona–Pescara line.

By April 26th effective blocks of the railway routes numbered eleven, temporary blocks thirty, possible blocks four. From roughly March 24th onwards no through traffic reached Rome. Trains were usually interrupted 120 miles away from the Capital, sometimes within fifty miles if travelling via Rimini–Fano–Fabriano–Foligno.

Impressive though these achievements might be, however, Strangle had not lived up to its name. It had not in fact strangled the German supply line. Given another 4,000 aircraft it was doubtful whether such a thing could have been done. According to Slessor:

> "Air power cannot, by itself, force a withdrawal by drying up the flow of essential supplies. It cannot entirely prevent the movement of tactical reserves from one part of the front to another, or of forward troops to fresh positions in the rear. It cannot absolutely isolate the battlefield from enemy supply or reinforcements. What it can do . . . is to make it impossible for the most highly organized and disciplined army to offer prolonged resistance on the ground; it can turn an orderly retreat into a rout, and virtually eliminate an entire army as an effective fighting force."

As a rider to the above he added:

> "It is doubtful whether anyone can be found to deny that if there had been no air force on either side the German army could have made the invasion of Italy impossible, except at a cost in national effort and life which the Allies would have been unwilling, if not unable, to face."

"Diadem"—the army plan to deal the knock-out blow against enemy forces in Italy—followed on the heels of Strangle. This, too, was doomed to fall short of the mark. Field Marshal Alexander, in his order of the day, made it clear that this was to be no local action with the aim of capturing Rome, but something far larger, the first instalment of victory.

> "From the east to the west, from the north to the south, blows are about to fall which will result in the final destruction of the Nazis and bring freedom once again to Europe. To us in Italy has been given the honour of striking the first blow."

Desert Air Force had a small but important part in the overall air plan. Because of the limited areas over which fighting was to take place, the control of their operations passed temporarily to 12th T.A.C. This control was exercised through two Headquarters; one mostly made up of D.A.F. officers attached to 8th Army H.Q.; and the other, in composition mainly American, attached to 5th Army Headquarters. D.A.F.'s particular sphere was the eastern area from a line east of Rome to the Adriatic coast, running northwards to the east of Lago di Trasimeno and Arezzo.

225 and 208 squadrons of 285 Reconnaissance Wing remained for a time on the eastern side, until moving to Aquino in June; 318 Polish squadron stayed in the east to aid the 2nd Polish Corps. 40 Squadron S.A.A.F., already on the eastern side, now performed some of their finest work. Throughout April and the early days of May the Liri valley was their main concern. Low-flying aircraft of the squadron had taken approach views of each objective. The photographs were produced in enormous numbers and distributed down to Battery and even Company commanders. When, an hour before midnight on May 11th, a forty-minute counter-battery barrage fired by over 1,000 guns from behind the Polish and 13 Corps fronts marked the beginning of the 8th Army's offensive, there was hardly a single gun position in the whole of the Liri valley that had not been recorded. The Poles converged on Cassino from the north-west as 13 Corps attacked across the Rapido river from the south; and the French Corps, from their bridgehead across the Garigliano, veered north to the Liri river and north-west to Ausonia and San Giorgio, whilst 40 squadron was on a constant aerial reconnaissance patrol from dawn to dusk between the Liri river and Highway 6. The pilots carried large-scale maps (1:50,000) and gridded aerial photographs (the products of earlier flights) which enabled them to pinpoint enemy guns opening fire. Pilots could, by pressing a button, be in immediate contact with the Headquarters of the 6th Army Group Royal Artillery. Acting as spotters for the guns the airmen directed the artillery engagements of the targets. On some occasions the reconnaissance planes, like Rover commissionaires, whistled 239 Wing out of the Cab-rank and led fighter-bombers against chosen positions.

Rover Cab-ranks were taking on plenty of fares. Special Observation Posts on Mount Trocchio, staffed by R.A.F. and 8th Army Air Control Officers, directed over seventy Kittyhawks and Mustangs; on the 15th against communications, on the 16th against the Cassino mortars.

Before the start of the battle, an observer from the hills above Venafro would have seen layers of smoke curled lazily on the plain drifting upwards towards where the Germans, like bees, clustered in rock-hewn honeycombs, and would have heard only occasional air-bursts. From a distance, nothing else suggested preparations for an offensive. Flowers caressing the roadside half hid the coils of telephone wire; the song of innumerable birds, which had grown used to the fighting, only served to emphasize the fevered stillness of anticipation. The peeling pink plaster of a roofless house, the twisted balcony rails, shimmered like an artificial eighteenth-century ruin in the liquid sun. An inscription on a wall in black Gothic lettering, *Wein müss alt und mädchen junge sein*, appeared to have been painted by deliberate intent to beguile the senses. Spring in Italy had scattered false elegance over the tragedy of ruined farmsteads, had softened contours with a green haze, and had created beauty out of the most scarred and pockmarked gun-site. But now, though the setting retained the same unyielding charm, activity transformed the tranquillity of the original picture. If, before, such surroundings had seemed to invite a *fête galante* rather than a battle, now their incongruity was even more marked; for the air was alive with gunfire and the noise of aeroplanes, whilst the ground reverberated to the clash of arms.

A German machine-gunner wrote in his diary:

> "In spite of it all we are still holding out. The weather seems to be improving. Spring in all its beauty has come to the valley below us. Here I have to suffer the worst privations, and want so badly to get home to my wife and son. I want to be able to enjoy something of the beauty of life again. Here we have nothing but terror and horror, death and damnation. When will the day come again when I will be able to devote myself to my wife and baby, and take pleasure in the birds and flowers?"

The offensive was soon to provide the grim answer, for Allied land and air power joined hands to ensure that the obstacle which had delayed them for so many weeks should at last be overborne. As our troops battled a way round and through the Gustav Line, tactical air forces by day and night gave them every aid, not only in the front, but in the more distant rear. At the close of May 18th, it was known that all railway lines were satisfactorily blocked as far north as the line Cecina–Certaldo–Incisa–Cesano. And on the other side of Italy, Marauders, Baltimores and Spitfires attacked bridges and railway tracks. By night Baltimores joined with Bostons in armed reconnaissance of the roads.

The collapse of the Gustav Line laid bare the Adolf Hitler Line. Impressed, it was rumoured, by the Russian defence of Stalingrad, the *Führer* had lent his name to these threaded strongpoints in the hope of investing them, too, with an aura of impregnability. However, in order to prevent the superstitious from reading a symbolic significance of its breaching, the line was hurriedly retitled "D" (Dora).

Dora was soon overrun. A break in the weather dampened air effort, but the enemy was now in retreat; and from Anzio troops were preparing to turn retreat into rout. Amidst the German lines, Allied aircraft caused continuous confusion, whilst in our own, congested roads could be ignored; camps and Headquarters could be moved at will. On the 24th, fighters and fighter-bombers claimed 563 vehicles damaged; the next day 1,171 (610 destroyed); and in the last six days of May a total of 1,148 destroyed and 766 damaged. Although these figures might seem incredible, it was later proved that pilots, if anything, had tended to underestimate their successes, for between Cori and Artena, where 173 were claimed, 5th Army troops counted 211 abandoned wrecks definitely put out of action from the air.

Part of D.A.F.'s contribution to this overall result was made on May 14th, when 200 vehicles attempting to escape from the battlefield were hemmed in by bombs at either end near Subiaco. At this sitting bird, 239 Wing shot all day long, claiming by evening 90 destroyed and 30 damaged. Reversing the tenets of the coverts, pilots longed for such targets, creating them with considerable efficiency whenever the opportunity offered.

In the fourth week of the offensive, after some bitter fighting amid the environs, the biggest sitting bird in Italy, yet the least molested, was captured intact upon its nest. Our troops entered Rome in force, to pass straight through on their way to the Pisa–Rimini Line.

—

CHAPTER XXXVI

HINDRANCE AND HEALTH

ROME, that eternal city, welcomed the liberators with flowers, handshakes, and requests for food, as though to remind the troops that they were still in southern Italy. But from the honey-coloured palazzos issued forth people who still had their homes whole, and who still retained their urban aspect, smart, busy, and full of curiosity. Roman society, though not intact, was ready with its cards of invitation and its formal dinners; and if the ghosts of German commanders seemed occasionally to interrupt the feasts, the new guests were not over-anxious to see their hosts bundled into a van to be taken to prison; protests of "*Mai Collaboratore!*"[1] were received, for the moment, without comment.

Rome, the city devoted to the worship of "Bella Figura",[2] owed its continued existence to the physical presence of Vatican City. All roads and all railroads led to Rome. It had been within easy reach of Allied bombers for some time past; but although, in spite of incredible precautions, part of the residential area lay in ruins, only the marshalling yards had suffered severely.

There was to be little time to wander through the gardens of Mussolini's Villa Torlonia, or to be granted an interview with His Holiness the Pope. War passed through Rome and out on the other side, leaving a trail of Headquarters and Military Government Officers behind.

German newspapers warned their readers:

> "In Italy the war can neither be won nor lost, regardless of whether the battle line is to the north or south of Rome. . . . Once the Second Front is attempted nobody will talk about Italy any more. . . . It is a question in the last resort of outpost engagements before the real trial in battle."

Interest certainly switched to the Normandy landings on June 6th when airborne troops were dropped in the south-east part of the Cherbourg peninsular, and to the east of the River Orne. 244 Wing had their comment ready: "The Second Front opened, stealing our Italian thunder and muting its own. Rome and Normandy on the same stage are inclined to shout one another down." As convoys started to arrive in the assault area during the afternoon, and as the 1st United States Army and the 2nd British Army landed to the east

[1] "We were never Collaborators!"
[2] Something considerably more showy than Good Form.

of Cherbourg, the pursuit to Viterbo, to Civitavecchia, and to Tarquinia, attracted little world attention.

In Russia operations north-west of Jassy and preparations for the Karelian offensive continued. Moscow, claimed the Germans, was the culprit who at long last had succeeded in forcing the Allies to "stab Europe in the back, while the German army and its Allies are fighting Bolshevism". In Burma, the Japanese, driven out of Kohima, were retreating to the north and south; there was a prospect that the Kohima–Imphal road would soon be in our hands. In Upper Burma there was heavy fighting around Myitkina, but in the Arakan area there was little but patrol activity. In New Guinea, Mokmer airfield on Biak Island fell at the same time as Rome, whilst Australian troops were advancing up the coast from Alexishaven to Daloa. On all fronts there were signs of a steady Allied advance. The German retreat to the Pisa–Rimini (Gothic) Line, cautious rather than precipitate, was lost in the vastness of the struggle which now, at last, seemed to be drawing to a close. For the Gothic Line was the last prepared position in Italy.

On June 10th, those who could do so remembered the raid on El Adem four years ago, as Mussolini had entered the war. Nothing then would have seemed more fantastic than that, on the fourth anniversary, Allied Forces would be passing through his capital in pursuit of the Germans, that Allied air power would have defeated and then embraced the *Regia Aeronautica*, or that the *Luftwaffe*, reduced to a shadow, would be unable to affect the fighting.

. . . . .

In complete control once more of all its units, D.A.F. Headquarters, which had moved to Castrocieto before the fall of Rome, now advanced side by side with 8th Army to Valmontone and Trasimeno. Sea and land communications from the bomb line to Rimini were attacked day and night; and during the halt before Arezzo, D.A.F. fighter and light bombers were sent against gun positions on the approaches to the town.

Balkan Air Force had been formed on June 7th for operations in the Ægean and in Yugoslavia, but D.A.F. responsibilities were still to include aid to the Partisans. Flak over Yugoslav towns was always to cause some of the heaviest casualties.

As in the past, all the ancillary departments of D.A.F. were adjusting themselves to the fresh advance. The Medical services, concerned with the high incidence of malaria, took every opportunity of pointing out that mosquitoes in central and northern Italy were active in their seasons. At the start of the year, Allied Force H.Q. had asked for information as to future D.A.F. aerodromes so that anti-malarial plans could be sketched in advance; the answer had been, "D.A.F. will occupy aerodromes in any area where the army happens to be." In February it was stated that: "The Desert Air Force facilities at present consist of three Anti-malarial Control Units and one Lysander aircraft for the spraying of breeding areas with Paris Green." The D.A.F. authorities were applying for an anti-malarial flight of three light aircraft. They were not to be fobbed off indefinitely with one Lysander.[1] Fairchilds were what were really wanted; and duly, on May 27th, the first Fairchild arrived.

Meanwhile, there was the routine work of inspecting stagnant pools near camp sites and the evil-looking canals which were never far away. Under the direction of the Senior Medical Officer, a bulldozer had cut channels to the sea to drain flooded areas at Trigno. At Lago and Venafro, the doctors had stepped in with a guarded: "There must be considerable doubt as to whether or not it will be desirable to operate this landing-ground at the height of the malarial season."

As at Sangro, malarial control linked the two services; the D.A.F. flight continued to spray for the army as well as for the R.A.F. The medical authorities were to pool resources to drain land at Ravenna and Cervia, flooded by the Germans before retreat. The benefit ultimately devolved upon Italian civilians, who that year suffered less from malaria than ever before.

Venereal disease, often for some reason considered unmentionable,[2] continued to cause dismay. Precautionary measures, coupled with the instant treatment of infected civilians, was the approved solution, but the disease still accounted for a high percentage of all casualties. From Brindisi onwards, a specialized type of V.D. which had already in the case of civilians been half-treated with sulpha drugs, was found to defy further attempts at this particular cure. Penicillin arrived in quantity just in time to prevent a serious situation from developing.

Mobile shower-bath units were tireless in drawing attention to the advantages of cleanliness. Their 30-seconds hot—30-seconds off—formula must surely have established a record for speed in handling their patrons. Field Hygiene sections carried the war against dirt into the camps. They checked Wing arrangements for the disposal of waste and salvage and advised on the fly-proofing of food containers. The line of medical care extended from the latrine party to the squadron doctor and his assistants, to the Wing Senior Medical Officer and his centralized Sick Quarters, through to the Mobile Field Hospitals, the Hygiene Sections, the Malaria Control Units, the Air Evacuation organization, to the Base Hospitals. Medical activity touched every corner of Service life, checking, approving, preventing, and treating.

The Mobile Field Hospitals, No. 25 (which went to Corsica and southern France), Nos. 21, 22 and 30, continued to provide in the Apennines what they had provided in the Desert—treatment near at hand, in surroundings adapted

[1] That monument of unpopularity!

[2] But in Italy certainly not unnoticeable. In the towns large signs drew attention to the prophylactic stations, which were often easier to find than the N.A.A.F.I.s.

by ingenuity to their function. Many members of D.A.F. owed their lives to the treatment received in these hospitals, which were equipped to carry out emergency surgery, X-ray, and bacteriological work in actual field conditions. The hospitals were each commanded by a Wing-Commander; and to some of them were attached nurses from Princess Mary's Royal Nursing Service, whose cheerful acceptance of primitive conditions made them the heroines of the campaign.

In summer 1944, so rapid was the advance of the army that evacuation from casualty clearing stations to base hospitals became increasingly difficult. Italian autostradas in the north had been the envy of the pre-war English motorist, but in the south war had ravaged surfaces which had never been entirely satisfactory. To prevent ambulances from having to negotiate such a tyre-bursting, spring-breaking *via dolorosa*, Air Evacuation came more and more into its own; the brunt of the service being borne by the Americans, who not only provided aeroplanes, but trained air ambulance nursing orderlies. These aircraft were running up to twenty sorties and sometimes twenty double sorties a day from bases like Orvieto and Civita Castellana, where only improvised strips existed. Desert Air Force Wings, at the dispatching end on their forward airfields, were always ready to give every assistance to the air ambulances, regardless of the pressure of operations. From June 28th to the 30th, 1,176 patients were carried, bringing the June total to 15,979. But as winter brought its own special problems of weather, the number dwindled.

Thus the Medical services of D.A.F., like all the ground services, were adapted to, and organized for, mobility. These pages have surveyed the growth first of the idea and then of the practice of "moving and operating simultaneously". Signals, Maintenance, Supply—all sections were fluid in the forward areas, static in rear.

The Signals empire, for instance, constantly readjusted to fit D.A.F.'s career, could be extended to cover the split Headquarters (part in western Italy; part in Corsica), and the split Fighter Control unit (M.O.R.U. "A" on the west coast; M.O.R.U. "B" on the east coast). Every move entailed fresh Signals and Air Formation Signals arrangements.

Similarly the Supply and Maintenance organizations. There would be no object in mentioning each part by name, or in giving a detailed history of their doings; in Italy, much to their credit, they could be taken for granted. The high operational standard of air support was the best evidence of the efficiency of the mobile ground services.

CHAPTER XXXVII

OTHER EVENTS

DURING the third week in Italy, Leghorn fell in the west, Ancona in the east. D.A.F.'s River Po offensive, temporarily interrupted to fly, on the 17th, 500 sorties for the Polish troops of 8th Army, was resumed next day when Mustangs of 239 Wing destroyed ten barges.

There seemed to be no immediate prospect of capturing Florence. Kesselring continued to confound the critics by standing to fight on every possible intermediate line of defence, instead of withdrawing post-haste to the Gothic Line. D.A.F.'s attitude was summed up in the phrase, "Oh, very well!"[1]

The next few weeks saw a reduction in the tactical air strength in Italy. On July 19th the Headquarters of M.A.T.A.F. transferred to Corsica. Soon there was only D.A.F. left in Italy to provide close support for both the 5th and 8th Armies. From island bases, however, 12th T.A.C. could still extend an arm from the bomb line to the Genoa–Milan–Venice railway.

D.A.F. Headquarters (Main) stayed alongside Headquarters 8th Army, but a subsidiary section was attached to 5th Army. There they worked with liaison officers from 12th T.A.C. and passed requests through to the senior Headquarters which then assessed the relative needs of the two fronts. Desert Air Force, which as a Headquarters appeared to have gone into a decline at Vasto, had now re-emerged as the sole close-support authority for the Italian battlefield from coast to coast.

There were, however, other air cards on the table. Operation "Mallory Major" (the destruction of the Po crossings) was carried out by American medium bombers. Scheduled to take place in June, Mallory Major had been postponed by army request because it had then been thought that such activities might impede our advance. But optimism wilted in the midsummer heat. It soon appeared that Diadem might have to batter for some time against the Gothic Line. In July, Mallory Major at last made a début, its success coming too late to have any immediate effect on the German supply position.

. . . . .

For a short period in July, D.A.F. operations decreased. A distinguished visitor, referred to as "General Collingwood", toured the 8th Army front. His progress aroused enthusiasm and interest which the name of Collingwood

[1] Equivalent perhaps to the Italian *e'così!*—a favourite expression with which those in contact with civilians were by now familiar.

did little to justify. The first signals were guarded. A V.V.I.P.[1] was to inspect all units. M.O.R.U.'s diary commented:

> "From all that is going on he must be very important indeed! Half the officers and a number of the airmen's tents have been moved so as to give better dispersal, and mud is being thrown over the new 160-pounder tents which have been bleached to almost white in the strong sunlight. It is only to be hoped that no thunderstorms will visit us and wash off the mud before the V.V I P. arrives."

On the 26th, preparations for the General's visit reached fever pitch. Special tents were erected; a quantity of basket chairs, carpets, rugs, cups and saucers were borrowed for the occasion. All those not on duty were to line the route to cheer the visitor on his way. That no hitch or misunderstanding should mar the event, a rehearsal was held in the evening. Wing-Commander Eaton for a brief while acquired a very high acting rank when, impersonating General Collingwood, he was driven through the cheering lines by the Group-Captain in a jeep. The next day the visitor arrived. By then, even the least intelligent were expecting H.M. the King.

After the Royal party left, operations were intensified. Including the fourteen standing patrols and escorts for the modern Haroun el Raschid, missions amounted to 50, sorties to 287. Following an attack by Mustangs of 260 squadron on a concentration of troops and guns about six miles south of Florence, the army signalled: "Beautiful exhibition of bombing; all bombs in the target area, only one wide. Are grateful for engagement especially as heavy commitment at time of request realized." Accuracy in bombing was a particular preoccupation of D.A.F. It was their policy "to conduct bombing operations in such a way that they do the maximum damage to the enemy and, so far as possible, the minimum damage to civilians and their property".

The next day, Kittyhawks and Spitbombers acted upon a report that Heidrich, the Commander of the 1st Parachute Division, was attending a party in a villa about six miles west of Pontassieve; the festivities were interrupted.

A D.A.F. celebration, however, took place unhampered by enemy aircraft. In the actual words of the Wing diary:

> "At night 244 Wing gave a dance at the Rest Hotel in Assisi, the D.A.F. band supplying the jive. Special late passes had been provided by the Town Major for various popsies of not very exceptional beauty, who, to varying degrees of disappointment, were of the '*haut*' rather than the '*demi-monde*'. Their scruples did not deter them from toting away as

[1] The superlative of V.I.P.

much of the buffet as they could cram into their handbags. Two who sneaked in without passes spent the night in the 'cooler' when the Military Police checked up. We wondered what the nuns in the adjacent convent made of the strains of 'St. Louis Blues' and such-like, which floated out till 11 o'clock; also what other inhabitants made of it when certain members of the Wing strutted through the deserted streets chanting the '*Horst Wessel*' and '*Deutschland Uber Alles*'!"

• • • • •

The departure of units for the invasion of southern France had stripped the Italian front of air strength. This encouraged D.A.F. to put out more sorties to veil the deficiency. During the week ending August 10th, D.A.F. averaged 340 per twenty-four hours; and on the 15th—"D" day for the invasion of southern France—an improvement in the weather enabled D.A.F. to top the 500 mark.

When "the fourth front" opened, D.A.F. took a part by providing cover for the area between Cuneo, Genoa and Imperia, whilst the troop-carriers and gliders were going in to land.

D.A.F.-administered units had already gone to Corsica—322 Wing and 324 Wing, and the 79th Fighter Group. The latter, D.A.F.'s favourite American unit, had moved over to Corsica on June 11th to attack communications on the French coast. Their pilots met with particular success at Valence, where they claimed over twenty German aircraft destroyed. Soon the Group was to see the effects of its work with its own eyes, for the squadrons moved over to the mainland following rapid ground advances, to land on the beach near San Raphael. This field was a veritable dust-bowl and a pall like an awning hung over the entire countryside. But in their own words, "The dust hadn't been created that could stop a band of willing men, and this the Germans soon found out."

The next month, D.A.F.'s Americans moved up to Valence, to find not twenty but thirty German aircraft lying where they had been smitten. The men were given a heartwarming welcome by the French; the hero reception received *en route* was only one of the many joys of operating from French territory, as 322 and 324 Wings were also to discover.

When the time came to return to Italy, the 79th Group sadly commented, "The ground crew moved to a staging area outside Marseilles, to await formation of a convoy to take it to the land of no spaghetti, starvation, filth, disease, and the monuments to precision bombing as typified by the shambles of what were once clean, proud buildings."

By then the Pisa–Rimini Line had been overrun.

CHAPTER XXXVIII

THE GOTHIC LINE OFFENSIVE

THE Pisa–Rimini Line neither started at Pisa nor ended at Rimini. Hence it was more convenient to use "Gothic" Line, a term borrowed from the enemy, to describe the series of linked strongpoints running from Carrara to Pesaro. When work first began on this "last ditch", the enemy's chief concern was to fortify these two termini and to take precautions against any seaborne landings in the rear. Work on the defences in the mountain sector was postponed until later; Kesselring's *Fabius Cunctator* tactics were partly designed to gain time for the *Todt* slaves to build last-minute additions. A Partisan report of July 3rd spoke of "feverish activity" on the eastern sector; this was confirmed by air photographs. The enemy had evidently taken stock of the fact that there was only one natural and comparatively easy way into the Po valley from central Italy, namely the coastal route along the Adriatic.

Although Florence had been entered, but not occupied, on August 4th, prospects of breaking the Gothic Line from the west were not rosy. The surrounding hills, which had been such a source of delight for the prosperous foreigners who had once looked upon Tuscany as their spiritual home, were less appealing now that death lurked behind each bend in the road.

In the east, however, Pesaro, famous for its ornate pottery, was defended by a wide arc of machine-guns; west of the town the Foglia fortifications consisted chiefly of anti-tank ditches, machine-gun positions, and pill-boxes. The majority of the defences of the town itself appeared to be directed against an attack from the sea rather than from the land.

The new offensive aimed at cracking this eastern pivot and forging onwards into the Po valley. Accordingly the greater part of 8th Army in the central sector was to be transferred in conditions of as much secrecy as possible over the tortuous mountain roads. An elaborate system of code-signs and code-words was intended to deceive the local inhabitants that the 11,000 vehicles a day moving to the assembly area at Ancona represented no more than the normal road traffic of a holding force.

D.A.F. was of course to support 8th Army in their latest manœuvre; orders for the move were issued on August 17th. Inquisitive civilians were told that D.A.F. was moving up to Florence. Squadron crests, painted with infinite care on all vehicles, were now equally carefully removed. Matters reached such a pitch that a *contadino* with pencil and notebook near Macerata was arrested in spite of pleas that he was serving Art, not Mammon. Operation "Olive" was being prosecuted with considerable zeal.

The D.A.F. Signals organization was now used as a direct weapon of war.

Wireless stations on the west coast were to maintain normal traffic levels, using dummy traffic if necessary. Units already on the east coast could continue to operate, but no new ground stations were to start activity until the move became accomplished fact; aircraft had to adopt call-signs of squadrons already there. In order to pass messages from coast to coast, other than by teleprinter, air couriers plied twice daily between Siena and Jesi.

Until "D day minus 3" the D.A.F. units were to remain on their present fields to attack dumps and communications. From D minus 2 to D plus 5 "A" parties were to move across to the Adriatic. Aircraft were to fly over on the morning of "D" day to start intensive operations.[1]

M.O.R.U., now in two sections, could regroup without much difficulty, because the fighter sector of 287 (Coastal) Wing was already in operation near Ancona. M.O.R.U. "A", on the road with 8th Army, was to be set up as soon as possible at Fano; M.O.R.U. "B" was to take over M.O.R.U. "A's" old site.

An illuminating incident showed how wide was the chasm between a D.A.F. unit, trained for offence, and a Coastal unit, equally skilled, but mainly preoccupied with defence. On August 26th, M.O.R.U. Ground Controller asked the 287 Wing Air Controller to call up some aircraft of 239 Wing and direct them on to a target of enemy transport. The answer came back: "Sorry, old man, I'm far too busy; I've got three 'X' raids on the table."[2]

On the morning of the 26th, 8th Army launched its attack across the Metauro river to capture Fano the next day. On the left flank, the ancient town of Urbino, the birthplace of Raphael, fell to the Indians. On the right, Pesaro, stoutly defended by the 1st Parachute Division, was the scene of fierce fighting. But air attack intervened; on the second day the town was cleared. The eastern end of the Gothic pivot was in our hands. In the west, Pisa fell to the 5th Army.

Like all the offensives in Italy, this one began with high hopes and initial successes. An operation for reducing Pesaro from the air by intensive bombardment (operation "Crumpet") was arranged amidst an exchange of telegrams and conversations with 205 Group. Crumpet was so successful that the bombardment, planned to last for three days, required only two. When the 8th Army surged into the town it was to find scattered defenders and empty pill-boxes. Apprehensive of the air softening-up, the Germans had withdrawn.[3]

Crumpet provided a good example of the balance between strategical and tactical, of interdiction weighed against army support. The A.O.C. D.A.F. was in a position requiring considerable judgment. In his capacity as the commander of close-support air force, he was bound to press for aid from the strategic air forces in order to implement army plans. On the other hand, the interdiction campaign demanded all resources of the medium and heavy

[1] The details of the moves are best given in the form of a chart. See Appendix C.

[2] Suspect enemy raids.

[3] Night-bombers of 205 Group on three missions dropped in all 574 tons of bombs on Pesaro, i.e. about one-eighth of the total tonnage dropped on the island of Pantellaria.

bombers. If 205 Group operated over Pesaro, then for that period the war against German supplies had to be interrupted. Was the interruption justified?

A parallel situation had arisen just before El Hamma, when the battle for air superiority had seemed to demand a renewal of attacks on enemy aerodromes in Northern Africa. Air superiority in 1944 was no longer in doubt; but interdiction was every bit as exacting.

Dickson's solution was the *via media*. For a land operation of special importance he was prepared to throw his whole weight into the balance on behalf of the army. At other times his force was to divide its attentions between interdiction near the battlefield, close support to the 8th Army, and aid to the Yugoslav Partisans. The best witness to his discretion was that he somehow managed to satisfy all three claimants.

In furtherance of the A.O.C.'s policy, air support for the first day of the offensive reached 666 sorties, although the Wing which had flown across in such conditions of secrecy complained that targets were scarce. Of these sorties 115 were made by 7 S.A.A.F. Wing, which remained at Florence to support the 5th Army.

The "slogging match for Rimini" inspired the diarist of 244 Wing to describe an air-sea rescue containing unusual features:

> "Hit by flak, Lawton baled out into the sea near Rimini, and was picked up within thirty minutes by a Walrus of 293 squadron. It was near dark then and the Walrus was unable to take-off; the pilot and the crew prepared to spend an uncomfortable night rocked on the waters of the Adriatic. They didn't know how uncomfortable! Came dark, and two British motor-boats which mistook the Walrus for a mine-laying E-boat opened fire with cannon and machine-gun and fired the Walrus's petrol tank. In imminent danger of providing a choice roast for fishes, Lawton and the crew struggled out of the blazing Mercy Plane, and after a chill fifteen minutes were picked up by the apologetic crews of the launches which proceeded to take them on patrol."

The climax of his adventures came in the very small hours of the morning, when one of the motor-boats had its stern blown off by a mine.

The 8th Army was now held up by a heavily defended ridge, known as the Fortunata Feature, on the way to Rimini; a double hill which had to be ascended and descended in the face of strong enemy defences. Air Commodore Pike, in the temporary absence of the A.O.C., had to decide how best to meet the army plea, "We cannot go down this hill unless you help us."

El Hamma (of course) supplied the answer. El Hamma had remained the classic of fighter-bomber employment. El Hamma was even referred to as "D.A.F.'s secret weapon", in so many fresh guises could it make its presence known. For there the army had been told "to expect continuous Kittybomber attacks throughout this period at a density of two squadrons. . . ." Might not the same type of attack be repeated as so many of D.A.F.'s experiences had been repeated far across the Mediterranean?

The result was "Timothy"; a wave-blitz, a headsdown*fest*, a continuous attack for forty minutes on the corrugated approaches. Fighter-bombers were to strafe the near declivity, whilst others simultaneously bombed gun positions on the reverse slopes. At ten o'clock, in the midst of other air attacks which had been in progress since dawn and were to continue until 7.45 that evening, Timothy was unleashed.

But the feature was *fortunata* to the Germans rather than to the Allies. For various reasons the Canadians were delayed for half an hour. Heads that had already been down had by then re-emerged. And though the feature was in our hands the next day, casualties were heavier than had been expected.

Timothy, however, was the darling of the day. Desert reports were hastily scanned by those who had joined D.A.F. since El Hamma. Soon the legend which had inspired the new form of attack was given repetitive airings. Soon the army was asking for Timothy on every possible occasion. Soon reports were to speak of "Timothy's, mostly".

When Rimini fell the next day, rose-coloured spectacles seemed to have been earned by ground and air forces. The capture of the coastal terminus of the Via Emilia suggested a march on Bologna attended by a break-through to the Po valley.

If it had been a feature of the Italian gains in the Middle East in 1940 that "the logical result never by any chance accrued", now it seemed that a similar curious fate lay in store for those who battled through the Italian homeland. The country of illogical contrasts appeared militantly opposed to everything but the unexpected. The "soft underbelly" provided an excellent example of an "inch-by-inch campaign" fought without glamour amidst surroundings of implacable beauty; likewise Diadem, which had promised the first instalment of final victory, had eventually to be content with the lesser triumph of containing approximately twenty-eight German divisions. So perfectly was the terrain adapted to defence that each offensive manœuvre needed to be flawlessly executed with unopposed air support if it was to succeed. But each step of the Italian escalator rattled underfoot only to reveal other steps beyond, until it seemed that there was no last ditch, no final exit. When, by the end of September, Rimini in the east and the Futa Pass in the centre had been captured, the Gothic Line had been overrun at all points save in a few places to the west. But the war was by no means at an end. The Po valley, whose keys jangled loudly in our hands, eluded entry.

The tumult and the shouting from all over Europe drowned the rattling and jangling in Italy. The public ear inclined towards France, where a Maquis revolt in Paris had paved the way for the American occupation troops. By the end of August, France, except for certain strongholds on the east coast, was clear of the Germans. Soviet victory resounded throughout eastern Europe.[1] Cries of capitulation came from Roumania on the 24th and Bulgaria on the 26th. Finland, whose resistance had been unexpectedly stubborn, accepted the Russian peace terms early in September.

Meanwhile the Germans were starting to evacuate Greece, leaving only third-rate troops in their rear. Beset from every side, deserted by her satellites, the Reich was collapsing.

To the Italian front, echoes from the other side of the Alps scarcely penetrated. The Germans, in spite of air interdiction, continued to fight as fiercely as before. Their supplies had to be moved at night by vehicles with dimmed or no headlights. Ferries had to take the place of the blown bridges, ferries which had to be concealed during the daytime and used feverishly whenever the sound of *Pippo's* engines died away. Horses and mules replaced motor transport; ingenuity replaced sufficiency.

Ingenuity could barely keep them alive on the defensive; it would not allow them to mount a counter-offensive. But the defence was none the less tenacious, adapted to the country, and increasingly immune to the rising storm of air attack.

As though to offset the decreasing effectiveness of air bombardment against troops fully prepared for "*Jabo*"[2], D.A.F.'s close support during September had been memorable. Never in D.A.F.'s history had so great an effort been concentrated so consistently on targets immediately in front of our ground forces. A message from the G.O.C. 8th Army to the A.O.C. D.A.F. ran:

> "Please convey to all ranks of the Desert Air Force the gratitude and appreciation of the 8th Army for their magnificent close support throughout our recent operations. The relentless pressure exerted by the Desert Air Force on enemy gun positions and communications has powerfully aided us in every stage of the advance. Our forward troops have entire confidence in the accuracy of close-support bombing and express the greatest admiration for the dash and gallantry of your pilots. In the more open fighting ahead I know that you and your Desert Air Force will take every opportunity to harass the enemy and shatter his columns. My thanks and best wishes to you all."

D.A.F. had advanced a long way since May 1942, when, it will be remembered, "Army commanders anxious for the safety of their own troops were only too ready to allow for a margin of error". A happy state of affairs had been reached.

[1] Though not throughout Poland, where the Warsaw uprising was to end in tragedy.
[2] The German name for our fighter-bombers.

CHAPTER XXXIX

THE WINTER LULL

OCTOBER started with the entire 79th American Fighter Group poised on the springboard of France. The ground echelons drove off on the third day, the air units leaping into space on the fourth. As was to be expected, the air party reached Jesi airfield on the same day, whilst the rest took over a week. 79th Group was rejoining D.A.F. once more.

The reception was hearty but the elements were unkind. The bivouac area offered a true-to-life "Mudville"; intermittent rain swamped attempts to improve the site. There on the same field was congregated the whole of 239 Wing, 167 Maintenance Unit (whose changing flocks of Spitfires were in such demand as to give them almost operational status), anti-malarial Fairchilds (now in the plural), and drogue-towing Bostons. The Marauders of 3 S.A.A.F. Wing were soon to arrive, to be drawn up in olive mass alongside the grass strip.

On some days heavy bombers returning from raids on Germany could not struggle back to their bases at Foggia and Bari. With radios out of order, engines feathered, their petrol short, with wounded and dead aboard, they put down on the first concrete runway behind the Allies lines. On Friday the 13th a Liberator lay with collapsed undercarriage on the *pista*, another had landed and swung off on to the strip of rough grass, and on the end of the parallel grass runway two Fortresses were bogged down—and a third, a fourth, a fifth and a sixth, were coming in to land. Overhead circled more of the heavy bombers, firing distress signals and shouting for landing instructions by radio-telephone. In the circuit, too, were Mustangs and Kittyhawks, their tanks almost empty of petrol, waiting to hear which field could take them in, whilst Thunderbolts, flying low to "buzz" the control tower before fanning out to land, were having their instructions cancelled at the last minute before putting wheels down.

On the ground, ambulances and cranes scurried from wreck to wreck. Men were being impounded to act as messengers from the control tower to the relief parties. In the tower itself, radio on two separate frequencies issued and countermanded orders; red Verey lights shot upwards in clusters; signal lamps flashed towards aircraft out of wireless contact. And in the midst of these alarums, operations continued until sheer pressure of events led to their cancellation.

The *Luftwaffe*, no doubt, would have agreed with the famous *Punch* cartoon in which the ragged man staring at a drunken reveller commented, "I wish I 'ad 'alf 'is trouble." For air activity on such a scale, though bringing problems, was a promising augury of victory. To be too busy was better than being idle most of the time. The long miles of concrete taxi tracks linking runways like monster parade-grounds, the *Luftwaffen Festungen* which usurped so much of the Udine plain, lay in peace and quiet, the silence broken only rarely by the seventy aircraft left unharmed by crushing Allied raids.

Consider, then, D.A.F.'s fields. Falconara, where 253 Baltimore Wing and 287 Coastal Wing were soon to welcome a detached squadron and then the whole of 232 Wing; there P.S.P. was being laid over compacted gravel strewn on spongy soil. Fano, Borghetto, Loreto, and Rimini, where once again King Mud was only prevented from assuming absolute monarchy over 244 Wing, 285 Wing, 7 S.A.A.F. Wing and 8 S.A.A.F. Wing by the constant and unremitting efforts of the airfield engineers. Jesi itself, where petrol cans were being sunk in the ground at the end of the concrete, as foundation after foundation was tried and found wanting.

Squadrons from the west coast left behind when D.A.F. swung across country for the Gothic Line offensive were put into involuntary quarantine. Stationed at Cecina, 232 Wing operated uneventfully until the end of September. On the last night of the month they carried out armed reconnaissance north of Florence, as usual. The following day the rains came; Cecina turned into a paddy field. A hopeful Italian farmer even appeared with a gun, explaining that locally the duck-shooting season was now considered open. It transpired that the season was generally prolonged—five months out of twelve.

Baltimores lay amid the waters like ships becalmed. Wavelets lapped the fuselages of the high-stepping, tricycle-undercarriaged Bostons. Bulldozers could do little; the floods showed no signs of abating. Doves in uniform were released from the D.A.F. Ark to find out where else the aircraft could put down, provided that they could get into position for take-off from the one small section of the runway still relatively dry.

But the doves returned, messages of ill cheer in their beaks. Every airfield in Italy was "out" that day. Failing a magic carpet, all ranks combined to manhandle the aircraft, containing pilots only, to the edge of the shortened runway—linking hands, as it were, with the officers and men who in 1942 had worked with such inspired zeal on Antelat during the retreat to Gazala. The sodden craft rose into the air to descend on widely scattered fields from Pisa to Perugia.

There the tale of misfortune might fairly have ended. But this was Italy, the land of surprises uncannily sympathetic towards the unexpected or the unwanted. 13 and 55 squadrons were now scheduled to convert from Baltimores to Bostons. The Baltimores were withdrawn; the Bostons were elusive. Even had they been there, there would have been no chance of training the pilots, as all available airfields were, in the gaps between the weather, working to capacity, and were unable to countenance a training programme. Eventually, Perugia was allotted to the Wing; but there the runway was too short for Bostons save in emergency.

Matters then became so urgent that the extraordinary step was taken of permitting the squadrons to convert at Marcianise, which latterly had been the home of V.I.P.s only; for just over a mile from the aerodrome Allied Force Headquarters and Mediterranean Allied Air Forces Headquarters were "isolated in splendour and discomfort" in the Royal Palace of Caserta.

The permission contained various codicils. V.I.P.s retained first priority at the airfield; only minimum servicing echelons were allowed at Marcianise; crews had to be converted flight by flight. Further complications ensued; it was discovered that these detachments were messing with Americans, thereby violating some obscure clause in the Lend-Lease agreement.

The main stream of 232 Wing had divided into three tributaries before, at the time of the Anzio landings, but what had once been a delta was now to become a watershed. 18 and 114 squadrons were operating over Yugoslavia and northern Italy from Falconara; ground crews were living in a tile factory south of Ancona; technicians from 13 squadron, temporarily redundant, were at Jesi. Rear parties of all these units were left at Cecina to "tidy up". 55 squadron had four separate detachments at Cecina, Ancona, Perugia and Marcianise; an aircraft strength of two Bostons; one pilot capable of flying them.

A comparison might be wrung from those days in 1941, when, after the first advance into Cyrenaica, the same squadron "could never muster more than four aircraft at any one time". But the analogy could not be sustained in 1944; for though Cecina slumbered, and though Perugia was barely more than comatose, D.A.F. fields across Italy could not but keep awake. The ground reverberated to the spluttering roar of engines warming up for take-off, the humming crescendo of engines in the circuit, the staccato rattling of engines throttled back as aircraft came in to land.

No *Luftwaffe* was burgeoning at Tripoli, no Stukas were appearing on a Desert horizon, no aerial mines were being laid in Benghazi harbour. Instead, German-held Villa Orba, Campoformido and Rivolto lay like silent concrete monuments to a dying world, like gigantic ground signs put out to propitiate some Afrit released in malignant clouds of smoke by the Allied fishermen of the sky.

. . . . .

Hitler's intuition was held to be responsible for German policy in Italy. The Allies were to be prevented from entering upon the rich plains of Lombardy, Piedmont, and Veneto, even though German divisions were to be needed more and more urgently in South-eastern Europe.

The *schwerpunkt* of the German defensive system lay south of Bologna.[1] Ground yielded on the Adriatic front would be of secondary importance so

[1] Another last ditch. The reader will by now be familiar with the fact that almost all towns in Italy were potentially key towns. Likewise all rivers were key rivers.

long as this central position could be held. For beyond, rivers guaranteed line after line of defence—the Senio, then the Po, the Adige, and behind that the Brenta.

At the start of October, the 5th Army, sixteen miles south of Bologna, was baffled by resistance as tough as any in its experience. Dispatches mentioned "minor advances made against very stiff opposition and most difficult terrain". Even operation "Pancake"(the air blitz by strategic and tactical air forces against the town approaches, intensified on the 12th) could not be exploited by the ground forces. The carpet of air destruction could beunrolled, but the German troops failed to suffocate under its folds.

On the Adriatic front, D.A.F. continued its offensive against the bridges, over the river Savio, clearly the next German line of defence. This by the 15th had yielded the necessary results, for all the bridges were cut. Mustangs and Thunderbolts operating to the east of the Verona–Ostiglia–Bologna railway continued to keep open rail cuts between Verona–Modena and Ravenna–Bologna, destroying 17 locomotives on the 12th, 30 on the 21st, and 10 on the 30th. At the same time, the boats and barges on the canals suffered, 52 being destroyed, 166 damaged.

When the Canadians, in the third week of the month, reached the Savio, D.A.F. could turn its attentions to the river Reno. Apart from having cut the Savio bridges, D.A.F. had hindered the withdrawal of enemy troops whenever weather permitted. Their support had been praised but patchy and was to continue to be so. On five of the last sixteen days of October, sorties fell to under a hundred, and on three particularly disappointing days there was a nominal effort only. Every advantage was taken of the brief clear intervals, but these were few.

The high hopes of October encouraged a Partisan rising in the hills. German reprisals were prompt and scarifying, but, in spite of this, by the spring the movement claimed some 12,000 members in the Lombardy plain, with another 5,000 or so in the mountains. Supplies dropped by fighter-bombers prevented the patriots from feeling neglected.

D.A.F.'s aid to the Partisans in Yugoslavia during November took a different form. 239 Wing were given Balkan targets as their first priority. On four days at the beginning of the month D.A.F. damaged over a hundred locomotives on the Sarajevo–Brod and the Zagreb–Maribor lines, destroyed three Ju. 52's on the ground at Brezice, and sank a siebel ferry, a corvette and a merchant vessel, outside Fiume. The next week, pilots claimed sixty-four locomotives and fifty-five waggons. The window between Italy and Yugoslavia, already jammed permanently open by Balkan Air Force, had become a thoroughfare. During five operational days over Yugoslavia, more than 200 locomotives were destroyed. In the first three weeks these figures rose to 276—about one engine for each 1·58 sorties.

Again and again messages came through to indicate that results were warmly appreciated by Marshal Tito. Light bombers supplemented the work of the fighter-bombers. On November 19th, Baltimores of 253 Wing bombed Kocejve so effectively that Partisans were able to penetrate into the outskirts of the town immediately afterwards. Mustangs, Thunderbolts (now with the new rockets), Kittyhawks, Baltimores, and Bostons continued to destroy bridges, blow up waggons and locomotives, and attack shipping in Fiume harbour. The Yugoslavs enjoyed the full benefit of air superiority without the burden of its maintenance—an incalculable advantage indeed.

It might have been reasonable to suppose, at the start of November, that the Balkans would thieve air support from the 8th Army. Paul could presumably only exist at the expense of Peter. But if weather in Italy was bad, in Yugoslavia it was even worse, and at different times. D.A.F. was therefore able to split and switch whenever necessary. During the battle for Forli, the day before the town fell, of 526 sorties, 90 per cent were flown in attacks ahead of the advancing 5 Corps. A Brigadier's message of congratulation, "In my experience air support has never been closer or more accurate," showed that, as always, D.A.F. was still able to thrive best on a varied fare. For besides taking part in the assault on Yugoslavia, where ruined road and rail bridges gradually revealed a pattern of interdiction, besides continuing to concentrate on the tracks and bridges of the lines feeding south from Padua to the 8th Army front, besides providing close support to the army at critical moments, D.A.F. had shared in operation "Bingo" (the blitz on transformer stations between Verona and Trento designed to smash the power supply for trains on the Brenner Pass line). Two squadrons of Kittyhawks and a squadron of rocket-firing Thunderbolts were allotted a station south-west of Verona. The Kittyhawks claimed fourteen direct hits on the main buildings and two on the transformer, whilst the Thunderbolts claimed four on the former and twenty-one on the latter. Vivid blue flashes streaked a dense pall of black smoke to give the pilots a vision of the Inferno.

• • • • •

D.A.F. remained much the same size as before. 324 Wing, which had retired to Florence after being withdrawn from the south of France, came over to Rimini on the 6th, but in return, as it were, 8 S.A.A.F. Wing, the younger brother of 7 S.A.A.F. Wing, flew the last sortie for D.A.F. on the 16th, before transferring to 22nd T.A.C. 324 Wing, which had been so much under the operational control of 12th A.S.C., 12th T.A.C. and 22nd T.A.C., was now joined with its parent body.

3 S.A.A.F. Wing, long out of action at Jesi because the concrete runway was too short for Marauders, started to operate in support of the army drive to Faenza, bombing south of the town ahead of the Polish troops.

The weather, however, grew worse and worse. Although D.A.F. flew

1,500 sorties from November 21st to 24th (1,200 in close support), some days were completely unproductive.

Once more there were those who agreed with the verdict of the Ancients. Hibernation could have solved so many problems! Phantoms of Trigno seemed to trail their sighs over Savio as the wind-whipped rain collected in a thousand puddles on the battlefield. The spongy shades of Sangro presided in glutinous conclave over the approaches to the river Senio, where the Germans, from December 17th onwards, had established themselves on the east bank with a bridgehead to the west.

In general, with fresh divisions preventing a further advance along the axis of Highway 9, the enemy position was stronger at the end of the month than at the beginning. On the outskirts of the 5th Army the Germans even mounted a counter-offensive in the Serchio valley in Lilliputian mimicry of von Runstedt's drive on the Western Front.

For the second time running the Italian year was ending not with a bang, but a whimper. Road and rail interdiction, and supply dropping by the fighter-bombers to Italian Partisans, continued towards the end of December, although the weather was so bad that for six days out of the last fortnight D.A.F. was virtually inactive. Close-support requests were being met by Spitbombers whenever they could be put into the air.

Within D.A.F., December had brought a change of command. Air Vice-Marshal Dickson left for England; Air Vice-Marshal Foster took his place. The departing A.O.C., like all the former commanders, had made his own particular contribution to D.A.F. Apart from exercising the discretion of a Solomon in his dealings with both the army and the Higher Command of M.A.A.F., he had contrived to increase D.A.F.'s prestige at a time when not only the land campaign, but interdiction itself, had hardly come up to expectations.[1] D.A.F.'s close-support methods could scarcely be improved, nor could D.A.F.'s resources have been stretched further in so many different directions. The architect of 83 Group returned to the United Kingdom with a greatly enhanced reputation.

The new A.O.C., who had been A.O.C. Malta and had since headed the Air Commission Italy,[2] was, like his predecessor, taking over a force that was already a going concern. Under his guidance, D.A.F. was to finish the war with a flourish of exceptional activity before settling down to the woes and joys of occupation.

In December, although there were many signs that Germany would not long survive the battering from all fronts, there were few indications of collapse in Italy. There could be no sitting back, no hibernation, no concession to comfort. These could come later. Air Vice-Marshal Foster was called upon to display not only operational efficiency, but, later on, human under-

[1] Otherwise, I suggest, the war might have been at an end.

[2] Where he had been, so to speak, King of the Italian Air Force.

standing of the different standards necessarily obtaining in the aftermath of war.

For the moment, however, mud, rain and bitter fighting welcomed the new A.O.C. with soggy discourtesy. As the Officer Commanding 114 squadron commented:

> "Personally I have often had to operate under adverse conditions, but never in Greece, the Western Desert, Sumatra, Java, or even Shaibah itself, have I ever had to operate when conditions have been equally bad for both the living site and the airfield combined."

But in spite of it all, D.A.F.'s second Christmas in Italy could stand comparison with the festival at Sidi Haneish, for the good cheer, high spirits and happy informality remained unchanged. If the weather in 1944 was less favourable for D.A.F., then there were other consolations: the dances, the wine, the hospitality of Italians.

But chiefly there was the feeling that homecoming could not be long delayed. Loyal as each airman was to D.A.F., his first loyalty had always remained in England with his family. At Christmas, the great family festival, the airman's thoughts turned homewards across the Alps. He discounted the villa and the palazzo. Like the Jacobite exile in Italy, he "heard on Lavernia Scargill's whispering trees, and pined by Arno for (his) lovelier Tees". He longed for a familiar fireside. All the wine in Italy could not equal the pint of ale drunk amongst old friends in a favourite pub. These things, he felt, were drawing nearer. Such hope was indeed the breath of life. Present trials were of passing importance compared with this promise of the future.

The campanile bells at Christmastide rang with yearning melancholy in German ears. For the Allies, that joyful clangour sent messages of good cheer throbbing across the wintry skies. Captivity and despair for the vanquished, a weary delight for the victors, tolled the bells; urging all men, once more, to obey the Christian summons of peace and goodwill.

CHAPTER XL

THE LULL AT ITS HEIGHT

IN the Desert, a lull—at Gazala or El Alamein—had been almost as interesting and as important as the storm of war at its full blast. Lulls allowed reorganization, which in turn governed success. In Italy, however, lulls were dictated by the seasons rather than by the exhaustion of this or that side. Reorganization meant redeployment of existing resources rather than the creation of new model armies or air forces. The Allied war machine was so accurately geared for victory that nothing short of a German break-through could disturb the smooth running of all those innumerable cogs and flywheels. This, patently, was unlikely to occur. Thus, in so far as either side could take advantage of a lull which was more in the nature of a disguised submission to the elements, the Germans were more likely to benefit. They were on the perpetual defensive. They needed time to dig themselves in on the banks of the Senio, time to coax supplies through the air barrier of interdiction.

Roughly speaking, interdiction held the centre of the stage from January 10th to April 8th. 75 per cent of M.A.T.A.F.'s sorties were made to this end. Close support for the army offensive then took over, lasting until near the end of the month, when air pursuit of a routed mob mixed the two policies. German surrender, officially dating from May 2nd, provoked many a *cri de cœur* attesting to the decisive part played by the air forces in the final battle.

Lull, as always, is a relative term. Army attacks and counter-attacks, though leading to little territorial gains, could not be called unimportant, for men's lives were being lost. The oft-reiterated statement, "Active patrolling on both sides with occasional clashes," superficially sums up a period of three months.

The constant tension of those days provided the enemy with considerable time for uneasy thought. A German officer of 232 Infantry Division confided his inner conflict to paper:

> "Time flies. Boredom without end. What great deeds can one put into a diary? 'All quiet on the Southern front', as Remarque would say. Artillery fire, grenade-launchers, a machine-gun rattles . . . such is the unending chain of days. Mail from Getrud (she has not received any news from me for two months). Inspection of the position. One dead, one wounded . . . the High Command communiqué omits mention of this.
>
> "One starts to think about the war, one thinks of the future (do we have any future at all?). . . .
>
> "One starts philosophizing—but of what use is Schopenhauer's

philosophy, Goethe's 'Faust', Nietzsche's 'Man and Superman', and Fichte's well-intentioned speeches? We all, young or old, officer or other rank, are subject to the laws of this bitter war. Its iron fist forces us into the smallest hole when the splinters start flying around. We become animals. For seconds all instincts are being put *ad acta;* and then you think: once more it did not get you....

"Is that war?—yes, this is it. In such moments it loses all its glory.

"The telephone rings.... Here, 'Laternehalter', here, 'Stoerungstrupp!' A short dug-out intermezzo....

"Does war have any meaning? . . . Yes, it has a meaning. No, it can have no meaning! I really don't know. I am all mixed up. How can anyone put such a question to me? To me, who am doing what my feelings, my ego, command me. Leave me along with such questions, you tormenting thoughts!

"War is the father of all things. So wrote a great German (and a great German he was without any doubt), Karl von Clausewitz. Is it really the father? Is it not the basic evil of all things? Or are we, who may or must live through this last, murderous, phase of the war, so small, so abominable? Perhaps wars in all their terrible bitterness are tests for the small, ugly, and sometimes so wanton, human being. Perhaps the steel-helmet-crowned graves of the dead of all nations are proof of the truth in the words of God, 'Peace on earth, and good will towards men of good will'. Burn those words deep in your hearts, you men of all nations! Never again war! Now leave me in peace, you tormenting thoughts. I am of good will. . . ."

Before devoting itself mainly to interdiction, D.A.F. had carried out some notable close support on January 4th for the thrust by the 7th Armoured Brigade which eliminated the enemy salient east of the river Senio. Although the bomb line wriggled like a live snake even while requests for support were being sent in, Rovers were able to direct aircraft on to targets only a furlong in front of our armour. But soon D.A.F. began to reflect the change in M.A.T.A.F. policy. Up to the 10th, the ratio of close support to interdiction was one to one; from the 11th to the 20th, one to three, and thereafter, one to seven. The programme, however much interrupted by the weather, guaranteed that the offensive when it came, would meet with reduced opposition.

Snow fell over the countryside towards the end of January. Snow plans in every D.A.F. Wing relied on shovels and man-power, but not even a "band of willing men" could clear a landing-ground until the blizzard had run its course. 244 Wing called in a bulldozer fitted with a rubber sleeve, but the P.S.P. tore the improvised sweep to shreds. 3 S.A.A.F. Wing, with the 14th Airfield Construction Group, sent lorries up and down their runway all night long, to such effect that eleven Mitchells of Tactical Bomber Force, very short of fuel and unable to make base at Corsica, landed at Jesi just after lunch, when no other field in the whole area was in use.

Snow was a wicked uncle of brevet rank only, for barges, bridges, road and rail trucks all suffered during February. In the lull, interdiction was inevitably the most potent Allied weapon of offence. Partisans, however numerous, could still not vie with air power in inflicting damage behind the lines on a scale impossible for the most incendiary of saboteurs.

To follow D.A.F. round the clock, from sunset on the 5th to sunset on March 6th, is to trace a twenty-four-hour orbit of destruction. As darkness came upon the land south of the Po, six Bostons of 232 Wing and eight Baltimores of 253 Wing (converted in February to night-flying) bombed a factory and a stores dump under radar control, dropping leaflets *en passant* to drive home the lesson of the fires and explosions. Thereafter, road and rail reconnaissance—in this case uneventful—occupied them until the flare-path dimmed in the early morning light. North of the Po, a Mosquito of 256 squadron intruded over Udine, but haze prevented any sightings and the aircraft returned with engine trouble. Bostons and Baltimores were over the road and rail systems in north-east Italy and the barge routes between the Po and Caorle, dropping bombs on Monselice and Rovigo marshalling yards. Small clusters of lights indicated traffic and enemy transport moving between the Piave and the Tagliamento rivers. One Boston was lost.

Dawn, for the Germans, was no deliverer. Two Spitfires of 7 Wing on early-morning reconnaissance north of the Po reported about 800 waggons on the length of line near Conegliano. The chokepoint was attacked by thirty-nine Marauders from 3 S.A.A.F. Wing, whilst fighter-bombers (Spitbombers from 244 Wing and 7 S.A.A.F., Thunderbolts from the 79th Fighter Group, Mustangs and Kittyhawks from 239 Wing) claimed between them fifty-eight destroyed and seventy-nine damaged. Other attacks further up the line destroyed or damaged a locomotive and fifty waggons. Line-cutting missions created fifteen cuts at different points. Kittyhawks of 239 Wing made holes in the bridge at Ponte Longo. Mustangs destroyed the southern span at Longhere, and scored direct hits on the western approaches of the bridge at Gorizia. 79th Group Thunderbolts knocked the centre and western span out of Montereale and destroyed the north-eastern span at Citadella diversion.

Barges on the waterways were attacked by Spitbombers, Thunderbolts and Kittyhawks, the latter claiming the destruction of a landing stage, one barge, and three damaged. All three Spitfire Wings, 7 S.A.A.F., 244 and 324, flew escorts for Marauders, Mitchells, and for tactical reconnaissance aircraft of 285 Wing. Anti-flak missions were also flown by 7 S.A.A.F. Wing and the 79th Fighter Group. South of the Po, Spitbombers attacked two gun positions. 285 Wing meanwhile arranged tactical and artillery reconnaissances and took oblique photographs of the Senio river.

In the Balkans, five missions of Thunderbolts and Mustangs destroyed with rocket projectiles 22 waggons and 15 lorries, damaging 15 locomotives, 84 waggons, and 35 trucks.

Nor was this the sole air activity, for 22nd T.A.C. were performing similar feats for the 5th Army; tactical and strategic bombers maintained the heavier labours of interdiction. But the catalogue of results altered considerably from day to day. An imposing programme could be inundated by unfavourable weather.

Camouflage adopted by the Germans was reminiscent of Rommel's "Bedouin" encampments (which had shown such remarkable powers of multiplication on the eve of a *putsch*). On one occasion the pilots of four Spitfires of 417 squadron saw below them three shapes which on first inspection appeared to be three hayricks towed by three horses. The pilots insisted that there was an unnatural precision about the hay and a lack of animation about the horses, which led them to suspect that under each hayrick was a panzer, over whose gun was draped the semblance of a horse. After the first attack two wheeled off the road; the third chugged on. In a subsequent attack, bullets apparently bounced off the contraption, which was last seen careering towards some houses, its hay awry, the horses' hooves clear of the ground. The pilots remained unshakeable in their story.

• • • •

Sorties from mid-March onwards started to mount—777 on the 19th, to 863 on the 20th. A visit to the Udine *festungen* prevented any *Luftwaffe* counter-measures, for three aircraft were destroyed and nineteen damaged by rockets, fragmentation and phosphorus bombs. A German airfield was, however, becoming an unfamiliar target. Little was needed to remind the enemy that his air force had had its day.

On the 21st, operation "Bowler" gave the opportunity for a display of precision bombing. For ten minutes, starting from 3.30 p.m., fighter-bombers of D.A.F. attacked shipping in Venice harbour. Names of operations had often been descriptive. Bowler, too, contained a suggestion of its function. The A.O.C. told his pilots that he would be "bowlerhatted",[1] if bombs damaged any of the buildings of cultural or historic value.

Venice, as a target, had been cleared in February; photo-reconnaissance had revealed that barges and coastal traffic between the Lagoon and Trieste had increased as a result of road and rail interdiction. But the area which could be allowed to suffer, the shipping basin and the surrounding docks, was only 650 by 950 yards. War had already done enough harm to the unique monuments of Italy; to batter Venice when the fighting was almost at an end would have been inexcusable.

Shipping had been under the close scrutiny of 285 Wing. On March 18th,

[1] Returned to civilian life.

the S.S. *Otto Leonhardt* was taking on stores. Nearby were assembled a coaster and a number of barges. Poor visibility delayed the attack until the 21st, by which time the coaster lay next to the *Otto Leonhardt*, and one small vessel had disappeared.

Two squadrons of Thunderbolts and a squadron of Mustangs were to knock out the anti-aircraft defences. Forty-eight Mustangs and Kittyhawks were then to drop their bombs. There were to be no doubts as to who did what, for at 20,000 feet a Spitfire prepared to take photographs of the operation.

Forty-three flak positions had been strafed, bombed, and seared by rockets when the first wave of fighter-bombers dived on the docks, scoring two direct hits on the *Otto Leonhardt*, a near miss on a torpedo-boat at the northern end of the quay, damaging two warehouses. Flames and smoke rose high into the air, partly obscuring the target for the next wave; but three more warehouses, the coaster, and a supply barge appeared to have been set on fire.

The third wave broke over the escort vessel, lying between the eastern and the Scomenera quays. Two barges disintegrated; warehouses were once more covered in smoke. By then the *Otto Leonhardt* was aflame; clouds of smoke and dust made it impossible to judge the efforts of the fourth and last wave, but an explosion on the Palazzo quay shuddered upwards to where the reconnaissance pilot sat, like some impartial God of Battles, high in the air above the holocaust.

Only one aircraft was lost, and of this the pilot was saved. Warehouses were gutted, the *Otto Leonhardt*, severely damaged fore and aft, probably aground, a torpedo-boat sunk, the coaster sunk, the gasworks damaged—and only one small private building destroyed.

The Italians themselves were delighted at the *spettacolo*; many climbed on to rooftops to view this, their one aerial entertainment for some time past. But few of them could have known what infinite skill the pilots had been called upon to display; few could have realized how easy it would have been to have overshot, to have sent bombs hurtling over the proud buildings of the canals. As the pigeons[1] in Piazza san Marco fluttered back to their perches overlooking the crowded square, the flames and smoke from that small dockside area rose in cloudy witness to the efficiency of Desert Air Force. The bowler hat could be put away in a cupboard.

[1] Now reduced in number and considerably more wary; many a bird had already found its way into a Venetian cooking-pot.

CHAPTER XLI

PARTISANS. A NIGHT FLIGHT. THE MODERN ODYSSEY

ITALIAN Partisans were responsible for saving so many Allied airmen that this alone was reason enough for welcoming them as co-belligerents. In the Western Desert, the sea of sand had been neither friendly nor hostile; succour to the castaways had shared points in common with air/sea rescue; air crews had wandered until sighting signs of human life, and not until then had problems of escape or return to units arisen. Arabs had extended hospitality impartially, their attitude towards strangers of any nationality being regulated by traditions stronger than laws. In Italy, however, aircraft were often forced down in thickly populated country. The peasant, representing the only hope of avoiding captivity, was almost without exception friendly; but on the Partisans depended the airman's eventual passage through enemy lines.

Terrible reprisals sometimes followed in the wake of Allied air crews. Italian guides were shot or tortured by Germans; whole families were deported as slave workers. But the work of passing airmen from hand to hand went on.

For instance, a Boston of 55 squadron landed in flames after attacking marshalling yards north of Padua. The crew, one of whom was wounded, set off towards the mountains where they had been told that the Partisans were in strength. By day they slept in the fields and ravines; for food they relied on friendly farmers to supplement the contents of their escape boxes. On reaching the hills, they made contact with guerillas who gave them food, medical attention and civilian clothes, and hid them in their houses. There they remained for two months, despite constant raids by the Germans. On one occasion a Partisan, whose house they had only just left, was killed for refusing to betray them. Another Partisan, in whose cottage they had been seen, escaped death by a very narrow margin; as a reprisal his possessions were burned before his eyes. In March, a British Special Mission, operating behind the lines, gave them money, boots and maps with which to make a getaway through Yugoslavia. But the last offensive had already begun. As the bomb line snaked on its way up north they were rescued by men of the 5th Army.

D.A.F. had often dropped supplies to the Partisans. There was no reason to regret the time or money spent on these delicate missions, for every air crew who came back was a living witness to the wisdom of such investments.

The night-intruding Bostons and Baltimores helped to mask especial flights in aid of the Partisans. *Pippo* was a well-known frequenter of the darkened countryside. Supply-carrying aircraft, which would have caused comment had they been the only night-fliers in the area, went about their work like sheep in wolves' clothing, their passage marked by lights extinguished in relays on the ground below.

Pippo, besides provoking black-outs, causing road accidents, and providing a cloak of darkness for the Partisans, kept the Germans awake and disgruntled. But these were by-products; mainly the night-intruders helped to fill the gap in the interdiction programme, in so far as it could be filled.

Some idea has already been given of the work of daytime fighter-bombers, fighters and reconnaissance aircraft of D.A.F. Here, then, is an unadorned account of a complete operation, from start to finish, carried out by a Baltimore of 253 Wing:[1]

" 'Y' for Yoke is standing in the dispersal close by, her dew-covered wings shining in the moonlight. Leaping from the truck, we pull our parachutes and Mae Wests (1)[2] after us and dump them by the aircraft as the truck jerks into motion and hurtles down the taxi track.

"A fitter and a rigger are standing by and soon activity in and around the aircraft resembles six mice on a large lump of cheese. The fitter is hauling the tarpaulin covers from the engine, the rigger, sitting astride the nose, is wiping the dew from the perspex with a chamois. 'Cog' (the W.A.G. (2)) and 'Taffy' (the gunner) are in the back room stowing parachutes and checking equipment. The Nav. (3), Max, calls up to the pilot:

" 'Ready for bomb check, Mitch; all clear bomb doors.'

"Mitch, standing on the wing placing his 'chute in his cockpit, leans across and pulls a lever.

" 'HA-H-H-HA-A-A-A-A.' With a long heavy sigh the belly of the Balt. swings down and out, revealing two rows of sleek yellow bombs. Standing in the bomb-bays the Nav. checks the fusing gear, then ducks out from under and clambers up his door-cum-ladder into the office, where the bomb selection gear is checked.

" 'Load O.K.—Bomb doors closed,' and 'Whoosh', the doors swing shut and the belly of the aircraft is again a smooth unbroken line.

"By 21.30 all checking has been completed, the crew is aboard and the engines running. A rigger with two torches guides us out from the dispersal and gives the thumbs up as we turn down the taxi strip. Four hundred yards' taxying brings us to the end of the runway, where the pilot does his final cockpit drill and tests his engines, then calls the Control Tower by R/T.

" 'Hello Hillpath from Flippant 35—Ready for immediate scramble—Over.'

" 'Flippant 35 from Hillpath—clear to go—Over.'

" 'Roger (4) Hillpath; 35 Out,' and the night intruder lumbers forward, turns, and is soon thundering down the runway between the two rows of lights on the ground.

"At about 100 m.p.h. she bounces once or twice and becomes airborne. The wheels fold back into the engine nascelles and the flarepath falls rapidly

[1] Contributed by Warrant-Officer Knight, of 454 (Australian) squadron.
[2] See Glossary, p. 254.

below and behind. A few minutes later we are over the flarepath again, at 4,000 feet, and headed north for the Po river, our patrol area for tonight.

"A good moon is up and the coastline is clearly visible as it slides slowly backwards beneath us. On the way up a light on the sea is investigated but found to be a sea marker dropped by another aircraft. Soon the nav. lights are switched off and the bombs fused and selected.

"Looking out to port we can see the artificial moonlight and the flashes and explosions of the 8th Army's artillery fire. Just north of this, over enemy territory, an occasional flare appears in the sky. The night intruders are looking for enemy movement on the roads.

"Occasionally, too, the red and white chameleon-like tongues of tracer reach up from the ground trying to pull the intruders from the sky.

"As we pass Porto Garibaldi on the Comacchio Spit we ease away a little, for this is a definite 'hot spot'. Altering course at Goro we soon reach Taglio di Po and turn west along the river, beginning our patrol at 22.11. We are to cover a 40-mile section of the Po until 23.15. Passing Polesella, a noted hot spot, we are alert for any hostile action, for it was here one night that Jerry nearly claimed another aircraft destroyed—us.

"Stooging along we see a light switched off in a large building in a village. Noting this, we move on looking for better targets. The country 3,000 feet below us looks dark and still; the only lights showing are fires dotted around the area, and from the sky flares are still dropping intermittently. About four miles on our port bow a flare lights up a sharp bend in the river.

"Mitch's voice comes over the inter-com. 'I think I see a bridge down there Max. Should there be one there?'

" 'No,' replies the Nav., 'it is probably a pontoon affair—someone is bombing it now.'

"Three streams of tracer slide up from the south bank almost converging at 4,000 feet, and we see four bombs exploding in the river and on the bank quite close to the bridge.

" 'Let's go in and have a 'shooft'. (5) If it is still in one piece we'll come back and bomb.'

" 'Right. Here we go. Keep your eye on the bridge, Cog, and see if there are any holes in it.'

"Cog is over the open hatch in the rear of the aircraft and has a good view of anything directly below. We are over the bridge at 3,000 feet and the old Balt. is weaving like a bat. A single stream of tracer slides beneath us but it is not very accurate. Satisfied the bridge is in good condition, we peel off and scream for the deck heading back up the river—but we'll be back.

"Finding nothing along the river, we turn again towards our bridge, and as we approach a light blinks once near the centre.

" 'See that light, Mitch?' The Nav. is kneeling over his bomb sight in the nose of the aircraft.

" 'Yes, M.T., I think. The bridge is certainly in use. I'm turning in now,' and the wing dips as we do a diving turn onto the target.

"From the rear, the W.A.G.'s voice comes up, 'Do you want me to toss out a flare, Max?'

" 'No, thanks, Cog, I'll use the moonpath—O.K. Mitch, hold her there.'

"The plane levels out and the Nav. speaks again:

" 'Height 2,500 feet, Mitch?'

" 'Yep.'

" 'Oke . . . left—left . . . steady. . . . Bomb doors open . . . damn! Right 10 degrees. . . hold it. . . . Bombing, 1—2—3 bomb doors closed—break left.'

"As the aircraft makes its breakaway in a tight turn the invisible weight of the G. presses down on us, and Taffy speaks from the turret, 'A burst of light trace well below.'

"Cog reports on the bombing, 'Overshot to the southern bank—one on the bank, one near the road and one on a house.'

" 'O.K. Thanks, Cog,' the Nav. replies and thinks, 'Not good but better luck next time—yimkin.' (6)

"Last night we were photographing Francolino where Jerry was suspected to be crossing, so we circle here a few times dropping flares from 2,000 feet. Satisfied there are no pontoons or ferries crossing the river we stooge off. Activity was also expected near Polesella tonight, so we circle there doing bags (7) of evasive action and firing off illuminating cartridges. These light a section of the ground brilliantly for ten seconds each, but no movement or M.T. is seen.

" 'Let's go down a bit, Mitch, and have a shooft around the roads between the Po and the Adige.' Cog is becoming restless.

" 'Right. Going down.'

"At something like 500 feet our descent is checked, and we go weaving and turning around roads and canals.

" 'M.T. below us.' Cog has sighted a target.

"Turning, we fly back along the road and make three or four passes over a large truck parked by the roadside. Cog is strafing with his two belly guns and the smell of cordite fills the aircraft. We have only ten minutes left on patrol and we must dump our bombs on something, so we leave the truck and continue the search. During these few short minutes we see an exhibition of really good shooting but did not like it one little bit. Our aircraft was the clay pigeon.

"At 500 feet we flew over the moonlit countryside, the Nav.'s head thrust as far forward into the perspex nose as possible for better vision, the pilot concentrating on his flying and at the same time looking for M.T., the W.A.G. crouched over his open hatch and Taffy constantly turning his turret searching for enemy fighters.

"From the bank of a canal, without warning, a long thin yellow tongue of tracer licks out trying to caress old 'Y' Yoke. The Nav.'s head shoots back into the body of the aircraft like a scared tortoise. Mitch dives the aircraft to starboard and levels out quick—you can't dive far when you start from 500 feet That thin yellow line stays just over the turret, and weave as we did we could not lose it. We are clipping along at a smart 220 m.p.h. some fifty feet above the deck when the gun, probably a 20-mm., finally lost us and ceased firing. It is just after this that we all start to breathe again.

" 'Yah, missed me!' says Mitch, and his breath comes in uneven pants through the microphone.

"Max suddenly realizes that he is still alive after all and speaks up: 'We still have these bombs on and it is almost time we went home. I think we'd better go down to the river. We're sure to find something there.'

" 'What height?' the pilot wants to know as he turns south.

" 'About four thou.'

" 'Four thousand it is,' and we start climbing.

"Just as we turn along the river, a pontoon bridge is silhouetted in the moonpath.

" 'Target 40 degrees port. Start turning.' The navigator is over his bombsight again and his eyes keep the bridge in sight as his fingers feel along the bomb switches and select those required.

" 'Are you going for that bridge?' The pilot sighted it too.

" 'That's right. Weave right, then back again. . . . O.K., steady there . . . bomb doors open . . . left—left . . . hold it . . . bombing, 1—2—3, bomb doors closed, break left.'

"The bombs hurl up geysers of water about fifty yards east of the bridge. Not good enough. The Nav. speaks again.

" 'Your course 160 degrees more or less.'

" 'Are we going home now?' comes a query from the turret.

" 'Yes, Taff,' says Mitch. 'We're pointing right at it, more or less.'

" 'Goodie, goodie,' says Taffy.

"We are late leaving patrol, for it is now 23.25, so we try to send an E.T.A. (8) to base by W/T (9), but cannot get through.

"We fly down over the lake watching the terrific 8th Army barrage. Looking back over enemy territory fires can be seen scattered everywhere. Flares and bombs are still going down and tracer is still coming up. It will be like that all night. In the morning the fighter and daylight formation bombers will continue the harassing and the pounding. Reaching the southern shore of the lake we alter course and head down towards base.

"At 23.45 we are calling the Control Tower.

" 'Hello, Hillpath, this is Flippant 35. Landing instructions, please. Over.'

" 'Hello, Flippant 35 from Hillpath. You are No. 1 and clear to land. Over.'

" 'Roger Hillpath. 35 out,' and we complete the circuit of the 'drome and come in.

"Safety harnesses are fastened and we settle back into our seats as the aircraft is aimed as though to dive into the ground just short of the flarepath.

As usual, though, we level out, sink, bump once and we are rushing down a lane between the two rows of lights at 100 m.p.h. The Nav. enters in his log, 'LANDED BASE 23.48', as we taxi back to the dispersal.

"The aircraft is parked, engines stopped and we clamber out among the waiting ground crew.

" 'How was the trip, Mitch?' one of them asks.

" 'A PIECE OF CAKE,' is the reply. . . ."

Hillpath was the call-sign of Cesenatico, a P.S.P. aerodrome near the beach not far from the pinewoods of Cervia, where 239 Wing were congregated. The Army Airfield Construction Engineers had created the aerodromes from which the last offensive was conducted. Each time that an aircraft circled overhead they could look up and say, "There go our customers." But in common with the Army Air Formation signals they were hardly likely to do so. Co-operation was so much a matter of course that working evidences passed without comment.

. . . . .

A South African pilot from 239 Wing, Lieutenant Veitch of 260 squadron, was to show that co-operation between the different air force units was equally effective. His adventures made variations (and in three movements) on the theme of Air/Sea Rescue. Collectively, they were known as "The Odyssey". On three separate occasions during April the pilot was forced to bale out over the mine-infested waters of the Adriatic. Each time he returned to his squadron unharmed, except finally for a bruised arm.

After a rocket-armed reconnaissance of Maribor-Graz in Yugoslavia on April 2nd, Veitch, who was flying No. 2 in the formation, found that his aircraft had been hit by flak. He was ordered to return to base escorted by one of the other pilots. But glycol was leaking and the motor went dead over the Istrian peninsula. As his craft burst into flames, the pilot baled out. When almost at sea level he dropped a shoe on the water to judge his height. Soon he was in the dinghy, watched over by the escort until a Walrus arrived.

There the adventure might have ended. But much to the pilot's perplexity the Walrus continued to circle overhead, unable to land, as it happened, because of mines. Two Spitfires relieved the Walrus, were succeeded by two Mustangs with long-range tanks, and eventually by a Warwick. A lifeboat festooned with parachutes swung out of the sky, missing Veitch (who thought his last hour had come) by fifty yards; life-lines, automatically fired by rockets, sprayed across the sea. The gift from the clouds was soon boarded. Meanwhile an enemy air/sea rescue launch was chased away by bullets from the Mustang, for competition was unwelcome. A message in the lifeboat ran: "Steer course out to sea, Walrus will pick you up. We suspect mines in this area." But the South African found that of the twin motors mounted in the bows only the starboard would start. Finally, however, a Catalina appeared overhead, dropping a line of smoke floats, landing shortly afterwards. Veitch, a colourful figure in maroon pyjamas, was soon safe ashore.

Three days later the second movement departed only slightly from the original. This time he was hit over Ljubljana . . . glycol leaking . . . escort . . . baling out near Trieste . . . dropping a shoe . . . clambering into the dinghy. This time he found himself surrounded by what threatened to be the classical contents of the Augean stables. Decaying vegetables bobbed up and down on the waters; garbage bumped and gurgled against the rubber bolsters of his boat. Trieste, in the morning mist, was mercifully dim and distant, but, even so, two enemy rescue boats must have seen him; once more the competitors were driven off by guns and rockets. Later, a third boat with red sails put out from the shore. The sail was hauled down after a burst from the Mustang across the bows, but the four occupants continued rowing towards the stranded pilot. Another warning burst from the Mustang was disregarded. "There was nothing for it but to sink the craft." There were no survivors.

A Catalina circled Veitch for a while, unable to land because of mines. A Warwick arrived. Down swung the lifeboat; off shot the life-lines. This time, however, events took a different turn; further variations had unpleasant consequences. Both motors started, but the Germans opened fire from the shore with 40-mm. cannon. The Catalina reappeared, two Mustangs weaved overhead. But Veitch was still in the minefield by nightfall. Dropping flares, the escorts flew off home, to be relieved almost immediately by two Mosquitos.

Stopping the engines to prevent discovery by the enemy, the pilot settled down wrapped in a kapok-lined sidcot inner.[1] He spent the hours of darkness signalling with a torch to aircraft passing overhead and in watching the sea. After a quiet night he restarted the motors. At eight o'clock in the morning the Catalina reappeared, escorted by two Mustangs, but no smoke floats dropped out of the sky. There was a hitch, explained by the message: "Steer 200 degrees. We'll pick you up sometime yet—still mines."

A new variation chose this late moment to be introduced. The wind from the north freshened; a rising sea and a rainstorm counterpointed one engine spluttering to a standstill. The Catalina could not land for some while; when it did, the lifeboat drifted away from the air-amphibian, which had to be restarted and taxied nearer. One of the rescuers, however, had managed to jump into the lifeboat; he now dived overboard with a line and swam back to the Catalina. Veitch was hauled as far as the wing-tip float, whence he swam to the hull, to be greeted with, "Haven't we seen you somewhere before?"

This perhaps might have been the dramatic finale to the Odyssey. The immediate award of the D.F.C. seemed to have brought the theme to a fitting climax. But there was to be a delayed third movement presented at the end of the month, so near the end of the war that the drums of victory were already booming an accompaniment.

[1] Worn under a sidcot flying-suit.

On April 30th Veitch was attacking transport north of Udine . . . his aircraft was hit . . . oil, not glycol, came pouring out . . . the oil pressure dropped to zero, but the pilot climbed to his usual 7,000 feet . . . the engine cut . . . he had to bale out, catching one arm on the tail plane. "He was not so clever about it this time," commented an Intelligence Officer, "being a little out of practice." He landed five miles from Lignano, in a minefield, naturally enough.

The third movement developed the variations of the second, scorning the lesser pipings of the first. Discomforts intensified. Escorts remained overhead until a Warwick appeared, but the weather grew worse; and the aircraft had to leave. It was nearly dark when the storm abated. Veitch had already spent a night in a lifeboat, but this time he was faced with the unpleasant prospect of a vigil in a dinghy. Literary precedents were valueless; neither the Jumblies[1] (who "went to sea in a sieve they did"), nor the three men of Gotham (who were found adrift in a bowl, chanting "Water may not pass the brim") had ever needed to bale and swab. Veitch did little else; there was not much chance of sleep.

The next morning, at dawn, a Catalina, a Flying Fortress, and a Mustang were attracted to the dinghy by red Verey flares. The Flying Fortress made two runs over it, dropping a lifeboat on the third about two hundred yards away. The South African started paddling, but his arm was hurting and progress was slow. He decided to swim to it, for dry clothes were awaiting him there. The lifeboat this time was American, differing very slightly from previous models. The engines at first puzzled him, but he was soon moving on course eating a G.I.[2] breakfast of pork and beef paste, sweet biscuits, peanuts and candy. A Catalina rode in the air above; occasionally a Mustang flew low overhead, waggling its wings to indicate changes in the course. Later he saw a high speed launch which he reached at 11.15. He was given a good welcome, offered rum, but preferred chicken soup and sandwiches. That night he was back with his squadron at Cervia.

Official recognition had applauded the second movement; but since then the orchestra, as it were, had embarked incontinently on a third. Only a joke could supply the absolutely final note. The A.O.C. had his ready. The pilot received a special signal: "Personal from Foster to Veitch. I have appointed you Honorary Commodore of the Desert Air Force Yachting Club, when it is formed."

GLOSSARY

(1) Inflatable lifejackets.
(2) Wireless Operator-Air Gunner.
(3) Navigator.
(4) Message received and understood.
(5) *Shufti*—the Arabic for "look".
(6) Arabic for "maybe".
(7) Plenty of.
(8) Expected time of arrival.
(9) Wireless-Telegraph.

[1] Lear. The Jumblies, it will be remembered, not only possessed "a pinky paper all folded neat", but avoided the issue by passing the night in a crockery jar, as soon as their sieve started to leak.

[2] Government Issue (American).

CHAPTER XLII

THE END OF THE CAMPAIGN IN ITALY

APRIL 1ST, 1945, gave the ingenious fewer opportunities for displaying their wit than All Fools' Day, 1944. Instead of fourteen, 740 sorties were flown. Railway lines and bridges were bombed, armed reconnaissances sent over Yugoslavia and southern Austria; and seventy Marauders of 3 S.A.A.F. Wing started a blitz on methanol plants and sugar refineries in north-east Italy; factories which were producing synthetic fuels to replace petrol. The only *poisson d'Avril* was a Hungarian light aeroplane, reported by a D.A.F. Direction Finder Station to have landed near Ravenna. The two occupants refused to leave their seats, demanding the presence of a German- or Hungarian-speaking officer. Expectation ran high. A convoy of three vehicles duly set off from M.O.R.U., containing the Senior Signals Officer, Senior Intelligence Officer, two American interrogators, and a Field Intelligence unit sergeant. On the field they met the Senior Intelligence Officer of 324 Wing. The two Hungarians, it transpired, had seen no future in fighting for the Germans; they had stolen the aircraft and some seventy litres of fuel and flown over the Alps and the Adriatic with blankets, cigarettes, wine and tins of food. One had changed into a smart civilian suit.

After such preparations the sequel was disappointing. The men knew very little. They carried no top secret plans, no confidential orders, not even a blueprint of an atom-smasher. The interrogators were forced to listen to gossip about senior Hungarian officers at Zeltweg (who were apparently enjoying themselves with no thought of the morrow). It was not long before the visitors were driven off ingloriously to the prisoner-of-war cage at Rimini.

From then until April 9th D.A.F. continued attacking methanol plants. Interdiction and assaults on the Po barges wove a pattern already imprinted during the last months. There was no sudden lull in air activity to warn the enemy of the tremendous blitz due to start as the army moved forward.

The relative strength of the opposing forces left no doubt as to the outcome of the offensive. In a sense, the final battle had already started further east, where some German-controlled troops—mostly Croat divisions or Ustachi quislings—had been retreating before twice that number of Yugoslavs. Tito's offensive, planned in consultation with Field Marshal Alexander earlier in the year, had begun on March 19th, its aim, Fiume and Trieste. D.A.F.'s Marauders, Spitbombers, Thunderbolts, Mustangs, Kittyhawks, Baltimores and Bostons were thus already involved in helping to close one claw of the pincer upon the common enemy.

In considering the German position, it should not be forgotten that Vienna, after fierce fighting in the suburbs, was mainly in Russian hands, and that Königsburg, the heart of Prussia, had surrendered to the Red Army by the 9th. These disasters on the Eastern front from the Baltic to the Adriatic had for the moment more effect on the German Army Group "C" in Italy than Allied successes in the west. For von Vietinghoff, who had just taken over from Kesselring, found himself, like Sinbad, upon an encircled peninsula little better than the island back of a whale; at any moment the mammal might sink and there would be no chance of escape to other shores.

Army Group "C", however, on the eve of the final battle, was better equipped and stronger than any other German group engaged in Europe. Twenty-four German divisions, six Italian fascist divisions, 200 tanks (nearly as many as there were on the whole Western Front at that stage), and 400 assault guns lent weight to the Southern Redoubt theory.[1] Not all these divisions manned the river Senio, where in fact there were only some sixteen German and one Italian with two mobile divisions; a training division was in reserve near Venice.

In our favour, therefore, the ratio was three, or at worst two, to one. We were far stronger in supporting arms. Our supplies streamed in uninterrupted. No camouflaged horses and carts were needed in the Allied lines. In short, the sole German advantage—and a powerful one—was that the ground was suited to defence, so well suited even against air attack that the Senio river line and the Bologna *schwerpunkt* were still in their hands after four months of persistent Allied effort.

German air strength need not be considered; it was token, if that, as it had been for some time past. In D.A.F. there was only one change; 3 Wing was placed under the operational control of the 57th Bombardment Wing.

The assault had been planned for the 7th, but high winds sprang up, and during the 8th all D.A.F airfields were non-operational. Since the preliminary air softening-up was an essential part of the joint plan, operation "Buckland-Wowser" had to be postponed until the next day.

D.A.F.'s greatest air effort ever was Air Vice-Marshal Foster's aim. He knew that this was to be the swan-song; and if so, the melody was to embody the whole of D.A.F.'s past experiences, to bring the Desert theme to a crescendo before dying away suddenly at the height of its fury. It happened, that night, that the film *Henry V* was showing at the Garrison Theatre; the Shakespearian drama which so perfectly sums up the feelings and emotions of small bands of Englishmen fighting against odds all over the world. The odds in Italy were no longer there; St. Crispin's Day for D.A.F. had come and gone in the

[1] It was said that the Germans might retreat into the mountains of Austria and Bavaria, there to fight on until annihilation; or until, pulling secret weapon after secret weapon out of some goblins' cavern, the world was at their feet. Arab listeners to German broadcasts had already been assured that V2 rocket projectiles capable of reaching America were in production.

Desert; but there was something topical about "Silken dalliance in the wardrobe lies . . . for now sits expectation in the air".

It had been sitting there, in point of fact, intermittently since the start of the year. In the last three months 27,000 sorties had been flown; 1,064 motor transport, 5,007 rail trucks, 531 locomotives, 485 barges, and 26 ships had been destroyed or damaged. But in April the wardrobe might no longer have existed, for D.A.F. was to produce 21,000 sorties in the one month.

The 9th opened without any apparent change in the air programme. Armed reconnaissances and rail cutters went about their work to create the impression that the day was not to produce anything out of the ordinary. The planning, however, was a masterpiece of detail. Areas had been given code-names. Heavy, medium and light bombers were briefed and ready. A phalanx of navigational aids, radio beams, smoke ground-signals, even a line of anti-aircraft fire to indicate the front, fought for the attention of the pilots, some of whom had already inspected their targets.

Just after lunch Strategic Air Force laid down its carpet—1,692 tons in the pre-selected areas; the medium tactical bombers hit their three allotted gun positions; and the full weight of D.A.F. was brought to bear on the chosen points. The employment of day-flying heavy bombers in close support—a practice in abeyance since Cassino—led to a similar incident. Out of forty-two formations, one bombed the attacking Polish troops, who suffered casualties. This, however, caused little animosity. General Anders took the view that the amazingly high standard of heavy close support was ample compensation for an incident of such exceeding rarity.

Never had D.A.F.'s fighter-bombers been called upon to work within more delicate limits. The men who had bombed the docks of Venice were now being directed by Rover on to targets sometimes only five hundred yards in front of the army. Rovers, bearing cheerful christian names, clung tenaciously to the forward troops, always moving with them, maintaining a continuity of close support which the Desert had never known.

During the afternoon all the fighter-bomber wings dived on enemy positions from Imola to the river Reno, firing rockets, strafeing, and dropping fuel tanks filled with incendiary jelly, whose liquid fire, more terrible than molten lava, bubbled unquenchably in trench and dugout. On the 5th Corps front, successive waves of Spitbombers of 244 Wing broke across the Senio during ten-minute lulls in the artillery barrage. Four times, in quadruple Timothy, the Spitbombers sprayed death over the river defences. The fifth time their guns were silent; the spume of destruction stayed aloft in mid-air; and that was the moment of the ground assault.

There had, in the past, been no question of cracking the Senio defences from the sky; there was none now. But four times the enemy heads had been down; and on the fifth occasion habit guaranteed that heads would be down again. British, Polish, and New Zealand troops were soon across the river, battling amidst fortified floodbanks at which they had gazed enviously all the winter. They were on their way to the Santerno.

That night our forces were a mile from the new river. D.A.F. exceeded its most optimistic maximum. From Forli, from dusk to dawn, eighty-three Bostons and seven Mosquitos took off or landed every two minutes. From Cesenatico, another sixty Baltimores rose into the air, not to attack bridges and pontoons, but gun positions running from Castel Bolognese to Bagnara, from Imola to Massa Lombardo, bombing closer to our troops than D.A.F. had ever attempted at night.

From April 10th to the 13th, out of D.A.F.'s total of 3,513 sorties, 90 per cent were in direct support; and of these missions, anything up to one-third were Rover-directed. In order to be comprehended fully these figures should be imaginatively transformed; they should be linked with previous descriptions of particular raids; for they meant that during the next few days D.A.F. provided for the ground forces a flying artillery service of devastating intensity, ubiquitous and persistent.

This at first took place only on one front. But when the 5th Army offensive opened on the 14th, the heavy bombers were switched across to lay their carpets ahead of the troops in the areas south of Bologna. 22nd T.A.C., like D.A.F., gave its army an unending parade of close support. Mitchells and Marauders struck whenever and wherever they were needed, to demonstrate that a tactical bomber force had a valuable contribution to make to the fighting. The Hydra of Allied air power, which during the winter lull had remained ever watchful, surveyed a chaotic scene largely of its own making. The land forces needed to break through and pursue; air power would then guarantee a rout.

When the bastion of Bologna fell on the 21st, D.A.F. switched its air effort to the remaining Reno bridges and the Po crossings, at which the Bostons and Baltimores had been hammering since their initial phase of close support. With D.A.F., 57th Bombardment Wing now concentrated on the makeshift pontoons, the traffic of a desperate enemy milling from Ostiglia to Crespino. Near Polesella—"the noted hot-spot"—76th Panzer Corps had tried in vain to withdraw in good order. Nine hundred vehicles, a hundred guns of all calibres, and fifty-nine tanks were found abandoned. And yet that Corps considered itself more fortunate than others. 15th Army Group reported "crippling losses in armour and equipment south of the river".

Movement by day was, as the Germans knew well, suicidal. Even in darkness there was little safety; for the night-intruders, with skill born of experience, were effective out of all relation to their numbers. The background to their work was typical of D.A.F. Air and ground crews rose to the occasion, determined that nothing should stand in the way of victory. When the bomb line was the river Po, 114 squadron flew twenty-six sorties from fourteen aircraft. Air crews, awake from dawn to dusk on their double errands, were operating two nights out of every three. The armament section re-armed and re-bombed in the dark with unparalleled speed; three aircraft were prepared for a second trip within thirty-five minutes. The servicing flights, who on average were maintaining fourteen out of sixteen (80 per cent), on the last night of the month succeeded in producing 100 per cent serviceability. 114 and 18 squadrons, originally from a Wing which had never been in the Desert, showed how completely they had absorbed the D.A.F. traditions; as if to give added proof that D.A.F. was indeed a conception, an idea, alive and dominant, exacting allegiance from each labourer in the vineyard whether at the first or at the eleventh hour, with the same reward for all, veteran or late-comer.

In the crumbling days, from the fall of Bologna to the end of the month, D.A.F.'s swan song grew louder and louder as town after town collapsed before the two armies. Von Vietinghoff had not been allowed by Hitler to give the order to withdraw until 13 Corps had broken through the Argenta gap, until 5th Army troops reached Highway 9 west of the town. By then, all his reserves had been committed to battle. By then, he had no chance of masking his retreat, or even of fighting delaying actions along the Adige or the Brenta. In the headlong rush towards the Alps, the last traces of organization disappeared. And the Partisans rose all over the north to hinder and harry the exit of the hated *Tedeschi*.

Tactical air activity of the last few days of the campaign was a matter of hunting down German transport, whilst the heavy strategic bombers severed and severed again the escape routes to the north. Aircraft flew in ever decreasing circles round the "vast prisoner-of-war cage" until all resistance ceased.

South of the Po the enemy had elected to stand and fight; south of the Po he was destroyed. The remnants of four divisions offered little hope of preserving the Southern Redoubt. On the 29th, the Instrument of Surrender was signed in the Royal Palace at Caserta, heralding the Armistice, effective from May 2nd. The war was over.

. . . . .

The most important function of the air forces had been to prevent an army from crossing the Po. D.A.F.'s share was large, though not of itself decisive. The integrated efforts of Allied air power, however, evoked testimonials from the enemy commanders, which should not be discounted as mere excuses for defeat. To assess the degree to which land, sea, or air forces have been decisive in any campaign is an unrewarding, perhaps impossible, task for a chronicler. Let von Vietinghoff therefore give his views; for he and his troops were in the best position, as victims, to know:

> "The fighter-bomber pilots had a genuinely damaging effect. They hindered practically all essential movement at the focal points. Even the radio and telephone communications were delayed threefold. Local

reserves, which should have been moved by day, often arrived with great delay at the ordered position.

"Even tanks could not move during the day because of the employment of fighter-bombers. The effectiveness of fighter-bombers lay in that their presence alone over the battlefield paralysed every movement. The artillery-spotting pilots were unpleasant as well. Their mere presence enforced silence upon our artillery. Each soldier felt himself observed and recognized by the artillery-spotting pilot, even when this was not the case. In this manner, in decisive phases of the battle, the centre of gravity of our defence, the artillery, fell away.

"From the 9th to the 20th of April, 1945, was the period of the most effective employment of the Allied Air Forces. In the attack on the Senio fortifications, the number of casualties was increased by the dropping of numerous small-calibre fragmentation bombs. Especially in the region of Ferrara and Lake Comacchio, the resistance of the troops was greatly reduced and communications and command were disrupted as never before. Through the destruction of almost all crossings of the numerous canals, transhipment was made much more difficult and we had to leave much heavy equipment behind.

"The smashing of all communications connections was especially disastrous. Thereafter the orders failed to come through at all or failed to come through at the right time. In any case, the command was not able to keep itself informed of the situation at the front, so that its own decisions and commands came, for the most part, too late.

"The crossings of the Reno and the Po rivers were decisively influenced by the employment of the Allied Air Forces. The smashing of almost all ferries and bridges made an ordered retreat across the Po no longer possible. The troops amassed at the crossing points, and often had to swim to the other bank without heavy weapons. After April 20th, less use was made of the air force.

"In considering the most important effects of Allied air power, the morale effect upon the German troops must not be underestimated. However, it was here decisive in that, as a result of their complete lack of an air force of their own and without the promise of the help of a like force, the troops felt still more the enemy's superiority of materials.

"Rail traffic was stuck in the most protracted fashion by the destruction of bridges. Restoration of bridges required much time; the larger bridge sites were detoured or the supplies were reloaded. With the increasing intensity of the air attacks, especially on the stretch of the Brenner, the damaged sections were so great and so numerous that this stretch, despite the best of repair organization and the employment of the most powerful rebuilding effort, became ever worse and was only locally and temporarily usable. A few bad weather days, in which Allied Air Forces could not have flown, would often have sufficed to bring the traffic again to its peak. Only in February and March was it again possible to travel by rail through the Brenner to Bologna."

To this General von Senger of 14th Corps provided a postscript:

"The effect of Allied air attacks on the frontier route of Italy made the fuel and ammunition situation very critical. We had no difficulty with food since we bought it locally.

"The night-bombing was very effective and caused heavy losses. We could still move when required at night, but we could not move at all in the daytime due to air attacks.

"It was the bombing of the river Po crossings that finished us. We could have withdrawn successfully with normal rearguard action despite the heavy pressure, but due to the destruction of the ferries and river crossings we lost all our equipment. North of the river we were no longer an army."

CHAPTER XLIII

CONCLUSIONS

D.A.F. alone does not provide the data from which the proper conclusions as regards the air side of the Italian campaign can be drawn. The successes and failures of interdiction have been surveyed in brief detail, too brief perhaps for a clear understanding of all the issues involved. D.A.F. played a relatively small part in the overall interdictory policy; within its sphere it was consistently effective.

In close support, D.A.F. improved its Desert reputation, developing new methods such as Rover, bombing enemy positions nearer and nearer the front line. Train-wrecking and bridge-busting showed that the fighter-bomber, particularly the rocket-armed fighter, had superseded the small formation of light bombers; but not, it should be added, the large formation of medium bombers.

If D.A.F.'s sphere of policy was small, the field of its activities was at various times very large. The invasion of France temporarily claimed some of its units; Yugoslavia was a more permanent responsibility. D.A.F. was competent enough, when need arose, to take over the entire close support for both armies on the Italian front. It was flexible enough to switch from interdiction to close support, and back to interdiction again. It was mobile enough to keep up with 8th Army; self-sufficient enough to provide its own ground services by day and night, leaving the higher air aims to be interpreted by specialist strategic air forces.

Throughout the campaign, the German air force could, for all practical purposes, be discounted. Raids on enemy airfields still had to take place occasionally to maintain this absolute air supremacy; and a few times—a very few times—German aircraft caused some damage behind our lines. The *Luftwaffe* had hardly recovered from disaster in North Africa; it was never to recover from fresh blows in Sicily.

In Italy, therefore, the air war never needed to be fought. The controversy as to whether or no the air battle should take precedence over the land battle never arose. Allied Air Forces thus gained freedom of action, which in the Desert would have been incredible. The argument was not between air superiority, interdiction, and close support, but solely between interdiction and close support. There were, if such a thing can ever be said, plenty of aircraft for both tasks.

Air supremacy, unshattered, unshakable, automatically diminished the value of implications to be drawn from this or that method of employing the air forces. The Italians in Abyssinia had previously demonstrated what an air force could do against no opposition, yet the *Regis Aeronautica* had not been outstandingly successful when faced with the Desert Air Force.

In Italy, as in North Africa, the chief merit of Allied air power remained in the fact that, starting from very little, R.A.F. Middle East and Mediterranean Allied Air Forces built up a vast empire whose sway, after the initial fight for air superiority, was unchallenged.

The application of such power was experimental, subject like all experiments to unexpected disappointments and sudden delights. Air Marshal Slessor's post-mortem on interdiction—"It cannot of itself . . ." etc.—indicated that, in the tactical sense, air power had its limitations.

As with the whole, so with the part. The improved tactics of D.A.F.'s air crew in Italy took place under conditions of air supremacy, conditions for which they themselves had fought. How they exploited their position has been shown in detail in the preceding chapters.

Two comments can be made. Firstly that they acquitted themselves superbly. Secondly, that German antidotes—anti-aircraft fire, cleverly arranged defences, fresh methods of evading interdiction—grew increasingly effective. Necessity being the mother of invention, where once the Allies had needed all the ingenuity at their command, in Italy the Germans were compelled to call every possible device into play to offset the grave disadvantage of air impotence. An unimpassioned assessment would give high marks to their efforts.

D.A.F., though liable to promote interdiction wherever necessary, was the finest instrument of close support on any side throughout the war. It had been the prototype; it remained the model, even when its aircraft grew gradually more obsolescent. Like some mother of parliaments, the products of its traditions could be bodily transplanted. 83 Group in Normandy was a good example of its influence.

D.A.F. never ceased to grow in importance because offshoots were taking root elsewhere. D.A.F. was built around the legend of the Desert. Adaptability was in the blood; variety was the perpetual stimulant; hardship was the highroad to success. The persistence of the Desert Air Force myth has been the theme of this history; for this persistence was a constant factor, ever at work binding the members of D.A.F. of all nations together, giving them a phenomenal loyalty to their group, dictating their modes of behaviour, and even their outward appearance. It was never difficult to recognize a D.A.F. man. Everything about him proclaimed his origin in an instant. Just as those who took part in the Battle of Britain were unmistakable, so the members of D.A.F., conscious of belonging to a *Corps d'Élite*, were curiously similar to those pioneers of 1940. Like the citizens of ancient Rome, they had won their privileges and were proud of their especial position.

The message of congratulation from General McCreary, G.O.C. 8th Army, was a remarkable tribute from one Service to another:

"In this hour of our complete victory I feel my first duty is to convey to you and to all the officers and men under your command my heartfelt gratitude for the magnificent support that the Desert Air Force has rendered to the 8th Army throughout our long association. This last great battle has been won as a result of complete confidence and co-operation between the 8th Army and the Desert Air Force. Our aim was to destroy the enemy south of the river Po; how completely we succeeded is proved by the vast numbers of enemy vehicles and equipment destroyed on the southern bank of the river as a result of your attack. The Desert Air Force has achieved a degree of high efficiency in close support of the ground forces that has never been equalled in any other partnership. Throughout the long struggle the gallantry of the pilots in the Desert Air Force has been the continual admiration of the 8th Army. Their dash and courage has never been more evident than in the great battle that has brought about the final collapse of the enemy. These decisive results could not have been achieved without the most skilled leadership and planning, and I should like to express my admiration at the manner in which you and your staff handled the intricate problems that have faced us. In particular I refer to the planning that was undertaken by your Headquarters with M.A.T.A.F. in connection with the heavy bomber attacks. The record number of sorties that the Desert Air Force have flown in a single day during the recent weeks is evidence of the unstinted labours and efficiency of your ground organization. I wish to thank you personally for all the help and co-operation you have extended to me while we have worked together towards the attainment of our common goal. My most earnest hope is that the comradeship and trust that has been built up between the 8th Army and the Desert Air Force will have a lasting influence on the relations between our two Services in the years to come. I am confident that this will be the case and feel sure that the results that have been achieved on the battlefields of Africa and Italy will long be quoted as a perfect example of inter-Service co-operation."

WESTERN DESERT

Australian Gladiators returning to base after patrolling over Bardia

SICILY

An Italian aircraft captured by Desert Air Force and repainted with R.A.F. markings

ITALY

Assembling rocket projectiles for Desert Air Force Mustangs. The aerodrome, practically on the seashore, was made of pierced steel plating

THE PRICE OF WAR

Figures and facts, this is what they really represent. The photograph happens to be of a German vehicle and its crew after a Desert Air Force fighter-bomber attack in 1944. In 1943 such a picture might have symbolized the Italian, and in 1942 the British, position. Reminders such as this should hang in every council chamber where the fate of nations is discussed. For this is the price of war

Desert Air Force's starting point. H.Q. 202 Group at Maaten Bagush

SKETCHES BY TEDDER

And the end of the trail: Advance H.Q. Desert Air Force at Klagenfurt, Austria

ENVOI

M.A.A.F. in April had taken the precaution of sending a message to all its formations; all aircraft save those ordered on special operations were to be grounded immediately after the end of the war. It was obvious that victory would be celebrated with warlike intensity. Accidents had to be avoided.

Those who took part in the rejoicings need not be reminded of that night. Their relatives in England would have been shocked, perhaps, or envious. Imagine a boom town at the height of the gold rush, and multiply it all over Italy. The revolvers, however, were fortunately less lethal; Verey lights flared into the sky all night long, and not even the severest Equipment Officer dared to disapprove. Most airmen for a few hours went happily and comfortably mad. For the end of the war in Italy was too great a thing for the mind to absorb in a moment. There would be long days of inactivity to come, when sober reflection could be given fuller scope.

At the fly-past[1] in May, Desert Air Force spread its wings to signal the passing of an era. As squadron after squadron swept across the grassy plain of Campoformido, memory might have recalled one after another the stages on the long journey from Cairo, the countries, the towns, the rivers which had become part of the D.A.F. tradition. The birthplace, 12 Sharia El Comanos Pasha . . . out into the Desert as Advanced Wing . . . Maaten Bagush, the starting-point . . . into Cyrenaica . . . Benghazi . . . Barce, and Headquarters Cyrenaica . . . Tobruk . . . and others in Greece.

Forward and backward, forward and backward swung the pendulum. Battleaxe and Winston Churchill's pronouncement . . . Crusader, and air parity for the first time . . . Tobruk again . . . Cyrenaica again . . . back to Gazala . . . Gambut, the enormous fairground . . . Bir Hakim and the Free French . . . air cover for the retreat to Alamein . . . the battle for Egypt. . . . Forward with the pendulum for the last time—Cyrenaica again, Gazala again . . . the air lift to Marble Arch . . . Tripoli . . . El Hamma . . . Khasr Rhilane and the Free French . . . on to Tunis.

Consolidation then; together at Tripoli for the assault on Sicily . . . Malta . . . Pachino . . . Gerbini, the mosquitos and dry earth . . . the interdiction of Catania . . . Brindisi . . . Foggia, for the strategic bombers . . . little landing-strips at Salerno, the whole fury of air power . . . the mud and rain by the rivers of Trigno and Sangro . . . the Anzio bridgehead . . . the air experiment at Cassino . . . Rome . . . the Gothic Line . . . Florence, the switch-over to Pescara, whilst others were in the south of France . . . then rivers again; the Savio . . . winter delay at the Senio . . . the Reno, the Po, the Adige, the Brenta

[1] *See* Appendix E.

. . . Yugoslavia—those places which nobody knew how to pronounce. And now Udine.

So many years, so much effort, such constant variety, from such small beginnings. There at Campoformido were the results; wave upon wave roaring overhead, the crews symbolizing all the men with wings, whilst there on the ground were the men without wings, symbolizing all who had made such results possible; men of many nations in one great unified force.

That night, at Brazzaco, the country house where D.A.F. Headquarters had come to rest, the A.O.C. held a party. There visitors from other commands who had attended the fly-past met the leaders in every branch of D.A.F. activity. Fairy lights festooned convenient branches; a flarepath lit the hazards of a sloping gravel walk; a chancelight[1] lurked in the background, casting leafy shadows over the cheerful company.

In tents nearby, food and drink drew the visitors away from the arena of grass where a band played at intervals to fill the glade with music. D.A.F. had expanded in all its glory; and this was its farewell.

The *fin de siècle* was ushered out with fanfares which sounded the louder because they were never to sound again. The happy band of brothers had come together for the last time, their witness no less sincere because the men themselves were not all veterans. All members, however recent, were proud to belong to D.A.F.

The fly-past and the party; those were the symbols of finality. But the force itself continued to exist, diminishing, always diminishing. Air Commodore Falconer, assuming command in August, presided over a dwindling concern. Where once there had been the pressure of operations there was now at least plenty of time for ease and enjoyment. The Lido, which had climbed to social heights throughout the pre-war years, was now exclusive in quite another sense. Its hotels were commandeered for men of the Allied armies and air forces. The bare backs outstretched on its beaches had perhaps been browned by the sun of North Africa, tanned by the winds of Sicily.

Venice itself was outwardly transformed. "Ducks" chugged their way along the canals, gondolas swayed under the weight of men in uniform. The Piazzo san Marco, where tourists had once aped the native Venetians—gossiping at an outdoor table, sipping a *café*, nibbling a tiny cake—was now a busy crossroads for men who, on pleasure bent, had dispensed with the siesta. The Italians claimed that their pearly town had even changed its native odour. "Carbolic instead of garlic; it all seems so unfamiliar. . . ."

Northwards, in Austria, the sparkle of Italian gaiety grew dim. For there the order was "No fraternization"! There were dances in Klagenfürt, there was boating on the Würtersee; but men alone do not make a holiday. Whatever the sentiment in England, no explanation of the order convinced any airmen in Austria save those who had other, personal, reasons for continuing to hate.

[1] A floodlight used to help pilots landing at night.

Austria was a silent, tragic land that summer. The noise, the dirt, the ragged glitter of Italy, lost the saving grace of humour on crossing the Alps. Clean white houses, prudently built with double windows, suggested preparations for harsh weather; whereas in Italy, villas elegant but carpetless maintained the persuasive fiction that winter was a passing accident rather than a yearly institution. In Austria, too, the huge trees sweeping upwards from curving hills, the lakes lying in calm majesty, all possessed a brooding quality. "Life," said the Würtersee, "is transitory; youth is fleeting; pleasure is the stepping-stone to pain." In Italy no such sermons waylaid the Allies. There the people of all ages seemed to have tamed, or adjusted themselves to, their environment. Few things disturbed or even affected profoundly. Life could be called artificial, rootless, but at least never fruitless. Old folk were frail figures who had their uses; in Austria they appeared more like grim symbols of approaching death.

Italy was recovering with surprising elasticity from occupation, war, and finally liberation. Much of the recovery was superficial, but the intention, the hope, was there. Austria, divided and divided again, its over-ambitious capital apportioned to the conquerors, was sunk in helpless, hopeless gloom.

On holiday, or at work, the men from D.A.F.'s remaining units were scarcely involved in problems of local conditions. The magic circle of a squadron life was no longer, as in Sicily, intact, but an aerodrome was still a sealed, self-supporting entity. The Service ministered to all their wants. Commandeering supplied what the shops could not. Rations, supplemented by purchases from the N.A.A.F.I., provided plenty of good food.

Training, "Just in case", continued. For although the war was at an end, units were enjoined to remain fit for further operations if necessary. Unease on the borders, incidents, disappearances, and civil clashes maintained a state of tension. D.A.F. was still kept on a mobile basis. It was still capable of being transplanted like a Christmas tree to spread protection over an army. Its presence guaranteed that the Allied Military Government would not rest on prestige alone.

D.A.F., claimed the querulous, was becoming "a pawn in the game of *Weltpolitik*". It was to stay within reach of Yugoslavia. Relations with Tito, which had been so excellent during the war, started to deteriorate; and the airmen were perplexed. A pilot of 239 Wing probably stated the popular case: "We saved his life more than once. We were always shooting things up for him. We lost a lot of men over 'Jugland'. It's hard to see what's gone wrong."

"Pawn" was partly descriptive, for D.A.F. became a midget air force. There were to be only 324 Wing in Austria, 244 Wing near Venice, and 239 Wing at Udine.

Thus, gradually, D.A.F. grew small, its purpose changing, its men leaving, until there was little but the name—the accolade of honour for a force which in 1943 had been about to leave the Desert for ever—to show that this command had been some special, unique phenomenon of the Royal Air Force. Some of the benefits lingered on to remind newcomers of glories past. Life was easier, less subject to interference. The older members still wore those variegated non-uniform clothes which they had carried with them from the Desert, though few of the tyros dared to imitate their example. There were not so many forms to be filled; a car or lorry was less difficult to come by. All those things, products of the D.A.F. tradition, were envied by other parts of the Royal Air Force. In principle, the men who had worked for them were allowed to retain them, but the regulations became in time more and more strictly applied as the veterans retired. D.A.F. slowly ceased to live.

D.A.F. died intestate; for its legacies had already been distributed during its lifetime. Mobility, self-sufficiency, of an Allied, polyglot air force, these lessons had been learned in the Desert, applied in Sicily, Italy and the south of France, and reapplied by others in Normandy and Germany.

The Desert Air Force myth lay coiled in the heart of victory. It should not be forgotten. But nor on the other hand should it be misinterpreted. Here is a legend that is the antithesis of "spit-and-polish", arising in direct opposition to the imported traditions of a Potsdam *élite*. For D.A.F.'s nomadic, individual way of life owed as much to Arabia as to Europe. Those men were finely disciplined as regards their work; in everything else they enjoyed a freedom not normally associated with Service existence. It is quite inadequate to say that they might have been even more efficient had they been subject to innumerable parades, obeyed without question any orders that might have been given, dressed correctly at all times—had they, in short, attempted to emulate manners not of their own making. D.A.F. was a phenomenon as a whole, not as a part. Those faults, if faults they could be called, were inherent in those other virtues.

At the end of the war it was generally supposed throughout D.A.F. that "They'll bring back all the old rules; they'll make us into proper airmen now." But in their hearts the men of D.A.F. knew that they were proper airmen already. Their banner with a strange device they had proudly borne from Cairo to Klagenfurt. No more orthodox standard could have suited the journey. If the peacetime purpose of an air force was different, then they were proud to be anachronisms—if indeed they really were.

APPENDIX A

(*See* page 64)

D.A.F. ORDER OF BATTLE, OCTOBER 1941

There were

Fighters:

229, 238, 1, S.A.A.F. (Hurricanes).
112, 250, 2 S.A.A.F. and 3 R.A.A.F. (Tomahawks).
33 Long-range Hurricanes.
A Royal Navy Fighter Squadron (Hurricanes and Martlets).
451 (Army Co-operation).

Light Bombers:

11, 45, 55, 113 (Blenheims).
12 and 21 S.A.A.F. (Marylands).
A detachment of 39 (Marylands and Beauforts) for G.R.

Medium Bombers:

257 Wing. 37, 38, 70, 148 (Wellingtons).
And to increase this number still further, fighters of 30, 94, 274 and 4 S.A.A.F. were brought in from Egypt.
260 from Haifa.
80 from Syria.
A detachment of Beaufighters from 201 Group.
The fighter squadrons were split into 3 mobile Wings, 258 (formed November 11th), 262 and 269 (formed within a month).

Light bombers were still further increased by bringing 14 and 84 squadrons from Iraq. A Free French squadron was also formed. 24 squadron S.A.A.F. was brought into the Desert and converted from Marylands to Bostons, and a flight of 8 squadron arrived from Aden. Just before the opening of the offensive, 451, at that time the only Army Co-operation squadron in the Western Desert, was joined by 208 and 237 (Rhodesian) squadrons. Strategical reconnaissance was to be carried out by a mixed unit comprising Marylands from 12 S.A.A.F., with crews from 12, 24 S.A.A.F. and 39 squadrons attached to 24 S.A.A.F. squadron. Lastly No. 1 Air Ambulance unit flew in from Ghaza. The pilots were to use De Havillands, Loadstars, Bombays of 216 Air Transport squadron, and even De Havillands on loan from British Overseas Airways Corporation.

APPENDIX B

(*See* page 66)

GERMAN AIR FORCE IN JULY 1941

Mediterranean, Greece, Ægean, Rhodes and Crete:

Bombers	120
Dive-bombers	50
Single-engined Fighters	—
Twin-engined Fighters	30
Recce.	40
	240

Sicily	Nil

North Africa:

Bombers	30
Dive-bombers	40
Single-engined Fighters	40
Twin-engined Fighters	10
Recce.	30
	150

Total:

Bombers	150
Dive-bombers	90
Single-engined Fighters	40
Twin-engined Fighters	40
Recce.	70
	390

APPENDIX C

(*See* page 231)

D.A.F. ON THE MOVE IN AUGUST 1944

PHASE 1

Present until D minus 3 (*approx.*)

West Coast	*Central Sector*	*East Coast*
Main 5th Army H.Q.	D.A.F.	Main 8th Army H.Q.
Ops. "A"		
M.O.R.U. "B"	M.O.R.U. "B"	287 Wing
ROSIGNANO	FOIANO	FALCONARA
600 Squadron	7 Wing	241 Squadron
Flt. 92 Squadron		Flt. 318 Squadron
		Det. 255 Squadron
		15 Squadron
		454 Squadron
CECINA	CRETE	
232 Wing	239 Wing	
	MALIGNANO	PESCARA
	285 Wing	3 Wing
	PERUGIA	
	244 Wing	
	SIENA	
	Comm. Flight	

PHASE 2

D minus 3 *to D plus* 5

West Coast	*Central Sector*	*East Coast*
	D.A.F. (Admin. Signals Branch of Advanced H.Q.)	Main 8th Army H.Q. D.A.F. (Main elements of Adv. H.Q.
F.F.C	Main 5th Army H.Q.	287 Wing (Augmented)
ROSIGNANO 600 Squadron Flt. 92 Squadron	OPS. "A" M.O.R.U. "B" PESCARA 3 Wing	FALCONARA 15 Squadron 454 Squadron Det. 255 Squadron Flt. 600 Squadron Comm. Flight
CECINA 232 Wing	FOIANO 7 Wing (rear) MALIGNANO 208 Squadron 12 (U.S.)	CHIARAVALLE 285 Wing (including 241 Squadron) Flt. 318 Squadron (ex Falconara) JESI 239 Wing LORETO/BORGHETTO 244 Wing

---

PHASE 3

D plus 5 *to D plus* 10

West Coast	*Central Sector*	*East Coast*
F.C.	Main 5th Army	Main 8th Army H.Q. D.A.F. (Adv. H.Q. complete)
		M.O.R.U. "A"

West Coast	*Central Sector*	*East Coast*
ROSIGNANO	OPS. "A"	FALCONARA
Det. Flt. 92 Squadron		253 Wing
H.Q. and Flt. 600 Squadron.	M.O.R.U. "B"	Det. 255 Squadron
		Flt. 600 Squadron
CECINA/FANO	FLORENCE (1)	JESI
232 Wing	7 Wing	3 Wing
	FLORENCE (2)	BORGHETTO
	208 Squadron	244 Wing
	12 (U.S.) Squadron	
	CRETE/FLORENCE	MAZZOLAIO/PIAGIOLINO
	239 Wing	
		285 Wing.
		? Comm. Flight.
		CHIARAVALLE
		8 Wing (??)

In actual fact, though, there were some modifications to this plan. 239 Wing stayed at Jesi instead of moving back to Crete. 3 S.A.A.F. Wing stayed at Pescara until driven out by weather. Then they became non-operational at Jesi.

APPENDIX D

Where abbreviations or initials have been used, the words for which they stand have been written out in full in the first instance.

To refresh the memory, here is a recapitulation of such as have occurred frequently throughout these pages:

R.A.F.M.E. ..	.. Royal Air Force, Middle East.
T.A.F. ..	.. Tactical Air Force.
T.B.F. ..	.. Tactical Bomber Force.
B.A.F. ..	.. Balkan Air Force.
M.A.A.F. ..	.. Mediterranean Allied Air Forces.
N.W.A.A.F.	.. North West African Air Forces.
M.O.R.U. ..	.. Mobile Operations Reporting Unit.
12th A.S.C. ..	.. 12th Air Support Command } American.
22nd T.A.C.	.. 22nd Tactical Air Command } American.
A.O.C. ..	.. Air Officer Commanding.
G.O.C. ..	.. General Officer Commanding.
S.A.S.O. ..	.. Senior Air Staff Officer.
M.T. ..	.. Motorised Transport.
R.T. ..	.. Radio Telephone.
M.U. ..	.. Maintenance Unit.
R.S.U. ..	.. Repair and Salvage Unit.
A.S.P. ..	.. Air Stores Park.
M.F.H. ..	.. Mobile Field Hospital.
Me.	.. Messerschmitt.
He.	.. Heinkel.
Mc.	.. Macchi.
Ju.	.. Junkers.
F.W. ..	.. Focke-Wulf.
Do.	.. Dornier.

ng (L.B.)
ston IV & V)
ston IV & V)
ston IV & V)
oston IV & V)

ved by
A.S.P.

253 Wing (L.B.)
454 (R.A.A.F.) Sqdn.
(Baltimore V)
15 Sqdn. S.A.A.F.
(Baltimore V)
500 Sqdn.
(Baltimore V)

Served by
31 A.S.P.

600 Squadron
(Night Fighter)
(Mosquito XIX)

Served by
31 A.S.P.

285 Wing (Recce)
208 Sqdn. (Spit. 9 M. 63, 66)
225 Sqdn. (Spit. 9 M. 63, 66)
318 (Polish) Sqdn.
(Spit. 9 M. 63, 66)
683 Sqdn. (Det.) (Spit. XI)
(Local Control)

Served by
36 A.S.P.

M.E. Stations Operating into M.O.R.U.
.S. 15852 A.M.E.S. 21021 A.M.E.S.
.S.
.S. } Operating for 3 Wing, S.A.A.F.
.S.

g A.M.E. Stations are at present non-operational

S.	6004 A.M.E.S.	6042 A.M.E.S.
.S.	6061 A.M.E.S.	6075 A.M.E.S.
.S.	8033 A.M.E.S.	374 A.M.E.S.
E.S.	14027 A.M.E.S.	21033 A.M.E.S.
E.S.	67005 A.M.E.S.	

and Administrative

nin. control only)

nit
nit
Jnit

n

Units in Austria under the Operational control of D. A. F. KLAGENFURT and administrative control of Rear Headquarters, Desert Air Force.

40 A.S.P.
21 M.F.H.
12 Met. Unit
1320 Wing H.Q., R.A.F. Regt.
1744 Field Squadron
2825 Field Squadron
2866 Rifle Squadron

2926 L.A.A. Squadron
A.P.O. Z.42 (attached from Army)
1328 Wing H.Q., R.A.F. Regt.
2771 Field Squadron
2914 L.A.A. Squadron
2932 L.A.A. Squadron
*651 (AOP) Squadron

* Operated by Corps

324 Wing (F.B.)
43 Sqdn. (Spit. 9 M. 66)
72 Sqdn. (Spit. 9 M. 66)
93 Sqdn. (Spit. 9 M. 63)
111 Sqdn. (Spit. 9 M. 66)
40 Sqdn. (S.A.A.F.) Spit. 9 M. 66)

Served by
40 A.S.P.